Pacific Island Economies

Toward Higher Growth in the 1990s

Copyright © 1991
The International Bank for Reconstruction
and Development/THE WORLD BANK
1818 H Street, N.W.
Washington, D.C. 20433, U.S.A.

World Bank Country Studies are among the many reports originally prepared for internal use as part of the continuing analysis by the Bank of the economic and related conditions of its developing member countries and of its dialogues with the governments. Some of the reports are published in this series with the least possible delay for the use of governments and the academic, business and financial, and development communities. The typescript of this paper therefore has not been prepared in accordance with the procedures appropriate to formal printed texts, and the World Bank accepts no responsibility for errors.

The World Bank does not guarantee the accuracy of the data included in this publication and accepts no responsibility whatsoever for any consequence of their use. Any maps that accompany the text have been prepared solely for the convenience of readers; the designations and presentation of material in them do not imply the expression of any opinion whatsoever on the part of the World Bank, its affiliates, or its Board or member countries concerning the legal status of any country, territory, city, or area or of the authorities thereof or concerning the delimitation of its boundaries or its national affiliation.

The material in this publication is copyrighted. Requests for permission to reproduce portions of it should be sent to Director, Publications Department, at the address shown in the copyright notice above. The World Bank encourages dissemination of its work and will normally give permission promptly and, when the reproduction is for noncommercial purposes, without asking a fee. Permission to photocopy portions for classroom use is not required, though notification of such use having been made will be appreciated.

The complete backlist of publications from the World Bank is shown in the annual *Index of Publications,* which contains an alphabetical title list (with full ordering information) and indexes of subjects, authors, and countries and regions. The latest edition is available free of charge from the Publications Sales Unit, Department F, The World Bank, 1818 H Street, N.W., Washington, D.C. 20433, U.S.A., or from Publications, The World Bank, 66, avenue d'Iéna, 75116 Paris, France.

ISSN: 0253-2123

Library of Congress Cataloging-in-Publication Data

Pacific Island economies : toward higher growth in the 1990s.
    p. cm. — (A World Bank country study)
  ISBN 0-8213-1938-8
  1. Oceania—Economic conditions. 2. Oceania—Economic policy.
3. Economic forecasting—Oceania. I. International Bank for
Reconstruction and Development. II. Series.
HC681.P295 1991
338.99—dc20
                                      91-33516
                                      CIP

PREFACE

This work on economic development strategies and policy options for the Pacific Island economies was initiated in 1989. The report was prepared and discussed with member Governments and donor agencies at a seminar in Singapore in November, 1990. A final version of the report was presented at the Forum Secretariat meeting on regional aid coordination in Fiji in February 1991.

This report is the first of its kind for the six Pacific island countries that are members of the World Bank--Fiji, Kiribati, Solomon Islands, Tonga, Vanuatu and Western Samoa. The first volume is a regional overview that examines the growth performance of the South Pacific countries in the 1980s, assesses the factors underlying the relatively weak performance, and develops a framework for achieving higher rates of growth in the 1990s. Chapter 1 reviews the economic performance of the South Pacific countries in the 1980s; Chapter 2 reviews the underlying policy environment during the past decade; Chapter 3 suggests strategies for accelerated and sustained growth and explores development prospects in the 1990s; and Chapter 4 examines the past and future role of development assistance in the growth process. The second volume contains country surveys on each of the six countries. These surveys provide more detailed background on the economies, review recent economic developments, assess development prospects and policies, and provide medium-term prospects including that of external financing requirements.

The World Bank would like to express its appreciation to all the member Governments, donor agencies and several research and regional organizations that cooperated in support of this review. The World Bank would also like to acknowledge the support provided for this study by the AIDAB South Pacific Facility.

This report is based on a mission that visited the region in November 1989, with follow-up missions in May-June, 1990. The principal authors are Amar Bhattacharya, Steven Tabor, Lloyd Kenward, John Kerr-Stevens, Ranji Salgado, Mark Baird, R. Kyle Peters, Graeme Thompson and Zaidi Sattar. Other contributors included: Te'o Fairbairn, Paul Flanagan, Colin Pratt and Jayshree Sengupta. Statistical support for the study was provided by Anna Maripuu, Peter Osei, and Cyrus Talati. Fay Willey provided editorial assistance and Sharon E. Gustafson provided administrative support and coordinated the processing of the document.

ACRONYMS AND ABBREVIATIONS

ADB	-	Asian Development Bank
AIDAB	-	Australian International Development Assistance Bureau
CB		Commodity Board
CER	-	Closer Economic Relationship
DAC	-	Development Assistance Committee
EEC	-	European Economic Community
GSP	-	Generalized System of Preferences
IBRD	-	International Bank for Reconstruction and Development
IDA	-	International Development Association
IFC	-	International Finance Corporation
IMF	-	International Monetary Fund
NIC	-	Newly Industrialized Country
ODA	-	Official Development Assistance
OECD	-	Organization for Economic Cooperation and Development
PMC	-	Pacific Island Member Country
PSIP	-	Public Sector Investment Program
REER	-	Real Effective Exchange Rate
RERF	-	Revenue Equalization Reserve Fund
RTM	-	Round Table Meeting
SPPF	-	South Pacific Project Facility
STABEX	-	Export Earnings Stabilization System
UNDP	-	United Nations Development Programme
USP	-	University of the South Pacific

Table of Contents

Part II. Country Surveys

EXECUTIVE SUMMARY

Growth Performance in the 1980s

1.   The six World Bank Pacific Island member countries (PMCs)1/ have achieved relatively high living standards in the face of many constraints. GNP per capita is at the upper-end of the low-income to middle-income range. Social indicators compare favorably with developing countries at the same or higher levels of income. One disappointing aspect, however, is sluggish growth performance in the 1980s--despite some of the highest inflows of per capita development assistance. Viewed across the span of an entire decade, economic growth was quite modest, while year-to-year growth in individual countries showed much volatility. As a group, the six recorded an average growth rate in real GNP of only 0.6 percent per annum during 1980-88, while population grew an annual 2 percent. As a result, there was a significant decline in per capita incomes.

2.   The poor economic performance for the PMCs stands in sharp contrast to the more than 5 percent GNP growth averaged by comparable countries in the Caribbean and the nearly 7 percent growth of the Indian Ocean islands of Maldives and Mauritius. PMC growth was not as unfavorable, however, as that of many Sub-Saharan African countries where dependence on primary exports is similar.

3.   <u>Factors underlying performance</u>. By standards of the broader developing world, the external environment for the PMCs was generally favorable in the 1980s. The terms of trade, although volatile, remained roughly unchanged over the decade. Natural disasters had an impact on growth; all the island economies except Kiribati suffered major devastation at one time or another. Political developments also adversely affected economic performance. The two 1987 coups in Fiji and political disturbances in Vanuatu led to a temporary halt in aid, declines in tourism, and a drop in private sector investment.

4.   Balanced against the negative factors, the PMCs benefitted from high levels of foreign assistance. Massive aid flows enabled the six to cover their domestic resource gaps and maintain high investment levels relative to GDP.

5.   Thus far, the high investment rates have not meant correspondingly high rates of growth. This is in part because most investments in the 1980s concentrated on building physical infrastructure and on human resource development. Such investments do not necessarily yield immediate output gains.

6.   But there is a more basic reason for the PMC's sluggish and volatile growth performance. Comparisons with the more dynamic island economies of the Caribbean and Indian Ocean indicate that among the PMCS, there has been an inability to stimulate private investment in productive sectors. This has

---

1/   The six World Bank Pacific Island member countries are Fiji, Kiribati, Solomon Islands, Tonga, Vanuatu and Western Samoa.

reflected, in part, a lack of a supportive policy environment and an absence of dynamic growth strategies.

7.   Although delayed macroeconomic responses to shocks sometimes required austerity measures, macroeconomic management has largely been sound in the PMCs. The policy shortcomings were more related to growth strategy. In particular, the islands' inward-oriented development has not produced satisfactory results during the decade. In choosing key sectors, Governments have not been able to pick industries with bright futures. Protection from foreign competition has contributed to high-cost local economies unable to compete in the world marketplace. Investments in infrastructure (largely financed by foreign assistance) have not made a substantial contribution to growth. State enterprises have been a burden on the public finances. Growth of a dynamic private sector has been stifled by over-regulation. Potential foreign investors have set up operations in other countries where the environment is more conducive to doing business.

8.   All six countries have the potential for more rapid growth on a sustainable basis. Fiji is now demonstrating its capacity for growth under a revised strategy and policies. In Solomon Islands and, to a lesser extent, in Vanuatu, pressing fiscal problems must be overcome before there can be improved performance based on the substantial resource base; moreover, human resource constraints will need to be addressed, and population growth is excessive. Western Samoa's GDP growth in 1990 may be negative; however, the net effects of even the most disastrous cyclone should not be exceptionally severe or protracted. Like Tonga, Western Samoa has the capacity for 3-4 percent annual growth and significant improvement in per capita income, employment, and living standards. Even Kiribati, with its fisheries resource and competent labor force, can attain enduring growth.

Shared Development Challenges in the 1990s

9.   Increasing the pace of development is an imperative for the 1990s. And given the weak outlook for primary commodities, the PMCs need to develop new sources of growth. Because of resource constraints, it is important that development strategy be geared to growth in the few areas where there is a clear comparative advantage. The experience of other small island economies is instructive. In the Maldives, concentration on just two major activities, tourism and fisheries, has produced remarkable results. Fiji's strategy, paralleling that of Mauritius, has achieved some success in manufacturing growth and exports. For a time, Solomon Islands grew rapidly as a forestry, fisheries and agricultural exporter. The key to resumption of sustained economic growth in the PMCS is a leading sector approach in which public policy facilitates the private sector's search for profitable niches in domestic and world markets.

Macroeconomic Management

10.   Maintenance of macroeconomic stability is a prerequisite for sustained growth. In the 1980s, all the Pacific Island countries, other than Fiji, ran a fiscal deficit of 20 to 40 percent of GDP. The generous availability of external grant financing enabled them to meet fiscal deficits without excessive recourse to domestic borrowing or inflationary finance, except in the cases of Solomon Islands and Vanuatu. A challenge for the 1990s

will be to maintain macroeconomic stability through policies that accommodate the fiscal deficit in a noninflationary manner.

11.   Fiscal policy. Given limitations on monetary policies and exchange rate management, fiscal policy is the main instrument that can be used to achieve macroeconomic stability. For the Solomon Islands and Vanuatu, restoring such stability through fiscal adjustment is a critical short-term concern. In both cases, a reduction in current expenditures will be required to reduce the fiscal deficit to more manageable proportions.

12.   Monetary policy. At best, monetary policy can play a limited role in the PMCs. The openness of these economies means that capital movements will tend to track fiscal policy and world market developments. Sound and efficient domestic financial systems are vital. While many PMCs have begun to move toward partial decontrol of commercial bank lending rates, deposit rates remain highly negative in real terms. Direct controls on interest rates reduce incentives for financial intermediation of economic activities and limit the availability of resources for private investment. A major effort is required to increase the soundness and competitiveness of PMC financial systems.

13.   External competitiveness. Maintaining external competitiveness will be an essential element in a more growth-oriented development strategy. Appropriate wage and exchange rate policies are particularly important since they exercise a major influence on international competitiveness and thereby on the viability of investment in both export and import-substituting industries. In particular, the the PMCs need to achieve greater flexibility in the setting of private and public sector wages by severing the rigid link between wages and the cost of living. Wage increases should be kept in line with variations in economy-wide productivity. To the extent that progress is made in improving competitiveness through wage policy, there will be less need for exchange rate adjustments and a smaller impact on the general level of prices.

Public Sector Management

14.   Taxes. The PMCs domestic resource mobilization is substantial, with tax revenues between 15 and 30 percent of GDP. There are problems in the tax systems, however. Direct tax rates are high, the tax base is narrow, and indirect tax rates vary widely across sectors. Taxes tend to reduce incentives to trade. The elasticity of nontax revenues to growth is low. The challenge for the decade will be to broaden the tax base, lower direct tax rates while reducing exemptions, eliminate trade-inhibiting taxes, and shift toward an indirect tax base that does not discriminate across productive sectors.

15.   Current expenditures. Sound management of current expenditures is a priority. While maintaining essential services, the Pacific Island countries must pay careful attention to restraining the administrative budget. Excessive growth in the wage and salary bill has tended to crowd out other current outlays, and, through transmission of public wage awards to the private sector, there has been a rise in wage costs throughout the economy. Much greater attention must go to the operations and maintenance (O&M) of physical infrastructure. The PMCs should improve institutional arrangements for

operating and maintaining physical infrastructure. Since donor assistance has not typically focused on augmenting current expenditures, O&M needs call for a reordering of donor commitments.

16.   Public enterprises. The role of public enterprises in these six nations is very large. To avoid excessive burden on the fiscal budget, public enterprise tariffs have to be sufficient to cover operating and investment costs. Programs should be put into place to improve the operating efficiency of public enterprises, to reduce the fiscal drain and, in many instances, to increase public savings. For the enterprises that are nonviable, that are crowding out private investment, or that could be more effectively managed in the private sector, the PMCs should institute a program of privatization. Candidates for privatization include the many commodity marketing boards established for primary product exports. Governments will need to ensure, however, that there are still adequate mechanisms to ensure quality control and quarantine requirements.

17.   Future investment focus. The future thrust of public expenditures should center on core activities in which public intervention is clearly warranted. High on the priority list should be the provision, operation and maintenance of essential infrastructure and of those services associated with human resource development. As in the past, investment programs will rely almost completely on external assistance.

Private Sector Development

18.   To restore sustained growth, there needs to be greater private sector participation in investment and in economic affairs. Efficient use of private investment will hinge on the capacity of entrepreneurs to identify and exploit the profitable niches. The most promising areas are expanded exports and services catering to the world market.

19.   Source of growth. New sources of growth must be developed as the traditional sources--public investment and primary commodity exports--show little scope for sustained increase. The combination of small domestic markets, a narrow economic base, high transport costs, and a shallow labor market implies that the island countries will not be able to support a broad base of economic activities. By achieving a critical mass of investment and support services in key subsectors, specialization can be the cornerstone of growth and development led by the private sector. In each economy, there will be many different niches to be explored. Government may facilitate this process--not by selecting or supporting specific areas for private investment, but by maintaining macroeconomic stability and by providing the necessary infrastructure, human resources and policy environment conducive to private initiative.

20.   Policy reform. The provision of a policy environment that facilitates private investment is a primary challenge in the 1990s. All six nations require a significant effort to put in place an outward-oriented and relatively undistorted incentives regime. A move from quantitative trade controls, high and uneven tariffs and complex systems of duty drawbacks and exemptions should be an early priority. Corporate tax rates should be set on a uniform basis at rates conducive to private investment and growth. Exemptions from enterprise taxes should be reduced. In view of the importance

of institutional arrangements in the labor market, efforts should go to introducing greater flexibility in wages and to better link wage awards to productivity.

21.   Facilitating investment. It is important, too, for PMC Governments to provide an atmosphere where regulatory impediments do not hinder private investment. Licensing requirements should be streamlined and consolidated. Where possible, there should be one-stop centers for licensing new domestic and foreign investment. Government will still have to play an important regulatory role, ensuring community safety and environmental standards, setting and monitoring product quality standards, and fostering awareness of export markets. But they should minimize the reporting and registration burden on the private sector. In addition, there is a need for Government support to develop entrepreneurial capacity.

22.   Policy stability. The 1980s saw a PMC policy environment notable for high volatility and frequent change. While it is important to alter policies to improve economic conditions, the uncertainty induced by frequent policy changes is itself a disincentive to private investment. The credibility of a policy regime hinges on the degree of certainty an investor can attach to its eventual implementation. The direction of policy reform should be made known and changes implemented in an orderly fashion.

23.   Financial markets. The financial sector will have to play a much more important role in the 1990s if the private sector is to lead in growth. Competitiveness of financial markets must be improved and controls on the cost and allocation of capital need to be phased out. Financial institutions must be adequately capitalized and new capital market instruments actively encouraged. The problem of failing development financial institutions will require solution.

The Medium-Term Outlook

24.   The external environment in the 1990s will likely be difficult--but less so than in the 1980s. Uncertainties in the Middle East and the prospect of higher petroleum prices dominate the short-term outlook. Over the long term, the fall in primary commodity prices is expected to continue, but erosion in relative prices is expected to be far less severe than in the 1980s.

25.   The petroleum price increase is expected to lead to a larger import bill and to higher transport costs in the near term. Should higher prices persist in the medium-term, unit costs of imported manufactures will rise, while orders from OECD nations for developing country exports may drop. With higher air transport costs and slower growth in OECD nations, demand for tourism services may also dip.

26.   For the Pacific Island nations, short-term stabilization policies will likely include a reduction in official reserves and, where possible, additional external assistance. In the event higher prices continue, increasing attention must be devoted to energy conservation and to development of alternative energy sources.

27.   Although difficult to assess in light of the Mideast uncertainty, the outlook for primary commodity prices in the 1990s is not particularly promising. There are considerable prospects, however, for exploiting high value markets in primary products, for expanding exports under favorable conditions to New Zealand and Australia, for developing ties to a dynamic European Community and for capturing foreign investment from the United States and the Pacific Basin nations.

28.   Resource gaps are projected to persist among the PMCs and continued donor support will be essential for steady growth in productive investment. Strong economic growth is predicated on the achievement of high rates of investment, increasingly in the commodity-producing sectors. The projections assume that, thanks to strong donor support, the availability of resources for investment will not be a constraint. Real levels of development assistance are expected to increase moderately in the 1990s.

29.   Country projections for 1990-94 suggest that the PMCs could achieve per capita income growth of 2.5 percent per annum, about the average expected for developing countries (excluding the rapidly industrializing Asian economies). More tentative projections for 1995-99 suggest that this pattern could be broadly maintained and, in the smaller countries, even improved.

30.   The total external financing requirement is expected to grow from an annual $270 million (U.S. dollars) in 1985-89 to $385 million per annum in 1990-94. On a proportionate basis, there would be less reliance on external grants, somewhat more dependence on official borrowing, and a considerably increased role for other capital inflows, especially direct foreign investment.

The Effective Use of Aid in the South Pacific

31.   The following are notable points concerning aid flows to the South Pacific:

o   While the PMCs have benefitted from high levels of aid, the net financial transfers have been substantially lower than the gross ODA flows. In consequence, the financial impact of aid flows has been somewhat less than might be expected from the size of the gross flows.

o   Aid accounts for a substantial part of total resources, a major part of Government expenditure and the bulk of public investment financing. Aid has clearly had a positive effect on overall development.

o   After a decline in the early 1980s, aid flows have increased steadily. There are good prospects for further growth in aid availability, given the recent Lome IV agreement with EEC and the indications from other bilateral and multilateral donors.

o   Virtually all aid is provided as grants or on highly concessional terms. Bilateral donors account for more than 90 percent of aid, with relatively new donors (EEC, Japan) diversifying the base and providing the impetus for recent growth. Multilateral donors play a very modest role.

32.   A case can be made that the high volume of official assistance provided to the PMCs in recent years should have led to much higher real growth rates. Bank analysis indicates, however, that linkages are not entirely clear. Actual flows of financial resources are in fact far smaller than recorded in official (Development Assistance Committee) aid figures, mainly because of sizable technical assistance and of other expenditures financed externally. In addition, the major part of aid goes to activities with long gestation periods, such as human resource development; these have little immediate impact on economic growth. Even the considerable flow of resources to infrastructure development has only a temporary effect on growth during the construction stage of projects; its full effect, through encouragement of output in other sectors, may take some time.

33.   During coming years, a new issue likely to arise concerning the allocation of aid is the means by which it should be channelled to the private sector to support that area's role in development strategy. Financialization (the channelling of resources to recipients through the commercial financial system) of some portion of aid is likely to be necessary in order to ensure that resources go to private entrepreneurs. The main question will be how to financialize most efficiently. Donor assistance may in fact be necessary for the reform of some PMC financial sectors.

34.   The bulk of donor resources, however, will still be needed for basic infrastructure and for human resource projects. And clearly, the PMC's utilization of their extensive aid resources would be made more effective if they increased their absorptive capacity. Several improvements are most important.

35.   First, it is necessary to improve elements of the planning process. Today, these processes generally concentrate on the production of unwieldy five-year plans that waste resources and, in some cases, appear to represent little more than lists of projects intended primarily for donor financing. Island governments would be well advised to adopt a new approach to planning, emphasizing macroeconomic assessment and the preparation of broad development strategies. Within this framework, each Government should concentrate on defining sectoral expenditure priorities, and give increased emphasis to program and project planning and to preparation capacity in key line ministries. These improvements imply a reallocation of staff within Government structures and an increase in capacity through training and other technical assistance.

36.   Second, there must be improved coordination of external assistance at both the national and international levels. The UNDP Round Table format seems appropriate organizationally, but a more complete discussion of the wider policy environment is required. At the national level, donors will have to engage in a realistic policy dialogue with the national authorities. For major donors, this will imply a move away from the current project-driven approach to one that looks at the wider impact of their assistance on the economy as a whole. For island countries, it will require Government commitment to policy actions, such as increased O&M expenditures, that are necessary to improve the effectiveness of aid investments. Island Governments

should also take the initiative in encouraging donors to focus their resources more efficiently through, for example, concentrating resources on sector-wide programs, reducing the number of projects, and improving coordination to ease pressures on the small PMC administrations.

37.   Finally, renewed attention must go to factors that directly affect efficient use of external assistance. Although there are many areas that require greater emphasis, two cry out for most urgent action: the problem of recurrent costs and the need for better human resource development.

38.   Donors will have to make at least selective provision for recurrent cost funding; paying the increasing O&M costs of new donor-financed investment is one of the major budgetary problems facing the PMCs. It could be more productive to use aid for some O&M costs than to finance new investment. PMC Governments must henceforth ensure that they do not accept new investments unless some provision has been made for recurrent costs. This may imply a temporary decline in the growth of aid levels until these Governments have increased their revenue capacity for supporting further aid-financed investment. A measure of donor support must help in dealing with the severity of the O&M problem, but the prime responsibility for funding recurrent costs rests with the PMCs.

39.   Human resource development must remain a major area of emphasis for the six island countries. Current policies should be examined to see whether external resources can be used more efficiently. As example, the balance among local, regional, and nonregional training should be scrutinized, as should the type of training, particularly in nonregional institutions. Donors may have to consider direct budgetary support to the education sector to ensure full use of facilities and greater access to basic education.

Part I

Regional Overview

I. Economic Performance in the 1980s

A. Introduction

1.1   The six World Bank Pacific Island member countries (PMCs)1/ have achieved relatively high living standards in the face of many constraints. GNP per capita is in the upper end of low-income to middle-income range. Social indicators compare favorably with developing countries at the same or higher levels of income. One disappointing aspect, however, is sluggish growth performance in the 1980s--despite some of the highest inflows of per capita development assistance. Viewed across the span of an entire decade, economic growth was quite modest, and year-to-year growth in individual countries showed much volatility.

1.2   This modest growth performance cannot be attributed simply to the fact that these are small, remote, open island economies. Comparable economies in the Caribbean and the Indian Ocean registered far stronger growth while facing a less favorable external environment during the same period. Indeed, the experience of the more successful small island economies during the 1980s helps identify the causes of the weak economic performance in the Pacific Island countries.

1.3   Looking ahead, the main objective for the PMCs in the coming decade is to resume strong and sustained economic growth, consistent with varying social, political, and environmental circumstances. Central to charting a strategy for restoring growth is an understanding of the disappointing experience of the 1980s--especially an identification of the principal factors responsible. This report is the first of its kind for Pacific Island countries that are members of the World Bank; it examines past performance and develops a framework for achieving higher growth rates in the future. Chapter I reviews economic performance in the 1980s; Chapter II reviews the underlying policy environment during the decade; Chapter III suggests strategies for accelerated and sustained growth and explores prospects for the external economic environment in the 1990s; Chapter IV examines the past and future role of development assistance in the growth process.

Geography and Society

1.4   Prospects for economic development are conditioned to a large extent by the Islands' geographical endowments and social patterns.2/ What is notable

---

1/   The six World Bank Pacific member countries are Fiji, Kiribati, Solomon Islands, Tonga, Vanuatu, and Western Samoa.

2/   There is a great deal of cultural, historical, physical, and demographic variation among the six PMC economies. While aware of the limitations of cross-country comparisons, this report focuses principally on issues that do cut across all of the island economies. For this reason, only limited attention is provided to the nexus of country-specific factors that may have effected particular development outcomes.

is the vastness, remoteness, and cultural complexity of the islands as a group. This mosaic of physical and cultural endowments exerts a profound influence over the pattern and prospects for development.

1.5   Together, the six countries occupy a central position in the South Pacific region. Except for Kiribati, whose islands are spread across the equator, the others stretch from Solomon Islands (northeast of Australia) to Vanuatu, southeast to Fiji, and then farther east to Tonga and Western Samoa. The total land area, dispersed among hundreds of small islands and atolls, is only 62,000 square kilometers, of which Solomon Islands and Fiji account for 45 percent and 30 percent, respectively. By comparison, the total sea area (controlled through exclusive economic zone agreements) is enormous: 7.6 million square kilometers or 124 times the land area. The fragmentation of the land mass contributes to the PMCs' remoteness and isolation: access to major metropolitan markets is limited; transport costs are high; flight and freight services are, for most countries, infrequent. On the other hand, geographic spread does provide the PMCs with certain natural advantages in the form of a vast array of climatic, agronomic, and oceanographic conditions.

1.6   Climate. The climatic patterns are characterized by relatively even temperatures and a change in seasons associated with a greater or lesser amount of rainfall. While the climate is conducive to a wide range of activities, the islands are subject to severe tropical cyclones and occasional droughts. In February 1990, Western Samoa experienced the worst cyclone in recent history. Only Kiribati lies outside the cyclone belt.

1.7   Natural resources. Natural resource endowments vary considerably across the PMCs. Fiji, the Solomon Islands, and Vanuatu have relatively abundant fertile soils, timber lands, minerals, and fish resources. Western Samoa and Tonga have no known mineral resources and relatively limited areas suited to permanent agricultural cultivation. Kiribati, a small coral-atoll microstate, lacks arable land, running water, pastures, and forest resources.

1.8   Population. The total population of the six is roughly 1.5 million. Fiji accounts for about half, while Kiribati has only 67,000 persons (1988) or 5 percent. The population growth rate is relatively high, averaging just over 2.2 percent per annum for the group. Growth rates are particularly high in the two Melanesian countries--Vanuatu and Solomon Islands--reflecting declining mortality rates and extremely high fertility rates. In the other countries, fertility rates are lower but still high by international standards. In the case of Polynesia, population pressures have been eased by emigration; thus Western Samoa and Tonga show net population growth of less than half a percent per year.

1.9   Emigration. A large number of Polynesians have emigrated to New Zealand, Australia, and the United States. As many as 100,000 Samoans, equivalent to 60 percent of Western Samoa's population, reside overseas. An estimated 40,000 Tongans, 44 percent of the total, have emigrated. Departure on this scale has had a major effect on the Polynesian economies. While it relieves population pressures and provides large remittance flows, such massive emigration carries with it the loss of skilled manpower and the demographic burden associated with caring for a population that is disproportionately aged or young.

Table 1.1: POPULATION AND DEMOGRAPHIC TRENDS

	Population 1988 ('000)	Total fertility rate		Natural population growth rate 1980-88 (percent)	Net migration rate 1980-88 (per '000)	Net population growth rate 1980-88 (percent)
		1980	1988			
Fiji	732	3.5	3.2	2.2	-5.2	1.8
Kiribati	67	4.6	4.3	2.3	-4.3	1.9
Solomon Islands	304	7.2	6.6	3.5	0.0	3.5
Tonga	101	4.8	4.2	2.2	-18.8	0.4
Vanuatu	151	6.1	5.8 /a	3.1	-2.5	2.9
Western Samoa	168	5.6	4.7	2.9	-25.7	0.3

/a 1987.

Source: World Tables, 1989-90, and staff estimates.

1.10   Population density. Although the populations are small, settlement
is generally concentrated on one or two main islands in each nation; this can
lead to the social issues associated with overcrowding. For Fiji, Solomon
Islands, and Vanuatu, population density is quite modest, at 39, 11, and
12 persons per square kilometer respectively; still, there are urban
population problems. Tonga and Western Samoa are more densely populated at
127 and 59 persons per square kilometer. More crowded still is Kiribati;
South Tarawa, the principal island, registers 2,500 persons per square
kilometer, one of the highest concentrations in the South Pacific.

1.11   Culture. The Pacific Islands are rich in cultural traditions and
practices. Although English is widely spoken, hundreds of local Austronesian
dialects continue in use. Cultural traditions exert a powerful influence on
social practices and are particularly important in influencing the choice and
pattern of political leadership, the distribution and access to land, and,
within an extended family structure, the provision of welfare services to the
poor and needy. The blending of diverse cultural traditions with modern
commercial practices provides each nation with a unique set of characteristics
and constraints.

1.12   Endowment constraints. Remoteness, massive geographic span, a high
degree of vulnerability to natural disasters, a limited natural resource base,
small but densely populated land areas, a net outflow of skilled labor from
some countries, and the persistence of traditional patterns of economic
organization: these constitute a set of formidable constraints to
socioeconomic development. In many ways, however, the six PMCs are better
endowed in resources than most other small island economies (table 1.2).
Moreover, the experience of those other island nations demonstrates that all
the above factors can be overcome, particularly given technological advances

in communications and transport, <u>provided there is a concerted effort to
follow policies that foster sustained economic growth and development</u>.

Living Standards

1.13   <u>Incomes</u>. Despite the constraints they have faced, <u>the Pacific
Islands have achieved quite high levels of income</u> compared to other developing
countries. GNP per capita among the six is in the low- to middle-income range
for developing countries. Fiji has the highest GNP per capita, over $1,500,
followed by Vanuatu and Tonga, $800 (all $ are U.S. dollars). The Solomon
Islands and Kiribati are at the lower end of the spectrum, with incomes of
$400-$600 per capita.<u>3</u>/ Fiji's higher income levels result from a fairly
broad-based growth process involving agriculture, tourism, and manufacturing.
In Western Samoa, Tonga, and, to a lesser extent, Kiribati, remittances have
been important in underpinning incomes and consumption standards.

1.14   <u>Welfare indicators</u>. Low income levels disguise a surprisingly
good--albeit mixed--performance in raising living standards. Such standards
for Fiji, Tonga, and Western Samoa are well above the level of a typical low-
to-middle income developing nation. In these three countries, life expectancy
at birth is 66-70 years, higher than the average for Asian countries and near
that for industrialized nations. Infant mortality rates are low; basic
literacy rates are high; primary education coverage is fairly complete; and
access to qualified medical staff is comparable to that in many middle-income
countries.<u>4</u>/ Modern transport and communications infrastructure are readily
available in Fiji, Tonga, and Western Samoa, and a large share of the
population has access to safe water supplies.

1.15   Performance in improving living standards has been less successful in
Kiribati, Solomon Islands, and Vanuatu. Infant mortality rates are high and
life expectancy low. In the two Melanesian countries, a large part of the
adult population is illiterate; only half the people have access to safe
water; intestinal diseases and malaria are endemic. Even so, significant
attempts are being made to improve living standards. Investments in education
have increased primary education coverage ratios to about 48 percent in the
Solomon Islands and 84 percent in Vanuatu; overall literacy rates will rise in
the coming decades.

<u>3</u>/   Average income figures should be treated with caution as a measure of
     welfare in the South Pacific. Wide disparities in income distribution
     occur as a result of: (1) the presence of a substantial resident
     expatriate population; (2) a small, educated, urban-based indigenous
     population; and (3) traditional patterns of asset allocation. On the
     other hand, national income accounts tend to under-estimate the value
     of nonmarketed goods and services, which represent an important share
     of consumption in the large, nonmonetized segment of the PMC economies.
     Overall, while absolute poverty is virtually nonexistent in the PMCs,
     relative poverty is still a concern, particularly in Kiribati, Solomon
     Islands and Vanuatu.

<u>4</u>/   In Fiji, access to qualified medical personnel was adversely effected
     by the outflow of professional staff following the 1987 political
     disturbances.

Table 1.2: GEOGRAPHICAL ATTRIBUTES & RESOURCE ENDOWMENTS

	Land area (sq. km)	Sea area (sq. km)	Arable land per person (ha)	Forest area (sq. km)	Major minerals	Nominal freight factor
Pacific						
Fiji	18,270	1,146,000	2.1	11,850	Gold	13.8
Kiribati	710	2,641,000	na	20	None	na
Solomon Islands	27,990	1,526,000	1.4	25,600	None	19.9
Tonga	720	543,000	1.8	80	None	15.3
Vanuatu	12,190	638,000	1.4	160	None	19.9
Western Samoa	2,830	131,000	3.5	1,340	None	na
Caribbean						
Antigua & Barbuda	440	110,000	1.0	50	None	10.0
Barbados	430	167,000	1.3	na	None	12.4
Belize	22,800	na	2.5	10,120	None	11.2
Dominica	750	15,000	0.9	310	None	10.1
Grenada	340	27,000	0.5	30	None	11.7
St. Kitts & Nevis	360	11,000	1.9	60	None	10.1
St. Lucia	610	16,000	0.4	80	None	10.0
St. Vincent & the Grenadines	340	33,000	1.2	140	None	11.1
Trinidad & Tobago	5,130	77,000	0.6	2,250	Oil	na
Africa & Indian Ocean						
Cape Verde	4,030	790,000	1.1	10	na	na
Comoros	2,230	249,000	1.8	350	None	na
Maldives	300	959,000	0.2	10	None	23.0
Mauritius	1,850	1,171,000	1.0	580	None	12.3
Sao Tome & Principe	960	128,000	0.2	na	na	22.4
Seychelles	270	1,349,000	0.1	50	None	17.8

Source: International Economics Department, World Bank.

1.16   Although the moderately high standards of living clearly are an encouraging sign, they have been maintained more through adherence to good education and health administrations established during the colonial period than through recent economic development. Further improvements in social indicators will depend upon what can be achieved in broad-based, more rapid growth.

B. Economic Performance in the 1980s

1.17   There are several common patterns in the growth performance of the PMCs during the 1980s. Economic growth was highly volatile but on a generally flat trend, leaving per capita incomes for the group at a lower level than at the outset of the decade. Despite high rates of domestic investment--financed largely by external grants and transfers--there was neither sustained growth nor significant expansion in formal sector employment.

1.18   Economic management was geared more to year-to-year stabilization than to a pattern of adjustment conducive to sustained growth; external balance was achieved by offsetting wide gaps in the merchandise trade account with positive transfers and inflows on the capital account. Despite low and volatile growth, financial stability and creditworthiness were maintained by observing a cautious fiscal stance.

Growth: Low and Volatile

1.19   Growth performance during 1980-88 is summarized in table 1.3. Growth rates were quite low, and, in general, below the rate of population growth. Fiji, Kiribati, Solomon Islands, and Vanuatu registered negative growth in per capita incomes during the decade. Without large-scale emigration, Tonga and Western Samoa would have suffered a similar per capita income decline.

1.20   Average growth estimates disguise enormous volatility in growth rates. Throughout the 1980s, surges and declines in GDP with swings in growth of 10-20 percent per annum occurred with disturbing regularity. Growth has been the most volatile and erratic in the largest and the smallest PMCs, Fiji and Kiribati. Tonga and Western Samoa were able to maintain positive growth rates for a more sustained period.[5]

1.21   As a group, the six countries recorded an average growth rate in real GNP of only 0.6 percent per annum during 1980-88, below the annual population growth rate of 2 percent. As a result, GNP per capita declined during the period. This is in sharp contrast to the growth performance of other small island economies (figure 1). Comparable countries in the Caribbean and the two Indian ocean economies (Maldives and Mauritius) achieved much higher growth rates--over 5 percent and 6 percent per annum respectively--with corresponding improvements in per capita incomes.

---

[5] A more detailed discussion of the economic performance of each individual Pacific Island member country can be found in Volume II.

Table 1.3: COMPARATIVE ECONOMIC & SOCIAL INDICATORS, 1988 /a

	GNP (US$ million)	GNP per capita (US$)	Life expectancy (years)	Infant mortality rate (per '000 births)	Population per doctor (persons)	Access to safe water (% of population)	Caloric intake per capita	Gross enrollment ratio (%)
Pacific								
Fiji	1,130	1,540	71	20	2,028	69	2,763	129
Kiribati	40	650	55	61	1,970	44	2,952	84
Solomon Islands	130	430	64	51	7,474	na	2,115	48
Tonga	80	800	66	25	1,667	99	2,980	na
Vanuatu	120	820	64	73	5,148	61	2,530	na
Western Samoa	100	580	66	49	3,568	69	2,477	99
Caribbean								
Antigua & Barbuda	230	2,800	73	21	2,863	na	2,222	na
Barbados	1,530	5,990	75	16	1,123	100	3,228	110
Belize	265	1,460	67	49	2,215	65	2,649	na
Dominica	130	1,650	74	18	3,124	na	2,877	na
Grenada	139	1,370	69	33	2,116	na	2,979	na
St. Kitts & Nevis	120	2,770	69	39	2,183	na	2,801	na
St. Lucia	220	1,540	71	20	3,831	na	2,821	na
St. Vincent & the Grenadines	130	1,100	70	24	4,163	na	2,818	na
Trinidad & Tobago	4,160	3,350	71	16	954	98	2,960	100
Africa & Indian Ocean								
Cape Verde	243	690	65	43	5,283	63	2,436	108
Comoros	200	440	56	97	12,290	na	2,046	80
Maldives	80	410	60	75	15,000	24	2,177	na
Mauritius	1,890	1,810	67	22	1,899	100	2,679	106
Sao Tome & Principe	30	240	65	47	1,988	42	2,657	na
Seychelles	260	3,800	70	18	2,200	97	2,146	na

/a 1988 or most recent year available.
Source: International Economics Department, World Bank.

Savings and Investment

1.22   Growth was low in the Pacific Islands despite very <u>high, sustained</u> <u>levels of domestic investment</u> (tables 1.4 and 1.5). During a decade in which many Latin American and African countries witnessed pronounced erosion in investment, the PMCs managed to sustain levels that were extremely high. For most years, gross domestic investment ranged from 25 to 35 percent of GDP in practically all countries. Indeed, the gross domestic investment rate was in excess of 30 percent for Solomon Islands, Kiribati, and Western Samoa throughout the decade. Only in Fiji did levels decline appreciably, primarily as a result of fiscal contraction in light of pronounced external imbalances.

<u>Table 1.4</u>: PACIFIC ISLANDS: ECONOMIC PERFORMANCE, 1980-88
RATE OF GROWTH OF REAL GDP

	1980	1981	1982	1983	1984	1985	1986	1987	1988	Est. 1989	Average /a 1980-88	Per cap. GNP US$ 1988
Fiji	-1.7	4.7	0.1	-3.9	8.3	-4.7	8.8	-7.8	0.4	12.5	0.9	1,540
Kiribati *	-47.8	-5.0	7.6	-3.4	5.0	-1.9	-1.5	0.5	17.0	1.1	1.3	590
Solomon Islands	-5.5	7.0	-0.3	4.1	6.8	3.8	-0.5	-4.6	4.5	5.7	1.8	430
Tonga	6.0	0.0	12.5	1.2	2.4	5.6	3.0	3.5	-2.0	3.6	4.1	800
Vanuatu *	-11.1	3.6	11.6	3.0	6.9	1.1	-2.0	0.7	3.0	n.a.	3.0	820
Western Samoa *	-5.6	-5.7	0.0	0.5	1.3	6.0	0.5	1.0	-1.9	0.2	0.4	600

*   Kiribati, Vanuatu, and Western Samoa have been given UN least-developed country status.
/a Estimated on the basis of three-year moving averages; Kiribati (1981-88).
Source: World Bank staff estimates.

Table 1.5.   PACIFIC ISLANDS: SAVINGS AND INVESTMENT, 1980-88
(% of GDP)

	1980-85		1985-88	
	Gross domestic savings	Gross domestic investment	Gross domestic savings	Gross domestic investment
Fiji	19.9	25.1	18.6	16.1
Kiribati	-40.7	35.4	-37.6	31.0
Solomon Islands	11.0	31.0	-0.3	29.8
Tonga	n.a.	n.a.	n.a.	n.a.
Vanuatu	12.6 /a	25.9 /a	4.7	30.8
Western Samoa	-6.0	31.4	-6.3	31.3

/a 1983-85.

Source: World Bank Staff estimates.

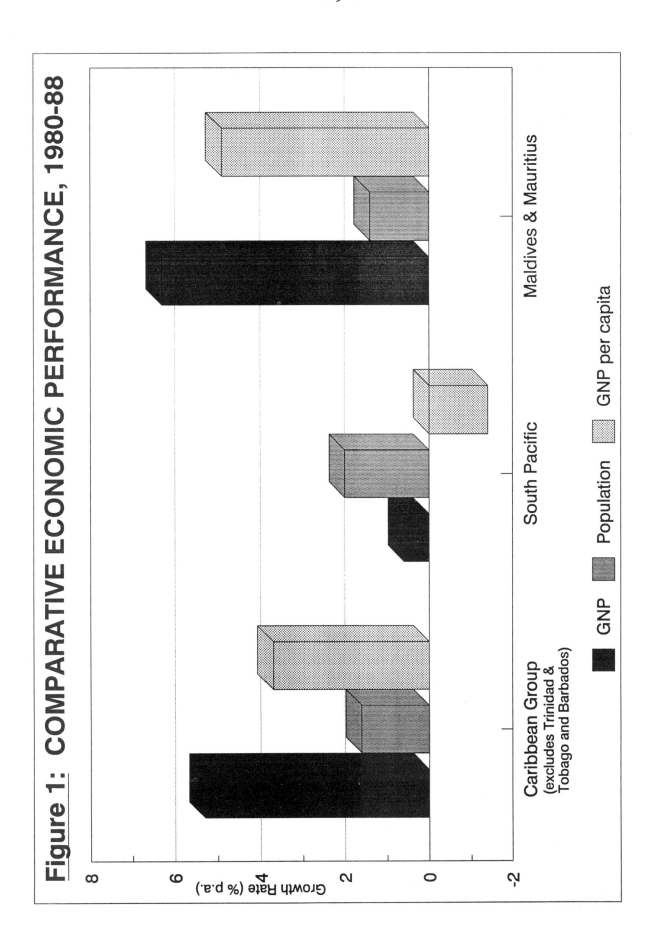

Figure 1: COMPARATIVE ECONOMIC PERFORMANCE, 1980-88

1.23   Domestic savings rates in the six countries are low, reflecting high propensities to consume, shallow financial systems, and the narrowness of the monetized portion of the economy. High rates of investment have been sustained primarily from remittances and official transfers in the case of Kiribati, Tonga, Western Samoa, and Vanuatu. Indeed, gross domestic savings were negative (consumption exceeded GDP) through parts of the decade for all countries except Vanuatu and Fiji. Only in Fiji was domestic investment largely financed from domestic savings.

1.24   National savings. In Fiji, gross domestic savings were the largest source of national savings. For Tonga and Western Samoa, remittances followed by official transfers were the largest national savings sources. For Kiribati, Vanuatu, and the Solomon Islands, net official transfers were major sources, particularly during the latter half of the decade.

1.25   Foreign aid. Foreign aid has played a major role in financing the high rates of investment in all countries except Fiji.6/ Among the five other than Fiji, external grant aid ranged from 7 to 35 percent of GDP and provided 30 to 84 percent of Government revenues; except for Solomon Islands, grant aid was greater than the merchandise trade deficit.7/ On a per capita basis, net annual disbursements of foreign aid in 1988 were equivalent to $74 in Fiji,

Table 1.6: PACIFIC ISLANDS: GROSS NATIONAL SAVINGS, 1986-88
(% of GDP)

	Fiji	Kiribati	Solomon Islands	Tonga	Vanuatu	Western Samoa
Gross national savings	16.2	57.9	22.9	23.6	35.0	41.6
Net factor income	-3.1	30.1	-1.2	5.2	-1.7	0.3
Net current transfers	0.9	64.8	26.9	36.1	33.9	48.0
Private	-0.8	7.6	2.2	29.2	6.8	32.1
Official	1.7	57.2	24.7	6.9	27.1	15.8
Gross domestic savings	18.3	-37.0	-2.8	-17.7	2.8	-6.7
Gross domestic investment	15.0	30.8	30.9	29.4	31.7	31.5
Current account deficit (+) /a	-1.1	-27.0	8.0	5.8	-3.3	-10.0

/a Including official transfers.

Source: World Bank Staff estimates.

6/ In particular, foreign aid has been the major financing source of public investment, underpinning in most cases the entire development budget. The bulk of this assistance has been on grant or highly concessional terms.

7/ The role of development assistance is discussed in greater detail in Chapter IV.

$243 in Kiribati, $192 in Solomon Islands, $186 in Tonga, $260 in Vanuatu, and $182 for Western Samoa. Such levels compare favorably with those obtained by the small Caribbean Island nations and are well in excess of aid received by the small African and Indian Ocean nations.

Employment

1.26   Except in Fiji, most employment in the PMCs stems from the traditional sources--agriculture, forestry, and fisheries. Among them, these sources account for 50 percent of total employment but contribute only 30 percent of GDP. In Vanuatu, Solomon Islands, Western Samoa, Tonga, and Kiribati, a large share of agricultural production is in the form of smallholder-operated, semisubsistence, household enterprises; Fiji's agriculture (especially sugar production) is organized more along commercial lines, although the subsistence sector is still important.

1.27   Despite high rates of investment, the Pacific Island countries registered only modest gains in providing wage-earning employment opportunities outside the traditional economic sectors. In the six economies combined, there are only some 150,000 wage-earning positions in the formal sector, of which 80,000 are in Fiji. In the total labor force, regular wage-earning employment accounts for 17 percent (Vanuatu) to 48 percent (Tonga); the figure is 33 percent for Fiji and 18 percent in the Solomon Islands. The balance of total employment is in own-account professions such as small-scale trade and subsistence agriculture.

Table 1.7: PACIFIC ISLANDS: EXTERNAL GRANTS TO PMCs, 1985-89

External grant as	Fiji	Kiribati	Solomon Islands /a	Tonga /b	Vanuatu /c	Western Samoa
% of GDP	4.4	34.5	7.6	19.3	21.0	15.6
% of revenue	4.0	77.3	32.3	64.4	83.6	39.0
% of budget deficit /a	..	95.0	49.0	86.9	81.1	116.8
% of trade deficit	48.7/c	187.7	68.0	134.3	111.8	223.3

/a 1985-88
/b 1985/86 - 1988/89
/c 1985-87

Source: World Bank staff estimates.

1.28   Where formal employment does exist, public service provides the single largest share of positions. In Fiji, public service accounts for roughly 20 percent of total paid employment.8/ In the other nations, the public sector provides 40-50 percent of total paid employment. As a result, there are only 100,000 wage-earning employment opportunities in the combined private sector of the region. This is a particularly adverse outcome and reflects both widespread underutilization of the available labor force and the low employment impact of high, sustained rates of public investment.

External Balance and Trade Performance

1.29   Openness. The Pacific Island member economies are extremely open ones in terms of merchandise trade. On average, exports amount to 55 percent of GDP and imports to 67 percent of GDP. During the 1980s, external trade was marked by a decline in export growth, a widening of the merchandise trade gap, and the maintenance of external balances principally through increased remittances and external assistance.

1.30   Declining export growth. All the PMCs suffered a sharp decline in export earnings growth compared with the previous decade. There were three main factors behind this slower growth. First, the six were not as successful as some other developing countries (for instance, the Southeast Asian economies) in expanding the volume of primary commodity exports in the face of weak commodity prices. Second, the PMCs were largely unable to diversify their merchandise exports beyond traditional primary products. Third, they

Table 1.8:   PACIFIC ISLANDS: FORMAL SECTOR EMPLOYMENT

	Wage labor ('000)	Share of labor force %
Fiji	80	33
Kiribati	9	24
Solomon Islands	25	18
Tonga	14	48
Vanuatu	10	17
Western Samoa	20	31

Source: Data provided by Fiji authorities; Fiji, Solomon Islands, Western Samoa, Vanuatu, and Tonga Country Profiles, 1990-91.

8/ In Fiji, a significant portion of those classified as wage laborers in the private sector are, in fact, in the employ of parastatal corporations. Actual private sector paid employment estimates for Fiji may be reduced by another 15,000 persons to approximate actual private employment opportunities.

were not able to exploit their tourism potential to the same extent as other island economies. The only area where the PMCs recorded a substantial increase in earnings was remittances. The overall increase in export earnings for the PMCs was quite modest (figure 2).

1.31   In contrast to the PMCs, comparable countries in the Caribbean achieved a substantial increase in export earnings, and this came to a large extent from developing tourism. The Maldives and Mauritius recorded even larger earnings increases; these were from tourism and also from expanded merchandise exports (garments for Mauritius, fish for Maldives).

1.32   Among the PMCs, Fiji has been the most successful in enlarging and diversifying its export base. Although Fiji's weak export performance during 1980-87 is in sharp contrast to that of Mauritius, Fiji has been quite successful in expanding manufactured exports and reviving tourism following policy adjustments since 1987. Sugar remains the largest export, with 55 percent of earnings; other important merchandise exports include gold, fish, timber, and garments.

1.33   Among the other countries, Tonga has achieved a measure of success in diversifying its small export base. No substantial export diversification or expansion has occurred elswhere. In Solomon Islands, fish accounts for 40 percent of export earnings; appreciable sums come from timber, copra, cocoa, palm oil, and gold. For Western Samoa, Kiribati, and Vanuatu, copra and coconut oil account for half of total export earnings. Other notable earners are timber and taro in Western Samoa; beef, timber, and cocoa in Vanuatu; and fish in Kiribati.

Table 1.9: PACIFIC ISLANDS: REAL EXPORT GROWTH

	1970s	1980s
Fiji	17.3	3.6
Kiribati	n.a.	12.7
Solomon Islands	33.0	1.6
Tonga	21.8	4.9
Vanuatu	26.8	-6.2
Western Samoa	26.0	6.0

Source: World Tables and staff estimates.

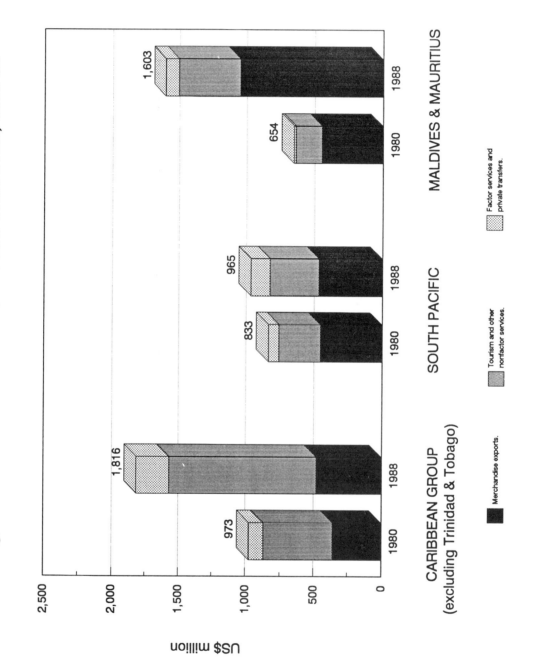

Figure 2: COMPARATIVE EXPORT PERFORMANCE, 1980-88

Box 1: <u>The Success of Mauritius in export-led growth</u>

Manufacturing played a small part in Mauritius' sugar-based economy before independence in 1968. Low income and small domestic markets offered little opportunity for efficient import substitution.

After independence, export-oriented manufacturing and tourism emerged as leading sources of growth, along the lines of small Asian economies such as Hong Kong, Singapore, and Taiwan. Mauritius' success in these areas stemmed in part from policies to attract domestic and foreign investors in export-processing. Exchange rate and wage policies designed to safeguard the competitiveness of export-oriented production, played an important role, as did the Export Processing Zone Act of 1970, which provided for duty-free imported inputs, easy repatriation of capital and dividends, land and factory space, and tax holidays on retained earnings and dividends.

The results in the 1970s were impressive. Industrial investment quadrupled in a few years and was financed largely through profits from the buoyant sugar industry. Real GDP grew at an average annual rate of around 10 percent during the first half of the decade.

Manufacturing growth halted in 1979-82, however, as the decline of sugar prices, the second oil price shock, and worldwide recession generated serious financial and economic imbalances. The Government responded rapidly with short-term stabilization measures, exchange rate adjustment, trade policy reform, and an effective incomes policy to hold down labor costs. Other measures to revive industrial exports included bilateral agreements to avoid double taxation of dividends, an export credit guarantee scheme to protect commercial banks against default, duty drawbacks for new exports by firms previously oriented toward the domestic market, and export promotion abroad.

These adjustments coincided with the emergence of capital from Hong Kong searching opportunities abroad, especially in countries in which the growth of textile exports was not constrained by quotas. Industrial investment surged in 1983-84; the number of export-processing industries increased from 195 in 1984 to 408 in 1986 and to 586 in 1988. Led by woven and knitted garments, manufactured exports grew at 30 percent a year and overtook sugar as Mauritius' main export (box table 1).

Box Table 1: COMPOSITION OF MAURITIUS' EXPORTS, 1970-88

	1970-71	1980-81	1987-88
Sugar	93.5	60.0	33.9
Export processing zone	-	32.6	61.2
Other	6.5	7.4	4.9
TOTAL	100.0	100.0	100.0

Source: World Bank data.

Figure 3: COMPOSITION OF MERCHANDISE EXPORTS, 1980-89

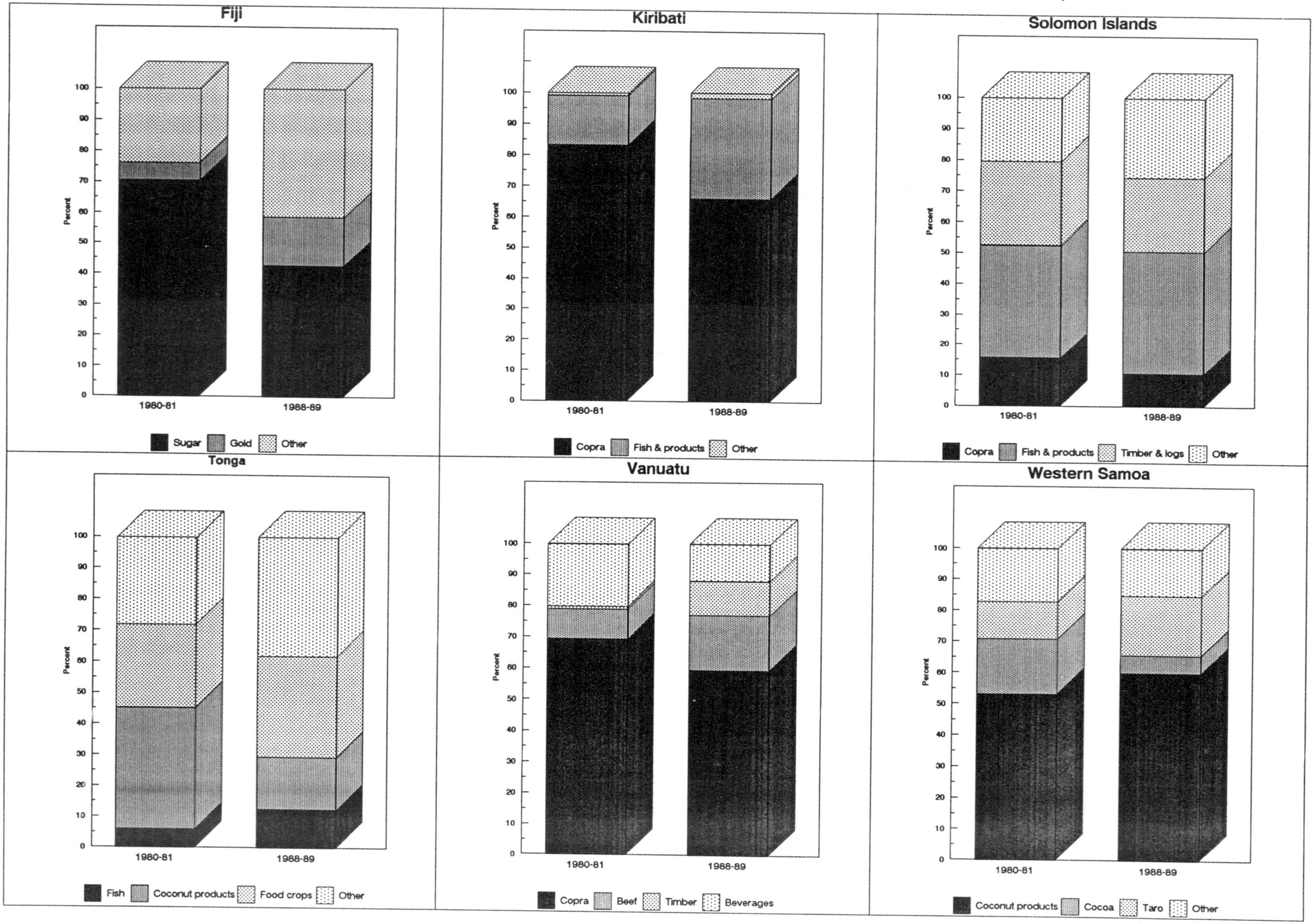

1.34   While growth of export earnings slowed in the 1980s, there was no reduction in import demand; this led to large deficits on the merchandise trade accounts. At times, these trade deficits were substantial. In the case of Kiribati, the trade deficit in 1988 ($17 million) was equivalent to three times total export earnings. In the same year, the deficit for Western Samoa was equivalent to total export earnings; for Solomon Islands, 70 percent of export earnings.

1.35   Trade deficits have largely been offset by official transfers, workers remittances, and tourism receipts. Fiji's tourism earnings have been the principal item serving to offset the merchandise trade deficit. In Kiribati, the Solomon Islands, and Vanuatu, external grants have been the primary source of financing to meet the external resource gap. For Tonga, Kiribati, and Western Samoa, worker remittances have been the most important source of external financing.9/ As a result of ample sources of external financing, the Pacific Island member countries were able to sustain a deficit on the merchandise trade account with only very modest recourse to international capital markets.

1.36   Creditworthiness. Measured in terms of the standard indicators of indebtedness, the PMCs have a modest debt exposure. This stands in marked contrast to many other low- and medium-income countries that experienced great difficulty in meeting debt service obligations during the 1980s. In 1988, the ratio of debt outstanding and disbursed (DOD) to GDP reached 43 percent for Fiji, 59 percent for the Solomon Islands, and 66 percent for Western Samoa but stood at less than 20 percent for Kiribati and Vanuatu. For Fiji, debt service obligations were a comfortable 10 percent of export earnings; for Western Samoa, they accounted for 8 percent. For the other countries, debt service obligations were the equivalent of less than 5 percent of export earnings. The PMCs' emergence from the 1980s with little external debt is the result of a cautious fiscal and monetary stance, good access to external grant financing, and increased worker remittances. Still, excepting Fiji, the PMCs are constrained in their creditworthiness by their narrow production and export base and by their small size. Based on the experience of the past decade, it would be difficult to justify commercial borrowing to finance public investment, given that past high levels of public investment have resulted in virtually no change in per capita GDP.

C.   The External Environment

1.37   A question often asked in assessing the performance and potential of the South Pacific countries is whether they faced a particularly difficult external environment or circumstances that would account for their weak growth

---

9/   Tonga and Western Samoa receive substantial amounts of personal remittances (roughly $30-35 million per annum) from kinsmen working overseas in New Zealand, Australia, and the United States. Remittance flows for Kiribati derive from workers employed on overseas vessels and in the phosphate industry. For Vanuatu, a substantial source of earnings is workers employed on foreign fishing boats.

Table 1.10. PACIFIC ISLANDS: EXTERNAL FINANCING REQUIREMENTS AND SOURCES, 1985-89
(US$ million per annum at current prices)

	Fiji	Kiribati	Solomon Islands	Tonga	Vanuatu	Western Samoa
Requirements	69	16	55	34	44	53
Merchandise imports	360	18	94	39	54	61
Merchandise exports	-264	-3	-72	-7	-14	-13
Principal repayments /a	37	-	2	-	1	4
Interest payments /a	25	-	2	1	1	1
Other service payments	-110	-3	28	-1	-4	-11
Change in NFA	21	4	1	2	6	11
Sources	69	16	55	34	44	53
Private transfers	-9	2	3	22	9	32
External grants	24	16	33	6	32	16
Public loan disbursements	24	-	13	3	3	5
Other capital (net)	30	-2	7	3	-2	-

/a Public MLT debt only.

Source: World Bank staff estimates.

performance.10/ To address this question, this section examines the key elements of the external environment facing the PMCs in the 1980s: the terms of trade; susceptibility to natural disasters; instability of output; and, access to finance.

Terms of Trade

1.38   Part of the reason for a modest and volatile growth performance is adverse movements in the world market prices for key PMC commodity exports. However, the net barter terms of trade currently facing the PMCs is little changed from the beginning of the decade; following a marked improvement

10/ See, for example, A. Thirlwall, "The Performance and Prospects of the Pacific Island Economies in the World Economy," Pacific Island Development Program, East-West Center, 1990.

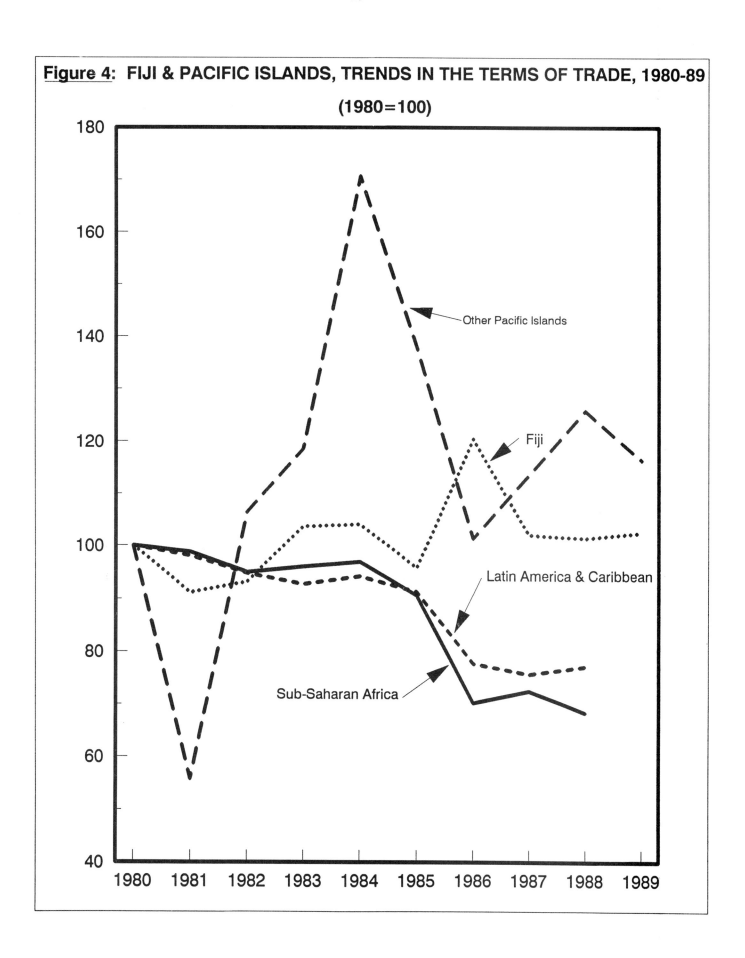

Figure 4: FIJI & PACIFIC ISLANDS, TRENDS IN THE TERMS OF TRADE, 1980-89

(1980=100)

Table 1.11. PACIFIC ISLANDS: INDICES OF TERMS OF TRADE, 1980-89 /a
(1984 = 100)

	FIJI	KIRIBATI	SOLOMONS ISLANDS	TONGA	VANUATU	WESTERN SAMOA
1980	96.1	n.a.	n.a.	n.a.	56.4	n.a.
1981	87.6	93.5	n.a.	n.a.	44.8	51.0
1982	89.6	67.2	84.1	n.a.	39.9	53.2
1983	99.7	63.9	75.7	n.a.	61.9	69.1
1984	100.0	100.0	100.0	100.0	100.0	100.0
1985	92.1	78.6	87.7	95.6	65.9	74.4
1986	115.8	34.7	67.3	95.0	27.5	50.9
1987	98.1	39.3	78.2	94.2	45.7	53.8
1988	97.5	45.8	89.5	90.1	n.a.	62.8
1989	98.6	n.a.	79.6	89.9	n.a.	55.1

/a SDR terms.
/b IECSE's weighted commodity price index of agriculture and timber.
Source: IMF and World Bank staff estimates.

during the period 1980-84, the terms of trade drifted downward.11/ Many developing countries such as those in Sub-Saharan Africa, whose exports are predominantly primary products and whose imports are largely manufactured goods, experienced a sharp decline in the net barter terms of trade (figure 4). While the Pacific Island member countries finished the decade at approximately the same level of relative prices, the developing countries as a whole faced a 20 percent decline. Clearly, the terms of trade environment for the PMCs was not particularly adverse in 1980s by the standards of the broader developing world.

Natural Disasters

1.39   Part of the explanation for the weakness and volatility of growth performance lies in the heavy economic and human burden of periodic natural disasters--especially cyclones, which damaged every PMC during the 1980s. The 1986 cyclone in Fiji affected nearly a third of the population; the 1990 cyclone in Western Samoa destroyed a quarter of the homes and contributed to the loss of more than half the food supply. Fiji has also suffered massive floods and hurricanes. In the wake of such events, generous donor support has enabled the PMC economies to mount vigorous reconstruction campaigns without jeopardizing other elements of public investment.

11/ This result occurs in part because of favorable movements for high-value exports, such as gold and timber, and because of the importance of basic foodstuffs and petroleum (which experienced a sharp decline in the import basket of the PMCs).

Box 2: DISASTERS IN THE PACIFIC ISLAND COUNTRIES /1 (1985-1990)							
Year	Country	Type	Killed	Affected	Homeless	Damage /2 US$'000	Comments
1985	Vanuatu	Cyclone	9	117,500	..	..	3 cyclones; 6 islands; thousands homeless; 75% of copra crop destroyed.
1985	Fiji	Cyclone	28	100,000	..	..	Cylones Eric and Nigel; Lautoka area; building insurance claims reached US$73 million.
1985	Fiji	Cyclone	3	2,000	..	..	Cylone Gavin; at least 2,000 evacuated.
1985	Solomon Islands	Cyclone	0	650	650	..	Utupia, Vanikolo, and Tikopia Islands; 131 homes and other buildings destroyed.
1985	Fiji	Cyclone	1	20,000	..	..	Western and Central Divisions; floods/landslides; extensive damage to crops; property damage estimated at US$3 million.
1986	Fiji	Floods	19	215,000	..	15,400	Central Division; torrential rains; figures include undeclared disaster from Cyclone Martin in Vanua Levu.
1986	Solomon Islands	Cyclone	101	90,000	60,000	..	Islands of Malatia, Guadalcanal, Ulawa, Makima, Rennell, and Bellona; Cyclone Namu; heavy damage to crops, homes, and infrastructure.
1986	Fiji	Cyclone	1	3,000	..	20,000	Northern Vanua Levu/Taveuni/ Lau Group; Cyclone Raja; damage to crops, roads, bridges, water/power supply systems; preliminary estimate of damage.
1987	Vanuatu	Cyclone	48	48,000	..	25,000	Efate, Erromango, Tanna and Aniwa; Cyclone Uma, damage to houses, crops, and utilities.
1988	Vanuatu	Cyclone	0	3,100	1,600	..	Torres and Banks Groups and W. Espiritu Sanio; Cyclone Anne.
1989	Western Samoa	Cyclone	0	..	..	15,500	Countrywide; especially Savai'i Island; Cyclones Fili and Gina; Heavy rainfall and flooding caused damage to roads and bridges; several houses washed away; unofficial damage figures.
1990	Western Samoa	Cyclone	11	80,000	25,000	140,000	Cyclone Ofa; widespread devastation across Northern Upolu and Savai'i; severe damage to roads, airstrips, port facilities, and other infrastructure and to agricultural productive capacity, with loss of 50% livestock and 70% national food production.

/1 Fiji (5 reports of disasters); Kiribati (0); Solomon Islands (2); Tonga (0); Vanuatu (3); Western Samoa (2); total 12 for 4 countries.

/2 Estimates for those affected, homes lost, and damage incurred are shown wherever available.

Source: Disaster History, Significant Data on Major Disasters Worldwide, 1900 - Present. Office of U.S. Foreign Disaster Assistance, Agency for International Development, Washington, D.C. July 1989. Information for 1990 added from World Bank sources.

Instability of Output and Incomes

1.40   What is implied by PMC susceptibility to natural disasters and the
narrowness of the production and export base is potential instability of
output and incomes. Domestic output growth of most PMCs was indeed
characterized by considerable volatility during the 1980s because of variable
weather conditions and natural calamities (table 1.4). Yet despite these
year-to-year fluctuations, the PMCs demonstrated their ability to rebound
quickly from the effects of cyclones or droughts, in part because of the
resilience of the subsistence economy. Moreover, the instability of export
revenues and imports was not significantly higher than in other small
economies and many larger economies (table 1.12). As previously noted, the
availability of external grant assistance also acted as an important
stabilizing influence.

Table 1.12: INSTABILITY INDEX, 1980-88

	Exports	Imports
PACIFIC		
Fiji	0.06	0.07
Kiribati *	0.13	0.06
Solomon Islands	0.09	0.12
Tonga	0.15	0.12
Vanuatu *	0.39	0.37
Western Samoa	0.15	0.13
CARIBBEAN	0.08	0.15
Antigua and Barbuda	0.09	0.07
Barbados	0.08	0.09
Dominica	0.15	0.07
Grenada	0.10	0.09
St. Kitts and Nevis	0.09	0.10
St. Lucia	0.12	0.02
St. Vincent and the Grenadines	0.08	0.15
AFRICA AND INDIAN OCEAN		
Comoros	0.39	0.08
Maldives	0.22	0.08
Mauritius	0.22	0.25
Sao Tome and Principe	0.27	0.14
Seychelles	0.13	0.10
OTHER		
Brazil	0.10	0.08
Chile	0.18	0.18
Ghana	0.27	0.22
India	0.07	0.06
Indonesia	0.09	0.11
Kenya	0.09	0.18
Pakistan	0.09	0.04
Thailand	0.17	0.18
Tunisia	0.15	0.17

Source: World Tables, 1989-90
* 1982-88

Availability of Finance

1.41   Since the PMCs benefited from high and rising levels of official
assistance during the 1980s, they were able to cover their domestic and
external resource gaps and maintain high investment. In per capita terms, aid
levels in the PMCs have been higher than in other island nations--and a large
multiple of aid received by most low- and middle-income developing countries.
While the Caribbean countries also receive substantial aid, the concessionary
element to the South Pacific is much higher; except for Fiji, virtually all is
in the form of grants. Thus, in contrast to most developing countries, the
PMCs do not have a substantial debt burden despite high levels of external
assistance.

Conclusion

1.42   The preceding assessment of external factors indicates that in the
1980s the South Pacific countries did not face an environment sufficiently
difficult to account for their weak economic performance. Although more
volatile than for larger countries, the PMCs' terms of trade did not decline
as did those of many developing nations. When natural disasters occurred, the
international response was swift and sufficient. The Pacific Island countries
did not have to service large amounts of external debt. Real per capita grant
aid receipts increased over the decade.

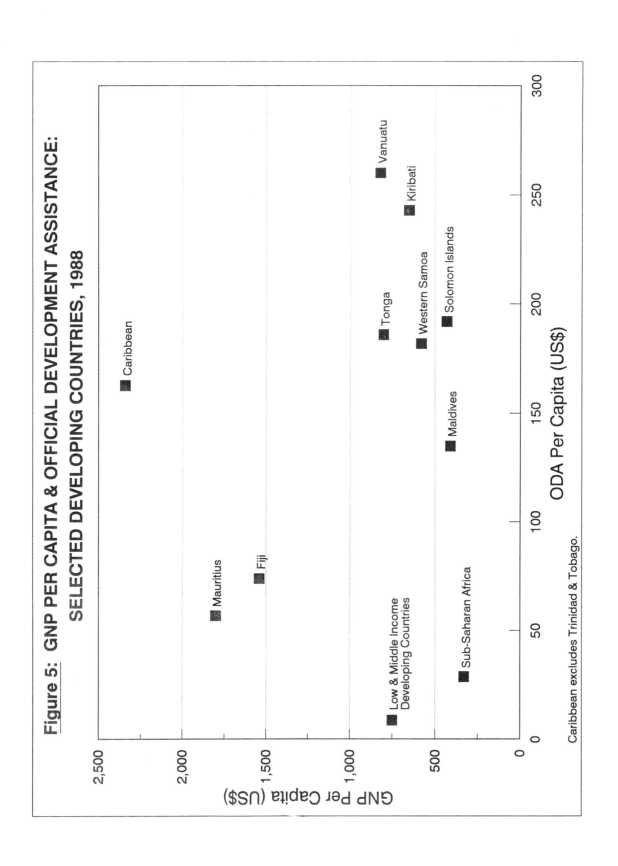

Figure 5: GNP PER CAPITA & OFFICIAL DEVELOPMENT ASSISTANCE: SELECTED DEVELOPING COUNTRIES, 1988

Caribbean excludes Trinidad & Tobago.

II. The Domestic Policy Environment in the 1980s

A. Overview

2.1   The PMCs' weak growth performance in the 1980s came not so much from an adverse external economic environment as from an inability to adopt needed structural reforms. Although delayed macroeconomic responses to shocks sometimes required austerity measures, macroeconomic management was largely sound. The policy shortcomings were more related to growth strategy. In particular, the islands' inward-oriented development has not produced satisfactory results in the past decade. In choosing key sectors, Governments have not been able to pick industries with bright futures. Protection from foreign competition has contributed to high-cost local economies unable to compete in the world marketplace. Investments in infrastructure (largely financed by foreign assistance) have not made a substantial contribution to growth. State enterprises have been a burden on the public finances. Growth of a dynamic private sector has been stifled by over-regulation. Potential foreign investors have set up operations in other countries where the environment is more conducive to doing business.

B. Macroeconomic Management

2.2   By and large, the PMC's were quite successful in maintaining macroeconomic stability during the decade. Their efforts were assisted by the generous availability of external grant financing that permitted them to meet fiscal deficits without excessive recourse to domestic borrowing or international finance and to meet their external deficits without significant external borrowing.

Fiscal Policy 1/

2.3   Fiscal policy is the main instrument of macroeconomic management for all of the Pacific Island member countries; this results from the large share of public expenditures in GDP and the limitations on monetary policy in small, extremely open economies.2/ Although current governmental expenditures are high in relation to GDP, revenue mobilization has been generally sufficient to cover the expenditures in all except Solomon Islands and Vanuatu. In these two countries, relatively weaker revenue mobilization and the phasing out of budgetary assistance and STABEX grants have led to large fiscal imbalances.

1/ This section briefly reviews the macroeconomic aspects of fiscal policy; a more detailed assessment of the role of the public sector is contained in section C.

2/ Limitations on the use of fiscal policy as an instrument of stabilization are discussed in "Macroeconomic Stabilization Policy with Special Reference to Fiscal Policy" by James Guest, Chapter 3 of Selected Issues in Pacific Island Development (R.V. Cole and T.G. Parry, eds.), The National Centre for Development Studies, Canberra, 1986.

Table 2.1: SELECTED MACROECONOMIC INDICATORS, 1980-88

	Fiji	Kiribati	Solomon Islands	Tonga	Vanuatu	Western Samoa
GDP (1988, mil US$)	1076	33	176	87	140	116
GNP per capita (1988)	1540	590	430	800	820	600
Growth rates (% p.a.)						
Real GDP	0.9	1.3	1.8	3.1 /a	1.5 /a	1.9 /a
Consumption	0.5	1.0	5.0	n.a.	-7.7	2.6
Investment	-9.3	6.0	3.5	n.a.	6.4 /d	-4.6
Consumer prices	7.7	5.1	12.9	12.3	9.7	8.4
Population	2.1	1.9	3.5	0.6	3.2	0.3
Ratios to GDP (%) /b						
Gross domestic investment	11.9	27.8	38.6	28.7 /c	31.7	29.5
Gross domestic savings	15.5	-19.2	-3.0	-5.7 /c	9.8	-8.9
Current account	0	-30.0	-39.2	-19.5	-20.0	-7.8
DOD/GDP	43.4	n.a.	59.5	50.9	19.2	65.5
Debt service/exports	10.5	1.3	5.3	2.5	3.0	8.3

/a 1983-88.
/b For last year of the period; current account excludes official transfers.
/c 1980.
/d 1983-87.

Source: World Bank staff estimates.

2.4   One PMC, Kiribati, has been notable for exceptional foresight in responding to a major contraction in its resource base and in acting with great prudence in the conduct of its financial policies. While committing itself in principle to a balanced budget, the Kiribati Government in practice permitted interest income from the Revenue Equalization Reserve Fund (RERF) to be reinvested in most years; after adjustment for reinvested interest income, it recorded significant surpluses in the current account and the overall balance for all but one year during 1985-89.

2.5   Development expenditures as a share of GDP are relatively high in all the PMCs, with the notable exception of Fiji. As a result, all except Fiji have run large fiscal deficits (before grants) during the 1980s. The bulk of development expenditures have been financed by external grant financing. Consequently, the fiscal deficits after grants have been relatively small except for Solomon Islands.

2.6   During the period under review, none of the PMCs resorted to substantial domestic bank financing of the overall deficits.3/ Domestic nonbank borrowing contributed significantly to the financing of these deficits in Fiji, Western Samoa, and Vanuatu; in the first two countries, the National Provident Funds were a major source of such borrowing. External borrowing to

___

3/ Fiji, Solomon Islands, and Vanuatu engaged in significant domestic bank financing of the overall deficits in some years of the period under review, but there were also net repayments in other years.

Table 2.2: FINANCING OF GOVERNMENT BUDGET DEFICITS, 1985-89
(as percent of GDP)

	Fiji	Kiribati	Solomon Islands /a	Tonga /b	Vanuatu	Western Samoa
Total revenue	23.8	46.4/e	23.4/c	29.9	25.8	40.2
Current expenditure	23.0	46.8/d	26.1	27.2	36.1/d	21.3
Savings (= current account surplus)	0.8	-0.4/e	-2.7	2.7	-10.4	18.9
Development expenditure	5.0	37.8	12.6	22.0	17.8	31.2
Overall balance, before grants	-4.2	-38.2/e	-15.3	-19.3	-28.2	-12.3
Financing						
External grants	1.0	36.7	7.6	19.3	25.8	15.6
External borrowing	-0.5	..	6.7	2.6	1.5	2.1
Domestic nonbank	2.9	..	0.3	-0.5	1.1	1.4
Domestic bank	0.8	..	0.7	-2.1	-0.2	-6.8

/a 1985-89.
/b 1985/86 - 1988/89.
/c Includes a very small amount of capital revenue.
/d Includes technical assistance.
/e In Kiribati, total revenue and the current account would be considerably
    higher (by about 12 percent of GDP) and the overall deficit, before grants,
    correspondingly lower if reinvested RERF income were included in revenue.

Sources: Official documents; IMF Consultation Reports; World Bank staff
          estimates.

finance deficits was heavy in Solomon Islands and rather substantial in Tonga
and Vanuatu. Western Samoa also engaged in extensive borrowing abroad but the
proceeds of both this and domestic nonbank borrowing were used to repay
domestic bank loans.

2.7   The PMCs' record in fiscal management is a positive one. In the face
of budgetary imbalances most countries have taken corrective action without
undue delay so as to avoid major inflationary pressures or the buildup of
debt. A recent example is Vanuatu, which has made difficult expenditure
reductions to parallel declining external grant financing. Only in Solomon
Islands has there been a tendency for budgetary imbalances to widen in recent
years.

Monetary Policy

2.8   The PMCs' small size and the openness of their capital accounts
places strict limits on the use of monetary policy; any domestic
disequilibrium will soon be transmitted through capital movements into

pressures on the external reserves position. The use of monetary policy is also restricted by other institutional and structural constraints. These include the existence of a large nonmonetary sector;4/ the rudimentary state of capital markets, which hinders smooth financial intermediation;5/ a shortage of monetary instruments to implement policy;6/ and high consumption propensities that limit the savings flowing into the financial system, particularly in the Polynesian nations.

2.9   Average rates of monetary expansion per year have ranged from 10 percent (Fiji) to 24 percent (Western Samoa). In the case of Western Samoa and Vanuatu, high rates of expansion reflected high inflows of foreign exchange in remittances and factor payments. Monetary expansion was also used to accommodate the effects of higher import prices (table 2.3). As a result of a cautious fiscal stance and a conservative monetary policy, inflation in most PMCs was held to a level that compares favorably with their closest industrialized trading partners. Inflation rates in Fiji, Kiribati, and Vanuatu were in fact significantly below those in Australia and New Zealand; in Western Samoa and Tonga, inflation mirrored that of the two industrialized countries. Only in Solomon Islands did monetization of the fiscal deficit result in an inflation rate well in excess of the region's as a whole. And even in the case of Solomon Islands, inflation was still well below 20 percent, the level generally used to denote a "high inflation" country.

C. The Role of the Public Sector

Overview

2.10   The public sector occupies a dominant position in the economy of all six PMCs. This has come from three principal factors: (1) the dispersal of population among several often remote islands has made it necessary for PMC Governments to undertake larger investments per capita in physical infrastructure and administrative and social overheads than has been the case in most developing countries; (2) the public sector has taken the lead in performing economic activities because private initiative has been lacking historically for social, cultural, and land tenure reasons; and (3) large aid inflows have been used primarily for public sector projects.

4/   Estimates for 1986 suggest that the nonmonetary sector may be as high as 20 percent of GDP in Kiribati and 30 percent in Tonga.

5/   Notable exceptions include Fiji, which partly financed its fiscal deficit during the period by the placement of Government bonds, and Western Samoa, which has relied upon captive markets (for example, the National Provident Fund) as a market for Government securities. However, in neither case is there any evidence of the growth of secondary or interbank markets for debentures or securities.

6/   Variations in reserve requirements of commercial banks has been widely used as the instrument for control of credit and liquidity. There has also been a shift from the use of interest and credit ceilings to a more market-based pricing of capital.

Table 2.3. PACIFIC ISLANDS: MONEY AND PRICES
(average annual rate of increase, 1980-89)

	Money and quasi money	Consumer prices
Pacific Islands		
Fiji	10.0	6.6
Kiribati	n.a.	5.5
Solomon Islands	14.2	12.5
Tonga	14.0 /a	10.1
Vanuatu	17.7	8.4 /b
Western Samoa	23.9	11.1
Sources of imported inflation		
Australia	15.5	8.2
New Zealand	18.7 /b	11.9 /c

/a 1982-89.
/b 1980-87.
/c 1980-88.

Source: IMF International Financial Statistics (various issues).

2.11   Incompleteness of data on the public enterprises in most PMCs (and the absence of consolidated public sector accounts in any of them) makes it difficult to determine precisely the size of the public sector. However, one firm indication of the sector's size is the size of the central Government.[7] For 1985-89, the ratio of central Government expenditures to GDP ranged from 28 percent in Fiji to 85 percent in Kiribati (table 2.4). The role of local government is still small, except perhaps in Solomon Islands. On the other hand, the public enterprises are generally extensive--although the available

---

[7]   A ranking by size of PMC central Government sectors in terms of the ratio of total central Government expenditure in GDP should not be taken as a reliable guide to a ranking by size of PMC public sectors. For example, Vanuatu, with its dual administrative setup, has a larger central Government sector (51 percent of GDP) than Solomon Islands (39 percent). However, available data indicate that Solomon Islands has a much larger public enterprise sector, and probably also a larger local Government sector, than Vanuatu. At the other end of the scale, consolidated public sector accounts would probably indicate that Fiji has both the smallest central Government and the smallest public sector.

data suggest significant variation in the relative contribution of the public enterprise sector to the countries' aggregate output or employment.8/

2.12   The dominance of the public sector in practically all PMCs has magnified the importance of fiscal policy. In addition, limitations on the use of monetary and exchange rate policy have reinforced the key role of fiscal policy in macroeconomic management. PMC Governments have generally recognized the importance of prudence in fiscal policy in avoiding inflationary pressures and balance of payments crises, aiming for the most part at surplus Government current accounts while relying on foreign grants for the financing of development expenditures.

2.13   As is evident from table 2.4, during 1985-89 there were rather wide variations among the PMCs in the ratios to GDP of both Government revenue and Government current expenditure. The revenue to GDP ratios ranged from 23 percent in Solomon Islands to 58 percent in Kiribati (after adjustment for reinvested RERF balances). The current expenditure to GDP ratios ranged from 21 percent in Western Samoa to 47 percent in Kiribati. There were also marked differences in experience with regard to the current balance, before grants. This varied from a deficit of 10 percent of GDP in Vanuatu to a surplus of 19 percent of GDP in Western Samoa.

Revenue Structure and Policy

2.14   While there is a wide spread in the ratios of Government revenue to GDP, the spread in the ratios of tax revenue to GDP is considerably less. These ranged from 18 percent for Kiribati to 31 percent for Western Samoa. Fiji, Tonga, Vanuatu, and Solomon Islands have tax revenue to GDP ratios clustered in the 19-21 percent range. Leaving aside Kiribati, which has a very high nontax revenue (41 percent of GDP), the nontax revenue to GDP ratios are low, ranging from only 2 percent in Solomon Islands to less than 10 percent in Tonga and Western Samoa.

2.15   The PMCs' tax revenue has been fairly income elastic, mainly because import duties are on an ad valorem basis and because taxes on income and profits have made up a substantial part of tax revenue (except in Vanuatu). Nontax revenue has generally been less elastic than tax revenue because specific fees and charges usually form an important component of nontax revenue. In general, the buoyancy of total revenue appears to have been higher than its elasticity; a proliferation of tax exemptions has been more than offset by the introduction of new taxes and by upward adjustments of existing levies.

2.16   It appears that there is no widespread need for large additional revenue generation, in view of generally high ratios of Government revenue to GDP and the absence of major budgetary deficits. In the Solomon Islands and to a lesser extent Vanuatu, however, measures need to be taken to augment revenue, unless expenditure growth can be effectively controlled. If there were to be a reduction in the availability of concessional aid to any of the PMCs or if a Government were to take a decision to reduce its dependence on aid, additional revenue mobilization would become important.

8/ In most PMCs, the reach of the Government has been further extended through marketing or commodity boards, which have generally been established as public enterprises.

Table 2.4: FISCAL INDICATORS, 1985-89

	Fiji	Kiribati	Solomon Islands /a	Tonga /b	Vanuatu	Western Samoa
			(as percentages of GDP)			
Revenue	23.8	46.4 /e	23.4 /c	29.9	25.8	40.2
Tax revenue	19.4	17.5	21.1	20.3	20.5	30.6
Nontax revenue	4.4	28.9	2.2	9.5	5.3	9.6
Grants	1.0	36.7	7.6	19.3	25.8	15.6
Expenditure and net lending	28.0	84.6	38.7	49.2	54.0	52.4
Current expenditure	23.0	46.8 /d	26.1	27.2	36.1 /d	21.3
Development expenditure & net lending	5.0	37.8	12.6	22.0	17.8	31.2
Current balance, before grants	0.8	-0.4	-2.8	2.7	-10.4	18.9
Overall balance, before grants	-4.2	-38.2	-15.3	-19.3	-28.2	-12.3
Financing						
External grants	1.0	36.7	7.6	19.3	25.8	15.6
External borrowing	-0.5	..	6.7	2.6	1.5	2.1
Domestic nonbank	2.9	..	0.3	-0.5	1.1	1.4
Domestic bank	0.8	..	0.7	-2.1	-0.2	-6.8
Memorandum Item						
Overall balance, after grants	-3.3	-1.5 /e	-7.8	-0.1	-2.4	3.3

/a   1985-88
/b   1985/86 - 1988/89.
/c   Includes a very small amount of capital revenue.
/d   Includes technical assistance.
/e   In Kiribati, if reinvested RERF income were included in nontax revenue, the
     figures for total revenue, nontax revenue, current balance before grants,
     overall balance before grants, and overall balance after grants would be 58.0,
     40.5, 11.2, -26.6 and 10.1 respectively, as percentages of GDP.

Sources: Official documents, IMF Consultation Reports, and World Bank staff
          estimates.

2.17   In all six countries, there is need for changes in revenue policy to
make it more conducive to savings, investment, and growth. The revenue
systems need to be adapted, primarily with a view to making them more broad-
based, more elastic, less distortionary and thereby more supportive of
development objectives. As means to this end, it would be helpful if the
elasticity of total revenue were raised by the introduction of sales taxes, by
the conversion of existing specific taxes, duties, fees, and charges to an ad
valorem basis, and by extension of the coverage of income tax in those
countries where the coverage is limited (or, in the case of Vanuatu,
nonexistent). Concurrently, the tax systems need to be made as equitable and
administratively efficient as possible.

2.18   The composition of revenue in the PMCs during 1985-89 is shown in
table 2.5 and figure 6. Taxes on international trade and transactions
constituted the largest source of revenue, except for Fiji, where taxes on
income and profits dominated. In the other PMCs, taxes on income and profits
constituted the second most important source of revenue (except in Vanuatu,
which does not levy such taxes). Domestic taxes on goods and services made a

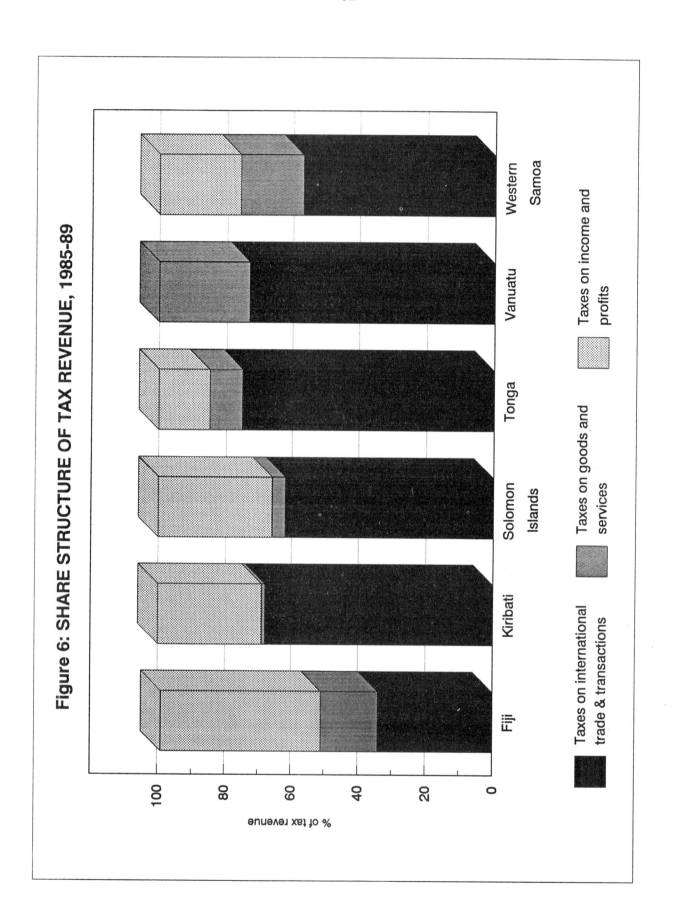

Figure 6: SHARE STRUCTURE OF TAX REVENUE, 1985-89

less substantial contribution to revenue. More detailed features of the tax systems are discussed in Appendix I.

2.19   Nontax revenue. The PMCs' very wide variation in the ratio of nontax revenue to GDP--from 2 percent in Solomon Islands to 41 percent in Kiribati--has been noted. Kiribati has been unique among the six in consistently raising more nontax than tax revenue in recent years, mainly in the form of interest income on a trust fund established before exhaustion of the country's phosphate deposits. Most other PMCs, particularly Solomon Islands, appear to have considerable scope for raising additional nontax revenues, mainly from fees and charges for Government services and from larger public enterprise surpluses. To maintain fees and charges as a fairly buoyant revenue source, regular adjustment is needed to keep pace with inflation as well as to ensure adequate cost recovery. In PMCs with a sizable public enterprise sector, there is considerable potential for increasing nontax revenue by larger transfers of public enterprise surpluses attained through greater efficiency.

Table 2.5: GOVERNMENT REVENUE AND GRANTS, 1985-89

	Fiji	Kiribati	Solomon Islands /a	Tonga /b	Vanuatu	Western Samoa
			Percent of GDP			
REVENUE	23.8	46.4	23.4 /c	29.9	25.8	40.2
TAX REVENUE	19.4	17.5	21.1	20.3	20.5	30.6
Income and profits	9.3	5.4	7.2	3.0	..	7.2
Goods and services	3.2	0.1	0.8	2.0	5.6	5.7
International trade & transactions	6.6	12.0	13.1	15.3	14.9	17.4
Import duties	6.5	12.0	10.1	14.8	14.1	16.3
NONTAX REVENUE	4.4	28.9	2.2	9.5	5.3	9.6
GRANTS	1.0	36.7	7.6	19.3	25.8	15.6
			Percent of revenue			
REVENUE	100.0	100.0	100.0 /c	100.0	100.0	100.0
TAX REVENUE	81.6	38.3	90.4	68.0	79.4	76.4
Income and profits	39.0	11.8	31.0	9.9	..	18.1
Goods and services	13.6	0.3	3.4	6.6	21.6	14.3
International trade & transactions	27.7	26.1	56.0	51.5	57.8	43.4
Import duties	27.4	26.1	43.1	49.8	54.5	40.8
NONTAX REVENUE	18.4	61.7	9.3	32.0	20.6	23.6
GRANTS	4.0	80.9	32.3	64.4	99.2	39.0

/a 1985-88.
/b 1985/86-1988/89.
/c Includes a very small amount of capital revenue.

Source: Official documents, IMF Consultation Reports, World Bank staff estimates.

Current Expenditure

2.20   Level and structure. For reasons cited earlier, the PMCs' current expenditure has generally been high relative to GDP. Kiribati, the most geographically dispersed, had current expenditures nearly one-half of GDP during 1985-89. The ratios were next highest in dually-administered Vanuatu, in Tonga, and Solomon Islands. At the low end, Fiji and Western Samoa had current expenditures in excess of one-fifth of GDP. The ratio of current expenditure to GDP was fairly close to that of total revenue to GDP in most PMCs, the exceptions being Vanuatu, where it was substantially higher, and Kiribati (adjusted) and Western Samoa, where it was markedly lower.

2.21   In recent years, the six Governments have increasingly come to recognize the need to reduce the public sector's relative command over the economy's resources. Accordingly, most have made attempts to restrain the growth of central Government expenditures mainly by reducing current spending. This has proved difficult because of pressures for further extension of Government services, for higher salaries and wages, and for various types of subsidies and transfers, particularly to public enterprises.

2.22   The composition of current expenditures is indicated in table 2.6. The share of personal compensation (wages, salaries, and emoluments) in current expenditure has varied from roughly 40 percent in Kiribati to 53 percent in Fiji. Interest payments on the public debt, still low by the standards of developing countries, have been rising, especially in Fiji and Solomon Islands; in Fiji, they were almost one-fifth of current expenditure by 1989. Transfers and subsidies have formed a major component (over 25 percent) of current expenditure in Solomon Islands, mainly because of large subsidies to public enterprises and transfers to local governments. Elsewhere, transfers and subsidies have also been fairly substantial, mainly reflecting sizable subsidies to public enterprises. Purchases of goods and services, related to both the current operations of governmental agencies and the maintenance of physical assets, have accounted for the bulk of the remaining current expenditures.

2.23   Policies. Growth of the wage and salary bill (the largest item in current expenditure) can only be restrained by controlling wage and salary increases or the number of Government employees. Restraint in granting wage and salary increases has been pursued in several PMCs in the 1980s but with mixed results, partly because of the strength of labor unions and partly because of difficulties in recruiting and retaining skilled personnel.[9] Notwithstanding these difficulties, excessive wage and salary increases must be avoided: they create budgetary imbalances and have a spillover effect into private markets.

---

[9] These difficulties have been especially pronounced in Tonga and Western Samoa, where the Government has to compete with foreign job markets. To a lesser extent, similar difficulties occurred in Fiji in recent years.

Table 2.6: GOVERNMENT EXPENDITURE 1985-89

	Fiji	Kiribati	Solomon Islands /a	Tonga /b	Vanuatu	Western Samoa
			Percent of GDP			
EXPENDITURE AND NET LENDING	28.0	84.6	38.7	49.2	54.0	52.4
CURRENT EXPENDITURE	23.0	46.8	26.1	27.2	36.1 /c	21.3
Wages and salaries	12.2	18.6	12.0	..	15.6	11.0
Interest payments	3.6	..	2.2	..	..	2.8
Subsidies and current transfers	2.4	..	6.9	..	..	..
Subsidies to public enterprises	..	3.8	1.9	..	..	..
Transfers to local government	..	..	3.1	..	..	..
DEVELOPMENT EXPENDITURE & NET LENDING	5.0	37.8	12.6	22.0	17.8	31.2
			Percent of Expenditure and Net Lending			
EXPENDITURE AND NET LENDING	100.0	100.0	100.0	100.0	100.0	100.0
CURRENT EXPENDITURE	82.0	55.4	68.2	55.4	67.8 /c	40.6
Wages and salaries	43.4	22.1	31.5	..	29.1	20.9
Interest payments	12.9	..	5.6	..	..	5.3
Subsidies and current transfers	8.4	..	18.3	..	..	..
Subsidies to public enterprises	..	4.4	4.9	..	..	..
Transfers to local government	..	..	8.2	..	..	..
DEVELOPMENT EXPENDITURE & NET LENDING	18.0	44.6	31.8	44.6	32.2	59.4

/a 1985-88.
/b 1985/86-1988/89.
/c Includes technical assistance.

Source: Official documents, IMF Consultation Reports, and World Bank staff estimates.

2.24   Interest payments have not been an important claim on PMC current expenditures due to a combination of cautious fiscal policies and generous provision of concessionary foreign assistance during periods of budgetary shortfall. However, interest payments have been rising in recent years in Solomon Islands, Fiji, Western Samoa, and Vanuatu (in this case, from low levels). As a general guideline--particularly for PMCs that have experienced rising interest payments in recent years--overall budget deficits should be limited to levels that can be fully financed by concessional foreign loans.

2.25   Subsidies and transfers consist of three major items: (1) those to public enterprises and marketing boards; (2) agricultural and other producer subsidies (for example, fertilizer subsidies); and (3) consumer subsidies and social welfare transfers. Of these, the third has not been significant because social needs tend to be met through the extended family system. Producer subsidies have been fairly substantial in some PMCs but have shown a declining trend in the second half of the 1980s.10/ Subsidies and transfers to

_____

10/ It should be noted that not all the producer subsidies are explicitly identified in the budgetary presentation. In certain cases, subsidies have been made available to producers through the prices paid by commodity or marketing boards and have been reflected in the transfers made to these boards. In other cases, producer subsidies have been financed by commodity boards through extrabudgetary transfers (for instance, of STABEX funds).

public enterprises and marketing boards have been important in every PMC. In most, however, they have declined moderately in recent years. This reflects special efforts made by public enterprises to cut operating costs and adopt cost recovery pricing and also the privatization or reorganization of the least viable enterprises. Efforts to improve the financial performance of public enterprises need to be intensified, since these enterprises remain a major problem area in several PMCs.

2.26   Purchases of goods and services. In times of financial stringency, deepest cuts tend to be made in the purchase of goods and services. Some of these cuts have fallen on goods and services purchased for current operations (for example, fuel for vehicle use, travel allowances for field staff, seed for agricultural extension work), adversely affecting the delivery of Government services. More important, cutbacks have often reduced purchases for repairs and maintenance. In every PMC, expenditure on repairs and maintenance has been inadequate during the 1980s, with resulting deterioration in physical assets particularly evident in the Solomon Islands, Vanuatu, and Western Samoa. Apart from constrained budgetary resources, such neglect sometimes results from a lack of technical expertise and skilled manpower. In addition, it should be recognized that external grant aid has, with few exceptions, been available for new development projects--not for maintenance and repair activity. This can lead to an uneconomic but convenient strategy of permitting existing infrastructure to decay in the expectation that donors will fund replacement projects.

2.27   The issue of recurrent costs. The need to provide sufficient funding for adequate maintenance infrastructure, as well as to ensure that essential services function efficiently, is a continuing problem facing developing countries. In small countries the recurrent cost problem is particularly severe, since the provision of infrastructure and services is far more expensive per capita than in larger countries. In the South Pacific, the problem has also been exacerbated by the large number of projects undertaken in recent years and by the expansion in Government services, particularly in education and health.

2.28   The recurrent budgets of several Pacific Island countries have at times been in substantial deficit, seriously limiting Government ability to fund the local cost component of projects and, perhaps more important, to meet recurrent costs. The problem is probably most acute in Vanuatu and Solomon Islands. It is essential to note, however, that this difficulty is not restricted to countries with budgetary deficits. In the other South Pacific countries, the problem is one of insufficient budgetary provision for operations and maintenance (O&M).

2.29   The lack of budgetary resources is the major factor affecting developing countries' O&M. Domestic revenue is insufficient to meet the local and recurrent costs of the large number of aid activities undertaken and, at the same time, to provide the range of social and other services expected from the Government. Given the size of the economies and the competing demands on revenues, the scope for reallocation of expenditures to provide for O&M is limited. Other factors that contribute to this problem include scarcity of technical expertise and skilled manpower and a lack of priority for maintenance.

2.30   Donor practices may also be a factor. Donor aid programs tend to focus very strongly on new investment. In the project design and appraisal process, insufficient attention is given to recurrent cost capacity, which may lead to the use of inappropriate technology or over-specification. In addition during appraisal, overoptimistic assumptions are often made regarding governmental capacity to make budgetary provisions for recurrent costs.

Development Planning

2.31   Current planning practices. All the PMCs have adopted a broadly similar approach to economic planning using the multiyear plan as the central instrument. Fiji has the longest history of multiyear planning, having produced nine five-year plans. Country plans vary considerably in length, in the quality of the underlying analysis, and in the quality of data sources used. Fiji has been able to produce the most comprehensive plans due to its sound statistical base and availability of sufficient skilled staff.

2.32   The functions of central planning agencies usually encompass strategic and project planning, preparation of the development budget, and, in some countries, aid coordination. Implementation of these functions makes substantial staffing demands; scarce staff resources are devoted to the periodic preparation and review of multiyear plans, often removing them from other tasks. In particular, insufficient priority has been given to the critical task of strategic planning.

2.33   Planning in most PMCs has concentrated almost exclusively on the public sector and on the allocation of Government resources, and appears to have largely been driven by aid considerations. Donors are clearly a key audience for the plan, since they are to provide virtually all the investment funding. In such circumstances, the plan documents often become little more than lists of desired projects prepared with donors specifically in mind. Even in this limited capacity they suffer from not giving donors a clear picture of the relative priority of project proposals. In some cases the projects listed are not entirely consistent with the stated plan objectives, and some proposed projects have had very little appraisal.

2.34   Since the development plans do not really indicate priorities (and in some cases are not finalized until well into the plan period) this information must be obtained in other ways. Donors use field staff reports, programming missions, and other forms of consultations to distill actual priorities; this inevitably influences the outcome.

2.35   Planning offices have a central role to play in working closely with the sector ministries in the early stages of identifying and evaluating projects. However, coordination between planning offices and sector ministries appears to have been weak in many PMCs, due in part to the competing demands placed on planning staff. In addition, since available staff resources are heavily committed to routine administration, only limited attention can be given to project preparation; beyond the initial conceptual stage, this is often left to donors--and they may give greater weight to their own considerations than to the recipient Government's strategic priorities.

2.36   <u>Towards more effective planning</u>. Despite the considerable effort that has gone into improving capacity and techniques, development planning in several countries still does not appear to achieve the primary objective, namely to ensure that resources are used as efficiently as possible to foster economic and social development. Existing planning processes therefore need to be examined carefully to see that: (1) they are not oversophisticated; (2) they provide Governments with a clear framework for establishing priorities for allocation of domestic and external resources; and (3) they do not absorb scarce staffing resources that might be better used elsewhere.

2.37   The vulnerability of the PMCs to external shocks makes detailed multiyear plans highly speculative at best. And since such plans do not presently provide a satisfactory framework for the efficient allocation of resources, their value is open to question. This is particularly the case in view of the unreliability of data in most PMCs and the substantial required inputs in administrative and technical resources.

2.38   The multiyear plans covered in this survey all contain national and sector objectives, a review of the previous plan, and a list of projects to be implemented or begun during the period. Most plans can be criticized on grounds that far too little attention went to the macroeconomic aspects of development and to formulating a set of consistent policies aimed at fostering development. Without such work, there is likely to be only a weak link between public investment and economic growth, while problems of absorptive capacity may be aggravated.

2.39   Governments must allocate a higher priority to the macroeconomic, strategic, and policy components of planning if aid and other resources are to be used more efficiently and effectively. Where it does not exist, the PMCs should consider establishing a distinct macroeconomic policy unit staffed separately from project planning and aid coordination. Fiji, for example, has recognized this need and has a well-staffed macroeconomic division within the Ministry of Finance. Donors should give a high priority in their programs to meeting requests for resources to staff these units.

2.40   While the development plans typically enumerate national and social objectives, insufficient effort has been made to assign them a timeframe or relative priorities or to use them as a way of concentrating donor assistance on priority areas. A more appropriate approach would be to give the strategic planning function greater priority; the planning process should be limited to the identification and clear statement of medium- and long-term economic and social objectives and to the formulation of a coherent strategy to achieve them. The task of plan preparation would thereby change from one of emphasis from a listing of project proposals to that of strategic and macroeconomic planning at national and sectoral levels.

2.41   Strategic planning should encompass all Government activities--not just those funded by aid--and should be extended into the full annual budget process. The preparation of budgets that include forward estimates would enable in-line ministries to be more readily aware of overall staffing and cost considerations of aid projects. The procedures to establish the above processes are not overly complicated; both Papua New Guinea and Fiji already offer good examples of how these processes might be implemented.

2.42   Existing detailed planning documents should be replaced by two shorter, related statements, which would be issued and updated annually:

(1)   A statement of national economic strategy and policies.
(2)   A public sector investment or expenditure program.

2.43   <u>The strategy and policy statement</u>. This should be a short but comprehensive expression of Government strategies and policies for economic and social development. It should include enough information on recent performance to place the issues in context and should be specific as to policy intentions. It need be only 25 or 35 pages long.<u>11</u>/

2.44   <u>The public sector investment program</u>. Most PMCs have well established budgetary systems that encompass recurrent expenditure and those items of capital development expenditure for which the central Government is directly responsible. But, the present systems do not always provide information sufficient to allow Governments to manage the development plan and assign priorities effectively. The development plan, aid flows, and the budget could all be integrated through public sector investment programs (PSIPs), which project expenditure on a two-, three-, or four-year basis and clearly specify all costs and planned sources of finance.

2.45   The advantages of an annually updated PSIP are clear: it is not technically possible to identify a comprehensive list of projects covering a five-year period. In practice, the projects identified for the early years of the plan are already relatively firm, since they are mostly approved and financing has been obtained. As time passes, projects identified for the outer years are often dropped and other projects added; priorities change in response to changing domestic requirements and to external events. As examples within the last five years, the public investment programs of Solomon Islands, Vanuatu, Fiji, and Western Samoa have had to be substantially modified because of the impact of cyclones. This demonstrates the doubtful value of detailed long-term planning.

2.46   <u>Improving the use of staff resources</u>. There is no need for larger central planning agencies to prepare ever more comprehensive documentation. Some countries have already decided to try to integrate the planning process into other central coordinating departments such as the prime minister's office or those responsible for annual budgets. The latter approach has the advantage that greater attention is likely to be given to recurrent funding pressures arising from proposed projects while allowing priorities to be set between the recurrent and development budgets. The longer-term strategic

---

<u>11</u>/ A possible list of contents of such a statement, modified from a recent strategy and policy document from Grenada, would include: (1) <u>General Overview</u>. (2) <u>Economic Review</u>: Growth Trends; Balance of Payments; Wages, Prices, and Employment; Money and Credit; Public Finance. (3) <u>Development Issues and Strategy</u>: Employment Creation; Investment and Savings; Human Resource Development; Absorptive Capacity; Trade; Land Issues; Role of the Private Sector; Environmental Protection. (4) <u>Fiscal Policy and Strategy</u>: Fiscal Trends; Constraints; Strategy; Debt Policies; External Assistance. (5) <u>Sectoral Policies and Strategies</u>: Agriculture; Fisheries; Tourism; Industry; Infrastructure; Education; Health and Nutrition; Housing; Institutional Development.

planning functions must, however, be given sufficient priority to avoid domination by the pressures of an annual budget.12/

2.47   Integrating the planning function with the budget process is likely to lead to more effective use of scarce staffing resources. Staff currently involved in the preparation and review of multiyear plans can be diverted toward improving project identification and appraisal--a key factor in increasing absorptive capacity. It is doubtful whether most Pacific Island countries have enough experienced people to decentralize project planning across the full range of sector ministries; in the short term, central planning staff will retain some functions in this area. As a first step, however, Governments should ensure that key ministries such as education, agriculture, and public works are the best staffed and capable of detailed project identification and preparation.

2.48   Accountability and review. Plan reviews prepared by planning authorities have not always received endorsement by Government, which considerably reduces their value. In addition, the lack of a proper review function undermines the Government's accountability for achieving plan objectives. In this regard, a change from multiyear plans to annual statements of strategies by the Government would readily accommodate realistic review. If increased responsibility for project planning were to be allocated to individual line ministries, it would result in improved parliamentary scrutiny of departmental proposals and performance, further improving accountability.

Public Enterprises

2.49   As noted, public enterprises have played a dominant role in the economic development of the PMCs, expanding rapidly following each country's independence through the mid-1980s. Outside the financial sector, public enterprises are heavily involved in the provision of basic services as well as commercial goods and services. A total of more than 100 publicly owned nonfinancial enterprises operate in these island economies, with relatively heavy concentrations in Kiribati, Solomon Islands, and Western Samoa; public enterprises occupy a relatively less commanding position in Fiji.

2.50   Public enterprises have been a burden on the fiscal budget in all the PMCs. Operating surpluses of the enterprises have generally been insufficient to meet capital expenditure requirements, causing the enterprises to rely heavily upon external aid to finance their investments. High wage costs, overstaffing, inflexible pricing policies, bureaucratic management techniques, and political interference in management have been commonplace.

2.51   Prompted by financial losses and by concerns expressed by bilateral donors as well as by multilateral agencies, several of the Pacific Island nations have undertaken reform of their public enterprises since the mid-

---

12/ The Solomon Islands, in a recent reorganization of the planning structure, has gone further and has separated the ministerial responsibilities for planning. The policy and strategy functions are now under the prime minister while project planning and aid coordination are divided between the Ministries of Finance and Provincial Government. Such an approach requires careful management to ensure that there are no failures in coordination between ministries.

1980s.13/ In some cases, the annual budgetary process has been strengthened with the aim of enforcing greater financial discipline on the enterprises. In other cases, monitoring units have been set up to track and analyze enterprise financial performance.

2.52   Notwithstanding the steps taken to date, a great deal remains to be done to restructure the system of public enterprises in the PMCs. In the case of nonviable enterprises, liquidation should be given serious consideration. For enterprises that perform activities more effectively managed by the private sector, a program of privatization should be undertaken. Such a program could involve the outright divestiture of enterprises, the partial sale of ownership in enterprises (including through the public sale of shares on stock exchanges), conversion to joint ventures with a foreign partner, and the placement of certain activities under management contracts or leases. For those enterprises that remain within the public domain, tariffs should be set at levels that will generate revenues sufficient to cover operating and investment costs. In addition, management of the remaining enterprises should operate in an environment subject to the same market criteria as private firms.

Marketing and Commodity Boards

2.53   Marketing and commodity boards (CBs) represent a form of specialized public enterprise that is common in the PMCs. Such boards typically aim at stabilizing producer prices (and thereby producer income) for specific export crops,14/ while passing on to producers the benefits of centralized purchasing and marketing operations. The prices paid to producers are generally determined on the basis of a formula linked to an average of recent export prices.

2.54   The experience with CBs in the Pacific Island nations has not been fully satisfactory. As with other public enterprises, high wages and overstaffing have been commonplace, causing large markups between the price paid to producers and the export price. In addition, small countries are often short of the skills necessary to operate a successful CB (for example, management efficiency in purchasing, storage, transport, and sale of the product and sophistication in marketing, price setting, and the investment of revenues). The experience of the PMCs indicates that lack of management

---

13/ Western Samoa has moved furthest in this regard. In 1987, the Government began a rationalization program that resulted in the privatization or liquidation of a number of unprofitable enterprises. Recently, the Government has announced a further program of privatization and disengagement of the Government from direct involvement in enterprise. Fiji has also made notable progress in this area since 1987.

14/ It is generally acknowledged that CBs have been successful in stabilizing prices. For example, in B. Hardaker and E. Fleming "Policy Issues in Agricultural Market Development in the South Pacific Region" (Islands/Australia Working Paper No. 86/17, 1986), it is estimated that the variation in producer prices was reduced by 40 percent in comparison with export prices for Fiji and Tonga; in Western Samoa the comparable figure was 60 percent; it was 70 percent for Vanuatu and Solomon Islands.

autonomy often results in producer prices being set too high; this leads financial losses by the CB and to costly Government subsidies of their operations. Following experience with such losses, steps were taken in the late 1980s to begin reform of the operations of several CBs, particularly in Tonga and Western Samoa, where the performance of marketing boards has been weak.

2.55   Many of the recommendations for other types of public enterprises (paragraph 2.52) are relevant to commodity boards. Even so, the key to eliminating the fiscal burden of CBs centers on a gradual withdrawal of Government subventions, encouragement of greater competition in export marketing and, in the long term, development of risk bearing contingency markets.15/ In view of the difficulties experienced by CBs in following this strategy, greater consideration might be given to the possibility of stabilizing prices through more active use of trade taxes and levies. As to the role of CBs in marketing, this function can often be carried out more effectively by competitive private traders; in such cases, the CB should be restructured or rationalized without its marketing function. In phasing out or reducing the functions of commodity boards, Governments need to ensure that there are alternative mechanisms for quality control and adherence to quarantine requirements.

D.   The Environment for Private Sector Development

2.56   Although the PMCs' private sector has traditionally played an important role in smallholder agriculture, fishing, small industry, and the provision of many services, public sector participation in economic activity expanded appreciably after independence. By the late 1980s, central Governments owned over 100 enterprises that together with other governmental operations reached deep into most economic areas. The dominant role of the public sector, a general lack of competitiveness, an inward orientation, a regulatory rather than a promotional approach to private investment, and weak financial sectors all combined to stifle private sector development.

Competitiveness

2.57   Exchange rate policies. In contrast to the policies followed during the 1970s, most PMCs introduced flexibility in the setting of their nominal exchange rates in the 1980s.16/ Unlike many developing nations, however, the six made only moderate attempts to improve macroeconomic competitiveness through exchange rate adjustment. Exchange rate policies have primarily been used to restore price stability but at a level of competitiveness consistent

---

15/ Comparative experience indicate that commodity price stabilization schemes have not been effective and have resulted in considerable fiscal burden.

16/ With the exceptions of Kiribati and Tonga, all PMCs have adopted the system of determining the value of their currencies in relation to a weighted basket of currencies. Kiribati does not issue its own currency (the Australian dollar circulates as legal tender) and Tonga is pegged to the Australian dollar. During the 1980s, Fiji and Vanuatu made several large discrete changes against their respective baskets of currencies, while Solomon Islands and Western Samoa made small frequent adjustments.

Table 2.7: INDICES OF REAL EFFECTIVE EXCHANGE RATES, 1980-89 /a

(1985=100)

	PMCs						CARICOM								AFRICA & INDIAN OCEAN		
	Fiji	Kiribati /b	Solomon Islands	Tonga	Vanuatu	Western Samoa	Antigua/ Barbuda	Barbados	Dominica	Grenada	St.Kitts/ Nevis	St.Lucia	St. Vincent	Trinidad/ Tobago	Cape Verde	Mauritius	Seychelles
1980	95.1	108.4	109.0	..	..	118.3	91.4	75.2	76.9	72.4	91.7	85.3	87.6	59.9	87.0	107.5	77.5
1981	97.6	117.5	116.3	..	..	122.3	95.7	82.0	83.1	83.7	94.5	93.6	92.6	65.9	91.3	111.8	90.7
1982	98.1	117.8	119.7	..	..	125.2	97.1	88.7	86.2	88.8	97.2	96.0	95.9	73.1	96.5	108.5	89.9
1983	97.5	115.4	108.5	..	93.5	114.9	97.9	93.2	91.5	93.7	98.2	97.5	99.4	83.2	100.9	106.5	94.6
1984	98.6	118.8	109.8	..	100.7	110.0	101.4	98.5	99.2	99.9	100.0	100.5	101.0	95.8	100.9	103.2	99.2
1985	100.0	100.0	100.0	100.0	100.0	100.0	100.0	100.0	100.0	100.0	100.0	100.0	100.0	100.0	100.0	100.0	100.0
1986	89.9	87.5	84.8	101.6	91.2	92.9	93.4	93.2	93.1	93.1	96.3	94.1	98.4	89.5	97.4	96.8	95.3
1987	76.5	87.3	73.2	91.9	88.2	89.0	89.5	88.0	89.2	83.7	90.8	92.4	93.8	64.1	100.0	88.2	93.0
1988	64.9	96.1	75.2	95.7	..	88.9	89.1	85.7	83.8	81.5	84.4	86.5	88.1	60.5	100.9	84.9	91.5
1989	64.9	103.1	77.5	124.8	..	86.0	89.9	88.0	86.9	84.9	86.2	88.1	..	59.3	99.1	86.0	89.1

/a Period averages.
/b Australia's index. Because of inflationary differentials, caution must be exercised in interpreting the index. Nevertheless, the Australian dollar is the medium of exchange in Kiribati.

Source: IMF International Financial Statistics (various issues); World Bank IEC.

with a widening trade gap and heavy reliance on external assistance. While there have been sizable declines in the real effective exchange rate (REER) for Solomon Islands and Western Samoa, only in Fiji has exchange rate management been geared specifically to enhancing competitiveness. In Tonga and Kiribati, by contrast, the REER appreciated during the second half of the 1980s.

2.58   Wage rates and labor markets. Although most PMCs adopted more flexible exchange rate policies in the 1980s, several countries have simultaneously followed centralized systems of wage-setting arrangements that have resulted in de facto indexation and considerable downward rigidity in real wages. The combination of generous public sector wage awards, a high degree of unionization, and centralized wage setting, wage controls, and minimum wage restrictions has effectively severed the link between wages and productivity.17/ Rigidities in labor markets have driven up domestic wage costs well in excess of productivity gains, largely offsetting the competitive gains that would otherwise have accrued from nominal exchange rate flexibility. As a result, the average level of real wages in the South Pacific are well above the levels of other countries of a similar or higher level of national income (table 2.8). This loss of potential competitiveness has reduced incentives for export and import substitution activities, thereby reducing investment demand and paid employment. Linking wage awards to inflation rates has also tended to reinforce a cycle of higher prices and wages, reducing the impact of exchange rate adjustments as a tool for enhancing competitiveness.

Table 2.8:   PACIFIC ISLANDS: AVERAGE MONTHLY EARNINGS
IN MANUFACTURING INDUSTRIES, 1979-86
(US$)

	1979-81	1984-86
Fiji	159.4	370.6
Tonga	85.1	n.a.
Vanuatu	n.a.	142.0
Western Samoa	80.1	n.a.
St. Lucia	76.1	128.9
Mauritius	58.3	49.7

Source: ILO Yearbook of Labor Statistics, 1988; IFS.

17/ Historically, labor market rigidities have been most pervasive in Fiji, Solomon Islands, and Vanuatu. In recent years, encouraging flexibility in this regard has been shown by Kiribati, Vanuatu, and Western Samoa, which adopted more restrained public sector wage policies in 1983-87, and in Fiji, which implemented a 15-month wage freeze in 1984.

Inward Orientation and Regulation of Investment

2.59   Compounding rigidities in the labor market has been a policy of inward orientation in trade and investment policy. Key facets of this policy included use of quantitative restrictions (for example, bans, government import limits, monopoly trade rights), punitive tariffs, domestic administration of commodity prices, and direct public sector involvement in commercial activities. In addition to a widening merchandise trade deficit, the net effects of this policy have been: (1) to discourage private sector investment as a whole; and (2) to bias private sector investment toward production for the small home market instead of for world markets. Industries such as tourism, which naturally cater to world markets, were especially disadvantaged by the high cost of imported goods and high wage rates.

2.60   In most PMCs, external trade policy represents an area where policy reforms would encourage outward-oriented private initiative. Although PMCs have tended not to rely excessively upon quantitative controls, a dismantling of remaining such restrictions on external trade--including export and import bans--should be an early priority. Along similar lines, the taxation of imports, which tends to be high and uneven because of its importance as a means of raising revenue, should be brought into harmony with that of domestic production. Simplification of complex duty drawback schemes would also be helpful.

2.61   An inward oriented trade policy, high wage rates, domination by public enterprises in key commercial sectors and public administration of market prices served as disincentives to new domestic and foreign private investment. In addition, private sector investment--particularly foreign direct investment--is impeded by an excessively regulatory environment. Potential new investors often find themselves bewildered by complex licensing systems, regulations, and procedures that may be administered by Government agencies designed to control new investment; by contrast, these agencies should promote new investment. This complex system of regulations has acted to stifle competition, to inhibit flexibility in resource use, and to retard productivity improvements; in turn, these have raised production costs and damaged international competitiveness. The adverse effect of these policies on investment and growth can be seen most clearly in the case of inflows of foreign direct investment, which have tended to stagnate throughout the 1980s. In Fiji, foreign direct investment remained strong, except for the 1987 period of political unrest, but has been mainly due to expansion by existing foreign enterprises; there has been relatively little investment by new enterprises. Only Vanuatu, with its offshore financial center and range of tax free privileges, has managed to attract growing amounts of foreign direct investment. Again, progress in small Caribbean nations and in the Indian Ocean countries has been far more promising in this area (table 2.9), demonstrating that a commitment to growth and an enabling policy environment will, in fact, generate an investment response regardless of the remoteness and size of the economy.

2.62   To stimulate private sector investment and growth, policy reform should be directed toward a prompt reduction of such regulatory hurdles. Licensing requirements need to be streamlined and consolidated, usually in a major way, including by making procedures more automatic. Wherever possible, "one-stop" centers should be introduced to clear the way for new investors to satisfy legitimate licensing requirements without undue difficulty. As to foreign investment, regulations concerning ownership need in many cases to be eased and additional areas opened.

Supporting Institutional Framework

2.63   Substantially narrowing the scope of regulations does not imply elimination of Government involvement in this area. Important regulatory roles will remain, including the maintenance of local safety and environmental standards, the setting and monitoring of product quality standards, and supervision of newly created monopolies (for example, privatized marketing boards). There must be a serious commitment to minimize the reporting and registration burden borne by the private sector, however. The Government can also play an important supportive role in entrepreneurship development by providing information and by filling gaps in key underdeveloped domestic markets -- for instance, export financing and venture capital. All the PMCs currently lack an institutional framework to support private sector development.

2.64   One of the challenges facing island Governments will be to find ways to facilitate a higher level of indigenous participation in private sector development. One promising approach to this problem 18/ stresses the central role likely to be played by small business; policy recommendations to make progress along these lines involve ambitious development of venture capital markets and educational courses at regional universities to foster entrepreneurial skills. Under this approach, Governments would play a catalytic role through the adoption of certain foreign programs that use governmental strengths in the aggregation of capital for investment and private sector strengths in the effective use of capital. The International Finance Corporation has taken a lead role in addressing this issue through that institution's South Pacific Development Facility, (SPPF), which has just begun operations. The facility will assist mainly small- to medium-scale private sector enterprises by providing technical assistance to help screen project ideas and to develop viable project proposals suitable for funding by existing financial institutions.

Financial Sector Development

2.65   Over the years, development of the PMCs' financial sector has been hindered by heavy reliance on external aid, which is disbursed primarily through the public sector. Governments, finding it unnecessary to rely upon funds mobilized locally, have accorded low priority to the development of a well-functioning financial system. These priorities will need to be reconsidered as part of a developmental strategy based upon growth rooted in the private sector. The capacity of the private sector to respond to a stronger incentive system will depend to a substantial extent upon complementary policies that improve the cost of availability of funds to finance investment.

18/ "Blueprint for Stimulation of Small Business Development and New
     Venture Creation in the Pacific Islands Region," by Taturoanui Graham
     Crocombe, Pacific Islands Development Program, East-West Center, March
     1990.

Table 2.9: NET DIRECT FOREIGN INVESTMENT, 1980-89
(US$ million)

| | PMCs | | | | | CARICOM | | | | Africa & Indian Ocean | |
	Fiji	Solomon Islands	Tonga	Vanuatu	Western Samoa	Antigua/ Barbuda	Dominica	Grenada	St. Vincent	Mauritius	Seychelles
1980	34.2	2.4	..	n.a.	..	19.6	..	..	1.1	1.2	5.7
1981	37.8	0.2	..	n.a.	..	22.4	..	..	0.5	0.7	2.8
1982	35.9	1.0	..	6.9	..	23.0	0.2	1.9	1.5	1.8	5.1
1983	32.0	0.3	..	5.9	..	5.0	0.2	2.5	2.1	1.6	5.9
1984	23.0	1.9	..	7.4	..	4.4	2.3	2.8	1.4	4.9	5.9
1985	42.8	0.9	0.02	4.8	..	15.6	3.0	4.1	1.8	8.0	1.1
1986	30.0	2.1	0.11	2.0	..	17.7	2.7	5.0	3.0	7.4	8.4
1987	6.3	10.4	0.19	12.9	..	29.2	8.8	12.7	3.6	17.1	14.0
1988	44.7	1.7	0.06	10.8	..	n.a.	6.9	17.0	3.6	23.6	15.6
1989	32.4	n.a.	n.a.	n.a.	n.a.	n.a.	n.a.	n.a	n.a.	25.6	n.a.
Growth rates (%) 1980-88	3.4	-4.2	44.2	7.8	n.a.	5.9	80.4	44.1	16.0	45.1	13.4

Source: IMF International Financial Statistics (various issues).

Box 3   Cook Islands: Private Sector Development

A member of Asian Development Bank (but not the World Bank) and one of the smallest self-governing Pacific Island countries, Cook Islands exhibits much of the growth potential for small countries discussed in this report.

It has a resident population of about 17,000 on 15 islands; a small land base (240) and only 0.15 hectares of arable land per capita, spread over 2 million square kilometers of the south central Pacific; a high level of external assistance (over $600 per capita in 1987 or about 25 percent of estimated GDP), half of this in the form of budgetary support from New Zealand; and the right of migration to New Zealand. Presently, the Cook Islands dollar (CKI$) is pegged to the New Zealand dollar.

According to official estimates, real GDP growth averaged 7.3 percent per annum in 1982-87, largely because of growth in tourism. Visitor arrivals increased from 10,000 in 1972 to 32,000 in 1988, which is over 3 times the population of Rarotonga, the main destination. There was also rapid growth in manufacturing, construction, and utilities (which doubled their contribution to GDP between 1982 and 1987) and in special initiatives such as the development of an offshore finance industry and a pear and pearl shell industry in the Northern islands. Exports tripled in CKI$ terms between 1982 and 1988, with the most rapid growth in fruit and vegetables, pearl shell, clothing and footwear, and miscellaneous categories.

The main development thrust appears to have come from private sector initiatives encouraged by the official interest in fostering a more effective partnership between public and private sectors. In tourism, for example, the official emphasis is on that sector's status as a "front-line" industry; strong support is given in marketing, negotiated increases in airline capacity, opportunities for local investors, training, and the extension of tourism further into the outer islands.

Despite development options that have been limited by size, remoteness, and the need to preserve its cultural and physical environment, the Cook Islands made great strides during the past decade.

2.66   Despite the low priority accorded their development, the PMCs' financial sectors exhibit a surprising degree of institutional diversity (table 2.10). The typical financial sector includes a central bank, a few commercial banks, a development bank, some insurance companies, a national provident fund, and several credit unions or cooperatives. Notable exceptions include Kiribati, which has a particularly small financial system, and Vanuatu, which also has a well-developed offshore financial center of some 100 banks and nonbank financial institutions.

2.67   Commercial banks represent by far the most important type of financial institution in these islands. For funding, deposits at banks consist of current or demand deposit accounts and fixed term deposits (from the business sector) and savings deposits (often raised through a large number of very small passbook accounts). In lending, the banks normally offer credit for short-term trade financing, overdraft loan facilities (for working capital purposes with terms up to two years), and term financing (three to five years) for asset acquisition. In recent years, lending for home mortgages has been expanding rapidly from a small base while personal lending has been relatively unimportant. Wholesale and retail trade finance is usually the dominant type of lending, and agriculture is least important.

Box 4: The South Pacific Project Facility

In early 1990, the International Finance Corporation introduced the South Pacific Project Facility (SPPF) to help the private sector in the island countries develop small and medium-sized enterprises. The Facility does not provide project financing; rather, it works with enterprenours to start projects and to secure financing from existing sources of capital. In addition, SPPF sponsors special training programs to refine entrepreneurial skills; where appropriate, it also assists governments in the island countries in the privatization of selected public sector enterprises.

SPPF identifies projects during regular country visits and receives proposals directly from project sponsors and from the ADB, IFC, UNDP, and local or regional development banks. After an initial assessment, SPPF selects promising project ideas and works directly with the sponsors in developing them. Once the Facility develops a project idea into a viable proposal, it selects consultants to prepare feasibility, market, and technical studies required for a bankable document; it may also advise on export marketing.

The Facility agrees with the project sponsor on a work program, budget, and time schedule for the necessary development work. The cost of such preparatory work, including additional assistance from consultants and other experts, is provided mainly by SPPF and by funding from other agencies. On occasion, SPPF requires the project sponsor to contribute a token amount, usually as a success fee, to demonstrate commitment to the project. During implementation, SPPF follows project development work closely and assists in defining the terms of reference for consultants; thereafter, SPPF helps in negotiations with investment authorities, equipment suppliers, contractors, financial institutions, and potential technical partners. Furthermore, SPPF will help to identify and select professional staff and to design management organization structures.

SPPF has begun operations. Following a series of staff visits to the region in the first half of 1990, a pipeline of potential projects has been identified and follow-up action will be taken during future staff visits. To date, the Facility has been supported by five donors (Japan, Australia, Canada, New Zealand, and the IFC), receiving pledges for about 60 percent of its five-year budget. Funds are in place for two years of operation. With the continuing assistance of donor countries, the SPPF is expected to make a much-needed contribution to the region.

Table 2.10: TYPES OF FINANCIAL INSTITUTIONS IN THE SOUTH PACIFIC

	Fiji	Kiribati	Solomon Islands	Tonga	Vanuatu	Western Samoa
Central banks	1	..	1	1	1	1
Commercial banks	4	1	3	1	3	2
Offshore banks	..	..	..	8e	100e	4
Development banks	1	1	1	1	1	1
Savings banks	..	..	..	..	1	1
Housing finance inst.	2	..	1	..	(p)	..
Finance companies	1	..	1	..	..	..
National Provident Funds	1	1	1	(p)	1	1
Other provident funds	..	..	1	yes	yes	..
General insurance	5	1	6	4	10	3
Life insurance	3	(a)	4	1	2	2
Credit cooperatives	173	..	yes	65	yes	3
Credit unions	395	..	86	44	yes	29

(a) The same company offers both life and general insurance.
(p) Planned.
(e) Estimated; many may have ceased operation.

Sources: Various World Bank and official documents.

2.68   Development banks represent another important source of financing in
the PMCs. The great bulk of their funding is obtained from international and
bilateral sources channelled through the Government. They are mainly involved
in medium- and long-term lending and in providing clients with some project
management advice. In most cases, these institutions are experiencing
considerable problems with the quality of their portfolios.

2.69   Historically, the main issues in development of the PMCs' financial
sectors center around traditional reliance upon interest rate ceilings[19] and
credit targets, both of which work against innovation and retard private
sector development. In recognition of these problems, many PMCs have
initiated reforms of their financial sectors, most notably toward decontrol of
commercial bank lending rates; during the past decade virtually all PMCs[20]
have removed interest rate ceilings and moved toward market-determined
interest rates. These reforms improved incentives for financial
intermediation in support of economic activity while effectively eliminating

_____

19/ A notable exception is Vanuatu, which has maintained internationally
    competitive interest rates on foreign currency operations in
    conjunction with its offshore banking facility. On domestic currency
    operations, an average interest rate ceiling officially remains in
    place, but this appears to be a general guideline not strictly
    enforced.

20/ Effective July 1, 1989, Tonga raised a 50-year old ceiling of 10
    percent on lending rates to 13.5 percent for new loans.

the need for credit rationing in the private sector. In the case of Kiribati, there was also a reflow of substantial amounts of funds that had been invested abroad.

2.70   Notwithstanding these advances, much remains to be done to improve the financial systems of the PMCs, which generally do not have depth. Monetary authorities often lack adequate instruments for indirect monetary control; this forces reliance upon more blunt instruments (such as variations in reserve requirements) for the implementation of policy. Deposit rates remain highly negative in real terms, which limits the availability of resources to finance private investment. Greater efforts need to be made to safeguard the soundness of the PMC financial systems through stronger banking supervision (especially of locally owned banks) and through improved quality of loan portfolios at state-owned development banks.

Policy Stability

2.71   During the past decade, the policy environment of the Pacific Island economies was characterized by volatility and abrupt change, sometimes stemming from unsettled political conditions. While it is clearly important to improve policies and to adapt them to changing economic conditions, it must be recognized that frequent policy changes generate uncertainty, which acts as a strong disincentive to private investment. Overcoming uncertainties depends to a large extent upon establishing and maintaining credibility of the policy regime. Once the Government has determined the desirable direction of policy reform, it can greatly reduce investor uncertainty by announcing publicly the direction of policy changes, by maintaining the direction of announced reforms, and by implementing the changes in an orderly fashion.

E.   Human Resource Development

2.72   Despite generally high rates of literacy, the acute shortage of qualified and experienced personnel represents a fundamental constraint to development in all the PMCs. Even Fiji, which has larger reserves of trained manpower than most, relies on expatriates to fill some key positions. This acute shortage is the result of a failure to link educational programs with national skills requirements, insufficient or insufficiently advanced educational and vocational training opportunities, and, in some countries, a high rate of emigration.

2.73   Although they vary from country to country, overall educational opportunities have increased more than threefold in the last 15 years. Total expenditures for education and training activities are high, particularly in the Melanesian countries, where over 20 percent of Government expenditure went to the education subsector. Education systems generally cover six years of primary/basic education, three years of junior secondary, and two or three years of senior secondary. Tertiary or higher education programs, which have greatly increased during the last 10 years, include teacher and vocational training and degree programs, particularly in the arts and humanities.

2.74   There are substantial differences in educational performance between the Melanesian countries of Solomon Islands and Vanuatu and the other countries covered in this survey (table 2.11). Despite higher expenditures on education as a percentage of GDP, Melanesian literacy levels are substantially lower, drop out rates are higher, and levels of teacher training are less advanced.

2.75   Notwithstanding the impressive growth in access to the education system over the past decade, many problems remain that affect the quality and number of appropriately trained personnel. In particular, countries are having difficulties sustaining programs and facilities originally funded by external assistance and often built to high-cost Western standards. The significant, often uncoordinated, involvement of many donors in this sector also places substantial administrative pressures on local staff, leaving them little time to devote to the qualitative improvement of programs. Because of the high dependency on donor funds for new activities in the sector, and in some cases for ongoing activities, projects and programs may at times respond to the donor objectives rather than national sectoral goals.

2.76   Better management and administration are needed if improvement in educational quality is to occur. Curriculum development has to be upgraded; too often existing programs were prepared by expatriates and lack effective scope and sequence of learning materials. There is insufficient planning capacity in the sector ministries and a shortage of educational managers in each country. National institutional weaknesses in the areas of management and planning capacity are also exacerbated by difficulties of regional coordination.

Table 2.11: REGIONAL EDUCATION INDICATORS /a
(as percent)

	Fiji	Kiribati	Solomon Islands	Vanuatu	Western Samoa	Asia Region
Primary						
Gross enrollment /b (6-11 cohort)	106	63	48	87	99	105
Teacher/pupil ratio	1/30	1/28	1/26	1/24	1/27	1/36
dropout rates	10	..	26	25	16	6
Transition to secondary	85	..	74	71	82	64
Secondary						
Gross enrollment (12-18 cohort)	52	16	11	12	..	72
Teacher/pupil ratio /c	1/17	1/20	1/18	1/16	1/18	1/24
Teachers trained						
Primary	100	..	64	60	99	97
Secondary	82	..	72 /d	82 /d	78	67
Tertiary						
Gross enrollment	4	/e	2	/e	..	7
Adult literacy rate	85.5	90	20*	30*	98	60.5
Public expenditure on education (% total)	16.3	..	24	23.5	..	11

/a   Varying years 1987-89.
/b   Gross enrollments include average students.
/c   International average: 1/32.
/d   For Solomon Islands 28 percent expatriates and Vanuatu 70 percent.
/e   Less 1 percent.

* Bank estimates.

2.77   Many PMCs have not prepared sound policies and strategies in the education sector to guide potential donors. There is a need for countries to improve their policies and project designs, basing these on coordinated national platform/strategies. There is also a need for donors to agree to more coordinated inputs supporting these national strategies. Periodic country and donor meetings should be organized to enhance coordination and long-term implementation of qualitative improvements within the education sector.

2.78   In addition to the above problems, which apply to the education system as a whole, there are issues that require attention at all levels of education--primary, secondary, and tertiary. All the countries have made impressive progress during the last 10 years in the provision of primary or basic education, with coverage varying from 48 percent in Solomon Islands to virtually 100 percent in the Polynesian countries. However, considerable problems remain:

   (1)   Because of the island nature of these countries, ensuring universal access to primary education is costly; it is difficult for most PMCs to sustain all the required inputs (teachers, educational materials, management, and facilities).

   (2)   Adequate facilities, equipment, and materials (particularly student textbooks and teacher guides) necessary for quality education are lacking throughout the region.

   (3)   The availability of well-trained teachers, particularly in the outer islands, remains a serious issue for all countries and especially in Melanesia. In-service training programs are few, leaving teachers with few opportunities to improve their skills.

   (4)   Wastage/dropout rates tend to be high, ranging up to 26 percent (compared to 6 percent in the Asia region).

   (5)   With a high proportion of teachers either untrained or poorly trained, particularly in Solomon Islands and Vanuatu, some core subjects are not being taught at a satisfactory level. This reduces the quality of basic education and often deprives children of basic literacy skills.

2.79   Secondary education opportunities have greatly expanded in recent years. Unfortunately, however, efforts have been directed primarily toward quantitative expansion with little attention to quality. Due to their smallness and isolation, many islands do not have the necessary population base to justify a local secondary school; despite large increases in enrollments, the secondary output is unsatisfactory due to the quality of the training provided; inadequate emphasis is placed on core subjects. Further problems are the failure to plan teacher training outputs to effectively match subject needs (this often results in surpluses in the humanities and shortages in other subject areas) and the low number of secondary graduates qualifying to train as teachers.

2.80   Recent expansion of educational opportunity has been particularly noticeable at the tertiary/postsecondary level. The region's two established universities (the University of Papua New Guinea, with 4,000 students, and the University of the South Pacific with 2,000) are now being supplemented with the development of several institutions at the national level offering, in some cases, degree level studies as well as vocational/technical and teacher education. These institutions respond to perceived national needs and run a multiplicity of training programs, usually with low enrollments and high unit costs; about 2,000 trainees were enrolled in 1989/90. The lack of resources at these small vocational institutions (in particular qualified and experienced teachers), their internal efficiency, and high unit costs related to the small scale of the national higher education programs are issues that need to be examined.

2.81   There are also substantial opportunities for tertiary training overseas, largely in New Zealand and Australia, with costs usually met by these countries. Unfortunately, external fellowships are not necessarily matched to national skills needs. Thus this training often does not benefit the home country to the extent desired: many trainees do not find employment in their area of training and return to opportunities in their country of training. There is an urgent need to link national and external training opportunities with countries' needs.

2.82   A lack of information on tertiary programs offered in the region results in duplication and gaps in the range of courses offered. Programs are often run with low enrollments and shortages of facilities, personnel, and materials. Links between secondary and tertiary programs need to be improved, since secondary graduates often require an additional year of training/upgrading so they can cope with basic tertiary programs. Finally, many existing programs are not sufficiently relevant to national needs or employment requirements. The lack of responsiveness of existing programs to the acute shortages of middle- and higher-level staff within the Government services and private sector require special attention.

2.83   Future actions. The provision of education and training services represents a major burden on Government expenditure; in the face of young and expanding populations, funding requirements for these services will increase.21/ Given the current budgetary situation facing most of the island Governments, emphasis should therefore first be placed on ensuring that existing facilities are fully used before undertaking costly construction of new facilities. In view of the critical importance of human resource development to the islands' development prospects, donors should continue to increase assistance to this sector to support revised policies and should examine the possibility of financing operating costs until governmental revenue expands.

2.84   Of equal importance in increasing educational opportunity is improved resource allocation. The region-wide assessment of opportunities for postsecondary education being undertaken by the Bank (in association with the USP) is expected to identify options to maximize the use of limited resources. Australia and New Zealand, the main providers of overseas scholarship opportunities to island students, should review their policies to ensure that the nature of courses undertaken outside the island countries is cost-effective and could not be substituted by lower-cost courses in the region itself. They should also examine other measures to provide lower-cost training--such as twinning some of their educational institutions and public authorities with local counterparts.

21/ This includes Polynesia, where low population growth rates largely come from adult emigration.

F. Sectoral Strategies and Performance

Agriculture and Fisheries

2.85   As discussed above, the agriculture sector is the most important
source of productive employment in the Pacific Islands economies. Taking the
six PMCs as a group, agriculture accounts for 28.5 percent of GDP (figure 7).
The services sector, which is largely public, accounts for 56 percent of GDP.
Excluding services, the share of agriculture rises to 74 percent of GDP.
Throughout the 1980s, agricultural growth has been modest, averaging less than
2 percent per annum. Although there is reason to believe that agricultural
production and exports have been underestimated in many cases, the performance
of the sector has been generally disappointing.

2.86   While conditions vary geographically, the traditional farming systems
of the islands are generally efficient, allowing rural populations to maintain
reasonable nutritional levels with relatively low labor inputs and few
purchased inputs, although in some areas increasing population pressures are
threatening the sustainability of the system. On the other hand, attempts to
introduce new sources of growth have often been unsuccessful. Domestic
markets are small, and the scope for economic forms of import substitution
very limited. The focus of agricultural development efforts and external
assistance in the region has therefore been on the production of export
commodities. But, despite these efforts, the traditional exports, such as
copra, sugar and cocoa, have tended to stagnate or decline in face of
declining world market prices. With some exceptions, such as the development
of vanilla in Tonga and coconut cream in Western Samoa, it has also proven
difficult to promote new exports, which typically require better production
techniques and quality control and more sophisticated marketing techniques
than are readily available in the islands.

The Forestry Sector

2.87   The forestry sectors of the Pacific Island nations are strongly
influenced by two major variables: supply from Papua New Guinea (which
dominates supply from the region as a whole), and market developments in
Australasia (which remains the major consumer of products from the Pacific
Islands).

2.88   Fiji is the major forestry producer and exporter among the PMCs. It
has extracted large volumes from its natural resources over the recent decade
and has also developed a major softwood plantation resource; it is in the
process of developing a substantial high quality plantation hardwood resource.
Solomon Islands also has a significant natural forest resource and is engaged
in plantation activity--most notably a large area of fast grown hardwoods on
the island of Kolombangara. Vanuatu has significant areas of natural forest,
but relatively little is known at this stage about its commercial viability.

2.89   According to a recent World Bank study of forest product market
prospects for the region, three major issues face forestry planners in the
area:

(1) Major international markets for commodity grade timber are not
     growing quickly and are subject to increasing competition from
     coniferous plantation suppliers.

Figure 7: ECONOMIC STRUCTURE OF PACIFIC MEMBER COUNTRIES a/

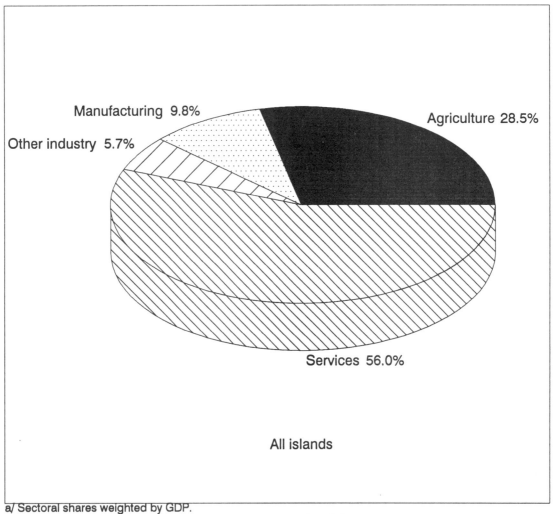

a/ Sectoral shares weighted by GDP.
Agriculture: Agriculture & livestock production, fishing, logging, & forestry.
Other Industry: Mining & quarrying; construction; and electricity, gas, & water.
Services: transport, storage, & communications; wholesale & retail trade; banking, insurance, & real estate;
 ownership of dwellings; public administration & defense.

Source: Various official sources and World Bank staff estimates.

(2) Critical supply and processing decisions will soon need to be made in the region. Fiji's high quality hardwood plantations will probably find lucrative markets, but the situation facing the Fiji pine and the large processing plants is less sanguine. The Solomons has little option in the short term but to rely on log exports, but improved management of this program, including greater efforts in the areas of classification, grading, and marketing, will be required if the resource is to produce a sustainable revenue base. All forest producing countries in the region aspire to greater processing facilities, but all will need to give careful consideration to the type of production developed. A movement from raw resource export to forest product manufacturing should not be considered as automatically preferable for any of these countries.

(3) Important environmental concerns must be addressed to ensure sustainable management of forest areas. Soil and water resources are extremely limited in all countries, and in many cases the forested areas are vital in retaining these.

Tourism

2.90   Tourism is an area in which the PMCs have some natural advantages. But it was not a leading source of income growth and employment during the 1980s. The islands' share of tourism to GDP ranges from 2 to 20 percent; for the small islands of the Caribbean and Indian Ocean, the comparable statistic is 30 to 60 percent. Growth in tourism earnings in the PMCs has been low -- in the Solomon Islands and Vanuatu, negative. Only in Fiji is tourism a major economic activity. In contrast, the rise in tourism earnings in small Caribbean Ocean and Indian Ocean island nations has been between 10 and 25 percent per annum, representing a major source of economic growth. A variety of factors are cited for the lackluster performance of the PMCs, including: (1) lack of frequent air service; (2) insufficient investment in hotels and recreational facilities; (3) high cost policies with regard to imported inputs to service the tourist industry; (4) lack of effective market promotion strategies; (5) distance from major markets; and (6) inadequate supplies of potable water. Inability to develop tourism as a major growth industry was one of the reasons for the significant differences in growth performance between the PMCs and other small island economies.

Transport

2.91   A number of geographic, population, and trade circumstances condition the structure and relative performance of the transport sector for each PMC. Terrain, climate, the size and number of populated islands, and remoteness from major international markets impose constraints on the cost and development of transport systems. While the relative importance of different modes varies, inter-island, coastal, and international shipping play a central role in most countries.

2.92   In all PMCs, the principal direct linkages of the transport sector are with three key activities: trade, tourism, and agriculture. International trade, predominately served by shipping, is of major significance; its limited size and composition shape the nature of transport services. With the exception of Solomon Islands, merchandise imports substantially exceed exports. Outbound shipments (mainly agricultural products) are generally

Box 5   Tourism: A growing sector

        As an export industry, tourism is unhampered by small domestic markets or a
relatively undeveloped local manufacturing sector. Its main disadvantages lie in its
potential it represents for encroachment upon local cultures and degradation of environment.
On average, tourism receipts are about 25 percent of export earnings in the PMCs, compared to
over 35 percent for the Caribbean islands. Natural disasters, political instability and
inadequate tourism infrastructure (air services and hotel accommodation) constitute the major
impediments to tourism expansion in the region. Earnings from tourism and visitor arrivals
remained stagnant for Fiji and Solomon Islands during the decade, but grew rapidly for
Tonga, Vanuatu, and Western Samoa. With rising global demand for tourism, considerable
potential exists in this sector in each PMC.

        In small island nations, tourism could have major economic impacts: (1) as a
source of foreign exchange earnings; (2) for its contribution to GDP; and (3) as a source of
employment for unskilled and semiskilled labor. In all these categories, the PMCs are
likely to derive significant benefits, the scope of which would increase if policies are set
on the right track to reduce the import content of tourist services by increasing the share
of indigenous inputs, management, and control. Greater regional cooperation on matters of
marketing strategy and improved air access would also be helpful. There is considerable
merit in the use of external aid for tourism development in the region.

Box Table 5:   TOURIST ARRIVALS AND RECEIPTS

		1980	1981	1982	1983	1984	1985	1986	1987	1988
Fiji	(1)	89	104	132	134	150	147	162	122	181
	(2)	190	190	204	192	235	228	258	190	208
Kiribati	(1)	..	..	..	1	1	1	1	1	1
	(2)	..	..	..	3	3	3	3	3	4
Solomon Is.	(1)	3	3	4	4	2	2	1	2	2
	(2)	11	11	11	8	11	12	12	13	11
Tonga	(1)	4	5	5	4	5	5	6	9	8
	(2)	13	13	12	14	14	14	16	17	19
Vanuatu	(1)	7	7	20	22	24	19	14	12	14
	(2)	22	22	32	32	32	25	18	15	18
W. Samoa	(1)	5	5	7	5	5	7	9	9	10
	(2)	34	34	29	37	40	41	46	46	46

(1) Tourism receipts, in millions of U.S. dollars.
(2) Tourist arrivals in thousands.

Source: Yearbook of Tourism Statistics, World Tourism Organization.
        Vol. 1, 1988.

destined for Europe (with the exception of Solomon Islands, which sends timber and fish to Japan). Imports (mainly manufactured goods and food) come from Australia and New Zealand. Thus international transport services for the PMCs are subject to directional and composition imbalances, long distances, and relatively low traffic density. In transportation associated with tourism, remoteness from major sources of visitors, thinness of routes, relatively high ground costs, and competing alternative destinations all constrain the growth in tourism. Limited passenger air services (especially with wide-body aircraft) also reduce the low cost availability of belly-hold air freight capacity.

2.93   These market and service characteristics significantly raise unit transport costs. As a consequence, the efficiency of the PMCs' transport infrastructure (for example, ports and roads), distribution systems, and transport service markets is especially important to their international competitiveness.

2.94   In concert with policy initiatives in other key factor markets--labor, capital, and land--policy initiatives in the transport sector need to be considered to improve service efficiency, to lower unit costs, and to widen support for export activities. Internal transport from source of production to international ports is especially important for agricultural and other primary products. Road maintenance is not well provided in all countries. Institutional, technical, management, and financial areas need to be strengthened and opportunities for private sector involvement in road construction and maintenance considered. In the maritime subsector, attention needs to be given to domestic shipping and ports/wharves. Opportunities for efficiency improvements through regulatory reform, commercialization, and privatization (for example, of shipyards) all warrant thorough examination.

2.95   The principal areas for transport infrastructure development are likely to be: (1) rehabilitation of existing infrastructure, especially roads (particularly in Fiji and Western Samoa); (2) landings and wharves on outer islands and some upgrading of major ports (particularly in Kiribati, Solomon Islands, Tonga, and Vanuatu); and (3) upgrading of rural roads to support agricultural and resource development. Detailed economic and financial analyses of individual transport projects and their priorities need to be developed and considered in the context of an overall transport sector strategy for each country.

2.96   Strengthening of institutions is a cornerstone for transport's improved performance and its future development. Improved capabilities are needed in policy and strategy formulation, management and implementation of maintenance for infrastructure, project planning, and the setting of priorities. Moreover, improvements in these areas should facilitate more effective management and coordination of donor assistance in keeping with the established national priorities.

III. DEVELOPMENT CHALLENGES AND PROSPECTS IN THE 1990s

A. Development Strategy and Policies for Sustained Growth

3.1   The paramount development goal of the Pacific Island nations in the 1990s will be to overcome the stagnation in income growth experienced in the decade past. Efforts in this regard are likely to be hampered by the inescapable realities faced by these economies: small and fragmented domestic markets, limited natural resources, and high transportation costs due to the islands' remoteness. In addition, prospects appear gloomy for a recovery in the sectors that usually have generated growth--most notably traditional primary commodity exports and public investment.

3.2   Despite these limitations, a clear method exists for setting the PMCs on a sustainable and more rapid medium-term growth path. To judge from the experience of other small island economies, it seems necessary to adopt a strategy based upon new sources of growth rooted in the private sector. Given the market and resource constraints of the PMCs, growth needs to be geared to a few specialized areas where there is a clear comparative advantage. By achieving a critical mass of investment and support services in key subsectors, specialization leads to sustained growth and development. Critical to the success of this approach will be significantly greater reliance upon the capacity of entrepreneurs to identify and develop niches for investment opportunities, probably with an outward orientation. The role of Government in this strategy is to provide: (1) a policy environment conducive to expansion of private sector activity; and (2) the the necessary infrastructural and institutional support.

3.3   The detailed policy agenda to underpin this strategy would vary across countries and would require much more specific analysis. However, several key elements of the policy agenda stand out, based on the review of the policy environment in the 1980s and cross-country experience. The key policies for accelerated growth are described below. The main themes underlying this agenda are:

(1)   The necessity to pursue macroeconomic policies that will provide financial stability as a precondition for growth and employment creation.

(2)   The importance of increasing the role of the private sector in development by providing an enabling incentives regime, the necessary infrastructure, and the human resources needed to promote international competitiveness.

(3)   The need to seek new sources of growth, since there are limited prospects for traditional sectors. Especially important in this respect will be Government support for private sector initiatives to develop profitable niches in the world economy that exploit individual countries' comparative advantage.

(4)   The importance of investing in human resource development to reduce the shortage of well-trained personnel.

Box 5 Specialization in Development

Maldives is an archipelago of nearly 1,200 tiny coral islands, grouped into 19 atolls, in the Indian Ocean, about 645 kilometers southwest of India and Sri Lanka. The total land area is estimated at 300 square kilometers, and the sea area at about 10,700 square kilometers. More than a fourth of the total population of 200,000 lives in the capital, Male (area 2 square kilometers), the only urban center. Tenuous inter-island transport and communication mean that the atols and Male remain isolated from each other. This dispersion greatly increases the cost of distributing commodities and social and economic services resulting in the concentration of incomes, resources, and services in Male.

Marine resources and tourism attractions constitute the principal natural endowments of the country. Agricultural production meets only 10 percent of food consumption; all major food staples other than fish are imported, and little scope exists for expansion in agriculture, given the extremely small cultivable area. Industrial activity is confined to industries, small-scale fabrication and repair, and recently established export-oriented garment factories. The lack of resources and the small size of the domestic market rule out any major import-substituting enterprise. The openness of the economy and its specialized nature make Maldives highly vulnerable to external shocks.

Notwithstanding its resource constraints, Maldives has successfully adopted a specialized approach to development--its two leading sectors being fishing and tourism. Despite the constraint of high transportation costs (with a nominal freight factor of 23 percent compared to 17 percent for the PMCs), GDP has risen at an average annual rate of over 10 percent in the last decade due primarily to the dynamism of the export sectors, fishing, and tourism.

Tourism is now the largest sector of the economy, accounting for about 18 percent of GDP, 60 percent of the foreign exchange earnings, a quarter of Government tax revenue, and a growing proportion of total employment. Tourism growth was encouraged by the completion of Male International Airport in 1981, the scheduled routing of airlines through Maldives, and increasing numbers of charter flights direct to Male. Growth in the sector in recent years has been supported by Government policy initiatives that have opened up new opportunities to private investors.

Fishing currently accounts for about 15 percent of GDP. The principal factors underlying its strong growth performance have been mechanization and improved design of the fishing fleet and infrastructure improvements.

(5)   The need for greater attention to environmental management and the sustainable use of natural resources.1/

3.4   To underpin this growth strategy, the PMCs will need a continued high level of external assistance. But, as discussed in Chapter IV, there must be a significant improvement in the absorption and effectiveness of such assistance.

Macroeconomic Management and Fiscal Policy

3.5   The PMCs' principal macroeconomic challenge in the 1990s will be to maintain stability through policies that foster renewed growth and contain fiscal deficits to levels that can be financed in a noninflationary manner. Given the weak outlook for commodity prices and considerable uncertainties in the prospects for the rest of the world, this will not be an easy task.

3.6   For Solomon Islands and to a lesser extent Vanuatu, fiscal policy should be set on a path that achieves the overriding short-term objective of greater financial stability. Attainment of this necessitates narrowing fiscal deficits to amounts that are roughly consistent with external resource availability. Once that objective has been achieved, there is greater convergence among the PMCs as to the desirable direction for fiscal policy. This direction suggests that: (1) total public expenditures should be set on a declining trend relative to GDP in order to make room for greater private sector activity; (2) adequate provision should be made for operations and maintenance; and (3) public investment expenditures should be focused on essential infrastructure and human resource development. On the revenue side, resource mobilization has been substantial. Even so, there is scope for improving the PMCs' tax structure (Chapter II and Appendix I).

External Competitiveness

3.7   Maintaining external competitiveness will be a key element of a more growth-oriented development strategy. Appropriate wage and exchange rate policies are particularly important in this context, since they exercise a major influence on international competitiveness and thereby on the viability of investment in both exporting and import-substituting industries. In particular, there is a need to achieve greater flexibility in the setting of private and public sector wages by severing the rigid link between wages and the cost of living. In the aggregate, wage increases should be kept in line with variations in economy-wide productivity to avoid the loss of competitiveness of domestic production. To the extent that progress is made in improving competitiveness through wage policy, the need for exchange rate adjustments will be reduced and there will be limited impact on the general level of prices.

1/   A major effort has been launched to prepare environmental statements at the country and regional level for the UN Conference on Environment and Development (UNCED). This will include identification of the policy and institutional steps needed to avoid environmental degradation and ensure the sustainable use of limited and often fragile natural resources.

Reform of Public Enterprises and Commodity Boards

3.8   As noted in Chapter II (section C), reform of public enterprises and commodity boards will yield considerable benefits in reduced budgetary burden and greater scope for private sector activity. For each country, specific reform programs need to be formulated that would include liquidation of nonviable enterprises and the divestiture of those that could be more efficiently run by the private sector. For those enterprises that remain under public ownership, greater accountability needs to be introduced in management practices, and tariffs should be set at levels that will generate adequate returns. With regard to commodity boards, many functions such as marketing should be transferred to the private sector and the scope of their activities substantially narrowed. Two areas where continued public support is likely be needed, although not necessarily through the commodity boards, are: (1) quality and quarantine control; and (2) assistance in market promotion.

Private Sector Development

3.9   The cornerstone for restoration of sustained growth will be greater participation of the private sector in investment and economic activity. The Government can facilitate this process by maintaining macroeconomic stability and by providing the necessary infrastructure, human resources, and policy environment conducive to private initiative. The provision of a policy environment that facilitates private investment is a key challenge for the 1990s. Although steps in this direction have been taken in many PMCs, further actions are needed in all countries to put in place an outward oriented and undistorted incentive regime. This, in turn, would require reduction in quantitative trade controls, rationalization of the tariff structure, and streamlining of duty drawback and exemption schemes. There is also a general need to shift from a regulatory to a promotional approach towards the private sector. Licensing requirements and other administrative impediments to both domestic and foreign private investment need to be reduced drastically. At the same time, the Government should turn its attention to core regulatory functions--environmental and safety standards and quality control. And it should provide positive support in areas such as the development of entrepreneurial capacity and the provision of information on export markets.

Strengthening the Financial Sector

3.10   The financial sector will have to be strengthened if private sector investment is to expand substantially. While elements of financial sector reform will differ by country, common elements will include: (1) phasing out of capital controls and sectoral credit allocation requirements; (2) a shift to indirect management of liquidity and foreign exchange reserves;
(3) improvement in surveillance procedures of all financial intermediaries;
(4) restructuring or closing of distressed institutions; and (5) promotion of capital market development.

Human Resource Development

3.11   The acute shortage of qualified and experienced personnel is a fundamental constraint to development in all six countries--even in Fiji, which has larger reserves of trained manpower than most. This acute shortage is the consequence of insufficient educational and vocational training opportunities and, in some countries, a high rate of emigration. The provision of education services represents a major burden on Government expenditure in the face of young and expanding populations. Given budgetary constraints, this implies that much greater emphasis will have to be given to reducing costs and improving the efficiency of education and training. (Chapter II section E). In view of the impact of emigration on the availability of skilled and qualified people, particularly in Polynesia, measures will have to be adopted to encourage more people to remain or return.

3.12   Another major development challenge is to reduce the very high fertility rates currently prevalent in the region, particularly in the Melanesian countries and Kiribati. Without more active family planning programs, population growth will continue to reduce substantially the benefits of growth and will further strain the limited capacities of Governments to provide basic services and maintain adequate nutritional standards.

3.13   Provided the above policy agenda is pursued vigorously, all PMC countries have the capacity to grow at a far faster rate than in the 1980s. Since the six are small, open, narrowly based economies, future gains will also depend on increasing trade and the provision of services to the rest of the world. International economic prospects will be among the key determinants of future opportunities for growth. Although world economic conditions are rarely amenable to accurate forecasts, an appraisal of international market prospects is an essential element in developing strategies for future growth.

B. The Oil Shock

3.14   The short-term outlook for petroleum prices is dominated by uncertainties in the Middle East. All PMC economies are net energy importers, and energy imports constitute a substantial share of total imports. In consequence, the petroleum price increase would lead to a higher import bill. The primary direct effect of higher petroleum prices will be to increase the value of merchandise imports and widen the merchandise trade deficit. Important indirect effects include greater freight charges, higher imported capital good costs, and a modest near-term decline in tourism and manufacturing earnings. In absolute terms, these effects will be substantially greater in Fiji than elsewhere.

3.15   To project the implications of the Middle East conflict on petroleum prices, a sustained increase in petroleum prices would have a substantial impact on the PMCs' because of the high share of shipment and trans-shipment costs in the total cost of fuel supply. Before the recent increases, the landed cost of petroleum products included a freight costs component of 5-10 percent at the primary distribution centers (Fiji, Papua New Guinea, and Noumea) and 27-40 percent (including storage and trans-shipment costs) at the secondary distribution centers in the smaller countries. Following the increase in petroleum prices, these proportions are likely to decline (fuel costs account for only 15-20 percent of shipping costs). Thus, with an increase in crude oil prices from $16 to $27 per barrel, the corresponding increase in the f.o.b. Singapore price of petroleum products (weighted on the basis of the structure of consumption in the Pacific) would be from roughly $22 to $33 per barrel. Such an increase in Singapore prices could result in an increase in landed costs from about $24 to $35 per barrel in Fiji and from about $27-29 per barrel to $39-42 per barrel in the smaller countries.

3.16   The estimated direct effects of hypothetically sustained higher petroleum prices on the merchandise account have been simulated for each of the PMCs using one set of hypothetical petroleum price projections. Under this scenario, for the period 1990-94, the average annual increase in the cost of petroleum imports is estimated at about $32 million for Fiji, $6 million for the Solomon Islands, $2 million for Vanuatu, $2 million for Tonga, $1.3 million for Kiribati, and $7 million for Western Samoa.2/ The total increase in the cost of imports will approximate $50 million annually for these six nations, or 5 percent of total import requirements. If, however, the oil price increase is sustained, then the impact in calendar year 1991 and beyond would be substantially greater.

3.17   In such a case, the PMCs would have to consider a combination of stabilization and adjustment options and would require additional financing from the donor community. In the near term, a combination of a drawdown in official reserves and a reduction in nonessential imports may be needed to maintain external balance. This could lead to some reduction in growth in the short term.

3.18   The magnitude of the medium-term impact will depend on the persistence of higher world market petroleum prices. Experience suggests that the full adjustment of petroleum prices (the assumption that the increase is permanent) is the better policy response for a petroleum importing country. Domestic adjustments should also include increased energy conservation and development of nontraditional energy resources (hydropower and solar). Despite these adjustments, the PMCs would face a financing gap if the oil price increase were sustained. An increase of 10 percent in Official Development Assistance levels or about $15 million in grant assistance would be needed to meet the financing gap for all of the Pacific Island countries except Fiji. In Fiji's case, an increase in external borrowing may have to be used to close the financing gap.

C. Income Growth and Primary Commodity Prices

3.19   Relatively slow rates of growth are forecast for major industrial economies for this year and next. The industrial economies are expected to grow by 2.9 percent in 1990 and 3.0 percent in 1991. Slower growth, combined with a resurgence in inflationary fears, is expected to lead to a policy of monetary restraint in the OECD nations. This will increase capital costs and, by reducing import demand, lead to downward pressure on real primary commodity prices, excluding petroleum. Although the recent developments in the Middle East are likely to lead to a downward revision of growth prospects for the

---

2/   For the PMC economies, under such a scenario, the bulk of the price adjustment would occur during the first two quarters of 1991, due to the lag of three to six months before world market prices are transmitted to domestic markets.

early 1990s in the industrial market economies, prospects for greater East-West cooperation and the creation of a unified European market are expected to provide a powerful stimulus to medium-term growth.

3.20   Although difficult to assess in light of Middle East uncertainty, the outlook for primary commodity prices in the 1990s is not particularly promising. According to the latest World Bank commodity price forecasts, sugar prices would soften early in the 1990s and then partly recover by the end of the decade. Coconut oil, copra, and palm oil are expected to increase over the next five years before weakening toward the year 2000. Timber prices are expected to increase marginally. Cocoa prices, after another five years of working through the glut of stocks overhanging the market, are expected to rise sharply toward the end of the decade. Expected price developments for a range of commodities, measured in real 1985 terms, appear in table 3.1.

3.21   The expected decline in sugar prices is likely to constitute a further setback for the Fijian economy but will be offset by short-term gains in the price of gold. Over the medium term as gold prices settle back to more normal levels, exports of manufactures are likely to compensate for losses registered in the sugar market; this will occur because of continued rises in real prices of manufactures.

3.22   The expected softening of coconut oil and copra prices has serious implications for many PMC economies. The combination of falling product prices and higher transport costs will place a heavy strain on processing and production margins. Comparative advantage in coconut production is increasingly expected to shift to the Southeast Asian countries, where a combination of scale economies, low labor costs, adoption of high yielding hybrid varieties, and low shipment costs combine to produce a significant cost advantage. Reorientation of output away from coconut production may be difficult for traditional farmers with little exposure to other technologies or marketing systems. PMC diversification into higher valued, specialized agricultural markets is central to restoring growth in agriculture in the 1990s.

3.23   Prices of manufactures are expected to rise 19 percent by 1995 and another 25 percent by the year 2000. The combination of higher petroleum and manufactured goods prices and stagnation and softening in primary commodity prices implies that the terms of trade could deteriorate for the PMC economies. Deterioration in the income terms of trade can be avoided, provided the PMC economies diversify export production towards markets with stronger price potential (high value tourism, hardwood production, recreational products) and engage in efficient substitution for high cost imports (energy conservation).

3.24   The most recent projections indicate that growth among the industrial countries will be maintained, on average, at about 3.0 percent a year during the 1990s. This would be slightly above the 2.8 percent realized in the 1980s. High rates of growth, combined with an easing of East-West tensions, are expected to lead to a sharp increase in consumer expenditures. If, as is expected, further reduction in trade protection measures take effect, growth in world trade is anticipated to exceed the record-breaking levels of the 1980s.

Table 3.1: SELECTED COMMODITY PRICE PROJECTIONS, 1990-2000
(in constant 1985 US dollars) /a

| | | Actual | Projected | | | Average Annual % change |
		1989	1990	1995	2000	1989-2000
Sugar	$/MT	204	198	189	221	0.7
Coconut oil	$/MT	373	235	375	381	0.2
Copra	$/MT	251	162	227	267	0.6
Beef	c/KG	185	176	199	213	1.3
Cocoa	c/KG	90	85	95	108	1.7
Coffee	c/KG	172	138	163	203	1.5
Bananas	$/MT	395	367	322	308	-2.2
Palm oil	$/MT	253	190	239	204	-1.9
Logs	$/CM	162	143	157	168	0.3
Gold	$/TOZ	275	262	236	242	-1.2
Weighted index of 33 nonoil commodities (1985=100)		85.9	77.9	72.0	79.2	-0.7
Index of primary products /b (1985 = 100)		106.7	100.9	121.5	153.4	3.3
Manufactures /c (1985=100)		141.3	150.3	178.5	212.1	3.8
Index of primary products/ MUV (1985=100)		75.6	67.1	68.0	72.3	-0.4
Petroleum	$/BBL	11.8	14.7	11.8	14.7	2.0

/a Unless otherwise specified.
/b Weighted index of food, nonfood, and timber in current US$.
/c Unit value index of manufacturing commodities (SITC 5-8), in current
    US$, from five industrial market economies to developing countries.

D. Trade Opportunities

3.25   Prospects remain promising for a deepening of ties with traditional
PMC trading partners (Australia, New Zealand). In addition, the resumption of
growth in the European Community, together with the expected broadening of
demand after the 1992 European economic integration, augers well for growth in
tourism and high-value exports. Although economic growth is expected to
soften in the United States, new opportunities for PMC exports will arise as
Singapore, South Korea, and Hong Kong graduate from the Generalized System of
Preferences (GSP) trade program. The PMC economies may be able to capture a
portion of the markets lost by the newly industrialized economies,
particularly in areas such as wood-based products, textiles, and decorative
items. If, in addition, the improvements registered in PMC airport and
tourism facilities are followed by direct flight agreements with major U.S.
cities, potential exists for considerable growth in tourism.

3.26   Economic adjustment programs underway in New Zealand and Australia are expected to benefit the PMC economies over the medium term. A resumption of sustained growth in both economies would increase import demand, investment, and resources available for development assistance. While abolition of trade restraints between Australia and New Zealand (as part of the CER agreements) may adversely affect some PMC economies, the continuation of the SPARTECA free trade agreement promises to provide opportunities for preferential access to these industrial markets.

3.27   Opportunities for increased trade among the PMCs remain limited because of similarities in production structures and high inter-insular transport costs. There are, however, important opportunities for cooperation in transport, investment promotion, communications, finance, energy, tertiary education, and other sectors. Mechanisms for more effective regional cooperation are established within the Forum Secretariat, the South Pacific Commission, and other organizations. Only modest achievements were registered in the use of regional cooperation to improve economic performance in the 1980s. Small island nations can ill afford to ignore opportunities to exploit economies of scale through regional cooperation. A key challenge for the 1990s will be to shift the focus of regional organizations to the launching of key initiatives for regional economic cooperation.

3.28   The growth in economic interdependence among the Pacific Rim countries continues to be one of the most dynamic forces in global economic growth and development. Central to this process has been the economic restructuring associated with a shift of labor- and natural resource-intensive industries from Japan and the middle income NICs to other Southeast Asian nations. The globalization of Pacific Rim production is expected to continue into the 1990s, as rapidly growing Asian enterprises seek new offshore investment opportunities. Special situations, such as the incorporation of Hong Kong into the People's Republic of China, are also expected to increase foreign investment opportunities. During the 1980s, many PMCs nations improved relations with Japan through development cooperation and investments in tourism and fisheries. The challenge for the 1990s will be to diversify business contacts with Japan while making inroads into other rapidly growing Asian economies.

E. Macroeconomic Projections

3.29   Projections have been made of macroeconomic performance in the 1990s, assuming that adjustments in economic policy and development strategy, outlined in Chapter II, are put into place3/ (table 3.2). Key assumptions include: (1) relatively stable prices; (2) high rates of investment; (3) an increase in the growth of exports and imports; and (4) maintenance of international creditworthiness. Most important, high rates of investment are expected to translate into higher rates of growth than those realized in the 1980s; investment is assumed to shift toward the productive sectors as past investments in infrastructure and human resources begin to yield positive returns. On average, the PMC economies are forecast to grow by 4.9 percent per annum in 1990-94, well in excess of the 2.9 percent realized annually in 1985-89. With population growth expected to average approximately 2.2 percent

---

3/   The policy assumptions involved in the macroeconomic projections are discussed in more detail in the individual country surveys contained in Volume II.

per annum, GDP per capita would increase by about 2.6 percent per annum. Such growth, although modest, would represent a marked improvement over recent performance. More significant, the resumption of growth in the early 1990s would lay the foundation for more rapid expansion in the latter half of the decade.

3.30   Volatility in growth is to be expected, since the PMC economies remain vulnerable to the vagaries of weather and the erratic behavior of primary product prices. Economic shocks must be absorbed by an appropriately tailored package of stabilization measures; important in this respect will be the addition of new monetary instruments (Chapter II) to reinforce fiscal policy as the mechanism for absorbing shocks. As to any natural disasters, it is important that adequate surveillance programs and contingency plans exist, that mechanisms for speedy donor response are in place, and that reconstruction campaigns are implemented in a timely and efficient manner.

Table 3.2: MACROECONOMIC PROJECTIONS, 1990-94

	Fiji	Kiribati	Solomon Islands	Tonga	Vanuatu	Western Samoa
Growth rates (% p.a.)						
GDP	5.4	3.3	4.6	4.5	4.2	2.8
Agriculture	4.4	3.5	3.7	2.6	3.0	1.6
Industry	8.3	6.0	8.0	5.8	4.1	4.3
Services	4.5	3.0	5.0	5.7	4.6	3.8
Consumption	3.5	2.5	2.8		3.7	3.0
Fixed investment	8.0	7.5	4.6		5.0	3.9
Exports of goods & services	7.5	5.0	6.2		3.0	5.3
Imports of goods & services	8.6	8.1	4.1		4.1	4.5
Consumer prices	5.0	5.0	6.2		5.0	5.0
Ratios to GDP (%) /a						
Gross investment	19.5	35.8	34.4		29.7	35.3
Domestic savings	17.5		2.3		12.2	-8.0
Other indicators						
Current account/GDP (%) /a	-2.0		-29.9	-16.6	-17.8	-5.1
Debt service/exports (%)	13.4	1.5	6.9	8.4	2.8	8.4
DOD/GDP (%)	27.8		50.9	37.5	25.7	90.5
Net foreign assets (as months of retained imports)	5.4		2.3	5.4	32.2	12.2

/a For the last year of the period.

Source: World Bank staff estimates.

External Financing Requirements

3.31   External financing requirements for the PMC economies will remain
substantial during the 1990s. Not only will donor assistance continue to be
very important, but so will remittances and foreign direct investment. In the
absence of adequate external financing, growth would be severely constrained
and external imbalances would risk financial instability. This underscores
the need for PMC economies to maintain good relations with the donor
community, overseas citizens, foreign financial institutions, and foreign
investors.

3.32   Estimates of external financing requirements and sources for 1990-94
are shown in table 3.3. These estimates are consistent with the macroeconomic
growth and external trade performance forecasts presented in table 3.2. Such
estimates are subject to a wide margin of error, particularly in the case of
natural disasters, when external requirements rise rapidly. An additional
source of uncertainty is the outlook for petroleum prices because of the
current Middle East crisis. Higher petroleum prices will lead to a widening
of the merchandise trade gap and to an increase in external financing
requirements. This, however, is expected to be offset in later years by
improved prospects for tourism, fisheries, timber, textiles, and other PMC
exports.

3.33   Overall, the figures suggest that external financing requirements
will increase from an average of $270 million per annum in 1985-89 to $385
million per annum in 1990-94. In real 1989 terms, external resource
requirements are expected to remain almost constant.

3.34   External grants will continue to be the most important source of
external financing for the PMC economies in the 1990s. Assistance in this
form is expected to increase from $127 million per annum (average 1985-89) to
about $160 million per annum, measured in current dollars. Viewed as a share
of total external financing requirements, external grant financing is
projected to decline, from 47 percent to about 40 percent by the end of the
forecast period, signalling a decline in aid dependency on the part of the PMC
economies. Nonetheless, continued steady support by the donor community will
be crucial to successful PMC growth.

3.35   Sovereign borrowing is expected to grow modestly from $48 million to
$75 million per year, on average, in 1990-94, with Fiji accounting for the
bulk of external borrowing. Total net transfers are anticipated to reach
about $20 million per annum, in view of relatively high debt service
obligations.

3.36   Approximately 20 percent of external financing is in the form of
"other capital" transfers, which would largely reflect net foreign direct
investment. Fiji would account for about 45 percent of external resource
requirements; for each of the other islands, the share is considerably less.
In the latter half of the 1990s, foreign direct investment is expected to play
an increasingly important role in meeting external financing requirements.

3.37   Remittance inflows are expected to provide approximately 20 percent
of total external requirements, with the proportions being particularly high
for Tonga and Western Samoa--60-65 percent. For these two countries, growth
prospects hinge on the ability to transform remittance inflows into a steady

stream of productive investment. Looking past the next decade, the outlook for remittance transfers is less optimistic in view of the changing demographic structure of Polynesian migrants. As remittances diminish, alternative sources of financing will have to be found.

Table 3.3:   EXTERNAL FINANCING REQUIREMENTS AND SOURCES, 1990-94
(in millions of US dollars per year)

	Fiji	Kiribati	Solomon Islands	Tonga	Vanuatu	Western Samoa
Requirements	111	21	75	48	61	68
Merchandise imports	666	25	137	55	62	94
Merchandise exports	-481	-5	-111	-11	-19	-17
Principal repayments /a	39	-	8	2	2	4
Interest payments /a	29	-	2	1	1	2
Other service payments	-173	-2	40	1	1	-29
Change in NFA	30	3	-1	1	15	14
Sources	111	21	75	48	61	68
Private transfers	-15	3	7	28	12	44
External grants	35	16	43	12	39	14
Public loan disbursements	38	1	9	3	8	16
Other capital (net)	53	1	16	5	2	-6

/a Public MLT debt only.

Source: World Bank staff estimate.

External Debt and Creditworthiness

3.38   By and large, the PMC economies remain creditworthy. They have a relatively small external debt exposure and can reasonably expect to meet debt service obligations without placing undue burdens on the fiscal accounts and the external sector. All these economies enjoy the option of external borrowing to meet sovereign needs, an option that not many developing nations have maintained following the debt crisis of the 1980s. However, with the exception of Fiji, which no longer has access to donor grant financing on a notable scale, commercial borrowing by the other PMC nations constitutes a substitute for cheaper external grant assistance (such as International Development Association). For these nations, external borrowing on commercial terms can only be justified when limits to development assistance have been reached.

3.39   In assessing creditworthiness for external borrowing, it is useful to distinguish between Fiji and the other countries in the region. For Fiji, total medium- and long-term debt outstanding and disbursed was $330 million at the end of 1988 (table 3.4), equivalent to 38 percent of GDP. Debt service payments amounted to 18 percent of total export income. Since 1988, Fiji's creditworthiness has improved due to a resumption of donor assistance, an increase in tourism earnings, and a reduction in capital flight. Given Fiji's modest accumulation of foreign debt, continued recourse to international financial markets should present no problems, provided borrowing is kept within prudent limits and an outward-oriented growth program continues.

3.40   The external debt obligation for the other nations is quite modest. As noted earlier, the great bulk of external financing has been provided to these nations in the form of official development assistance, predominantly grants. For Kiribati and Vanuatu, external debt is small, both in relation to national product and export earnings. However, both countries should avoid external borrowing in view of the ready availability of external grant assistance, the shallowness of domestic resources, and the fragility of the external accounts.

3.41   Tonga, Western Samoa, and the Solomon Islands have larger outstanding debts, measured in absolute terms and in relation to GDP. Nonetheless, debt service payments remain modest by international standards, in absolute terms and relative to total export earnings. Only in the Solomon Islands, where macroeconomic instability has recently taken root, is there concern that debt service obligations may grow to unsustainable rates. For all three countries, external borrowing on commercial terms should be avoided until incomes are higher and growth more steady.

Table 3.4: INDICATORS OF DEBT AND CREDITWORTHINESS, 1988
(in millions of US dollars)

	MLT debt outstanding (US$m)	Debt out- standing as % of GDP (%)	Debt out- standing per capita ($)	Debt service (US$m)	Debt service as % of exports (%)
Fiji	330.2	39.3	457	61.5	18.4
Kiribati /a	2.1	9.3	32	0.5	3.1
Tonga	41.0	44.3	414	2.3	3.8
Western Samoa	72.3	77.7	435	4.5	12.5
Solomon Islands	106.3	73.9	363	5.6	6.5
Vanuatu	16.8	6.8	121	1.6	2.9

/a Data for 1986.

Source: World Bank staff estimates.

F. Conclusions

3.42   Despite the PMCs' small size and remoteness, considerable untapped potential exists for economic growth in the 1990s. Even so, the traditional growth sources--primary commodities and public investment--offer little prospect of contributing to real growth in a significant way. New sources of growth will come largely from niches in the rapidly expanding continuum of world trade and investment. Identification and exploitation of new sources of growth is a task that Governments worldwide are poorly equipped to handle. It will therefore be the private sector that must take the lead if new sources of growth are to be tapped.

3.43   Near-term prospects for the world economy are overshadowed by unfolding Middle East events. Over the medium term, opportunities abound for markets in tourism, tropical forest products, fisheries, and textiles, and light manufactured goods; such markets are likely to be found in both traditional trading partners and in the Pacific Rim nations. If the PMC economies are able to successfully exploit such markets, real economic growth on the order of 2-3 percent per capita may be achieved during the first half of the 1990s.

3.44   Restoring growth will be possible only if the PMCs provide macroeconomic stability and an enabling investment climate for the private sector. External imbalances are expected to persist but should not adversely affect macroeconomic stability or creditworthiness, provided external development assistance is forthcoming. Efficient use of foreign assistance will be central to restoring growth and development in the 1990s.

IV. IMPROVING AID PERFORMANCE

A. The Role of Aid in the South Pacific

Trends in the Flow of Aid

4.1   Over many years, net flows of official development assistance (ODA) have been substantial for the PMCs (table 4.1). In 1988, for example, the six countries, with a combined population of 1.5 million, received $220 million, or $147 per capita. Traditional donors have been the United Kingdom, New Zealand and Australia (the largest since the early 1980s). Japan and the EEC have also begun substantial programs. Today, three-quarters of all aid to the region comes from these five donors; the World Bank and the Asian Development Bank provide 6 percent of net ODA.

4.2   The flow of ODA has fluctuated considerably. After rapid growth in the late 1970s, it declined from a 1980 peak of $185 million to some $120 million by the mid-1980s. Since 1986, the level has again begun to grow rapidly, because of: (1) the emergence of Japan as a major donor; (2) the provision of substantial payments to several countries under the EEC's STABEX scheme; and (3) a rise in disbursements by Australia. The fluctuation is less evident when ODA volume is measured as a percentage of GDP. The underlying trend is one of relative stability, with much smaller fluctuations, except in 1984/85 as a result of a decline in disbursements and in 1987/88 as a result of large disbursements of STABEX funds (particularly to Solomon Islands and Vanuatu).

4.3   In absolute terms, Fiji and Solomon Islands have received the largest amounts of aid. But the level of ODA for the smaller island countries is significantly higher than for Fiji when measured on a per capita basis, in relation to economic size, or as a percentage of Government expenditure. For the smaller countries, ODA has accounted for 25 to 50 percent of GDP; for Fiji, the figure is only 3 to 5 percent. High per capita aid levels are inevitable in very small countries due to limited financial resources and the relatively large cost of basic infrastructure. Even so, per capita aid levels to the South Pacific countries are among the world's highest (table 4.3).

4.4   The major part of the aid to the PMCs, for both capital development and technical assistance, is grants from bilateral donors and the EEC. Multilaterally, considerable technical assistance comes through the United Nations agencies, in particular the UNDP; the International Development Association and the Asian Development Fund provide concessional loans; Fiji also borrows from the IBRD and ADB. The IBRD and ADB loans apart, all other assistance falls within the definition of ODA as determined by the Development Assistance Committee of the OECD.

4.5   In the 1990s, external financing requirements for the PMCs will remain substantial (Chapter III, section E). The availability of donor resources is not likely to be a constraint on PMC development. Bank estimates indicate that the volume of assistance is likely to grow. Overall, aid for the six could rise by more than 40 percent over the next five years. This outlook is substantially more favorable that of other developing countries, though it does not constitute a significant increase in real terms.

Table 4.1 (A): NET DISBURSEMENT OF ODA FROM ALL SOURCES COMBINED TO INDIVIDUAL RECIPIENTS

	1974-1978	1979	1980	1981	1982	1983	1984	1985	1986	1987	1988
Fiji	107.3	31.0	36.1	40.5	35.4	32.7	31.3	31.9	42.5	35.9	54.3
Kiribati	32.4	9.1	19.2	15.3	15.1	18.8	11.9	12.0	13.4	18.4	16.3
Solomon Islands	97.8	28.5	44.5	31.1	28.4	27.5	19.4	20.8	30.1	57.1	58.3
Tonga	27.5	23.9	18.4	18.0	17.4	17.9	15.7	13.6	15.1	21.3	18.8
Vanuatu	93.2	38.4	44.0	30.4	28.0	28.9	24.5	21.8	24.4	51.0	39.3
Western Samoa	71.5	29.9	25.7	25.0	22.8	26.7	20.2	19.4	23.3	35.2	30.6
TOTAL	429.5	158.8	185.9	160.3	145.1	148.5	123.0	119.5	148.8	218.9	217.6

Table 4.1 (B): ODA AS A PERCENTAGE OF GDP

	1974-1978	1979	1980	1981	1982	1983	1984	1985	1986	1987	1988
Fiji	-	3.0	3.0	3.3	3.0	2.9	2.7	2.8	3.3	3.1	5.1
Kiribati	-	21.4	68.8	52.2	51.5	61.8	40.3	52.2	55.6	74.8	48.9
Solomon Islands	-	25.4	38.4	24.1	21.9	22.2	11.1	13.0	20.8	38.8	33.0
Tonga	-	53.0	31.5	28.9	28.0	28.9	23.4	22.3	21.9	29.2	21.6
Vanuatu	-	32.3	38.8	31.0	26.5	26.4	19.9	18.0	19.5	42.9	28.9
Western Samoa	-	27.4	22.9	23.8	21.1	26.7	20.8	22.8	25.9	35.6	25.7

Source: Table 4.1 (A) Geographical Distribution of Financial Flows to Developing Countries, OECD.
        Table 4.1 (B) World Bank

Table 4.2: NET DISBURSEMENTS OF OFFICIAL DEVELOPMENT ASSISTANCE BY SOURCE, 1984-88
(US$ million)

	1984	1985	1986	1987	1988	Totals 1984-88	1989-93/1
Australia	28.1	32.8	39.3	42.2	53.3	189.4	..
Japan	12.3	15.7	30.2	39.1	52.2	142.3	..
New Zealand	12.8	12.4	11.1	15.7	14.0	67.0	..
United Kingdom	21.4	18.3	17.7	20.6	22.4	101.0	..
EEC	13.5	9.2	14.6	53.9	31.0	135.4	..
IDA/IBRD	1.9	2.3	2.5	3.6	3.0	14.3	..
ADB	7.2	4.8	5.3	8.7	12.3	35.0	..
Other	25.8	23.7	28.1	35.5	29.4	150.1	..
Total	123.0	119.2	148.8	219.3	217.6	827.9	1,180.0

/1 World Bank staff estimates.

Source: OECD: Geographical Distribution of Financial Flows to Developing Countries, 1989.

Table 4.3: COMPARATIVE AID INDICATORS

	Population ('000)	Total ODA 1988	ODA per capita 1988	Gov't expenditure as % GDP	ODA as % of Gov't expenditure
Fiji	732	54.3	74	25.4	20.4
Kiribati	67	16.3	243	..	..
Solomon Islands	304	58.3	192	39.0	84.9
Tonga	101	18.8	186	44.0	49.1
Vanuatu	151	39.3	260	46.3	61.2
Western Samoa	168	30.6	182	46.3	55.5
Antigua & Barbuda	84	8.5	101	..	..
Belize	182	25.0	137	27.1	33.6
Dominica	81	17.0	210	45.6	33.8
Grenada	102	20.5	201	44.3	27.8
Guyana	799	27.1	34	..	..
St. Kitts & Nevis	43	14.0	326	39.7	31.6
St. Lucia	145	17.6	121	35.4	24.9
St. Vincent	122	16.6	136	40.5	27.4
Bhutan	1,373	41.5	30	..	..
Cape Verde	352	86.6	246	..	..
Comoros	442	51.4	116	37.6	66.1
Equatorial Guinea	397	43.4	109	20.1	147.1
Gambia, The	822	82.1	100	34.7	111.5
Guinea-Bissau	940	98.8	105	31.2	191.8
Macao	443	0.4	1	..	..
Maldives	203	27.5	135	35.1	57.0
Mauritius	1,048	59.4	57	27.5	11.1
Sao Tome and Principe	119	24.0	202	38.3	112.1
Seychelles	68	20.7	304	..	..
Suriname	429	21.4	50	..	..
Swaziland	737	38.7	53	..	..

Sources: 1989 World Bank Atlas; World Bank Country Briefs; and OECD Geographical
Distribution of Financial Flows to Developing Countries, 1989.

Nontraditional donors are expected to become more active, and the PMCs' two main bilateral donors, Australia and Japan, appear likely to enlarge their assistance. Multilaterally, the volume of aid disbursed by the EEC is expected to rise substantially. Assistance from the World Bank and the Asian Development Bank will depend on the availability of suitable projects and of grant aid, the preferred form of external financing for the island countries.

Aid and Its Relationship to Growth in the South Pacific

4.6   Aid has clearly had a very positive impact on development in the PMCs. It has raised levels of investment, including for human resource development. It has enabled the funding of imports critical for development. Technical assistance has been important, given gaps in management and technical skills. To date, however, aid has not had a substantial impact on growth in the South Pacific.

4.7   Several of the smaller PMCs depend on high aid flows to develop and support essential public services and facilities. Some of these services and facilities are not growth-oriented or at best have only a temporary effect on growth in the project implementation phase. Since a high proportion of aid allocated to these small countries falls into such categories, it is only tenuously related to short-term growth prospects.

4.8   Notably, too, the gross flow of ODA is not the same as the transfer of financial resources that actually reaches a country. ODA statistics come from donors and, for bilateral donors, reflect the amount of funds allocated in their budgets. In fact the flow of financial resources is significantly less, chiefly because a considerable part of ODA spending takes place outside the recipient country.[1] In the case of technical assistance, there is a transfer of skills that enables many essential services to remain in operation, yet the financial transfer is far smaller than the cost in aid dollars. Expatriate staff tend to remit savings home, and much of their cost is for air fares, education, and transfer. In all forms of aid, the costs of mobilization, administration, and implementation funded out of donors' aid budgets mean a lower financial transfer than official figures imply. No accurate figures are available and the percentage may vary from donor to donor, but estimates place the actual financial transfer below 60 percent of total ODA. The immediate effect on the recipient economy may, in fact, be limited only to wages paid to local workers and expenditures registered by experts, visiting consultants, and contractors. This may be only 5-10 percent of total program costs--though in a very small economy this can have important multiplier effects.

4.9   For the six PMCs, estimates of the sectoral allocation of aid can be drawn from the UNDP's 1988 Report on Development Cooperation in the South Pacific. Of a total of $87.3 million spent on bilateral and multilateral projects in five of the six countries,[2] $34.7 million, or about 40 percent, went to natural resources sectors--agriculture, forestry, and fisheries--and

---

[1]   For example, approximately one-fifth of Australia's assistance to each island country is allocated for overseas study awards.

[2]   These data exclude Western Samoa.

to industry, where a productive response could be expected. The remainder went to sectors including infrastructure and human resource development in which returns in economic growth would be more long-term. The pattern is similar in the Australian and New Zealand aid programs. In 1988 only 25 percent of Australian aid was allocated to PMC areas where private sector response might be stimulated directly; for New Zealand's aid the figure was 40 percent. And the net effect on short-term growth in the productive sectors is likely to be even much smaller since: (1) the net transfer of financial resources will be lower; and (2) much assistance will be for activities not aimed at generating an early productive response.

4.10   It has already been noted that the direct impact of aid on growth is far less than ODA flows suggest. There are also strong arguments that large aid inflows can actually hinder economic development or compound economic constraints. As one example, extensive foreign aid can cause an overvaluation of the real exchange rate by raising wages and prices of nontradables. The traditional trade sector is thus disadvantaged; this leads to its decline, to growth in imports, and to a deteriorating trade balance. Such effects may well be occurring in the smallest and most dependent PMCs.

4.11   In addition, large inflows of aid tend to foster growth in the Government sector at the expense of the private sector. Among the PMCs, Government dominates the formal economy and relies on continuing aid; these inflows underpin high wages in the Government and have disincentive effects on other sectors of the labor market, in particular agriculture. High levels of aid-financed investment have also contributed to a budgetary problem, since PMC Governments are unable to provide sufficient revenues for operations and maintenance (O&M).

4.12   In the absence of clearly articulated development priorities and projects--and with weak project preparation and implementation--aid has not contributed as effectively as it might to the development of PMC economies. As a final complexity, the costs of aid administration have been high. The absence of the effective aid coordination has heavily burdened the administrative resources of the island countries.

B.   Toward More Effective Aid Use

4.13   Given the dominant role of aid in the South Pacific, its optimal use is a key element in improving development prospects. Discussions with donors indicate that, despite some dramatic examples, the failure rate of PMC projects is probably not higher than that in other developing countries. But implementation is generally more difficult in the islands. And it is generally agreed that aid effectiveness can be much improved. (Within the region, performance in Fiji is far better than in the smaller countries).

4.14   Without question, improved aid utilization is the prerequisite for higher growth rates in the 1990s. To achieve better use of aid, the donor community must take a number of actions:

- Donors should give greater emphasis to the policy environment; they should provide support to PMCs to address policy concerns and strengthen development planning mechanisms.

- Donors should give concerted assistance to strengthen the capacity for project identification, preparation, and implementation.

- Donors should give much closer attention to the issue of recurrent cost financing.

- Donors should develop viable mechanisms to channel a larger proportion of aid to the private sector.

- The donor community must continue to place special emphasis on human resource development.

- And, as discussed in section C below aid coordination needs to be improved at all levels.

<u>Table 4.4</u>: SECTORAL ALLOCATION OF AUSTRALIAN AND NEW ZEALAND AID

A. <u>New Zealand</u>
<u>1988 NZ$</u>

	Fiji	Kiribati	Solomon Islands	Tonga	Vanuatu	Western Samoa	Total
Administration/Planning	0.4	..	0.2	0.3	0.1	0.6	1.6
Education/Health/Social	2.5	..	1.5	0.5	1.4	3.1	9.0
Economic infrastructure	..	..	..	0.2	0.5	0.1	0.8
Agriculture/Fisheries/Forestry	2.4	..	0.6	1.6	0.4	1.4	6.4
Industry	..	..	..	0.1	..	..	0.1
Trade/Finance/Tourism	..	..	..	0.3	0.1	0.2	0.6
Multisector	0.1	..	0.2	0.6	0.3	0.2	1.4
Total	<u>5.4</u>	..	<u>2.5</u>	<u>3.6</u>	<u>2.8</u>	<u>5.6</u>	<u>19.9</u>

B. <u>Australia</u>
<u>1988 A$</u>

	Fiji	Kiribati	Solomon Islands	Tonga	Vanuatu	Western Samoa	Total
Administration/Planning	1.1	0.3	1.8	0.2	1.9	1.8	7.1
Education/Health/Social	10.0	1.8	5.7	2.4	2.8	2.1	24.8
Unspecified/Unallocated /1	4.4	0.3	1.2	1.7	1.2	5.1	13.9
Economic infrastructure	0.1	0.4	0.2	4.3	1.0	0.1	6.1
Agriculture/Fisheries/Forestry	2.4	..	1.0	0.1	0.7	0.4	4.6
Industry/Mining/Construction	0.2	..	..	0.4	0.1	0.1	0.8
Trade/Finance/Tourism	0.1	0.1	0.5	..	0.1	..	0.8
Multisector	0.7	0.2	0.4	0.4	1.3	0.2	3.2
Other /2	..	..	0.2	..	1.3	..	1.5
Total	<u>19.0</u>	<u>3.0</u>	<u>11.2</u>	<u>9.5</u>	<u>10.4</u>	<u>9.8</u>	<u>62.9</u>

/1 Includes development import grants.
/2 Includes prog. aid, food, and other emergency support.

Source: South Pacific Economic and Social Data Base, National Centre for Development Studies, 1989.

(1) Improving Development Planning

4.15   More effective development planning represents the starting point in the process of using aid better. Development planning helps provide Governments with a clear framework for establishing priorities for the efficient allocation of resources. As this report has argued in Chapter II, development planning practices in the PMCs can be improved and simplified through Governments' allocating a higher priority to the macroeconomic, strategic, and policy components. Planning output should change from the detailed multiyear plan to a much shorter statement of national strategy and policies and a public sector investment program (PSIP), both annually updated. Donors can assist in this process by providing technical assistance. They should respond positively if such assistance is sought by central ministries for macroeconomic analysis or by sector ministries for support of planning and project preparation.

(2) Improving Project Preparation and Implementation

4.16   The capacity of most PMCs to identify, prepare, and implement projects is extremely weak. The factors that limit absorptive capacity include inadequate skills, lack of management capacity, institutional limitations, insufficient infrastructure, and cultural and social constraints; in the South Pacific, land tenure problems are a particularly difficult area. Inappropriate donor policies and procedures also affect the ability of small countries to use aid well and quickly.

4.17   Several donors have taken steps to tailor their aid to the capacity of these six countries. Yet much more could be done. The simplification and possible standardization of procedures would be particularly advantageous.3/ Donors can assist countries to build capacity for development planning at the macroeconomic level and also for project preparation and implementation; this can be accomplished through more intensive and coordinated technical assistance and training. Donors should consider whether provision of aid through numerous individual projects is transferring a satisfactory level of benefits. Increased benefits may result from a different, broader approach: providing support for sector-based programs involving larger projects in several related areas. Perhaps best, the donor should take the lead role in a sector and assist in the planning process. Providing aid to one or more related sectors for an extended period of time can also help the recipient with institutional strengthening.

(3) Supporting Recurrent Costs

4.18   The recurrent cost problem is particularly severe among the PMCs (Chapter II). Because of the large number of recent infrastructural projects and the expansion of Government services, both PMC and donor Governments need to cooperate to find a solution to inadequate O&M expenditures. PMC Governments could be more selective in choosing projects, according higher priority to the productive sectors and seek assistance only for projects that generate sufficient revenue to meet at least on-going recurrent costs. Donors could shift from current programs emphasizing new investment to support for effective use of existing facilities.

3/ "Guidelines for Improving Aid Implementation," issued by the OECD in 1979, is still a relevant reference.

4.19   Lack of attention to the problem of recurrent cost funding is detrimental to efficient aid use; it wastes donor money, drains administrative resources, and undermines the ultimate return from the development project. Donors must give more attention to the long-term viability of new projects, first through improving standards of project design and second by identifying all recurrent cost requirements. Prior to project implementation, donors and recipient must ensure that O&M cost implications are provided for. Based on this assessment, donors may have to make an explicit provision for recurrent cost financing.

4.20   Even so, any donor move toward financing O&M costs should in no way remove from PMC Governments the responsibility for raising adequate domestic revenues: Governments must implement policies that will enable them to fund their recurrent cost budget in the long term without recourse to foreign aid. In the case of new donor-financed projects, donors need to satisfy themselves that adequate provision will be made for recurrent costs and should, if necessary, earmark allocations for these costs on a declining basis. Any provision for recurrent costs, or budgetary support for a particular sector, should be made from within existing and planned appropriation levels; this would reduce expenditure on new investment to a level more in line with the Government's capacity to service it and would also encourage the development of clearer investment priorities. The following are specific mechanisms for donors to support recurrent cost financing:

- Trust funds. Donors could contribute to trust funds whose income is specifically dedicated to maintenance and recurrent costs associated with aid funded projects. Such trust funds would alleviate both constraints on new investment and current budgetary difficulties.

- Project funding. PMC Governments could require donors to provide 100 percent financing of project costs across the entire spectrum of aid activity. (This approach was recently adopted by the Government of Solomon Islands. After placing a temporary moratorium on new aid projects, it has now issued guidelines requesting donors to finance 100 percent of costs including project specific recurrent costs.) With this approach, it would be necessary for PMCs to adopt policies that would eventually bring enough revenues and enable PMCs to assume full responsibility for O&M.

- Budgetary support. Shortage of domestic revenues has led to inadequate financing for repair and maintenance of past investments. One donor response could be to shift emphasis toward supporting past investment through budget support. Any such move would require a comprehensive dialogue between donors and individual island countries to determine priorities for allocating of aid funds between new investment and O&M.

(4) Providing Finance for the Private Sector

4.21   A major challenge in the 1990s will be to give a portion of aid to the private sector. This will be necessary to facilitate private investment that, under a reformed policy framework, will catalyze growth. Greater financialization (channelling aid flows through the commercial financial system) of donor resources will be essential, particularly during the early half of the 1990s, since the PMCs have to low savings propensities and lack depth in financial markets.

4.22   Getting aid to the private sector will not be easy. PMC financial systems tend to be shallow, repressed (through allocation and interest rate controls), and volatile (from openness and reserve management). The long end of the financial market is generally absent. Except in Fiji, capital markets are in infancy, the deposit base is largely short-term, and inter-bank markets are sufficiently illiquid to hinder term transformation. Donor experiences with Development Finance Institutions have been disappointing. Weak lending policies, a high degree of politicization, and a loan-production incentives structure have eroded financial discipline and have saddled Governments with unsound portfolios.

4.23   Increasing the financialization of aid will require an improvement in the performance of the financial systems. In particular, donors must not exacerbate financial system problems with their efforts to channel resources to the private sector. It will be important to avoid lending at negative interest rates, targeting credit to noncreditworthy groups, and refinancing unsound financial institutions. Donors can help entrepreneurs to develop plans to the point where they are potentially bankable.4/

(5) Developing Human Resources

4.24   Since the acute shortage of qualified and experienced personnel is a fundamental constraint to development in all PMCs, human resource development must remain a major area of emphasis. Governments should examine current policies to ascertain whether the generous level of external resources already available can be better used. Donors should continue to increase aid to this sector in support of revised policies; they should consider adapting their assistance to allow for the funding of O&M expenditures. Donors could usefully review their policies and programs in this sector to ensure that the assistance given is the most cost-effective and relevant to national needs and employment requirements.

C. Aid Coordination and Policy Dialogue

Aid Coordination

4.25   With the amount of aid--and the number of donors--increasing markedly, effective coordination of flows becomes more vital than ever. Aid coordination can improve information on national and sectoral needs and allocate scarce external resources to meet priority objectives. It can help simplify aid administration and stimulate greater flows. It can provide an environment for needed discussion of policies.

4.26   In the South Pacific, aid coordination takes place at national, regional, and international levels. Most PMCs hold regular programming discussions with their major donors. At the regional level, a number of organizations, most notably the Forum Secretariat and the South Pacific Commission, provide the focus for discussion of sectoral issues. At the international level, there is increasing use of the UNDP Round Table process.

4/   The IFC South Pacific Facility is one example of the appropriate type of business consultancy assistance.

4.27   While these processes have improved the information flow between island countries and the donor community, they do not seem to have gone beyond that. Coordination processes are often seen as a means of garnering increased aid; insufficient attention goes to discussing the policy environment or the constraints to efficient allocation and use of aid. Policy dialogue between donors and recipients is a critical aspect of aid coordination. It should take place not only at international coordination meetings, where it often relates to macroeconomic considerations, but also in bilateral relationships. In this forum it should involve discussion of narrower sectoral policy issues.

4.28   National coordination. It is not unusual to find several donors active in the same sector and a number of relatively small projects underway. This puts considerable strain on counterpart staff, who must service each donor's administrative and reporting requirements. It is essential therefore that the PMCs take the initiative and move toward some degree of sectoral and/or geographic coordination in their respective countries. A good example of geographic coordination is found in Tonga: each of the main regions has been notionally allocated to a specific donor. This is an appropriate approach for small, location-specific projects.

4.29   Coordination of sectoral aid at the country level has been neglected. This should be remedied, particularly if, as is recommended elsewhere, development strategies focus more on sectoral priorities than on individual projects. The PMCs should consider allocating particular sectors to individual donors or nominating a lead donor in major sectors. Such a move will assist in defining sectoral plans, since wider responsibility will require more donor attention to broader policy issues. For some donors, in particular Australia and New Zealand, that will help increase the focus of assistance. Despite recent efforts to concentrate their aid on fewer sectors, these two nations still appear to act as donors of last resort; as a result, programs dissipate their efforts across too many activities.

4.30   Regional coordination. There are many issues that are best addressed on a regional basis. But the Pacific Island countries are already well-served by regional organizations and institutions; significant costs would be involved in a further proliferation of organizations. As one example, a regional development bank would strain already scarce administrative resources. Proposals for enhanced regional cooperation should be examined closely to see whether the need could be met by an existing institution such as the Forum Secretariat.

4.31   International coordination. The UNDP has sponsored a series of Round Table Meetings (RTM) in Geneva for the Pacific Island countries. These began with Western Samoa in 1983 and now include arrangements for Vanuatu, Solomon Islands, Fiji, Cook Islands, Tonga, and Kiribati. Meetings have proved successful in improving information flows and in providing an opportunity for potential new donors to become familiar with a country's development objectives, strategies, economic potential, and constraints.

4.32   Nonetheless, a number of concerns have been expressed about the present format. These include insufficient emphasis on policy framework, limited follow-up, unclear benefits in furthering relations with established donors with already agreed forward programs, and a widely held view that it would be more appropriate to hold the meetings in-country or in-region.

4.33   The location of the RTM meetings is for individual Governments to decide. They might usefully consider the benefits of holding a series of back-to-back meetings in the Pacific.5/   Such gatherings might attract more senior/relevant representation from bilateral donors, allow new and prospective donors to gain first-hand experience of the region, and be a more cost-effective option for ministers and officials of South Pacific countries.

Policy Dialogue

4.34   To make the RTM process more effective as an instrument for aid coordination and policy dialogue, greater attention should go to ensuring an open exchange of views on development strategies and on policies that affect the capacity to absorb aid. These discussions could cover the broad policy agenda and the supporting Public Sector Investment Program and focus selectively on specific policy concerns.

4.35   Policy dialogue is necessary at both the multilateral and bilateral levels. The reluctance of bilateral donors to engage in policy discussion and negotiation, especially where they provide small amounts of assistance, is understandable. But in the South Pacific, entire development budgets come from donors and recipient countries possess insufficient staffing resources for in-depth policy analysis; donor reluctance can thus adversely affect aid implementation.

4.36   Major donors such as Australia, New Zealand, and Japan have a particular responsibility to provide sound policy advice on the impact of aid in areas where they are the dominant donor. Where necessary, they should undertake background analysis to offer this advice. Until now, dialogue has often been limited to a division of project responsibilities, with no discussion of the policy environment in which that project is to be implemented; long-term effectiveness has been ignored. Without a satisfactory policy environment, the contribution of aid to securing growth and balanced development is diminished.

Administrative Costs of Aid Coordination

4.37   While improved coordination is essential to increasing the efficient use of aid, it can be time-consuming and extremely expensive in staff resources. This is particularly so where small administrations have a limited number of key officials with aid responsibility.

4.38   Donors have noted the high costs of administering aid and have argued for improved coordination to reduce the burden. Little attention has been focused on the costs of such coordination to the island countries themselves. The major meetings that ministers and aid officials can be expected to attend appear in table 4.5. As a conservative estimate, the time required to service these meetings would be 15 weeks per year; frequently an island delegation will consist of more than one person, with the burden falling disproportionately on a few key personnel.

5/   The organization of the World Bank Caribbean Group Meeting offers a possible model in this regard.

4.39   Table 4.5 lists only major meetings: at the multilateral level it does not include meetings of the United Nations or its specialized agencies; at the regional level, it does not take into account meetings of the numerous regional agencies and organizations such as the Forum Fisheries Agency and the University of the South Pacific. These meetings impose additional demands on officials in central coordinating agencies. Moreover, the table does not take into account the various bilateral and multilateral programming missions, the appraisal, supervision, and evaluation missions that impose burdens on central coordinating agencies, or the visits of senior officials and ministers.

Table 4.5: COORDINATION REQUIREMENTS IN THE SOUTH PACIFIC

Multilateral	Regional
IMF/IBRD Annual Meetings	South Pacific Forum and pre-Forum
ADB Annual Meetings	meetings
UNDP Round Table Meetings and	South Pacific Conference
sensitizing missions	Forum Secretariat Annual Meeting
EEC Consultations	SPC.CRGA
IMF Annual Consultations	Pacific Islands Development Programme

Bilateral: Annual high-level consultations and preparatory meetings

4.40   Because of the high human cost of servicing frequent missions, donors are urged: (1) to assess carefully the need for missions; (2) wherever possible to combine missions into multitask exercises; and (3) to provide adequate advance notice of missions that are planned--preferably a six monthly program. Within the region, the Forum Secretariat could play a larger role in coordinating the scheduling of regional meetings and arranging for back-to-back meetings. The human costs also extend to numerous studies and information-gathering exercises, often duplicative, undertaken by donors. In the case of studies covering more than one country, the Secretariat could maintain a register so that future duplication of effort could be avoided.6/

D. Conclusions

4.41   Aid is a dominant factor in South Pacific development. Except for Fiji, Pacific Island countries have relied almost entirely on external assistance to finance Public Sector Investment Programs. Much of the region's major infrastructure has been financed through aid grants or concessional loans.

4.42   Notwithstanding the very substantial inflows of external assistance, economic growth in the PMCs has been slow and uneven in the last decade. The major part of aid has been applied to activities, such as human resource or infrastructure development, that have little immediate impact on economic growth or only a temporary impact on growth during the expenditure phase.

6/ The research bibliography project being undertaken by the National Centre for Development Studies in Australia could form the basis of such a register.

4.43   While there may not be any direct causal linkage between high volumes of aid and slow growth, there is increasing concern that available assistance is not being used as effectively as possible in the PMCs. Several changes are possible in this regard.

4.44   Donors need to work closely with the PMCs to improve elements of the planning process. Island Governments would be well advised to adopt a new approach to planning, emphasizing macroeconomic assessment and broad development strategies. Increased emphasis should go to improving project planning and preparation capacity in key line ministries.

4.45   Renewed attention must be given to factors that directly affect efficient use of external assistance. Chief among these is the problem of recurrent cost financing. Governments must adopt appropriate policies that will enable them to provide for their recurrent costs. In the short term, donors will have to consider making at least selective provision for some O&M expenditures, which may in fact represent a more productive use of aid than financing new investment.

4.46   Donors need to provide greater support for private sector development, if necessary by channelling more aid resources to the private sector. Given the acute shortages of qualified and experienced personnel, donors must continue to place special emphasis on human resource development and technical assistance.

4.47   Finally, there must be improved coordination of external assistance. At the international level, the UNDP Round Table provides an already established organizational framework--but a more complete discussion of the wider policy environment is required. At the national level, major donors will have to engage in a realistic policy dialogue with the recipient authorities.

4.48   In the 1990s, a steady flow of development assistance will be essential to ensure the PMCs' macroeconomic stability, to realize the rewards of past investment, and to underpin growth. Improving the system for allocating aid and the partnership between donor and recipient countries will be major challenges. But along with structural adjustment in PMC economies, these improvements will be vital to support a resumption of growth.

Appendix I. Tax Systems of the PMCs

1.   This appendix discusses the main features of the tax systems of the
Pacific Island member countries. Appendix table 1 summarizes specific
elements of tax systems by country; the following commentary puts these items
in context, indicating the desirable direction for reform of the tax systems.

2.   Taxes on income and profits. Personal income taxes are high--though
not exceptionally so by the standards of developing countries--in most of the
PMCs. Exceptional cases are Tonga, which has a low flat rate of income tax,
and Vanuatu, which does not have an income tax.1/

3.   All the PMCs, except Vanuatu, provide for the taxation of company
profits. By and large, resident companies are taxed on their worldwide income
while nonresident companies are taxed on their income from domestic sources
only.2/ In Fiji, Solomon Islands, and Western Samoa, nonresident companies are
taxed at flat rates that are higher than the respective rates applicable to
resident companies by 9 to 15 percentage points. Kiribati applies a two-tier
tax system to resident companies while Tonga has differentiated two-tier tax
systems applying to both resident and nonresident companies. In Tonga, the
difference in the rates of tax for resident and nonresident companies is as
high as 27.5 percent over a certain income range. It is also noteworthy that
in the four PMCs with fairly high rates of personal income taxation, the rate
of tax on resident companies is lower by 5 to 15 percentage points than the
respective maximum rate of personal income tax.

4.   While the progressive rate structure of the income tax in Fiji,
Kiribati, Solomon Islands, and Western Samoa has tended to make the
distribution of tax burdens more equitable, the presence of numerous
exemptions from income tax has worked in the opposite direction. Urban-rural
inequities arise in Fiji, Kiribati, and Western Samoa as a result of the
exemption of agriculture and most other forms of primary production from
income tax (mainly because of anticipated difficulties in tax enforcement).
The tax holidays and other concessions common in the PMCs also detract from
equity while sometimes having unintended effects on resource allocation. The
general exemption of commercially oriented public enterprises from income
taxation also tends to have distorting effects on resource allocation.

1/ In 1986, Tonga reformed its income tax system, substituting a flat 10
    percent rate of personal income tax for a progressive rate structure
    with a maximum rate of 40 percent; at the same time, it introduced a
    tax on retail sales at 5 percent. The combined revenue yield from the
    10 percent income tax and the 5 percent sales tax greatly surpassed the
    previous income tax yield. Vanuatu has not introduced a general income
    tax because of concern that this might conflict with the country's tax
    haven status. Recently, for incentive reasons, Fiji, Kiribati, and
    Western Samoa revised their rate structures, moderately lowering the
    highest marginal rates and, in the case of Kiribati and Western Samoa,
    also reducing the number of tax brackets.

2/ In Solomon Islands, even resident companies are taxed only on their
    domestic sourced income.

5.   As to the direction of future income tax reform, most PMCs need to consider moderating the present rather steep progressivity of the rate structures for personal income tax while reducing exempted categories and improving enforcement.3/ More specifically, they should consider expanding the size of the income tax brackets, limiting the number of brackets to at most five (as Kiribati and Western Samoa already have done), and significantly lowering the highest marginal rates. In the area of corporate taxation, it would be advisable for the PMCs to adopt the guideline that the rate of tax on resident companies should be set at, or closely below, the maximum rate of personal income tax; also, the differential between the rate of tax on resident companies and that on nonresident companies should be zero or small. Clearly, if the scope of tax exemptions can be narrowed, all the personal and corporate rates of tax could be lowered without loss of revenue. The present situation, where nonresident companies are nominally subject to high rates of tax but benefit from tax holidays and other concessions that greatly reduce their average effective tax rates, is anomalous.

6.   Taxes on goods and services. In the PMCs, domestic taxes on goods and services consist mainly of excise duties, sales and turnover taxes, and license and registration fees. Excise duties are a fairly important source of revenue in Fiji and Western Samoa; they are levied on a specific or ad valorem basis on a fairly large number of selected goods, including the traditionally dutiable items such as alcoholic beverages and cigarettes. License fees and other similar taxes, applying at varying rates to certain categories of businesses and often to other specified activities, are a significant source of revenue in some PMCs. Some types of sales and turnover taxes are now levied in all the PMCs except Solomon Islands. Of these, the only tax with a rather wide coverage is that levied in Tonga on retail sales, with various exemptions. The "turnover tax" in Fiji and the "goods and services tax" in Western Samoa, as well as the taxes levied on hotel services in Kiribati and Vanuatu, have a more limited coverage. In recent years, sales taxes have, in general, been a growing source of revenue in the PMCs because of increases in rates and extensions in coverage; nevertheless, their revenue yields are still rather modest.

7.   In recent years, interest in making tax systems more development oriented has made PMC Governments receptive to proposals for adopting broad-based "consumption taxes," specifically value-added and general sales taxes, while at the same time reducing income taxes and export duties and rationalizing import tariffs. Value-added taxes tend to be preferred in principle, but considerations of administrative feasibility have ruled them out for the present. Instead, for example, Fiji is considering the introduction of a flat rate sales tax to be applied to imported and domestic consumer goods and to a range of services. In restructuring their tax systems, the other PMCs should also consider the adoption of a general sales tax on domestic sales of goods by manufacturers, imports of finished goods, and services sold by the organized sector; exports, raw materials, and intermediate goods used in domestic production as well as unprocessed goods should be exempted. Such a tax could be applied at a uniform rate, basically

---

3/   In most PMCs, the incidence of personal income tax now falls mainly on public sector employees.

as a single-stage tax, thus avoiding the administrative difficulties of operating a VAT type general tax credit system while minimizing cascading effects.

8. Taxes on international trade and transactions. As noted in the main body of the report, taxes on international trade and transactions account for well over one-half of tax revenue in all the PMCs except Fiji, where they account for one-third. In all the PMCs, import duties constitute the predominant, if not sole, component of taxes on international trade and transactions.4/ In recent years, export duties have generally declined in importance as a source of revenue; they are levied at present only in Fiji, Solomon Islands, and Vanuatu. Other taxes on international trade and transactions, such as the wharfage tax in Tonga and the tax on foreign currency sales in Western Samoa, do not constitute important sources of revenue.

9. For the most part, import duties in the PMCs are on an ad valorem basis, with the spread of ad valorem rates varying widely among the countries. While all the countries have large numbers of exempted (or zero-rated) goods, the rates at the upper end vary from 60 percent in Western Samoa to well over 200 percent in Fiji and Solomon Islands. Specific duties are also levied on a limited range of items (usually including alcoholic beverages and tobacco) in several PMCs. Despite high ad valorem rates, the average effective rates of import taxation (total import duties as percent of total imports c.i.f.) have ranged between 15 percent (in Fiji) and 31 percent (in Vanuatu).

10. In recent years, the Governments of several PMCs (Fiji and Western Samoa) have become aware of anomalies in the import tariff structures and have taken steps toward tariff reform. Nevertheless, the existing tariff structures are still unnecessarily complicated and somewhat lacking in economic rationale in practically all the PMCs. In general, the PMCs have followed the principle of taxing essentials at low rates and luxuries at high rates, although revenue considerations have led to departures from this principle. The resulting structure of effective rates of protection involved very high rates for luxury consumer goods and low (and sometimes negative) rates for widely used essential consumer goods. Such a structure of effective rates is likely to have undesirable effects on the general pattern of investment, especially in the case of a relatively developed PMC, like Fiji, with active import-substituting industries.

11. In most of the PMCs, the tariff structures appear to have evolved primarily under the pressure of revenue needs. It would be highly desirable for the PMCs gradually to revise their tariff systems so that these principally serve protectionist objectives, leaving the revenue raising function primarily to excise duties or sales taxes that apply to both imported and domestic goods. Such revision of tariff systems may have to be a phased process since it will have to proceed pari passu with the establishment of the administrative machinery for collecting the excise or sales taxes that replace the revenue-raising import duties. Pending such major tariff reform, the PMCs should take further steps to rationalize and simplify their tariff structures, reducing the present wide dispersion of ad valorem rates.

4/ The ports and services tax of Tonga, which is levied at a 15 percent rate on the value of imports, is classified here as an import duty.

12.   Export duties have been used for revenue generation at some time or the other in almost all the PMCs, mainly because of the ease with which they can be collected. At present, however, they contribute significantly to revenue only in Solomon Islands and Fiji. There is little theoretical justification for the use of export duties in the PMCs because of the elastic international demand facing their exports; the incidence of export duty falls almost wholly on the farmer-producers, thus conflicting with the general aim of providing incentives for exports. In addition, specific export duties create problems unless they are adjusted frequently to take account of changes in export prices and production costs. Export duties on a sliding scale linked to export prices, or export duties that are otherwise "graduated," have been used by developing countries to deal with these problems, but such sliding scales or "graduations" also need to be reviewed frequently. A case can sometimes be made, on a balance of considerations, to levy moderate export duties as an administratively convenient substitute for income taxation; such duties should also be graduated or adjusted frequently and be designed as a transitional step toward income taxation. Export duties may also appropriately be used as a strictly temporary measure in a special situation, as was the case recently in Fiji where export duties were increased with a view to siphoning off windfall profits following a currency devaluation.

13.   Tax exemptions and tax collections. A general problem with revenue generation in the PMCs is the tendency to exempt substantial classes of potential payers of such taxes as income and profits taxes or import duties for reasons of economic incentive, equity, or administrative convenience. Thus, private enterprises are granted income tax holidays and other concessions often on an ad hoc basis; public enterprises are exempted from income taxes and sometimes also from import duties; the agricultural sector and sometimes other primary sectors as well as unorganized enterprises are exempted from income taxation. A substantial reduction of such exemptions should be part of any major restructuring of the tax system of a PMC.

14.   All the PMCs need to take steps at an early date to strengthen their revenue departments, in order to improve collections from existing taxes and to prepare to implement new taxes, such as a sales tax. While there are expenditure constraints in most of the PMCs, additional spending on revenue administration (including adequate staff training programs) should be recognized as likely to yield large benefits relative to costs.

15.   Better use of available information, both qualitative and quantitative, could help improve revenue collection in almost all the PMCs. Tax assessment could be facilitated by making full use of information relating to incomes, transactions, and taxable capacity already available to agencies within the Government complex, by compiling other relevant statistics, and by using computerized information systems where feasible. The use of self-assessment procedures, combined with appropriate penalties for delayed payments and for non-compliance, and the levy of presumptive taxes (for instance, on the basis of employment or rough estimates of turnover when businesses do not furnish proper accounts or file tax returns) could be very effective in improving tax collection.

APPENDIX TABLE 1: MAIN FEATURES OF TAX SYSTEMS (JANUARY 1990)

I. TAXES ON INCOME AND PROFITS

	FIJI	KIRIBATI	SOLOMON ISLANDS	TONGA	VANUATU	W. SAMOA
	Individuals pay basic tax at 3.75% on total income plus normal tax (10 slabs with rates ranging from 4% to 40%) on taxable income (after allowances); highest rate of normal tax at F$40,000.	Individuals: Residents pay tax on worldwide income (after allowances); 4 slabs with rates ranging from 10% to 40%; highest rate at A$6,000 of taxable income. Nonresidents pay at 30% on Kiribati-source taxable income.	Individuals pay tax on incomes (after allowances for residents only) accruing or received in or derived from Solomon Islands; 8 slabs with rates ranging from 14% to 42%; highest rate at SI $14,700 for single persons and SI $17,500 for married persons filing jointly).	Individuals pay flat 10% tax on chargeable income (after allowances).	No general income or profits taxes. However, tax is payable at 15% on rental income from properties in Vanuatu.	Individuals: Residents pay tax on worldwide income after allowances; nonresidents pay tax on total income derived from W. Samoan source; 5 slabs with rates ranging from 10% to 45% for both resident and nonresidents; highest rate at WS$20,000.
	Resident companies pay basic tax at 3.75% plus normal tax at 35% on worldwide income. Nonresident companies pay basic tax at 3.75% plus normal tax at 45% on income from Fijian sources; shipping and insurance companies taxed on separate basis.	Resident companies pay basic tax at 25% on first A$50,000 of taxable income and at 35% thereafter. Nonresident companies pay tax at 30% on Kiribati-source taxable income.	Companies pay tax only on income accruing in or derived from Solomon Islands; rate of tax 35% for resident companies and 50% for nonresident companies.	Resident companies pay tax at 15% on first T$100,000 of taxable income, at 30% on balance. Nonresident companies pay tax at 37.5% on first T$50,000 of taxable income, at 42.5% on balance.		Resident companies pay tax at 39% on world-wide taxable income. Nonresident companies pay tax at 48% on income from W. Samoan sources.
	Withholding taxes e.g. on dividends (residents at 5%, nonresidents at 30%), on interest (nonresidents only at 15%); rates for nonresidents may be lower depending on tax treaty provisions.	Withholding taxes at 30% on receipts of dividends, interest, royalties, management fees, etc. by residents not filing tax returns.	Withholding taxes on dividends from resident companies at 20% for residents and 35% for nonresidents.	Withholding taxes e.g. on gross royalties (resident companies at 3%, nonresident companies at 15%), on income from lease of land (at 3%).	None.	Withholding taxes e.g. on dividends, royalties at 15%; on interest earnings at 15% (with WS$50 exemption); on commissions at 10%.

	FIJI	KIRIBATI	SOLOMON ISLANDS	TONGA	VANUATU	W. SAMOA
I. TAXES ON INCOME AND PROFITS (cont'd)	Capital gains on land (with various exemptions) taxed at special rates.		Capital gains on sales of business assets taxed at 35%.		None.	Capital gains (after annual 5% inflation adjustment) on assets sold within 3 years of acquisition taxed at 30%.
II. PROPERTY TAXES	None.	None.	Estate and death duties range from SI$2 up to a 40% rate on value of estate exceeding SI$4 million.	None.	None.	None.
III. TAXES ON GOODS AND SERVICES	Excise duties: Specific duties on cigarettes, tobacco, beer, spirits, matches, cement, sugar. Ad valorem duties at 10% on a range of goods manufactured in Fiji (but not for export). Turnover taxes at 10% on hotel and restaurant charges, betting, entertainment, car hire, overseas travel tickets, lotteries, etc.	Hotel services tax at 3%.	Specific excise duties on a few goods. Licence fees on retail businesses, motor vehicles, driving licences, work permits, etc.	Retail sales tax at 5%; exemptions for export goods, local agricultural and fishery products, and livestock sales in Government markets.	Business licence fees for banking and financial institutions, other overseas companies. Registration fees work permit fees tourist tax at 10% on all hotel and restaurant charges. Excise duties: None.	Excise duties on a range of domestic and imported goods (rates high on tobacco, alcoholic beverages, soft drinks). Goods and services tax at 10% applying to hotels, restaurants, movie theatres, sporting events, lotteries, most professional services, etc.

IV. TAXES ON INTERNATIONAL TRADE AND TRANSACTIONS

Import duties: Ad valorem "customs duties" at 5% or 7.5% plus ad valorem "fiscal duties" mostly at rates of 7.5%, 10%, 15%, 20%, 25%, 30%, 40%, and 50% but with rates on certain items (e.g. motor vehicles) rising up to 225%; also, some specific duties e.g. on spirits.	Import duties, mostly ad valorem, at rates between 0 and 80%; some specific duties.	Import duties, mostly ad valorem, at rates of 0-125% for food, 0-105% for chemicals, 0-255% for machinery and transport equipment. Additional 3% import duty on goods subject to ad valorem rates, except for petroleum products and other exempted goods. Specific duties on beverages and tobacco, and specific plus ad valorem duties on some minerals and fuels.	Import duties: 8 rates of import duty ranging from 0 to 45% plus ports and services tax at 17.5% of c.i.f. import value. Specific duties on fuel, tobacco, liquor, etc.	Import duties vary from 17% to 100%. Most rates fall in 20-35% range, but significant exceptions are fruits and vegetables (40%), carpets (47%), and meat (55-75%). Specific duties on alcoholic beverages and tobacco products.	Import duties at five "general" levels of 10%, 20%, 35%, 50% and 60% (examples: 10% or less for essential foods; 35% for raw materials).
Export duties at 5% on sugar, molasses, gold, and silver.	Export duties: None.	Export duties on copra (at 15% on value per ton in excess of SI$250), fish (5%), palm oil and kernels (10%), logs and lumber, gold, etc.	Export duties: None.	Export duties (Details?) Copra export tax? Others?	Export duties: None since January 1990.

V. OTHER TAXES

					Foreign exchange levy at 1% on tala value of foreign currency sales by commercial banks.
Stamp duties, mostly specific, on documents, agreements, transfers. Airport departure tax.	Stamp duties on agreements, various property and title transfers, some ad valorem, others specific.			Stamp duties on property transfers. Airport tax.	Stamp duties on selected documents at varying rates.

Sources: Official documents; IMF Reports; World Bank reports; various other publications.

BIBLIOGRAPHY

Browne, Christopher, and Douglas A. Scott. 1989. Economic Development in Seven Pacific Island Countries. Washington, D.C.: International Monetary Fund.

Cole, Rodney. 1988. "Creating a Climate for Investment in Fiji." National Centre for Development Studies, Islands/Australia Working Paper, No. 88/6. Canberra: Australian National University.

Cole, R.V., and T.G. Parry, eds. 1986. Selected Issues in Pacific Island Development. Pacific Policy Papers, No. 2. Canberra: National Centre for Development Studies, Australian National University.

Dornbusch, R. 1982. "Stabilization Policies in Developing Countries: What Have We Learned?" World Development, Vol. 10, pp. 701-708.

Dwyer, L. 1986. "Tourism in the South Pacific," in Cole and Parry (eds.) Selected Issues in Pacific Island Development.

Fairbairn, T. 1985. Island Economies: Studies from the South Pacific. Suva: University of the South Pacific.

-----. 1988. Island Entrepreneurs: Problems and Performance in the Pacific. Honolulu: University of Hawaii Press.

Fairbairn, T., and C. Tisdell. 1983. "Economic Growth Among Small Pacific Countries: Can it be Sustained?" Working Paper No. 83-5. Nagoya, Japan: United Nations Center for Regional Development.

-----. 1984. "Subsistence Economies and Unsustainable Development and Trade: Some Simple Theory." The Journal of Development Studies, Vol. 20, No. 2.

Fairbairn, T., and T. Perry. 1985. Multinational Enterprises in the Developing South Pacific Region. Honolulu: East-West Center.

Fairbairn, T., and H. Kakazu. 1985. "Trade and Diversification in Small Island Economies with Particular Emphasis on the South Pacific." Singapore Economic Review, 30(2), pp. 17-35.

Fisk, E.K. 1978. The Island of Niue, Development or Dependence for a Very Small Nation. Canberra: Australian National University.

Fleming, M., and R.R. Piggott. 1985. "Analysis of Export Earnings Instability in the South Pacific Region." Singapore Economic Review, 30(1), pp. 14-33.

Forsyth, P. 1986. "Economic Problems of International Transport for the South Pacific Island Economies." National Centre for Development Studies, Islands/Australia Working Paper, no. 86/10. Canberra: Australian National University.

Guest, James. 1985. "Macroeconomic Stabilization Policy with Special Reference to Fiscal Policy." National Centre for Development Studies, Islands/Australia Working Paper no. 85/1. Canberra: Australian National University.

Moran, Christian. 1983. "Export Fluctuations and Economic Growth: An Empirical Analysis." Journal of Development Economics, Vol. 12, pp. 195-218.

Pollard, S. 1987. "The Viability and Vulnerability of a Small Island State: the Case of Kiribati." National Centre for Development Studies, Islands/Australia Working Paper no. 87/14. Canberra: Australian National University.

------. 1988. "Atoll Economies: Issues and Strategy Options for Development." National Centre for Development Studies, Islands/Australia Working Paper no. 88/5. Canberra: Australian National University.

Price Waterhouse Information Guide:
Doing Business in Fiji, 1989;
Doing Business in Solomon Islands, 1983;
Doing Business in Western Samoa, 1979.

Robertson, M. 1985. "The South Pacific Regional Trade and Economic Cooperation Agreement: A Critique." National Centre for Development Studies, Islands/Australia Working Paper no. 85/2. Canberra: Australian National University.

Skully, M. 1987. Financial Institutions and Markets in the South Pacific, New York: St. Martin's Press.

Siwatibu, S. 1988. "Macroeconomic Policies Under Adverse Conditions: The Case of Fiji in 1987." Pacific Economic Bulletin, 3(1), pp. 17-25.

Srinivasen, T.N. 1985. "The Costs and Benefits of Being a Small, Remote Island, Landlocked, or Mini-State Economy." Development Policy Issues Series. Washington, D.C.: The World Bank.

Tanzi, Vito. 1984. "Is There a Limit to the Size of Fiscal Deficits in Developing Countries?" in Bernerd P. Herber (ed.), Public Finance and Public Debt, Detroit: Wayne University Press, pp. 139-152.

Thirlwall, A.P., and J. Bergevin. July 1985. "Trends, Cycles, and Asymmetries in the Terms of Trade of Primary Commodities from Developed and Less Developed Countries." World Development Report.

Thirlwall, A. 1990. "The Performance and Prospects of the Pacific Island Economies in the World Economy," Plenary Address, Third Pacific Islands Conference of Leaders, April 9-11, 1990. Honolulu: East-West Center, University of Hawaii.

World Bank Publications:

Fiji: Challenges for Development, Report No. 7724-FIJ, May 4, 1990.

Fiji: A Transition to Manufacturing, 1987.

Kiribati: Economic Developments, Issues, and Prospects, Report No. 6889-KIR, May 4, 1988.

Trends in Developing Economies, 1989.

World Development Reports, 1984, 1987, 1988, 1990.

Long-Term Prospects for the OECS Countries, Report No. 8058-CRG, February 15, 1990.

Caribbean Region: Current Economic Situation, Regional Issues, and Capital Flows, Report No. 8246-CRG, February 22, 1990.

Data Sources:

International Monetary Fund, Direction of Trade Statistics. Washington, D.C.: International Monetary Fund, 1990.

Organization for Economic Cooperation and Development. Main Economic Indicators. Paris: OECD, 1990.

United Nations Conference on Trade and Development. Handbook of International Trade and Development Statistics. New York: United Nations, 1988.

World Bank. Standard Tables. Washington, D.C.: World Bank, 1990.

------. World Bank Atlas: Gross National Product, Population, and Growth Rates, Washington, D.C., 1989.

------. World Tables, 1989-90, Washington, D.C., 1989.

World Tourism Organization. Yearbook of Tourism Statistics, 1988. Madrid: World Tourism Organization, 1988.

Part II

Country Surveys

FIJI

DEVELOPMENT SURVEY

FIJI

CURRENCY EQUIVALENTS

Annual Averages

1981	F$1.00 = $1.17
1982	F$1.00 = $1.07
1983	F$1.00 = $0.98
1984	F$1.00 = $0.93
1985	F$1.00 = $0.87
1986	F$1.00 = $0.88
1987	F$1.00 = $0.82
1988	F$1.00 = $0.70
1989	F$1.00 = $0.67

FISCAL YEAR

January 1 - December 31

ABBREVIATIONS AND ACRONYMS

EEC = European Economic Community
FDB = Fiji Development Bank

Table of Contents

FIJI: ECONOMIC DEVELOPMENTS AND PROSPECTS

A.   Background

1.1   Among the small Pacific Island economies, Fiji stands out in terms of
its relative size and levels of economic and social development. Its
population amounted to 720,000 in 1988, growing at present at about 1.4
percent a year. As a result largely of political developments in 1987 which
greatly affected the economy, GNP per capita dropped to the equivalent of
$1,540 in 1988 from $1,730 in 1986. Nonetheless, Fiji remains a diversified
middle-income country notable for its internationally competitive smallholder
sugar industry, its tourism development, a significant industrial base, and
substantial prospects for further forestry, fisheries and other agricultural
development. Its primary need is for more sustained growth.

1.2   Fiji's land area of 18,272 km^2 is spread across 330 islands, located
centrally among neighboring island countries but over 1,500 km from its
closest major markets, Australia and New Zealand. In the early stages of
development as a British colony, sugar came to dominate the economy, with
production growth averaging nearly 5 percent a year from the 1870s up to 1940
and by then accounting for close to 70 percent of export earnings. Copra was
the other main export. Entrepot trade developed early, as did tourism, and
both remain important today.

1.3   The sugar industry was developed by farmers of Indian origin, who
came originally to the colony as indentured laborers, on land leased by native
Fijians. On this base and through wider participation in the cash economy,
the population of Indian origin increased from 14 percent of the total in 1901
to 51 percent in 1966; at the time of the 1986 census, Indians comprised
49 percent of the population, Fijians 46 percent and others (Melanesian,
Polynesian, Chinese and European) the residual 5 percent. The Indian
community became prominent in commerce and industry, education, the
professions, the public service and public enterprises, and as an industrial
workforce, while continuing to dominate the smallholder sugar economy.
Fijians, however, still own close to 83 percent of all land (about 8 percent
is freehold, and the rest Government-owned). Fijian economic activity has
diversified with the growth of commercial agriculture, urban employment
opportunities, and tourism, with the Fijian community accumulating education
and wealth and retaining political and considerable economic power. Political
stability depended on a system in which a multiracial but essentially Fijian
government retained control.

1.4   This stability was assisted before and for a period after
Independence by a strong economic performance with large investments in
infrastructure and human resource development as well as in agriculture,
manufacturing and tourism which had widespread employment and income benefits.
From the mid-1970s, growth slowed and became more erratic. In 1980-85, there
was very little increase, on average, in real GDP, and per capita incomes
started to decline.

1.5   After much better growth performance in 1986, the economic situation deteriorated rapidly following the military take-over in May 1987 after the electoral defeat of the government in power since Independence, and a second coup in September. The effects on production, investment and incomes were immediate and severe; Fiji suddenly faced the need for short-term stabilization measures, for economy recovery, and for more basic structural adjustment measures. The economy was quickly stabilized, at reduced levels of activity, by an interim civilian government which has since taken steps both to promote economic recovery and to reestablish the constitutional and political basis for new development. A draft constitution is being discussed but some uncertainties are likely to persist while the political issues are being resolved.

1.6   The Government has concentrated its attention on measures that would promote economic recovery and stimulate investment in agriculture, for which incentives have been revised, and manufacturing, for which tax-free zones are being established to promote labor-intensive export activities. Special efforts have been made to revive tourism and attract new investment. Efforts are also being made to compensate for losses of skills through recent emigration. Some of the steps taken, including devaluation and changes in the agriculture, manufacturing and financial sectors, are contributing to the rapid restructuring of the economy and, significantly, to the restoration of confidence.

1.7   <u>Trends in Population, Employment and Access to Services</u>. Fiji's population increased at a rate of 1.9 percent per annum, between the 1976 and 1986 censuses, with higher rates of increase among ethnic Fijians. The most recent estimates of annual population growth is 1.4 percent per annum. This reflects the substantial emigration which occurred after the coups: the rate of natural increase remains closer to the 1.9 percent per annum recorded in the period 1976-86. The labor force increased much more rapidly, at 3.2 percent per annum, than total population, primarily because of rapid growth of labor force participation among women (5.7 percent per annum). Nevertheless, the workforce was much better educated in 1986, with 73 percent having completed some secondary or higher education compared to 27 percent in 1976. This expanding and more educated labor force could not be adequately absorbed in the conditions of low and diminishing economic growth.

1.8   Within the labor force of about 240,000 in 1986, the year of the latest census, 43 percent--about 100,000 in all--were employed in the formal wage sector. Of these, approximately 80,000 were employed on a continuous basis; the remainder, primarily casual agricultural and construction workers, were only seasonally or intermittently employed. The public sector accounted for about one-third of continuous employment. While total employment increased by about 2.9 percent per annum in 1976-86, only about 20 percent of this was in wage employment, two-thirds of it within the public sector. About 48,000 of the 60,000 new jobs were in the "own account" or unpaid family worker categories; however, virtually all of the latter was in cash cropping rather than in subsistence activities.

1.9   Open unemployment rates increased only slightly over the period from 1976 to 1986, from 6.7 percent to 7.5 percent, although the numbers of unemployed increased from about 12,000 to about 18,000. Unemployment was more severe in urban areas (12 percent) and among females (15 percent compared to 5 percent for males) and it was concentrated among young people; about 75 percent of the unemployed were aged between 15 and 24. The census also identifies a category of "discouraged workers", who were not actively seeking work because of perceived poor employment prospects; if this latter group were added to the actively unemployed, the effective unemployment rate would rise to over 11 percent. On this basis, the rates of urban unemployment for Fijian males aged 15-19 and 20-24 would have been 49 percent and 30 percent, respectively. By 1986, therefore, Fiji confronted major employment problems which could only be solved at higher rates of economic growth.

1.10   **The Loss of Skills**. Fiji's quite abundant supply of skills was threatened by the political events of 1987. Prior to them, about 500 workers emigrated annually; in the year following the coups d'etat, emigration rose sharply to about 2,500, or 1 percent of the work force. Emigration has particularly affected the supply of high- and middle-level staff. According to the Fiji Bureau of Statistics, of those employed at the time of the 1986 Census, about 7 percent of professional and technical, 17 percent of administrative and managerial, and 8 percent of clerical staff had left the country by late 1988. Key professions have been particularly hard hit: it is reported that 70 percent of lawyers, over 50 percent of doctors, 40 percent of accountants, and many architects, engineers and technicians, and teachers have recently left Fiji; vacancy rates for some key public service skills still range from 30 to over 50 percent.

1.11   **Education and Health**. Fiji has in the past given high priority to human resource development and has achieved remarkable coverage and performance in the health and education sectors; progress was maintained during the early 1980s. Table 1.1 gives some of the latest data. By 1986, about 68 percent of the labor force had some secondary education, and another 5 percent some post-secondary education or training. Mortality and health status indicators are also favorable compared to other developing countries. Utilization of education and health services is high, and service quality is good. Government expenditure devoted to education has been consistently close to 20 percent of the budget throughout the 1970s and 1980s, equivalent to 5-6 percent of GDP. The objective up to 1985 was to provide 10 years of education for every child wanting it; this was to be increased to 12 years in 1985-90. Public expenditure on health averaged about 8 percent of total government spending in the 1980s, nearly 3 percent of GDP, with health expenditures per capita rising by close to 20 percent in real terms in 1981-84 but later dropping back to 1981 levels. The emphasis has now shifted to efforts to maintain service quality and coverage within tighter budgetary constraints, while providing for expanded training programs to meet pressing needs. The loss of skills through emigration will make this adjustment process especially challenging.

Table 1.1: SOCIAL INDICATORS, 1988 /a

Indicator	Units	Fiji	Asia	Lower-Middle Income
Population	persons	720,000	-	-
- Growth rate	%	1.4	1.8	2.2
Crude birth rate	per 000	26.6	26.8	31.5
Crude death rate	per 000	5.0	8.8	8.6
Infant mortality rate	per 000 births	21.0	61.5	59.1
Life expectancy at birth	years	70.4	63.7	63.8
Population per:				
- Doctor	persons	2,028	1,422	1,547
- Nurse	persons	491	1,674	-
- Hospital	persons	364	733	-
Child immunization				
- Measles	%	24.6	41.0	62.6
- DPT	%	80.4	48.6	64.7
Access to safe water	%	69.0	-	-
- Urban	%	89.0	72.5	76.7
- Rural	%	56.0	-	46.3
Gross enrollment ratios				
- Primary	%	129.0	105.3	106.8
- Secondary	%	55.0	30.5	51.8
Adult illiteracy rate	%	14.5	39.5	26.2

/a Or most recent estimate.

Source: World Bank, Social Indicators of Development, 1989

B. Recent Economic Developments

1.12   In 1965-73, Fiji experienced robust economic growth; real GDP increased by close to 8 percent per annum. In 1973-80, growth averaged a lower but still adequate 3.8 percent per annum. International prices for sugar were favorable for much of this 15-year period. Tourist arrivals and tourism receipts expanded rapidly in earlier years. The expansion of these two sectors was supported by public investments in sugar production and basic infrastructure, as well as private investments in tourist facilities. Beginning in 1979 and persisting through 1983, however, there was a marked slowdown. The increase in oil prices in 1979-80 and the subsequent recession in the industrialized world resulted in a sharp deterioration in the terms of trade (about 25 percent) and reduced inflows of foreign capital. Fiji also suffered adverse weather conditions, with droughts in 1980 and 1983, and severe cyclone damage.

1.13   The slowdown in economic growth and export earnings during the early eighties led to increased deficits on both the current and fiscal accounts. The current account deficit rose to almost 16 percent of GDP in 1981; the fiscal deficit increased to nearly 7 percent of GDP in 1982. The Government responded by imposing monetary and fiscal restraints. Public investment was reduced, as major projects were completed, from a peak of 18 percent of GDP in 1981 to about 10 percent in 1984. Efforts to contain current government expenditures were frustrated in 1983 by a major salary increase awarded under arbitration to public sector employees. Later stabilization efforts proved more successful, as the Government instituted a wage and salary freeze while continuing to restrain development expenditures.

1.14   In 1984, the upswing in the industrial countries gave new impetus to tourism, and there was a substantial recovery in agricultural production and exports after the drought and cyclone the previous year. Real GDP growth exceeded 8 percent and the current account deficit was reduced from an average of 10 percent of GDP in the preceding three years to below 3 percent. In 1985, however, Fiji was again struck by cyclones. Sugar production declined by 25 percent in volume terms due to storm damage; tourism stagnated. While other sectors performed reasonably well, real GDP declined by about 3 percent.

1.15   The cumulative result of these annual swings, largely related to external developments and adverse weather conditions, was an increase in real GDP averaging only 1.2 percent a year in 1980-85. Growth rates in agriculture (0.5 percent a year) and tourism were low and, in manufacturing, negative. There was little structural change and almost no growth in wage employment. Per capita incomes declined, on average, by 0.7 percent a year though with large variations around the trend.

1.16   In 1986, almost perfect weather conditions boosted sugar production to 502,000 tons, the largest crop ever harvested in Fiji. Tourist arrivals also surpassed previous levels; gold production doubled, and several other industries--ginger, copra, cocoa, and poultry--proved buoyant. Real GDP increased by nearly 8 percent; domestic inflation, which had declined steadily since 1984, was less than 2 percent. Reduced oil prices, affecting about one-fifth of Fiji's imports, reinforced the strong gains achieved through increased export receipts. Similar improvements, however, were not achieved on the fiscal side during 1986. A major reform of the personal income tax reduced direct taxes and raised indirect taxes, but increased revenues from the latter did not materialize and, as a result, the budget deficit widened from 3 percent of GDP in 1985 to close to 5 percent.

1.17   The economy nevertheless entered 1987 in an apparently comfortable position. International reserves amounted to $170 million, equivalent to six months of imports. While economic growth was forecast to slow down, the balance of payments was projected to record a larger surplus, on the basis of a continuing rise in tourist receipts and increased nontraditional exports. These prospects, unfortunately, were upset by the political developments resulting in the May and September military coups and by the economic disruption they caused. The immediate results included a sharp loss of business confidence, increased emigration, and capital flight. The sugar harvest was interrupted and tourist arrivals dropped precipitously. Investment virtually ceased and the external position deteriorated. The stance of economic policies had to shift from support for a relatively strong economy to protecting foreign exchange reserves. A large drop in government revenues led to expenditure cuts ranging from 10 percent to 20 percent in wages and salaries and 40 percent in capital expenditures. The budget deficit nevertheless increased. While some recovery was evident later in 1987, it is now estimated that real GDP declined by almost 8 percent for the year as a whole.

1.18   Government action to stabilize the internal and external financial position of the country included credit restrictions and foreign exchange controls, supplemented by devaluations of about 18 percent in June 1987 and 15 percent in October, which together imply a real effective depreciation of about 30 percent during 1987. While this discouraged capital flight, and contributed to a rebuilding of reserves, little immediate stimulus to investment or output could be expected until business confidence recovered. Consequently, economic recovery, utilizing the gains from exchange rate adjustment, was consolidated.

1.19   This recovery gathered momentum in 1988. It has been assisted by measures to stimulate agricultural investment, for which incentives have been revised, and the manufacturing sector, for which tax-free zones and factories are being established to promote labor-intensive exporting. Special efforts have been made to revive tourism and attract new investment. Efforts are also being made to compensate for losses of skills through recent emigration. Further adjustments will be needed, however, to establish conditions for more sustained growth than Fiji has achieved in recent years.

1.20   Partly because of lower sugar production, in drought conditions, there was minimal growth (0.4) percent, in real GDP in 1988, and inflation increased from 6 percent to 12 percent largely because of the effects of the devaluation. The balance of payments strengthened, however, as nonsugar exports responded to the increased incentives, tourism began to recover, and external assistance returned to normal levels. This contributed to a substantial surplus on both current and capital accounts, and a level of reserves equivalent to about seven months of imports at the end of 1988.

1.21   In 1989 there has been a further demonstration of the resilience of the Fijian economy and its capacity, through structural adjustment, for improved growth performance. Real GDP growth of 12.5 percent is estimated, largely because of an exceptional increase in sugarcane production (31 percent) and the effects of this on processing and other activity, but also through healthy growth in general manufacturing, construction and services.

Commodity exports increased by nearly 15 percent to over $350 million with garment exports increasing from $18 million to $48 million (and from 6 percent to 14 percent of exports) as new markets were secured. Tourism arrivals increased by 20 percent to reach 250,000, close to the 1986 peak, and receipts could amount to $160 million, 30 percent more than in 1988. There were large increases in both private and public investment, rising aggregate fixed investment from 12 percent to over 14 percent of GDP. Paid employment increased by an estimated 13 percent with more than half of the new employment in manufacturing. The ground lost during 1987-88 has now been almost fully restored and the economy looks strong.

1.22   Table 1.2 summarizes the performance of the economy in 1980-84, 1985-87 and the two subsequent years. Among the factors most affecting performance in the 1980s were a set of economic policies which produced little in the way of market incentives for growth and, associated with this, a lengthy decline in investment levels.

1.23   Investment. Total fixed investment in Fiji increased to an average of 25 percent of GDP in 1981-82 but then declined to under 18 percent in 1985-86. In constant prices, investment expenditures in 1986 were only 57 percent of the 1981 level. In 1987, they amounted to only 14 percent of a reduced GDP and were below even that level in 1988.

1.24   The reductions were primarily in Government and public enterprise investment. Two factors explain this trend. A number of large infrastructure projects initiated in the 1970s raised public sector investment to unusually high levels. These projects were completed early in the 1980s. They had provided large increases in infrastructure capacity, especially in the transport, power and telecommunications sectors, and in agricultural production possibilities. Low growth in demand left areas of excess capacity. The public investment program was scaled down partly for these reasons, and also because of increased stringency in public finance. The reduction of public sector expenditures, as a proportion of total spending, was an explicit policy target from the beginning of the 1980s; provisions for the operation and maintenance of infrastructure as well as for new investments were affected. Public sector investment outlays fell from 14 percent of GDP in 1981 to 7 percent in 1986 and, in crisis conditions, to under 5 percent in 1987.

1.25   During the period, private investment fluctuated at around 10-12 percent of GDP with little tendency to increase. Few major new investments were undertaken in agriculture, manufacturing or tourism. The extent of regulation and control of private sector activity may well have been largely responsible. Incentives for foreign and new domestic investment were more effective in 1986 and early 1987, when a number of new projects, mainly in tourism and production for export, were approved. Many investments were postponed, however, when the political crisis occurred.

1.26   The Role of Government. Perhaps the most notable trend evident in Fiji in the 1970s and into the 1980s, other than the declining growth rate, was the increasing extent of government intervention in the operation of the economy. National development objectives emphasized import substitution, in agriculture as well as manufacturing, and the official promotion of diversification in exports, primarily of new agricultural products. Tariffs

Table 1.2: ECONOMIC INDICATORS, 1980-89

	1980-84	1985-87	1988	Estimate 1989
Production & Expenditure				
(growth rates, % p.a.)				
GDP	2.2	0.5	0.5	12.5
Agriculture	4.3	5.3	-2.3	13.8
Industry	-1.4	-1.2	-7.8	20.3
Services	2.6	-0.9	4.0	9.5
Expenditure	-1.2	-2.4	1.3	15.8
Consumption	2.9	0.2	2.3	12.7
Government	4.5	-2.3	-15.8	5.3
Private	2.3	0.9	7.4	14.3
Fixed investment	-9.8	-13.6	-8.2	29.8
Indicators				
Sugar production ('000 tons)	326	415	363	475
Copra production ('000 tons)	23	19	11	14
Paddy (tons)	19	24	32	37
Cocoa (tons)	177	377	238	370
Fish (tons)		26	27	28
Round logs ('000 cu. ft.)		258	397	421
Tourist visitors ('000s)	160	225	208	260
Central Government Budget (% of GDP)				
Revenue	25.3	23.1	24.5	22.9
- Tax	20.4	18.8	19.3	19.1
- Nontax	4.9	4.3	5.2	3.9
Expenditure & Net Lending	29.7	28.8	26.7	26.8
- Current	23.2	23.8	22.4	20.4
- Development	6.5	4.4	6.4	5.0
Overall Balance	-4.4	-5.7	-2.2	-3.9
Financed by:				
External grants	0.6	0.7	1.4	1.1
External borrowing (net)	1.2	-0.6	-1.4	0.2
Domestic credit	2.6	5.6	2.2	2.6
Money and Prices				
(growth rates, % p.a.)				
Domestic credit	13.7	11.1	-7.4	39.9
Private credit	14.5	6.0	4.6	32.4
Broad money	9.3	10.0	20.6	16.4
Money	7.8	8.8	61.4	...
Consumer prices	7.5	3.7	11.7	7.0
GDP deflator	4.0	4.0	7.3	6.6
Balance of Payments ($ million)				
Exports (fob)	196	244	310	354
Imports (fob)	400	310	358	482
Trade balance	-204	-66	-48	-128
Services (net)	98	67	55	99
Private transfers	-5	-12	-4	-7
Current Account	-111	-11	-3	-34
External grants	23	12	34	29
Public loan disbursement (net)	42	-17	7	-36
Other capital (net)	27 /a	43 /a	52	47
Use of NFA (increase)	-19	26	94	4
Ratios				
- Current account/GDP (%)	-9.3	0.0	3.4	-0.5
- Debt service/exports (%)	6.9	17.2	15.3	13.1
- DOD/GDP (%)	31.2	33.1	35.7	25.4
- Official reserves (months of imports)	3.9	5.8	7.9	5.9

/a Including errors and omissions.

increased, quotas were established, and other restrictive trade measures imposed. Detailed incentive arrangements and direct price supports were established to encourage and protect selected industries and, in effect, discourage others considered to have lesser priority. Lending was channelled into designated priority areas. Price controls developed to limit the gains available from protection and preferential treatment, and were complemented by price stabilization schemes for commodity exports. Production costs were nevertheless high in the small, secure internal markets, imposing increasing burdens on the main export sectors, including the tourist industry. The tight organization of most forms of production encouraged trade union development and more inflexibility in the small formal labor force. Entrepreneurship, and informal market enterprise, were quite effectively discouraged. In addition, therefore, to its external trading problems and the weather-related damage to the economy, there were forces repressing at least some of the private sector energy that had earlier benefitted Fiji.

C. Development Prospects and Policies

1.27   Fiji has the structure and capacity for much better economic performance than was registered in the 1980s. The most critical requirement to achieve this potential is the full recovery of private investment. The full restoration of normal political conditions will be an important factor not only in overcoming the wait-and-see attitude of some local and foreign investors, but also in stemming the outflow of Fijians with technical and managerial skills.

1.28   A sustained recovery in investment and growth will require, as is well recognized, major shifts in economic strategy. The vulnerability of the economy to external factors and the lack of diversification argue strongly for structural change to create a more resilient economy. But the approach of the past, with emphasis on regulation of private sector activities including the determination of wages and prices and reliance on import substitution policies, did not achieve this objective. The effects of external setbacks on the two dominant sectors--sugar and tourism--were reinforced by an unfavorable policy environment. Inward-looking and interventionist policies failed to spur manufacturing growth. Rather than playing a leading role, the contribution of the manufacturing sector to GDP declined from 16 percent in 1966 to less than 10 percent in 1988.

1.29   In order to achieve accelerated and broad-based growth, Fiji will need to exploit all the opportunities that are available to the economy. Although the relative share of sugar in the economy may decline over time, it continues to provide major opportunities for the expansion of output and employment. There is considerable untapped potential in agriculture other than sugar and in the forestry, fisheries and mining subsectors. Tourism can provide, given appropriate macroeconomic and sector policies, further diversified opportunities for employment and income growth. And despite the disappointing performance of the past, manufacturing development has been rapid in 1988-89 and this sector probably has the greatest long-term potential for employment creation. The policies that will consolidate economic conditions to utilize these opportunities, primarily through private sector development, are discussed below.

1.30   Macroeconomic policies. The basic need is for the maintenance of a macroeconomic policy framework conducive to further development. Policies pursued by the Government should therefore ensure that the competitive gains achieved through the 1987 devaluations are preserved through cautious fiscal and monetary policies, and if necessary, through further exchange rate adjustment. To support competitiveness and promote employment-intensive investment, wage moderation should be maintained in the regulated wage sector; increasing wage flexibility would be promoted by not reestablishing minimum wage regulations for ongoing and new manufacturing investments. Efficiency can be promoted throughout the economy by continuing to reduce distortions stemming from import restrictions, high tariffs, and remaining price controls and agricultural subsidies--in general, by stimulating economic activity through the removal of disincentives and the development of market rather than special incentives. In addition, it will be necessary to identify and implement priority public expenditures, with the emphasis on operations and maintenance, infrastructure bottlenecks, and human resource development.

1.31   The deregulation of activity within the economy should receive high priority, to provide more freedom for entrepreneurs to engage in informal as well as more structured enterprise, to compete more effectively and to produce goods and services more efficiently. The private contracting of services now provided by Government departments should be encourages wherever possible. Tax reform is also required to reduce the disincentive effects of some taxation, the distortions that exist, and the low revenue elasticity of the system. These are most evident in indirect taxation, which has narrow coverage, low buoyancy and multiple specific rates. Further consideration should be given to a general sales tax, levied at the manufacturing stage, to broaden the tax base and replace most domestic excises.

1.32   Sector development. Within this framework, more rapid development can be achieved in agriculture, manufacturing and tourism. The policy needs in each of these sectors are discussed in detail in the Fiji Country Economic Report. They are summarized below:

1.33   (a) Agriculture. This is still the key sector. Agricultural development remains essential for Fiji, with almost half of its workers engaged in agriculture, forestry and fishing, nearly 30 percent of them still classified as subsistence producers. Fijian participation in cash agriculture has been stimulated, outside the sugar areas, by the extension of rural roads and interisland shipping services and through forestry and fisheries development. This thrust needs to be maintained. Nevertheless, the critical decision to be made in this sector concerns the sugar industry, in which no major expansion has been contemplated for a number of years. There is a strong producer interest in expansion and this offers the best prospects for increased employment and incomes in agriculture. Increased sugar production could permit growth rates in agriculture averaging over 4 percent per annum in the expansion phase to 1994 and close to 3 percent per annum thereafter. This sectoral performance would also depend on other policies for agricultural development.

1.34   Such major changes have already been initiated. Reliance on input, service and price subsidies has been reduced and improvements in the credit system are being made. These changes can be seen as part of a broader agriculture strategy which will place more reliance on market forces and incentives and less on Government intervention and direct involvement in the promotion of new agricultural initiatives. Accordingly, and given the advantages derived by producers from the recent devaluations, it would be timely to review the protective arrangements still existing for a number of agricultural products, to move where possible to the abolition of quotas and prohibitions, and to reduce high tariff levels.

1.35   (b) Manufacturing. The promotion of export manufacturing has elicited strong domestic and external interest, especially after rapid growth in garment exports following the devaluations and the downturn in domestic markets. Preferential (and recently improved) access to Australian, New Zealand, EEC and US markets and the fiscal and other incentives offered by Fiji, including currently low labor costs, could result in substantially increased manufacturing employment and net export earnings. Constraints on this expansion could, however, quickly emerge unless a major effort is made to increase the supply of needed skills. Nevertheless, growth in manufacturing as a whole at rates averaging at least 7 percent per annum until 1994, and 6 percent per annum thereafter, now seems feasible.

1.36   To achieve this and promote wider structural adjustment in manufacturing, the proposed program of quota and tariff reform should be initiated without delay. Tariff reform should be seen as part of a more general tax reform, in association with proposals for the introduction of a manufacturing sales tax. Some of the benefits of the tax-free zones should be extended, in a graduated fashion, across the rest of the manufacturing sector, to encourage more firms to increase their contribution to exports. Training and skills requirements should be addressed in a coordinated manner for the manufacturing sector as a whole. Facilities are needed to improve entry-level skills as well as develop those of experienced workers, supervisors, and managers. Better provision of industrial advisory and research services, marketing assistance, and labor-relations services will be required.

1.37   (c) Tourism. Recent and proposed changes in economic policies, including agricultural and industrial reform and renewed emphasis on infrastructure maintenance and rehabilitation, have the potential to improve tourism standards and lower costs. The devaluations of 1987 helped to restore cost-competitiveness. While no major new incentive appear to be needed for the industry itself, some existing incentives could be extended for the renovation of existing accommodation and replacement of equipment, including vehicles. Fostering broader Fijian participation in tourism should continue to have high priority and be encouraged through geographic dispersion and the promotion of second-level tourism. The Fiji Development Bank, in cooperation with tourist organizations, the Ministry of Fijian Affairs and the National Land Trust Board, should have a leading role. The hotel turnover tax should be used more directly for the costs of tourism development, both domestically and to support the development of external markets and services. In these circumstances, growth of up to 15 percent in 1990 and at least 10 percent per annum thereafter could be secured.

1.38   The Financial Sector. Interest rate deregulation, in June 1987, introduced new flexibility into the Fijian financial sector. Currently the most serious constraint is the lack of investor confidence; a potentially more important limitation is that of human resources. Action in some areas could substantially encourage the flow of funds to private investment. These include the revision of acts and regulations no longer serving their original purposes, including among others provisions under the insurance, trustee, moneylenders, and credit union legislation and such controls as the agricultural lending ratio and limits on borrowing by foreign companies. Measures can also be taken to develop Fiji's small capital market and assist the process of privatization. Both would be facilitated by better provision for private share participation in major public enterprises.

1.39   Public Sector Management. Within the Government structure a major reordering of priorities is called for. Again, this has been recognized by the Government, and the basis for it has been established through the adjustments made in 1987-89. The starting point was the recognition that Fiji could benefit from less regulation, administrative intervention and direct government investment in productive activities than in the 1980s. The role of government can be more narrowly defined. This redefinition of the role of the public sector can be more readily accommodated in circumstances in which quite large numbers of civil servants have recently retired (the retirement age has been reduced to 55) and in some cases have left the country. Staff requirements can be further considered before vacancies are filled, to keep personnel numbers down to efficient levels. In an environment of deregulation, the need for specific service provisions can be questioned. The stated aim of the Government is to maintain its total expenditures, in relation to GDP, at no more than current, relatively moderate levels, while still providing the necessary infrastructure to support private sector investment and activity. This includes, of course, the educational and health provisions to build on the established capacity of Fijians to contribute to and benefit from development. As part of the reorientation, however, increased provisions for operations and maintenance seem essential. The net revenue requirements for this strategy to work seem likely to be modest. They could be met from improved revenue growth achieved through the tax and tariff policies indicated above to support early and necessary increases in expenditure in 1990 and modest growth thereafter, as the reforms within the public sector take effect.

1.40   The public sector investment program requires reorientation, in the changed circumstances facing Fiji, to give priority to high-yielding projects such as the rehabilitation of existing infrastructure and complementary investments in existing facilities. Other labor-intensive projects could also provide needed employment opportunities on a substantial scale. External assistance appears likely to be available for nearly all projects in these categories so that the direct budgetary costs of a modified investment program can be kept to low levels. Nevertheless, an overall review of the public sector investment program should be undertaken before major existing and new project proposals are confirmed. The program for 1990-92 has been subjected to such a review and it is evident that a recovery in public investment in economic and social infrastructure is now in progress. Compared with the depressed levels of 1988, an increase of over 60 percent in public sector capital outlays is programmed in current prices, including 150 percent in education and social services and an associated 43 percent in operating costs; investment in infrastructure is planned to rise by two-thirds and, in services directly related to production, by over 40 percent. Indicative figures suggest a nominal increase of public sector investment outlays of 15 percent in 1991 and 1992. Assuming that aid inflows rise moderately, this could be accommodated without undue pressures on domestic financial markets, and within intended overall public expenditure restraints.

1.41   These objectives would be facilitated by the effort now underway to reduce the budgetary costs and improve the efficiency of the public enterprises still dominating large areas of economic activity. To improve public enterprise performance, profit objectives should be established for all enterprises. As a corollary, they should be subject to income tax, further reducing their net costs to the Treasury. The Ministry of Finance, rather than individual sector ministries, should have the supervisory power over financial performance. The Public Enterprise Unit should be strengthened, and given technical assistance, to exercise supervision and control. Standard audit procedures for all enterprises should be established. External borrowing intentions should be carefully scrutinized and cleared. The reform of the public enterprise sector should include a program of privatization, both to reduce budget deficits and to provide increased scope for private sector initiatives. A study should be commissioned to determine the range of enterprises which would benefit. Quick action is recommended, however, in cases in which privatization or liquidation is the obvious solution.

1.42   <u>Investment in a Growth Environment</u>. As noted, total fixed investment in Fiji fell from an average of 25 percent of GDP in 1981-82 to under 18 percent in 1985-86 and 13 percent in 1987, and this contributed to the poor growth performance of the Fiji economy in the 1980s. Private investment fluctuated around 11 percent of GDP from 1981 to 1986, slipping to 8 percent of GDP in 1988; public investment fell to 5 percent of GDP. In seeking to reverse these trends the primary emphasis must be on new private investment, domestic and foreign, and concentrated in the growth sectors of the economy, manufacturing, tourism, and agriculture. Higher rates of GDP growth, following such investment, would allow for a strong recovery in private consumption levels. In addition, there would be more scope for real increases in recurrent public expenditures, as will be essential if, even after substantial reorganization within the Government, they are to provide adequately for maintenance and rehabilitation, the operating costs of completed development projects, and the efficient operation of social services.

1.43   <u>Human Resource Development</u>. As noted, Fiji has given high priority to human resource development and achieved remarkable coverage and performance in the health and education sectors. Current budgetary constraints, however, mean that the Government is not likely to be able to devote the same volume of resources to education and health as in the past. These sectors thus face a dual challenge: how to meet new demands with fewer resources. The immediate need, therefore, is to examine the efficiency and financing of the health and education systems, in order to increase their cost-effectiveness and mobilize nonbudgetary resources to address priority objectives. This process is now underway.

1.44   <u>Employment and the Supply of Skills</u>. Although employment in Fiji increased by nearly 3 percent per annum in 1976-86, only 20 percent of the increase was in wage employment. Unemployment increased sharply in 1987.

While the position has greatly improved with the economic recovery and paid employment is now higher than at any time in the past, employment for the continuing surpluses of school leavers still depends primarily on further growth in manufacturing, agriculture, and tourism. The greatest gains for Fijians in agriculture are likely to come from reforms that increase their participation in the sugar subsector, as well as the high rates of growth possible in forestry and fisheries. In the urban areas, manufacturing for export is the key to increases in employment and incomes. The activities most likely to flourish are those which make use of Fiji's abundant supply of relatively cheap labor. Consequently, the income gains are likely to be broadly based. In addition, new private investment activity would generate substantial further employment, concentrated in urban and major tourism zones. Increased public spending on rehabilitation and maintenance would help to alleviate the unemployment problem, as would labor-intensive development projects including the Government's low-income housing scheme. Significant reductions in open unemployment could therefore be achieved.

1.45   Overcoming critical shortages of technical, professional and managerial staff, following the loss of middle and higher level skills through emigration, will nevertheless be an exceptional challenge. Expanded training programs, both within and outside government agencies and private firms, will be an essential component of a successful structural adjustment program. Substantial technical assistance will be required. Within the training provisions, some special efforts to provide business and technical skills for Fijians could be made. In addition, there is a continuing need for measures to promote and support the entry of Fijians into new areas of business enterprise.

Medium-Term Projections and Financing Requirements

1.46   Given the economic policies now being pursued, and under reasonable external economic circumstances and climatic conditions, Fiji has the potential for sustained real GDP growth averaging close to 6 percent per annum in 1990-94 and probably 5 percent per annum in the succeeding 5 years. Its performance, taking into account the exceptionally high growth in 1989, was not unsatisfactory in 1985-89 as a whole. Projections for the later periods are summarized in Table 1.3.

1.47   In the 1990-94 period, the agricultural growth rates indicated could be sustained only if sugar production and exports expand. This depends, essentially, on a decision still to be made as to the desirability and feasibility of pursuing this course. Similarly, the high growth rate in industry relies on the persistence with policies which will keep Fiji competitive in markets for export manufacturing and attract further investors in that activity. And, while all basic ingredients for diversified tourism growth exist, this also will depend on the maintenance of conditions which, as at present, encourage investment in this key sector.

1.48   The projections assume growth primarily in private investment in all the above activities and a supportive public investment program. Most of this investment can be financed from the higher domestic savings generated within Fiji, as in earlier periods of sustained development. Nevertheless, substantial increases in private consumption levels could eventuate if, as is the Government's intention, recurrent public expenditure growth is restrained.

Table 1.3: MEDIUM-TERM MACROECONOMIC PROJECTIONS, 1990-99

	1985-89	1990-94	1995-99
Growth rates (% p.a.)			
GDP	3.3	5.8	5.1
Agriculture	5.4	3.6	2.9
Industry	2.0	7.1	6.3
Services	2.8	6.2	5.4
Consumption	3.7	4.8	4.0
Fixed investment	-2.9	9.4	7.3
Exports of goods & services	10.1	6.6	5.5
Imports of goods & services	10.2	5.8	5.5
Consumer prices	6.5	5.0	4.5
Ratios to GDP (%) /a			
Gross investment	15.9	17.3	19.1
Domestic savings	15.3	16.5	19.0
Other indicators			
Current account/GDP (%) /a	-0.5	-1.7	-0.5
Debt service/exports (%)	15.7	8.9	6.4
DOD/GDP (%)	31.8	23.6	21.4
Net foreign assets (as months of retained imports)	5.9	5.7	5.8

/a For the last year of the period.

Source: World Bank staff estimates.

1.49   Based on the above growth scenario, projected external capital
requirements and sources of financing are shown in Table 1.4. The estimates
suggest an increase in Fiji's external financing requirements from an average
of about $70 million in 1985-89 to about $140 million in 1990-94, in current
dollars. Although additional grant assistance is being sought by the
Government, initially for 1991 and 1992, and net official capital transfers
are likely to increase, the bulk of the extra funds could and should come from
increased private investment in Fiji.

Table 1.4:   EXTERNAL FINANCING REQUIREMENTS AND SOURCES, 1990-99
(\$ million per annum at current prices)

	1985-89	1990-94	1995-99
Requirements	<u>69</u>	<u>143</u>	<u>157</u>
Merchandise imports	360	752	1,265
Merchandise exports	-264	-449	-723
Principal repayments /a	37	59	74
Interest payments /a	25	33	32
Other service payments	-110	-298	-542
Change in NFA	21	46	51
Sources	<u>69</u>	<u>143</u>	<u>157</u>
Private transfers	-9	-5	-5
External grants	24	33	25
Public loan disbursements	24	65	74
Other capital (net)	30	50	63

/a   Public MLT debt only.

Source: World Bank staff estimates.

FIJI: STATISTICAL APPENDIX

Table 1.1: POPULATION BY ETHNIC ORIGIN, SEX AND AGE AT 1986 CENSUS

	Fijian			Indian			Others			Total			Percent of total
	Male	Female	Total	Male	Female	Total	Male	Female	Total	Male	Female	Total	
0 - 5	25,547	23,902	49,449	23,918	23,014	46,932	2,615	2,326	4,941	52,080	49,242	101,322	14.2
5 - 9	22,125	20,849	42,974	23,363	22,228	45,589	2,362	2,227	4,589	47,850	45,302	93,152	13.0
10 - 14	18,796	17,836	36,632	19,549	18,887	38,436	2,013	1,944	3,957	40,358	38,667	79,025	11.0
15 - 19	17,110	16,693	33,803	17,967	18,038	36,005	1,993	1,815	3,808	37,070	36,546	73,616	10.3
20 - 24	16,438	16,530	32,968	18,390	18,673	37,063	1,903	1,794	3,697	36,731	36,997	73,728	10.3
25 - 29	13,637	13,220	26,857	16,714	16,896	33,410	1,601	1,540	3,141	31,952	31,456	63,408	8.9
30 - 34	10,661	10,783	21,444	13,338	13,319	26,657	1,338	1,269	2,807	25,337	25,371	50,708	7.1
35 - 39	9,152	8,998	18,148	10,698	10,577	21,275	1,185	1,109	2,294	21,035	20,682	41,717	5.8
40 - 44	7,624	7,517	15,141	8,920	8,810	17,730	1,026	872	1,898	17,570	17,199	34,769	4.9
45 - 49	6,761	6,651	13,412	6,887	6,938	13,825	803	762	1,565	14,451	14,351	28,802	4.0
50 - 54	5,603	5,438	11,041	5,186	5,153	10,339	713	571	1,284	11,502	11,162	22,664	3.2
55 - 59	4,285	4,130	8,415	3,865	3,705	7,570	599	485	1,084	8,749	8,320	17,089	2.4
60 - 64	3,275	3,086	6,361	2,457	2,411	4,868	468	348	814	6,198	5,845	12,043	1.7
65 - 69	2,424	2,519	4,943	1,876	1,771	3,647	309	291	600	4,609	4,581	9,190	1.3
70 - 74	1,758	1,632	3,390	1,109	1,057	2,166	230	222	452	3,097	2,911	6,008	0.8
75 +	1,389	1,682	3,071	1,145	1,143	2,288	210	222	432	2,744	3,047	5,791	0.8
not stated	671	585	1,256	447	457	904	117	88	203	1,235	1,128	2,363	0.3
Total	167256	162049	329305	175829	172875	348704	19483	17883	37366	362568	352807	715375	100.0

Source: Bureau of Statistics.

Table 1.2: POPULATION BY ETHNIC GROUP, 1976-86

	1976	1977	1978	1979	1980	1981	1982	1983	1984	1985	1986
Ethnic Fijians ('000)	259	284	270	278	282	288	294	301	308	318	329
% of total population	44.3	44.3	44.5	44.4	44.5	44.6	44.7	44.8	44.9	45.3	46.0
Ave. annual growth rate (%)	..	1.9	2.3	2.2	2.2	2.1	2.1	2.4	2.3	2.6	4.1
Ethnic Indians ('000)	292	297	303	310	317	324	329	336	342	347	349
% of total population	49.9	49.8	49.9	49.9	50.0	50.2	50.0	50.0	49.9	49.8	48.8
Ave. annual growth rate (%)	..	1.7	2.0	2.3	2.3	2.2	1.5	2.1	1.8	1.5	0.6
Other ethnics ('000)	34	35	34	35	35	34	35	35	36	34	37
% of total population	5.8	5.9	5.6	5.6	5.5	5.3	5.3	5.2	5.2	4.9	5.2
Ave. annual growth rate (%)	..	2.9	-2.9	2.9	0.0	-2.9	2.9	0.0	2.9	-5.6	8.8
Total population ('000)	588	598	607	621	634	646	658	672	686	697	715
Growth (%)											

Source: Bureau of Statistics.

Table 1.3: POPULATION AND LABOR FORCE BY SEX, 1976-1986

Sex/ Age	September 1976			August 1986			Labor Force Change, 1978-86	
	Popula- tion No.	Economical- ly Active No.	LFPR %	Popula- tion No.	Economical- ly Active No.	LFPR %	No.	%
Males								
0 - 14	174,038			140,252				
15 & over		146,315	84.1	222,316	189,929	85.4		
Total		146,315		362,568	189,929	52.4	43,614	29.8
Females								
0 - 14	172,055			133,211				
15 & over		29,470	17.1	219,598	51,231	23.3		
Total		29,470		352,807	51,231	14.5	21,761	73.8
Both Sexes								
0 - 14	241,977			273,463				
15 & over	346,091	175,785	50.8	441,912	241,160	54.6		
Total	588,068	175,785	29.9	715,375	241,160	33.7	65,375	37.2

Source: 1976 and 1986 Population Censuses.

Table 1.4: ECONOMICALLY ACTIVE POPULATION BY EMPLOYMENT STATUS, 1976-1986

	1978 Total		1986 Fijians		Indians		Others		Total	
	No.	%	No.	%	No.	%	No.	%	No.	%
Own account worker	30,467	17.3	33,811	29.7	45,225	39.9	1,964	14.2	81,000	33.6
Public employed	30,939	17.6	18,285	16.1	16,981	14.9	2,856	20.7	38,102	15.8
Private employed	59,574	33.9	20,481	18.0	37,389	33.0	5,683	41.2	63,553	28.4
Unpaid family worker	13,878	7.8	32,257	28.3	4,664	4.1	2,310	16.7	39,231	16.3
Unemployed	41,129	23.4	8,660	7.6	8,618	7.6	911	6.6	18,189	7.5
Not stated	a/	a/	410	0.4	607	0.5	68	0.5	1,085	0.4
Total	175,785	100.0	113,904	100.0	113,464	100.0	13,792	100.0	241,180	100.0

Percent of each group by race

	Fijians	Indians	Others	Total
Own account worker	41.7	55.8	2.4	100.0
Public employed	48.0	44.5	7.5	100.0
Private employed	32.2	58.8	8.9	100.0
Unpaid family worker	82.2	11.9	5.9	100.0
Unemployed	47.8	47.4	5.0	100.0
Not stated	37.8	55.9	6.3	100.0
Total	47.2	47.0	5.7	100.0

Source: Census Office.

a/ Included in unemployed.

Table 1.5: PAID EMPLOYMENT BY INDUSTRY, 1976-89
(as at end-June)
(Number)

	1976	1977	1978	1979	1980	1981	1982	1983	1984	1985	1986	1987	1988	1989 Est.
Agriculture	2,599	2,441	2,787	2,303	2,627	2,509	2,274	2,517	2,238	2,577	2,165	1,900	2,000	2,100
Industry	22,431	23,102	25,022	26,811	27,788	26,185	23,978	24,883	23,522	24,268	24,213	23,200	23,200	28,900
Mining	1,550	1,841	809	724	1,055	1,068	1,145	1,226	1,239	1,214	1,206	1,300	1,400	1,500
Manufacturing	11,444	11,253	13,484	13,948	15,413	14,223	13,522	14,702	14,184	14,057	13,973	13,800	14,000	19,700
Electricity, Gas	1,765	1,879	1,834	2,336	2,285	2,750	2,168	2,231	2,065	2,141	2,070	2,100	2,500	2,500
Construction	7,672	8,129	8,895	9,803	9,035	7,146	7,143	6,724	6,034	6,856	6,964	6,000	6,300	5,200
Services	45,144	46,840	48,775	49,425	50,069	53,712	52,037	52,675	52,842	54,237	53,476	52,500	52,500	57,200
Trade	11,701	12,117	12,778	13,099	13,378	14,140	13,878	14,888	14,904	14,805	14,100	11,300	11,600	13,700
Transport	6,774	7,196	7,303	8,111	8,122	7,865	6,982	7,898	7,580	7,811	7,747	7,700	8,000	9,900
Finance & Real Estate	3,697	4,169	4,186	4,382	4,436	4,926	5,030	5,057	4,671	4,891	4,864	5,000	5,100	5,400
Community, Social & Personal Services	22,972	23,358	24,508	23,833	24,133	26,781	26,147	25,032	25,687	26,730	26,765	28,500	27,800	28,200
Total	70,174	72,383	76,584	78,539	80,484	81,406	78,289	80,075	78,602	81,082	79,854	77,600	77,700	88,200

Source: Data provided by Fiji authorities.

Table 2.1: GROSS DOMESTIC PRODUCT BY INDUSTRIAL ORIGIN AT
CONSTANT 1977 FACTOR COST, 1981-89
(F$ million)

	1981	1982	1983	1984	1985	1986	1987	1988	1989 Est.
Agriculture, Forestry & Fishing	172.6	175.6	143.8	181.0	156.2	186.0	173.1	169.2	192.5
Sugarcane	81.2	83.2	47.8	82.7	58.6	85.9	68.6	62.1	81.5
Other Crops	22.6	24.5	23.9	26.1	25.5	27.4	25.4	25.0	26.8
Livestock	6.5	6.6	7.2	7.2	7.1	7.4	7.5	7.5	8.2
Fishing	10.2	10.0	12.1	11.1	9.8	9.4	11.8	12.5	12.9
Forestry	6.4	4.8	5.4	5.5	6.0	5.7	9.3	11.6	12.3
Subsistence	45.6	46.5	47.4	48.4	49.1	50.1	50.5	50.5	50.8
Mining & Quarrying	0.4	0.6	0.6	0.7	0.8	1.3	1.3	1.9	1.8
Manufacturing	88.9	86.5	77.7	91.0	79.3	94.6	83.9	79.4	94.2
Sugar	31.2	32.2	18.3	31.8	22.6	33.3	26.6	24.1	31.5
Other	55.4	51.9	57.0	56.7	54.1	58.8	55.3	49.2	62.7
Self Employment	2.3	2.4	2.4	2.5	2.5	2.6	2.6	a/	a/
Electricity, Gas & Water	6.8	7.0	7.4	8.0	8.4	9.0	8.8	9.5	9.8
Construction	60.5	53.4	50.9	39.8	41.4	40.0	32.9	26.2	35.0
Wholesale & Retail Trade, Restaurants & Hotels	125.5	113.0	122.3	122.0	124.8	136.0	116.9	127.4	163.0
Trade	102.4	87.7	100.8	97.6	99.6	109.2	97.6	..	..
Hotels, Restaurants, Cafes	23.1	25.3	21.5	24.4	25.1	26.2	19.5	..	..
Transport & Communications	70.6	77.6	78.0	87.7	90.3	89.8	87.8	95.4	105.0
Transport	58.7	65.3	65.4	74.9	77.0	75.7	73.6	..	..
Communications	11.9	12.3	12.5	12.8	13.3	14.1	14.8	..	..
Finance, Insurance, Real Estate & Business Services	87.9	90.8	93.7	95.8	97.6	98.4	95.0	95.9	97.5
Community, Social & Personal Services	126.7	128.0	131.1	137.7	131.6	130.5	136.3	134.7	130.8
Less: Imputed Bank Service Charges	20.0	20.3	21.5	22.3	23.3	23.7	22.0	22.6	23.3
GDP at Factor Cost	719.9	712.2	683.9	741.3	707.1	761.9	714.0	717.0	806.3

Source: Bureau of Statistics and staff estimates.

a/ Included in "Other".

Table 2.2: GROSS DOMESTIC PRODUCT BY TYPE OF
EXPENDITURE AT CURRENT PRICES, 1980-89
(F$ million)

	1980	1981	1982	1983	1984	1985	1986	1987	1988	1989 Est.
Consumption	731.4	833.0	888.4	979.8	1039.0	1090.0	1146.0	1183.0	1299.0	1560.0
Private	574.7	660.0	684.7	748.2	794.1	838.0	873.0	923.0	1064.0	1296.0
Government	156.7	173.1	203.8	231.6	244.9	252.0	273.0	260.0	235.0	264.0
Gross Investment	313.2	362.2	284.5	241.5	241.2	251.1	266.0	198.0	202.0	293.0
Fixed Investment	249.8	280.5	262.6	239.2	218.0	239.1	215.0	193.0	190.0	263.0
Private	134.4	130.5	113.2	112.2	130.9	160.0	145.0	135.0	114.0	149.0
Government	45.4	72.8	61.0	36.3	37.9	41.0	43.0	28.0	40.0	61.0
Public Enterprises	70.1	77.2	88.5	90.7	49.2	38.1	27.0	30.0	36.0	53.0
Change in Stocks	63.4	81.7	21.9	2.4	23.3	12.0	51.0	5.0	12.0	30.0
Foreign Balance	-33.4	-152.1	-71.2	-62.0	-13.6	-5.0	32.0	40.0	37.0	-11.0
Exports (GNFS)	477.5	454.4	481.3	498.1	546.2	584.0	609.0	658.0	849.0	1063.0
Imports (GNFS)	510.8	606.6	552.6	560.1	559.8	589.0	577.0	618.0	812.0	1074.0
Statistical Discrepancy	-27.5	13.0	11.7	-17.1	8.7	-20.0	27.0	-	-	-
GDP at Market Prices	983.8	1056.1	1113.4	1142.2	1275.3	1316.1	1471.0	1421.0	1538.0	1842.0
Net Indirect Taxes	82.7	102.4	92.9	110.4	123.6	139.0	136.0	136.0	153.0	182.0
GDP at Factor Cost	901.0	953.7	1020.5	1031.8	1151.7	1177.1	1335.0	1285.0	1385.0	1660.0

Source: Bureau of Statistics and staff estimates.

Table 2.3: INVESTMENT AND SAVINGS, 1980-89

	1980	1981	1982	1983	1984	1985	1986	1987	1988	1989 Est.
				(In Millions of Fiji Dollars)						
Gross Domestic Investment	313	362	285	242	241	251	266	198	202	293
Fixed Investment	250	281	263	239	218	239	215	193	190	263
Private	134	130	113	112	131	160	145	135	114	149
Government	45	73	61	36	38	41	43	28	40	61
Public Enterprises	70	77	88	91	49	38	27	30	36	53
Change in Stocks	63	82	22	2	23	12	51	5	12	30
Gross National Savings	293	173	198	177	214	237	274	191	254	283
Gross Domestic Savings	280	175	222	188	238	254	305	249	257	309
Net Factor Income	-14	-16	-40	-36	-40	-44	-42	-46	-46	-58
Net Current Transfers	27	15	16	25	16	26	11	-11	43	33
Official	29	22	19	27	20	38	17	13	48	43
Private	-2	-8	-3	-2	-4	-12	-6	-24	-5	-10
Current Account Deficit 1/	20	189	87	64	28	14	-8	7	-52	10
Memorandum Item										
Resource Gap	33	188	63	54	3	-3	-39	-51	-55	-16
				(In Percent of GDP)						
Gross Domestic Investment	31.8	34.3	25.6	21.1	18.9	19.1	18.1	13.9	13.1	15.9
Fixed Investment	25.4	26.6	23.6	20.9	17.1	18.2	14.6	13.6	12.4	14.3
Private	13.7	12.4	10.2	9.8	10.3	12.2	9.9	9.5	7.4	8.1
Government	4.6	6.9	5.5	3.2	3.0	3.1	2.9	2.0	2.6	3.3
Public Enterprises	7.1	7.3	7.9	7.9	3.9	2.9	1.8	2.1	2.3	2.9
Change in Stocks	6.4	7.7	2.0	0.2	1.8	0.9	3.5	0.4	0.8	1.6
Gross National Savings	29.8	16.4	17.8	15.5	16.7	18.0	18.6	13.5	16.5	15.4
Gross Domestic Savings	28.5	16.5	19.9	16.4	18.7	19.3	20.8	17.5	16.7	16.8
Net Factor Income	-1.4	-1.5	-3.6	-3.1	-3.2	-3.3	-2.9	-3.3	-3.0	-3.2
Net Current Transfers	2.7	1.4	1.5	2.2	1.2	2.0	0.7	-0.8	2.8	1.8

Source: Data provided by Fiji authorities and staff estimates.

1/ Including official transfers.

Table 2.4: PRIMARY PRODUCTION, 1985-89

	Weight	1985	1986	1987	1988	1989 Est.
			(Index 1977=100)			
Crops	90.2	111.3	146.1	106.1	113.7	141.5
Sugarcane	77.7	113.8	153.7	110.7	119.1	148.8
Copra	7.7	68.3	72.8	42.1	34.6	43.7
Paddy	3.1	153.6	136.9	130.8	179.2	203.2
Ginger	0.9	143.1	207.1	180.7	146.8	177.0
Tobacco	0.7	70.1	54.5	38.7	26.8	45.2
Cocoa	0.1	232.0	294.8	482.5	245.4	381.4
Livestock	4.1	165.4	175.5	164.8	180.7	175.7
Beef	2.1	146.1	154.7	163.3	159.0	169.7
Other	2.0	185.7	197.3	166.4	203.6	181.9
Fish	5.7	211.4	202.4	241.7	248.0	260.4
Total	100.0	119.3	150.5	116.2	124.1	149.7
		(Volume in thousands of metric tons)				
Sugarcane		3042.0	4109.0	2960.0	3185.0	3980.0
Copra		21.1	22.5	13.0	10.7	13.5
Paddy		27.6	24.6	23.5	32.2	36.5
Ginger		3.8	5.5	4.8	3.9	4.7
Beef		3.4	3.6	3.8	3.7	4.0
Cocoa		225.0	286.0	468.0	238.0	370.0
Fish		25.1	24.9	26.9	27.4	28.2
Subsistence		15.0	15.2	15.4	15.6	15.8
Commercial		5.8	6.1	6.7	6.9	7.2
Industrial		3.9	3.2	4.2	4.3	4.5
Miscellaneous		0.4	0.4	0.6	0.6	0.7
Round Logs ('000 cu. ft.)		206.0	195.0	320.0	396.7	421.0
Indigenous Forests		194.0	185.0	222.3	187.0	200.0
Pine Forests		12.0	10.0	97.7	209.7	221.0

Source: Data provided by Fiji authorities.

Table 2.5: INDUSTRIAL PRODUCTION, 1985-89

	Weight	1985	1986	1987	Revised Weight	1988	1989 Est.
		(Index 1977=100)				(Index 1986=100)	
Gold Mining	2.8	121.5	186.1	172.4	5.0	149.6	146.2
Manufacturing Of which:	85.6	113.6	137.0	121.0	69.7	87.1	116.4
Sugar	31.4	94.2	138.6	110.8	14.8	72.3	94.7
Canned Fish	3.4	169.9	296.4	430.7	1.6	167.4	201.2
Coconut Oil	1.6	84.5	87.3	66.3	1.7	46.6	47.6
Flour	1.0	213.9	220.2	230.4	0.9	103.8	112.9
Beer	4.5	112.2	100.7	92.7	2.9	97.8	106.1
Cigarettes	1.4	108.8	101.2	86.9	2.4	85.9	104.4
Sawmilling	5.3	107.1	103.6	118.2	3.4	175.8	108.9
Veneer	0.7	350.7	356.8	385.7	6.6	108.6	106.6
Soap	1.4	133.1	149.6	160.7	1.1	113.6	118.5
Cement	5.0	119.2	117.9	75.4	5.4	114.9	103.5
Electricity and Water	11.6	138.9	149.6	147.2	25.3	106.7	109.5
Total	100.0	116.9	139.8	125.4	100.0	95.2	116.2

Volume of Output

Gold (kg)		1865.0	2856.0	2647.0		4272.0	4177.0
Coconut Oil ('000 metric tons)		12.9	14.1	8.4		6.6	6.7
Sawn Timber ('000 cu. m.)		90.7	78.0	85.0		96.5	...
Veneer ('000 cu. m.)		9.2	9.4	10.4		10.6	11.1
Plywood ('000 cu. m.)		1.2	1.4	1.3		1.3	1.4
Other Wood Products ('000 cu. m.)							
Cement ('000 metric tons)		93.2	92.2	58.7		44.2	51.3
Electricity (mn. kwh)		372.0	402.0	394.0		379.0	385.0
(of which: hydroelectricity)		304.0	332.0	330.0		...	...

Source: Data provided by Fiji authorities.

Table 2.6: Hotel and Visitor Statistics, 1985-89
(In thousands; unless otherwise indicated)

	1985	1986	1987	1988	Jan. - Aug. 1988	Jan. - Aug. 1989
Hotel Statistics 1/						
Rooms Available (end of period)	3.2	3.6	3.5	3.7	..	..
Beds Available (end of period)	9.0	10.1	9.9	10.4	..	..
Room Occupancy Rate (%)	61.6	60.6	44.8	48.0	..	..
Bed Occupancy Rate	43.7	42.6	30.2	33.4	..	..
Number of Employees	3.8	4.1	3.3	4.3	..	..
Visitor Arrivals 2/						
Australia	89.5	86.3	65.4	75.2	45.2	59.6
New Zealand	19.5	22.7	16.2	21.5	14.2	18.7
United States	49.6	69.7	47.0	42.1	25.4	22.0
Canada	18.9	23.7	16.8	16.9	9.9	10.6
Japan	12.6	11.8	5.5	3.4	1.8	8.6
United Kingdom	7.7	10.0	8.5	8.4	5.0	7.5
Other Europe	12.7	15.8	14.7	20.5	12.4	15.8
Pacific Islands	11.9	12.8	11.2	14.2	9.1	11.9
Other	5.8	5.8	4.5	5.7	3.6	4.4
Total	228.2	257.8	189.8	208.2	126.8	159.1
Memorandum Item:						
Average Length of Stay (days)	8.4	7.9	8.3	8.5	8.6	9.3

Source: Data provided by Fiji authorities.

1/ Excluding hotels with fewer than 25 beds and guest houses.
2/ Excludes cruise ship passengers.

Table 3.1: CENTRAL GOVERNMENT BUDGET, 1981-89

	1981	1982	1983	1984	1985	1986	1987	1988	1989 Est.
	(In Millions of Fiji Dollars)								
Current Receipts	263.4	265.3	298.3	334.8	346.1	345.9	342.2	398.6	441.9
Tax Revenue	214.0	210.5	237.3	273.4	279.3	276.0	266.7	296.7	351.1
Income & Profits	113.2	119.9	128.9	146.9	141.0	136.1	128.8	140.7	153.1
Goods & Services	23.4	27.2	31.0	36.2	40.9	43.8	44.9	52.8	65.0
International Trade	72.9	59.2	73.4	84.9	92.4	91.4	89.0	99.6	129.0
Other	4.5	4.2	4.0	5.5	4.9	4.7	4.0	3.6	4.2
Nontax Revenue	41.1	44.4	51.0	51.3	56.4	60.5	64.1	79.7	71.3
Grants	8.3	10.3	10.0	10.1	10.5	9.5	11.4	22.2	19.6
Current Expenditure	211.6	247.3	286.0	324.0	326.3	330.9	355.4	343.9	375.8
Wages & Salaries	116.1	138.0	166.0	186.0	177.3	186.0	187.5	166.8	197.6
Interest	19.2	25.6	32.0	37.0	40.6	45.1	53.3	65.8	69.5
External	9.5	13.0	12.0	14.0	14.1	13.7	15.9	20.6	20.3
Domestic	9.7	12.5	20.0	23.0	26.5	31.5	37.3	45.2	49.1
Subsidies & Transfers	40.3	45.0	47.0	55.0	50.0	51.0	60.0	54.8	58.5
Goods & Services	35.9	38.7	41.0	46.0	58.4	48.8	54.6	56.5	50.3
Current Balance (Deficit -)	51.8	18.0	12.3	10.8	19.8	15.0	-13.2	54.7	66.1
Capital Expenditure	79.2	79.4	48.0	49.0	52.9	52.6	48.7	63.4	94.8
Net Lending	16.1	12.0	7.0	3.0	3.4	31.6	12.0	3.6	23.3
Total Expenditure & Net Lending	306.8	338.7	341.0	377.0	382.6	415.0	416.1	410.9	493.9
Overall Balance (Deficit -)	-43.4	-73.4	-42.7	-42.2	-36.5	-69.1	-73.9	-12.2	-51.8
Financing									
External (net)	24.7	18.2	5.0	5.0	-0.3	-3.2	-15.0	-21.1	4.1
Borrowing	..	..	11.0	19.0	14.2	17.1	7.9	11.3	33.5
Repayments	..	..	6.0	13.0	14.4	17.2	22.6	25.3	31.4
Domestic (net)	18.7	55.2	38.0	36.0	36.8	72.3	88.9	33.3	47.7
Banking System	-1.4	18.4	13.0	-6.0	2.2	31.5	30.8	-15.6	8.0
Provident Fund	20.0	29.0	28.0	33.0	36.0	36.7	44.4	43.6	..
Other	0.1	7.8	-3.0	9.0	-1.4	4.1	13.7	5.3	..
	(In Percent of GDP)								
Current Receipts	24.9	23.8	26.1	26.3	26.3	23.5	24.1	25.9	24.0
Tax Revenue	20.3	18.9	20.8	21.4	21.2	18.8	18.8	19.3	19.1
Income & Profits	10.7	10.8	11.3	11.5	10.7	9.3	9.1	9.1	8.3
Goods & Services	2.2	2.4	2.7	2.8	3.1	3.0	3.2	3.4	3.5
International Trade	6.9	5.3	6.4	6.7	7.0	6.2	6.3	6.5	7.0
Other	0.4	0.4	0.4	0.4	0.4	0.3	0.3	0.2	0.2
Nontax Revenue	3.9	4.0	4.5	4.0	4.3	4.1	4.5	5.2	3.9
Grants	0.8	0.9	0.9	0.8	0.8	0.6	0.8	1.4	1.1
Current Expenditure	20.0	22.2	25.1	25.4	24.8	22.5	25.0	22.4	20.4
Current Balance (Deficit -)	4.9	1.6	1.1	0.8	1.5	1.0	-0.9	3.6	3.6
Capital Expenditure	7.5	7.1	4.2	3.9	4.0	3.6	3.4	4.1	5.1
Net Lending	1.5	1.1	0.6	0.2	0.3	2.1	0.8	0.2	1.3
Overall Balance (Deficit -)	-4.1	-6.6	-3.7	-3.1	-2.8	-4.7	-5.2	-0.8	-2.8

Source: Data provided by Fiji authorities.

Table 3.2: CENTRAL GOVERNMENT REVENUE AND GRANTS, 1981-89
(F$ million at current prices)

	1981	1982	1983	1984	1985	1986	1987	1988	1989 Est.
Total Revenue	255.1	255.0	288.3	324.7	335.6	336.5	330.8	376.4	422.3
Tax Revenue	214.0	210.5	237.3	273.4	279.3	276.0	266.7	296.7	351.1
Taxes on Income & Profits	113.2	119.9	128.9	146.9	141.0	136.1	128.8	140.7	153.1
Corporate	31.9	30.7	30.0	34.2	33.6	34.6	31.2	44.6	38.0
Individual	77.2	86.2	95.7	109.4	104.6	97.2	91.9	92.3	109.1
Unclassified	4.1	3.0	3.2	3.2	2.8	4.4	5.7	3.7	6.0
Taxes on Property	0.7	0.6	0.8	2.4	0.6	0.8	0.5	0.1	0.2
Estate & Gift Duty	0.7	0.6	0.8	2.4	0.6	0.8	0.5	0.1	0.2
Taxes on Goods & Services	23.4	27.2	31.0	36.2	40.9	43.8	44.9	52.8	65.0
Excise Duties	19.5	23.1	25.3	27.3	31.7	34.2	36.3	38.9	43.5
Turnover Tax	0.0	0.0	1.5	4.6	4.9	6.8	5.9	9.9	17.0
License Fees	0.4	0.4	0.4	0.4	0.4	0.4	0.4	a/	a/
Vehicle Taxes	3.6	3.7	3.8	3.9	3.9	2.3	2.2	4.0	4.5
Taxes on International Trade	72.9	59.2	73.4	84.9	92.4	91.4	89.0	99.6	129.0
Import duties	66.8	56.6	73.4	84.9	92.4	91.4	89.0	98.9	123.0
Export duties	6.1	2.6	0.0	0.0	0.0	0.0	0.0	0.7	6.0
Other Taxes	3.8	3.7	3.2	3.1	4.3	3.9	3.5	3.5	4.0
Stamp Taxes	3.3	3.1	3.2	3.1	3.7	3.4	3.1	3.0	..
Other	0.5	0.6	0.0	0.0	0.6	0.5	0.4	0.5	..
Nontax Revenue	41.1	44.4	51.0	51.3	56.4	60.5	64.1	79.7	71.3
UN Peacekeeping Forces	..	..	12.9	12.3	13.9	13.4	13.9	23.5	16.8
Monetary Authority Profits	..	..	7.8	5.9	6.4	6.3	6.3	8.0	10.2
Public Enterprise Dividends	..	..	0.9	0.0	1.9	1.9	5.6	5.9	2.8
Other	..	..	29.4	33.1	34.1	38.9	38.3	42.3	41.5
Foreign Grants	8.3	10.3	10.0	10.1	10.5	9.5	11.4	22.2	19.6
Total Revenue & Grants	263.4	265.3	298.3	334.8	346.1	345.9	342.2	398.6	441.9

Source: Data provided by Fiji authorities.

a/ Included in "Vehicle Taxes".

Table 3.3:   CENTRAL GOVERNMENT EXPENDITURES, 1981-89
(F$ million at current prices)

	1981	1982	1983	1984	1985	1986	1987	1988	1989 Est.
Current Expenditures	211.6	247.3	286.0	324.0	326.3	330.9	355.4	343.8	375.8
Wages & Salaries	116.1	138.0	166.0	186.0	177.3	186.0	187.5	166.7	197.6
Salaries	100.7	119.8	..	..	150.6	158.3	161.3	144.0	170.7
Wages	15.5	18.3	..	..	26.6	27.7	26.1	22.7	26.9
Employees' Contribution to FNPF	5.4	6.6	7.1	8.0	15.9	14.8	23.3	20.2	23.5
Purchase of Goods & Services	35.9	38.7	41.0	46.0	58.4	48.8	54.6	56.5	50.3
Interest on Public Debt	19.2	25.6	32.0	37.0	40.6	45.1	53.3	65.8	69.4
External	9.5	13.0	12.0	14.0	14.1	13.7	15.9	20.6	20.3
Domestic	9.7	12.5	20.0	23.0	26.5	31.5	37.3	45.2	49.1
Subsidies & Other Current Transfers	34.9	38.4	39.9	47.0	34.1	36.2	36.7	34.6	35.0
Development Expenditures	95.3	91.3	55.0	52.0	56.3	84.2	60.7	67.1	118.0
Acquisition of Fixed Assets	60.2	57.5	..	..	32.3	37.9	32.7	37.8	59.6
Capital Construction	..	..	..	..	29.7	33.1	25.5	..	..
Capital Purchase	..	..	..	..	2.6	4.8	7.2	..	..
Capital Grants & Net Lending	35.1	33.8	..	..	24.0	46.3	28.0	29.3	58.4
Grants	19.0	21.8	..	..	20.7	14.6	17.3	..	..
Net Lending	16.1	12.0	7.0	3.0	3.4	31.6	10.9	..	..
TOTAL	306.8	338.7	342.0	377.0	382.6	415.0	416.1	410.9	493.9

Source: Data provided by Fiji authorities.

Table 4.1: MONETARY SURVEY, 1983-89 1/
(F$ million at current prices)
(End of Period)

	1983	1984	1985	1986	1987	1988	1989 Sept
Net Foreign Assets	108.0	117.8	130.9	189.6	194.6	327.7	304.6
Net Domestic Assets	335.7	372.2	371.6	396.8	413.3	405.2	461.9
Domestic Credit	381.5	412.6	438.3	471.4	541.3	501.0	630.8
Government (net)	32.9	29.3	28.3	47.4	81.5	19.1	52.0
Official Entities	73.3	58.5	59.6	56.4	66.2	70.4	70.7
Private Sector	275.3	324.8	350.4	367.6	393.6	411.5	508.1
Other Items (net)	-45.8	-40.4	-66.7	-74.6	-128.0	-95.7	-169.0
Broad Money	443.7	490.0	502.5	586.5	607.9	733.0	766.5
Narrow Money	141.6	142.3	146.4	178.6	173.2	279.5	256.4
Currency	58.7	61.0	61.8	63.1	64.9	67.7	66.8
Demand Deposits 2/	82.9	81.3	84.6	115.5	108.3	211.8	189.6
Quasi-money	302.1	347.7	356.1	407.8	434.7	453.5	510.1

Source: Data provided by Fiji authorities.

1/ As of the last Wednesday of the month.
2/ Includes local bills payable.

Table 4.2: INTEREST RATE STRUCTURE, 1983-89
(End of Period)
(% per annum)

	1983	1984	1985	1986	1987	1988	1989 Mar.	June	Sept.
Reserve Bank									
Minimum Lending Rate	10.50	11.00	11.00	8.00	11.00	11.00	11.00	8.00	8.00
Deposit Rate									
Commercial Banks 1/	3.50	3.50	3.50	3.50	3.50	3.50	3.50	3.50	3.50
Other Depositors									
1-3 months	6.00	6.00	6.00	6.00	6.00	..	..	..	..
3-6 months	6.50	6.50	6.50	6.50	6.50	..	..	..	..
6 months or more	7.25	7.25	7.25	7.25	7.25	..	..	..	..
Commercial Banks									
Interbank Rate	6.36	9.21	13.16	2.03	3.70	1.00	0.60	1.10	4.80
Loan Rates									
Maximum	13.50	13.50	13.50	13.50	..	..	..	..	..
Average 2/	12.76	12.95	13.06	11.97	13.72	12.30	12.40	12.00	11.90
Deposit Rates 3/									
Savings Deposits	6.00	6.00	6.00	6.00	6.00	4.00	4.00	4.00	4.00
Time Deposits 3/									
7 days-1 month	..	..	..	5.50	9.00	4.00	--	--	--
1-3 months	6.00	6.00	6.00	6.00	6.00	4.00	4.00	4.00	4.00
3-6 months	6.50	6.50	6.50	6.50	8.00	5.00	5.00	5.00	5.00
6-12 months	7.25	7.25	7.25	7.25	7.25	6.00	5.30	5.30	5.50
1-2 years	8.00	8.00	8.00	8.00	8.00	8.00	7.00	7.50	7.50
2-3 years	9.00	9.00	9.00	9.00	9.00	9.00	9.00	9.00	9.00
3 years or longer	10.00	10.00	10.00	10.00	10.00	10.00	10.00	10.00	10.00
Unregulated Time Deposits 4/									
7 days-1 month	..	..	..	3.00	8.00	--	--	0.50	2.00
1-3 months	..	..	11.34	3.35	11.06	0.70	0.50	0.60	4.00
3-6 months	..	..	11.01	4.67	18.55	5.50	4.30	3.20	4.50
6-12 months	..	..	12.14	5.43	18.36	3.60	4.00	4.30	5.80
1-2 years	..	..	12.48	7.13	16.23	3.10	2.20	4.60	6.50
Public Sector Securities (yield)									
Treasury Bills 5/	6.63	7.18	6.70	6.30	11.20	0.80	0.40	2.60	3.90
3-year Bonds	9.00	9.70	--	8.10	9.00	--	--	5.40	5.50
5-year Bonds 6/	9.40	10.41	10.42	9.66	9.75	7.20	6.40	7.30	7.70
10-year Bonds 7/	9.45	11.48	11.06	10.39	9.60	--	7.90	--	--
Promissory Notes									
Fiji Sugar Corporation	9.45	9.01	7.75	8.78	12.90	1.10	0.70	3.10	3.50
Fiji Electricity Authority	7.73	9.01	7.75	8.78	19.99	..	..	..	..

Source: Data provided by Fiji authorities.

1/ Paid on statutory reserve deposits of commercial banks.
2/ 1981-84 estimates; 1985 onward - weighted average for the year.
3/ Maximum rates on regulated deposits of under F$250,000.
4/ Deposits over F$250,000. Weighted average figures from 1985.
5/ Weighted average for the year from 1984-89.
6/ Weighted average for the year for 5-7 year bonds from 1984.
7/ Weighted average for the year for 10-14 year bonds from 1984.

Table 4.3:   INDEX OF CONSUMER PRICES BY COMMODITY GROUP, 1981-89
(Annual average percentage change)

	1981	1982	1983	1984	1985	1986	1987	1988	1989 Est.
Food	..	..	33.9	5.9	8.3	-1.8	6.1	18.4	10.8
Drinks and Tobacco	..	..	6.4	8.9	8.2	16.0	7.0	9.4	2.7
Housing	..	..	18.6	13.0	1.2	4.4	1.7	-1.6	1.5
Heating and Lighting	..	..	4.9	0.7	0.7	-9.2	3.7	10.1	-1.4
Durable Household Goods	..	..	7.6	5.4	--	3.0	9.8	12.0	7.9
Clothing and Footwear	..	..	6.3	2.8	-0.4	1.5	3.1	18.2	10.4
Transport	..	..	11.3	6.8	4.6	2.9	6.6	9.9	2.9
Services	..	..	6.7	4.5	1.8	1.4	6.4	9.9	2.9
Miscellaneous	..	..	4.3	6.2	2.7	6.6	12.5	32.6	9.4
Combined Index	11.2	7.0	6.7	5.3	4.4	1.8	5.7	11.9	6.4

Source: Data provided by Fiji authorities.

Table 4.4: EXCHANGE RATES: 1978-88

	1978	1979	1980	1981	1982	1983	1984	1985	1986	1987	1988
						Annual Average					
Fiji $/SDR	1.1	1.1	1.1	1.0	1.0	1.1	1.1	1.2	1.3	1.6	1.9
Fiji $/US$	0.8	0.8	0.8	0.8	0.9	1.0	1.1	1.2	1.1	1.2	1.4
Japanese yen/Fiji $	248.6	282.3	277.4	258.6	267.3	233.8	219.7	207.0	148.9	118.2	89.6
Fiji $/Australian $	0.97	0.93	0.93	0.98	0.95	0.92	0.95	0.81	0.76	0.86	1.12
Fiji $/Pound Sterling	1.63	1.80	1.90	1.73	1.63	1.54	1.44	1.49	1.66	2.01	2.55
						% Change					
Fiji $/SDR	-1.02	1.85	-1.41	-5.34	2.15	5.61	2.07	5.54	13.47	19.13	21.50
Fiji $/US$	-7.67	-1.30	-2.17	4.37	9.20	9.08	6.40	6.61	-1.79	8.08	16.90
Japanese yen/Fiji $	-21.31	5.51	5.76	-6.80	3.43	-12.57	-6.01	-5.80	-28.07	-20.59	-24.21
Fiji $/Australian $	3.60	-3.61	-0.28	5.26	-3.33	-3.27	3.71	-15.08	-5.98	12.92	30.79
Fiji $/Pound Sterling	10.42	9.09	7.27	-9.02	-5.74	-5.49	-6.28	3.42	11.50	20.76	27.06

Source: IMF, IFS.

Table 5.1: BALANCE OF PAYMENTS, 1981-89
(US$ million at current prices)

	1981	1982	1983	1984	1985	1986	1987	1988	1989 Est.
Exports, f.o.b. (Domestic)	227.8	194.5	176.4	183.5	167.1	213.8	273.1	309.8	354.4
Sugar	154.2	134.3	110.1	101.5	97.0	118.1	152.3	138.7	144.8
Other	73.5	60.2	66.3	82.0	70.1	95.7	120.8	171.1	209.6
Imports, f.o.b. (Retained)	492.4	383.1	380.6	343.4	342.2	334.5	284.9	358.0	482.7
Trade Balance	-264.6	-188.6	-204.2	-159.9	-175.1	-120.7	-11.8	-48.2	-128.3
Services (net)	77.0	78.0	116.5	121.0	139.9	118.2	15.1	54.7	99.4
Private Transfers (net)	-8.8	-3.0	-2.1	-4.1	-10.4	-5.3	-19.1	-3.6	-6.9
Current Account	-196.4	-113.6	-89.8	-44.1	-45.5	-7.8	-15.8	2.9	-35.8
Official Transfers (net)	25.9	20.5	26.7	18.5	33.0	14.8	10.3	33.7	29.1
Current Account (incl. Off. Transf.)	-170.5	-93.1	-63.1	-25.6	-12.6	7.0	-5.5	36.7	-6.6
Official Capital (net)	74.2	42.4	40.6	11.3	0.4	-9.4	-25.3	6.7	-36.1
Private Capital, MLT (net)	32.6	33.7	31.0	18.5	31.6	31.7	14.6	36.8	37.8
Short Term Capital (net)	30.5	1.3	8.6	2.1	-24.0	-0.4	-32.8	14.7	8.8
Capital Account	137.3	77.4	80.2	31.8	8.0	21.9	-43.5	58.2	10.5
Errors & Ommissions	-15.9	-13.4	-21.4	1.0	6.2	19.3	53.1	-0.6	..
Overall Balance	-49.2	-29.1	-3.2	7.2	1.6	48.2	4.1	94.3	4.0
Memorandum Items:									
Current Account/GDP (%) (excl. Off Transf.)	-15.9	-9.5	-8.0	-3.7	-4.0	-0.6	-1.4	0.3	-2.9
Gross Reserves	135.1	128.7	122.6	130.0	146.5	170.7	131.6	232.3	236.3
Months of retained imports	3.3	4.0	3.9	4.5	5.1	6.1	5.5	7.8	5.9

Source: Bureau of Statistics.

Table 5.2:   VALUE OF EXPORTS BY TYPE OF PRODUCT, 1981-89
(US$ million at current prices, f.o.b.)

	1981	1982	1983	1984	1985	1986	1987	1988	1989 Est.
Sugar	154.2	134.1	110.1	101.6	97.0	118.1	152.3	138.7	144.8
Coconut Oil	7.5	6.6	10.4	17.1	6.6	3.7	2.5	2.4	3.7
Gold	13.9	16.7	16.6	18.9	18.9	34.1	41.4	57.0	49.0
Fish Products	..	10.1	14.8	13.9	11.9	16.1	20.5	33.7	35.1
Forestry Products 1/	..	3.7	3.9	6.7	6.2	7.0	13.4	18.6	21.6
Molasses	11.3	5.5	3.1	6.2	5.6	7.0	8.7	8.0	7.1
Other	..	17.7	17.4	18.9	20.9	27.8	34.4	51.5	93.1
DOMESTIC EXPORTS	230.2	194.3	176.2	183.2	167.1	213.8	273.1	309.8	354.4
Re-exports	85.0	92.6	66.0	76.0	69.9	62.2	60.9	58.2	64.6
TOTAL EXPORTS	315.2	287.0	242.2	259.2	237.0	276.0	334.0	368.0	419.0

Source: Data provided by Fiji authorities.

1/ Includes logs, sawn timber, veneer and plywood.

Table 5.3: VALUE OF IMPORTS BY SITC CLASSIFICATION, 1981-89
(US$ million at current prices, c.i.f.)

	1981	1982	1983	1984	1985	1986	1987	1988	1989
Food	102.0	75.9	76.8	69.0	69.4	68.6	70.1	81.0	82.5
Beverages & Tobacco	a/	4.3	3.6	3.3	3.7	3.1	a/	a/	a/
Crude Materials	5.2	4.0	5.1	3.2	2.9	2.6	2.7	2.9	6.1
Mineral Fuels	162.3	146.8	112.8	98.9	100.1	72.5	61.9	62.0	99.6
Oils & Fats	..	5.5	6.7	8.7	9.1	5.2	6.5	8.1	6.7
Chemicals	43.7	37.5	38.4	40.9	33.7	36.5	32.8	46.2	52.2
Manufactured Goods	..	84.7	90.0	84.0	87.4	93.9	84.6	108.5	138.4
Machinery	138.3	88.0	91.5	79.9	79.5	102.7	73.7	97.1	152.4
Miscellaneous Articles	..	50.0	46.6	47.3	43.4	39.3	47.9	54.9	69.2
Miscellaneous Transactions	21.1	13.4	13.4	14.5	11.4	14.4	b/	b/	b/
TOTAL	632.8	510.1	484.9	449.8	440.8	439.0	380.1	460.7	607.1

Source: Bureau of Statistics.

a/ Included in Food.
b/ Included in Miscellaneous Articles.

Table 5.4: DIRECTION OF TRADE, 1981-87
(F$ million at current prices)

	Origin of Imports							Destination of Exports						
	1981	1982	1983	1984	1985	1986	1987	1981	1982	1983	1984	1985	1986	1987
Australia	194.1	184.7	188.6	168.4	177.3	166.5	133.5	19.7	29.1	28.1	38.1	36.5	53.5	75.4
New Zealand	75.1	74.5	80.7	78.5	86.3	83.0	78.7	21.8	25.7	12.2	11.0	17.3	20.9	23.8
Japan	86.4	67.7	82.6	78.8	76.5	71.3	56.4	19.3	5.2	5.9	7.8	6.4	5.4	12.4
EEC	44.4	35.0	40.0	43.5	46.9	60.8	..	..	68.2	72.1	82.2	84.0	110.8	..
Of which: UK	29.5	19.8	24.9	24.6	24.5	21.6	21.9	67.4	60.0	60.8	80.2	83.0	108.7	138.8
United States	38.7	17.5	19.1	19.7	20.8	23.8	24.4	27.6	26.4	20.7	28.1	12.8	14.8	20.9
Pacific Islands	1.6	2.1	1.8	2.2	3.8	6.0	3.5	39.5	38.0	38.9	42.5	44.3	38.2	43.6
Asia	77.9	81.4	66.3	64.0	66.9	53.4	95.1	32.7	36.1	36.3	6.1	7.9	10.7	27.0
Others	21.7	12.7	14.1	24.3	22.8	21.0	45.6	30.3	40.7	36.0	65.9	62.5	59.1	65.5

Source: Bureau of Statistics.

Table 5.5:   CHANGE IN MERCHANDISE TERMS OF TRADE, 1983-89 1/
(1983=100)

	Export Unit Value	Import Unit Value	Terms of Trade
1983	100.0	100.0	100.0
1984	92.9	96.7	96.1
1985	78.5	89.2	88.0
1986	106.2	90.6	117.2
1987	111.2	89.1	124.8
1988	116.9	93.3	125.2
1989 (Est.)	121.6	100.7	120.7

Source: Data provided by Fiji authorities.

1/ US$ terms.

Table 6.1: EXTERNAL PUBLIC DEBT OUTSTANDING (INCLUDING UNDISBURSED)
(as of Dec. 31 1988)
(US$ million at current prices)

CREDITOR TYPE	DISBURSED	UNDISBURSED	TOTAL
MULTILATERAL LOANS	194.0	35.1	229.2
Asian Dev. Bank	56.6	18.2	74.8
EEC	13.1	0.9	13.9
European Invest. Bank	49.2	0.0	49.2
IFC	3.4	0.0	3.4
IBRD	71.9	16.1	87.9
BILATERAL LOANS	82.1	0.0	82.1
Australia	15.2	0.0	15.2
China	4.0	0.0	4.0
Nauru, Rep. of	17.1	0.0	17.1
Netherlands	1.5	0.0	1.5
United Kingdom	42.7	0.0	42.7
United States	1.5	0.0	1.5
SUPPLIERS CREDITS	24.2	0.0	24.2
Australia	9.8	0.0	9.8
Brazil		0.0	
Japan	0.3	0.0	0.3
Netherlands	0.4	0.0	0.4
Multiple Lenders	13.7	0.0	13.7
EXPORT CREDITS	2.9	0.0	2.9
Singapore	0.3	0.0	0.3
United Kingdom	2.6	0.0	2.6
FINANCIAL INSTITUTIONS	27.0	0.0	27.0
Japan	0.3	0.0	0.3
Multiple Lenders	20.1	0.0	20.1
Singapore	6.6	0.0	6.6
United Kingdom		0.0	
TOTAL	330.2	35.1	365.4
	-----	----	-----

Source: IBRD.

Table 6.2: SERVICE PAYMENTS, DISBURSEMENTS & OUTSTANDING AMOUNTS OF EXTERNAL PUBLIC DEBT, 1981-88
(US$ million at current prices)

	1981	1982	1983	1984	1985	1986	1987	1988
TOTAL EXTERNAL DEBT	372.1	402.0	437.4	413.4	443.7	440.9	466.2	466.6
	-----	-----	-----	-----	-----	-----	-----	-----
Long-Term Debt	333.1	365.1	397.3	378.2	410.2	413.0	437.9	431.2
Public & Publicly Guaranteed	237.4	265.5	292.3	279.4	302.2	311.5	334.2	330.2
Private Nonguaranteed	95.7	99.6	105.0	98.8	108.0	101.5	103.7	101.0
Use of IMF Credit	0.0	14.9	14.1	13.2	14.5	7.9	6.7	4.0
Short-Term Debt	39.0	22.0	26.0	22.0	19.0	20.0	21.5	31.4
PUBLIC & PUBLICLY GUARANTEED LONG-TERM DEBT								
Debt Outstanding & Disbursed	237.4	265.5	292.3	279.4	302.2	311.5	334.2	330.2
Official Creditors	179.1	209.8	229.6	210.2	220.1	241.4	280.2	276.1
Multilateral	84.2	106.2	136.5	130.9	144.0	165.2	193.9	194.0
IBRD	42.6	53.5	70.3	69.1	63.4	71.0	80.1	71.9
IDA	0.0	0.0	0.0	0.0	0.0	0.0	0.0	0.0
Bilateral	94.9	103.5	93.1	79.3	76.1	76.2	86.3	82.1
Private Creditors	58.3	55.7	62.7	69.2	82.1	70.1	54.0	54.1
Suppliers	9.3	6.4	8.4	19.4	25.0	21.8	15.5	27.2
Fianacial Markets	49.1	49.3	54.3	49.8	57.1	48.3	38.5	27.0
Disbursements	80.1	56.8	55.5	43.7	33.9	18.4	18.1	43.5
Official Creditors	72.7	56.0	41.8	20.9	6.1	16.8	17.7	29.7
Multilateral	22.9	27.7	40.0	16.7	3.9	10.5	13.9	29.7
IBRD	10.2	13.3	20.2	3.6	0.0	0.2	0.5	3.0
IDA	0.0	0.0	0.0	0.0	0.0	0.0	0.0	0.0
Bilateral	49.8	28.3	1.9	4.3	2.2	6.3	3.8	0.0
Private Creditors	7.4	0.8	13.7	22.8	27.7	1.6	0.3	13.7
Suppliers	0.0	0.1	4.7	9.8	15.4	1.6	0.3	13.7
Fianacial Markets	7.4	0.7	9.0	13.0	12.3	0.0	0.0	0.0
Amortization	9.5	11.9	14.5	26.7	31.2	31.3	36.6	36.4
Official Creditors	4.9	9.2	8.5	12.8	14.4	17.5	20.1	23.0
Multilateral	1.5	3.4	5.1	6.5	8.7	11.0	12.7	15.7
IBRD	1.1	2.5	3.3	4.3	5.5	5.9	6.9	8.0
IDA	0.0	0.0	0.0	0.0	0.0	0.0	0.0	0.0
Bilateral	3.4	5.8	3.4	6.2	5.6	6.5	7.4	7.6
Private Creditors	4.7	2.7	6.0	14.0	16.8	13.8	16.4	13.4
Suppliers	2.9	2.4	2.5	7.9	10.7	4.8	5.2	2.1
Fianacial Markets	1.8	0.3	3.5	6.1	6.1	9.0	11.2	11.3
Interest Payments	16.5	22.3	23.0	24.3	24.6	25.2	26.0	24.8
Official Creditors	9.6	14.1	16.6	17.9	17.6	19.0	20.8	21.1
Multilateral	5.0	6.2	8.0	9.9	10.7	11.9	13.1	13.4
IBRD	3.0	3.5	4.3	5.2	5.0	5.7	6.2	7.0
IDA	0.0	0.0	0.0	0.0	0.0	0.0	0.0	0.0
Bilateral	4.6	7.9	8.6	8.0	6.9	7.1	7.7	7.7
Private Creditors	6.9	8.2	6.3	6.3	7.0	6.2	5.2	3.7
Suppliers	0.9	0.7	0.7	1.4	1.7	1.6	1.7	1.0
Fianacial Markets	6.0	7.5	5.6	5.0	5.3	4.6	3.6	2.7
PRIVATE NON-GUARANTEED DEBT								
Debt Outstanding & Disbursed	95.7	99.6	105.0	98.8	108.0	101.5	103.7	101.0
Disbursements	..	..	..	..	..	..	..	..
Amortization	..	..	..	..	..	..	..	..
Interest Payments	..	..	..	..	..	..	..	..

Source: IBRD.

Table 6.3: FIJI: OFFICIAL DEVELOPMENT ASSISTANCE, 1984-88
(US$ million at current prices)

	TOTAL RECEIPTS NET					TOTAL ODA NET				
	1984	1985	1986	1987	1988	1984	1985	1986	1987	1988
DAC COUNTRIES										
Australia	2.0	12.8	11.1	5.9	-2.0	9.9	10.0	13.8	11.3	19.8
Belgium	0.0	0.0	0.1	0.1	0.1	-	-	0.1	0.1	0.1
Canada	0.2	0.4	0.3	0.2	0.2	0.2	0.4	0.3	0.2	0.2
Finland	0.3	-	0.0	0.2	0.3	0.2	-	0.0	0.2	0.3
France	0.5	-	0.6	1.9	10.2	0.5	-	0.6	1.9	10.2
Germany, Fed. Rep.	0.9	1.0	1.4	1.8	2.1	0.9	1.0	1.4	1.8	2.1
Japan	1.7	4.7	10.6	7.1	26.9	3.4	8.2	11.0	10.3	8.1
Netherlands	1.2	0.5	0.4	-3.2	0.4	1.2	0.5	0.4	0.6	0.4
New Zealand	3.4	3.4	2.3	3.8	1.3	3.4	3.4	2.3	3.8	1.8
Norway	0.0	0.0	0.1	0.1	0.1	0.0	0.0	0.1	0.1	0.1
United Kingdom	4.8	-0.7	8.7	-3.3	-2.1	1.7	1.8	1.6	0.9	0.5
United States	1.0	-	-	-	2.0	2.0	1.0	1.0	1.0	3.0
TOTAL	16.0	22.1	33.5	17.5	33.0	23.5	26.3	32.4	32.2	47.4
MULTILATERAL										
ASDB	7.1	0.2	1.8	0.8	20.0	0.5	0.2	0.4	-	1.5
EEC	7.3	4.2	10.2	8.6	0.8	4.3	3.6	8.8	1.4	2.7
IBRD	-1.3	-5.5	-5.6	-6.4	-1.0	-	-	-	-	-
IFC	-	-0.4	4.0	-0.6	2.8	-	-	-	-	-
UNDP	0.8	0.3	1.2	0.6	1.5	0.8	0.3	1.2	0.8	1.5
UNTA	0.7	0.3	0.8	0.9	0.5	0.7	0.3	0.8	0.9	0.5
WFP	0.5	0.1	-	0.0	-	0.5	0.1	-	0.0	-
Other	1.0	1.1	0.9	0.7	0.6	1.0	1.1	0.9	0.7	0.8
TOTAL	18.1	0.4	13.3	4.7	23.6	7.8	5.6	10.1	3.7	6.9
ARAB COUNTRIES	-	-	-	-	-	-	-	-	-	-
EEC + Members	14.5	5.0	19.4	8.8	10.7	8.6	6.9	10.8	6.6	16.3
TOTAL	32.1	22.5	46.8	22.2	56.6	31.3	31.9	42.5	35.9	54.3

Source: Geographical Distribution of Financial Flows to Developing Countries, 1984/88.

KIRIBATI

DEVELOPMENT SURVEY

CURRENCY EQUIVALENTS

Annual Averages

1980	$A 1.00 = US$1.14
1981	$A 1.00 = US$1.15
1982	$A 1.00 = US$1.02
1983	$A 1.00 = US$0.90
1984	$A 1.00 = US$0.88
1985	$A 1.00 = US$0.70
1986	$A 1.00 = US$0.67
1987	$A 1.00 = US$0.70
1988	$A 1.00 = US$0.78
1989	$A 1.00 = US$0.79

(The Australian dollar is the official currency and the sole circulating medium of exchange)

FISCAL YEAR

January 1 - December 31

ABBREVIATIONS AND ACRONYMS

EEC	- European Economic Community
EEZ	- Exclusive Economic Zone
MED	- Marine Export Division
NPF	- National Provident Fund
NPO	- National Planning Office
RERF	- Revenue Equalization Reserve Fund
SPMS	- South Pacific Marine Service
TML	- Te Mautari Limited (National Fishing Company)
TTI	- Tarawa Technical Institute

Table of Contents

This report was prepared by a World Bank mission which visited Kiribati in December 1989. The mission members were Graeme Thompson and Jayshree Sengupta (consultant).

KIRIBATI: DEVELOPMENT SURVEY

A. Background

2.1   Kiribati consists of 33 islands located in the mid-Pacific, astride both the equator and the international date line in three main groups--the Gilbert, Phoenix and Line Islands. The total land area, which amounts to only 725 square kms, is distributed over approximately 3.5 million square kilometers. Most of the islands are low-lying coral atolls except for Banaba, which is of limestone origin. The geographical fragmentation of the islands, their remoteness, and their small size represent fundamental constraints to Kiribati's development.

2.2   Kiribati faces difficult challenges in the agricultural sector due to an inhospitable natural environment. Only coconuts, breadfruits, pandanus, swamp taro, pawpaw, bananas and pumpkins grow in the infertile soils of Kiribati. There are no forest resources and no known exploitable mineral resources, except for residual phosphate deposits in Banaba. The nation does, however, possess abundant ocean resources, including both fish and a significant amount of manganese nodules in its 200 mile exclusive economic zone (EEZ).

2.3   Kiribati gained its independence from Britain in 1979. 1/ The I-Kiribati have a strong cultural tradition and possess an egalitarian ethic which is based on mutual help and cooperation. Kiribati's large subsistence economy has been self-sufficient in the past but as urbanization proceeds Kiribati is expected to become increasingly dependent on international trade to meet essential requirements.

Population, Education and Health

2.4   The population of Kiribati was estimated at 68,207 in 1988. Population distribution among the islands is highly skewed; South Tarawa, with only 2 percent of the land area, accounts for one third of the total population, implying a population density of 1,354 persons per square km. By contrast, the Line Islands 2/ (Christmas, Fanning and Washington) account for only 4 percent of the population and about 60 percent of the land mass. Over-crowding in South Tarawa is considered to be a serious problem and the government has already launched a resettlement scheme.

1/   The Republic of Kiribati adopted a system of government consisting of only one legislative body or House, the "Maneaba ni Maungatabu" which has 36 elected members. The President is elected by universal suffrage from among a short list of three or four candidates nominated by the Maneaba. Seventeen local government councils control rural island activities and two urban councils manage South Tarawa.

2/   Christmas Island in the Northern Line Islands is the headquarters for the Ministry for the Line and Phoenix Group.

2.5   The population of Kiribati expanded at 2.1 percent per annum during the 1979-88 period, close to the average for the region. A high fertility rate averaging five children per woman, was largely offset by the relatively low life expectancy of 53 years compared, for example, with 63 3/4 for Asia.

Table 2.1: KIRIBATI: SOCIAL AND DEMOGRAPHIC INDICATORS, 1988

Indicator	Units	Kiribati	Lower middle income	Asia
Population	Persons	68,207		
- Growth rate	% p.a.	2.1	2.2	1.8
GDP per capita	US$	470		
Daily calorie supply	per capita	2,935		
Crude birth rate	per '000	37.5	31.5	26.8
Crude death rate	per '000	14	8.6	8.8
Infant mortality rate	per '000 births	82	59.1	81.5
Life expectancy at birth	years	53	63.8	63.7
Population per				
- Doctor	persons	1,967	1,547	1,422
- Hospital bed	persons	209	-	-
Access to safe water	% population	44.0	-	-
- Urban	% population	95.0	76.7	72.5
- Rural	% population	54.0	46.3	-
School enrollment ratio	%	84.0	-	-
Adult illiteracy rate	%	10.0	43.3	39.5

Source: Data provided by Kiribati authorities and estimates by the World Bank.

2.6   Despite high levels of literacy, shortages of skilled labor represent a major development constraint in Kiribati. There is only one public secondary school together with five secondary schools that are managed by local church groups; few students complete secondary school education and go on for higher education. With the exception of a maritime training college, there is no vocational training institute. The available evidence suggests that there is also a shortage of fully trained primary teachers, with over 70 percent of positions filled by inadequately qualified incumbents.[3]

---

[3] A fully qualified teacher is defined as one who has completed at least Form 5 secondary schooling and at least two years of professional training as a teacher.

2.7   Kiribati also faces a number of severe health problems. Health
service capacity is inadequate with one doctor per 1,967 persons and only one
hospital in the entire country. As noted earlier, life expectancy is low
(55.6 years for women and 50.6 years for men) and infant mortality is high at
82 per 1,000 of the population. In addition, there is a general Vitamin A
deficiency among the children and evidence of dietary deficiencies (low
protein intake) is present in other age groups. Diabetes is also common.
Furthermore, there is a lack of potable water supplies in South Tarawa where
the water supply is being depleted, drought is endemic and salinity is on the
rise. The water supply on Christmas Island (Kiritimati) is also in a poor
condition.

Employment

2.8   The bulk of the working population in Kiribati is employed in the
subsistence sector. Formal wage employment is largely limited to urban
sectors where the civil service and public enterprises account for over two-
thirds of total paid employment. Data available from the 1978 and 1985 Census
indicate little change in indigenous employment suggesting that much of the
increase in the labor force during the intervening years has been absorbed in
subsistence activities.

2.9   Although no reliable survey data exist, the Ministry of Trade,
Industry and Labor believes that there is a substantial excess supply of
labor. As evidence, it may be noted that applications for entry level
positions in the civil service more than doubled during 1988-89. The labor
force situation is expected to become clearer when the findings of the 1990
ILO Employment and Manpower Survey are available.

B.   Recent Economic Developments

2.10   Prior to Independence, growth of the Kiribati economy was closely
linked to exports of phosphates from Banaba Island, whose deposits were
exhausted in 1979. However, the colonial administration established a Revenue
Equalization Reserve Fund (RERF) 4/ in 1956 to serve as a trust fund to
supplement revenues in the post-phosphate era. Notwithstanding revenues from
this source, real GDP fell dramatically when phosphate deposits ran out around
the end of the 1970s (see Chart 1) and had recovered to only US$15.4 million
by 1987, compared to US$35.2 million in 1978; a further output gain of 17
percent was recorded in 1988.

2.11   During the 1980s, output followed a highly erratic pattern (see
Chart 1), reflecting the vagaries of weather and the vulnerability of the
country's only export commodities (copra and fish) to price and environmental
shocks. Stabilizing influences have been exerted over the years by a steady

---

4/   The RERF is managed by a London firm of stockbrokers who invest the
       fund mainly in government bonds and cash in a variety of major world
       currencies. More recently (1988) transfers have made from the bond
       portfolio to an equity portfolio which now comprises 16 percent of the
       total RERF's market value.

Table 2.2: SELECTED ECONOMIC INDICATORS, 1985-89

	1985	1986	1987	1988	1989 Est.
Production and Expenditure					
Real GDP (mil 1978 US$)	17.35	17.84	16.45	19.25	19.44
Growth Rates (% p.a.)					
- Real GDP	-6.4	2.8	-7.8	17.0	1.1
- Agriculture	-25.2	-20.7	-25.6	87.0	-
- Industry	11.8	11.2	-23.6	1.2	-
- Services	2.2	11.7	0.0	2.9	-
Ratios to GDP (%)					
Gross investment	31.5	34.1	30.6	27.8	-
- Private	1.5	2.4	2.2	1.3	-
- Public	30.5	31.7	28.4	26.5	-
Domestic savings (% of GDP)	-55.2	-18.9	-35.3	-34.5	-36.2
National savings (% of GDP)	45.6	74.2	61.6	42.4	43.9
Central Gov't Budget (% of GDP)					
Revenue	52.6	38.6	54.9	44.4	40.9
Tax revenue	16.1	16.7	21.3	17.3	18.2
Non-tax revenue	37.6	22.7	33.3	28.3	22.5
Expenditure					
Current	51.2	46.3	47.8	45.4	74.6
Capital	33.5	45.6	41.4	34.3	43.1
Overall Balance	5.9	-9.5	5.1	-1.6	-5.3
(Excluding grants)	-32.2	-53.4	-34.6	-34.3	-39.2
Money and Prices /a					
Consumer Price Index (1975 = 100)	160.2	172.7	183.9	189.6	197.0
GDP deflators (1978 = 100)	168.2	179.3	191.0	196.9	204.6
Nominal effective exchange rate	85.2	75.0	68.3	80.3	77.1
Balance of Payments (mil US$)					
Exports (f.o.b.)	4.3	1.6	2.1	4.5	4.7
Imports (c.i.f.)	-15.1	-14.4	-12.6	-19.0	-22.3
Trade Balance	-10.8	-12.8	-15.5	-14.5	-17.6
Services	0.9	6.2	3.1	3.2	4.0
Private transfers (net)	0.9	1.6	2.2	2.4	2.9
Official transfers	12.5	14.8	16.4	13.2	16.5
Current account balance	3.5	9.8	6.2	4.3	5.8
Overall Balance	2.9	4.6	2.1	-1.2	6.3
Reserve movements [Increase in foreign assets (-)]	-2.9	-4.6	-2.1	-	-

/a The Australian dollar is legal tender in Kiribati, but no money supply
    figures are available.

Source: Data provided by Kiribati authorities and World Bank estimates.

KIRIBATI: GDP GROWTH, 1980-89 AND STRUCTURE OF PRODUCTION, 1989

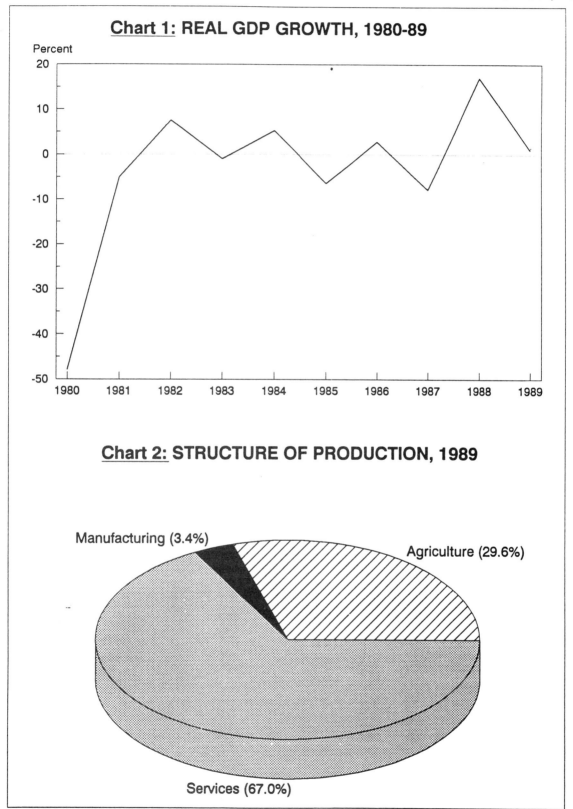

Chart 1: REAL GDP GROWTH, 1980-89

Percent

Chart 2: STRUCTURE OF PRODUCTION, 1989

Manufacturing (3.4%)

Agriculture (29.6%)

Services (67.0%)

Source: Data provided by Kiribati authorities and World Bank staff estimates.

KIRIBATI: TRADE INDICATORS, 1980-89

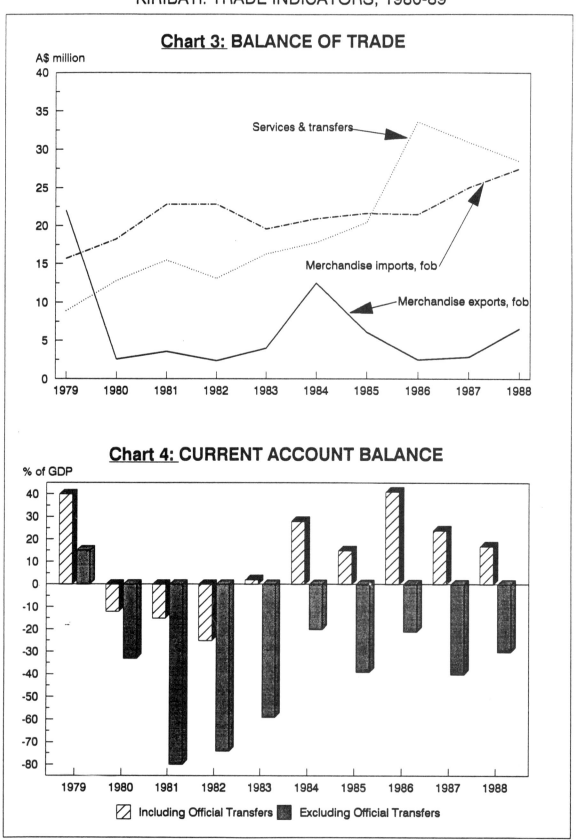

Chart 3: BALANCE OF TRADE

A$ million

Services & transfers

Merchandise imports, fob

Merchandise exports, fob

Chart 4: CURRENT ACCOUNT BALANCE

% of GDP

▨ Including Official Transfers   ▩ Excluding Official Transfers

Source: Data provided by Kiribati authorities and World Bank staff estimates.

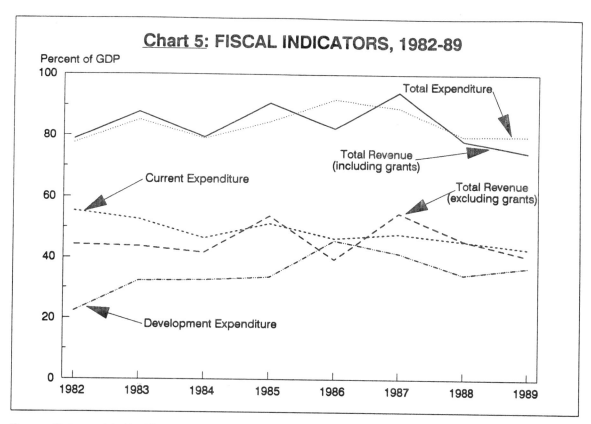

Chart 5: FISCAL INDICATORS, 1982-89

Source: Data provided by Kiribati authorities and World Bank staff estimates.

inflow of aid, budget grants and workers' remittances together with revenues generated by the RERF. In 1988, the per capita GDP of Kiribati stood at US$470, placing it in the category of low income countries.5/

Fiscal Stance

2.12   Available evidence on the fiscal balance of Kiribati indicates a prudent and conservative approach to public expenditure management (Table 2.3). Current and development expenditures of the Government have been guided by three main principles: (a) to avoid budgetary deficits; (b) to restrain outlays on public services to levels that could be sustained in the medium-term, and (c) to invest in the development of economic and social infrastructure as a foundation for future growth.

2.13   To restrain current expenditures, the Government has pursued a policy of containing the growth of real wages in the public sector and, on occasion, by observing hiring freezes for extended periods. Since 1979, nominal salaries have been increased on only three occasions, by 5 percent in 1982 and 1985, and by 10 percent in 1987; a further increase of 8 percent is expected in early 1991. Such modest increases in the face of an average annual inflation rate of around 7 percent, implies a substantial drop in the real income of government employees. As a further means to restrain current expenditures, several measures were introduced to improve finances of the public enterprises, such as the introduction of flexible pricing policies; consequently, subsidies to these enterprises dropped from 10 percent of GDP in 1980-82 to only 2 percent in 1987. As a result of these measures, by 1985 the level of current expenditures was down more than 25 percent from 1982 levels and it remained fairly steady until 1988. The reduction in current expenditure was sufficient to offset the loss of UK budgetary grants in 1986 and to provide a budgetary surplus sufficient to finance about 4-5 percent of capital expenditures. The balance of capital expenditures was financed by external grants.

Money Supply and Prices

2.14   There is no central monetary authority in Kiribati and the Australian dollar serves as legal tender. 6/ This currency constraint accounts in part for the prudent stance of fiscal policy adopted by the Central Government despite the low level of economic activity experienced during the 1980s. Inflation, which tends to reflect the rate of price increase in Australia, but which ultimately is transmitted to Kiribati through surpluses in the balance of payments, averaged less than 6 percent during the decade. This was the lowest among the PMCs.

5/   Kiribati was designated a "Least Developed Country" by the United Nations in January 1987.

6/   It appears that the Government intends to continue using the Australian dollar although plans are under way to replace Australian coins with domestic coins.

Table 2.3: KIRIBATI: CENTRAL GOVERNMENT BUDGET SUMMARY, 1982-89
(In thousands of US$)

	1982	1983	1984	1985	1986	1987	1988	1989 Budget	1989 Est.
Revenue	12,964	11,922	12,306	12,099	9,277	13,511	14,761	15,486	13,664
Tax revenue	4,543	4,156	3,990	3,467	3,798	5,274	5,613	5,683	6,104
Nontax revenue /a	8,421	7,766	8,317	8,632	5,479	8,236	9,148	9,803	7,561
Of which: Interest income									
From RERF /a	4,833	4,963	4,838	5,396	1,879	3,505	6,080	5,441	3,750
External grants	10,072	12,002	11,148	8,749	10,600	9,813	10,569	8,100 /b	11,366
Current /c	3,561	3,158	1,560	1,039	--	--	--	--	--
Development /d	6,511	8,844	9,588	7,709	10,600	9,813	10,569	8,100	11,366
Total revenue and grants	23,036	23,924	23,455	20,849	19,877	23,323	25,331	23,586	25,030
Current expenditure	16,168	14,368	13,717	11,778	11,158	11,837	14,691	15,411	14,468
Development expenditure /e	6,511	8,844	9,588	7,709	11,003	10,233	11,112	8,250	12,345
Total expenditure	22,679	23,212	23,306	19,487	22,161	22,070	25,803	23,661	26,813
Overall balance	357	712	150	1,382	-2,284	1,253	-473	-75	-1,784
Reinvested interest income from RERF	--	--	1,075	-1,538	5,446	4,264	2,812	2,360 /f	4,875
Overall balance including reinvested income from RERF	357	712	1,224	-178	3,162	5,517	3,664	2,285	3,091

(As percentage of GDP)

	1982	1983	1984	1985	1986	1987	1988	1989 Budget	1989 Est.
Tax revenue	15.5	15.2	13.5	16.1	16.7	21.3	17.3	17.1	18.2
Nontax revenue	28.8	28.6	28.2	37.6	22.7	33.3	28.3	29.5	22.5
External grants	34.5	44.0	37.8	38.1	43.9	39.7	32.7	24.6	33.9
Total revenue and grants	78.8	87.7	79.5	90.7	82.4	94.3	78.3	71.2	74.6
Current expenditure	55.3	52.7	46.5	51.2	46.3	47.8	45.4	46.4	43.1
Capital expenditure	22.3	32.4	32.5	33.5	45.6	41.4	34.3	24.4	36.8
Overall balance	1.2	2.6	0.5	5.9	-9.5	5.1	-1.6	--	-5.3
Adjusted overall balance	1.2	2.6	4.2	-0.8	13.1	22.3	12.2	6.8	9.2

/a Excludes reinvested interest income from RERF.
/b Excludes potential projects yet to be approved by the Government.
/c United Kingdom budgetary grant.
/d External assistance excluding STABEX, technical assistance, and food aid.
/e Includes local contribution of US$0.4 million each in 1986-88, and US$0.1 million in 1989.
/f Staff estimate.

Source: Data provided by the Kiribati authorities and staff estimates.

2.15   The prevalence of interest rate ceilings in the early 1980s reduced
domestic liquidity and fostered outflows of capital. The resultant shortage
of bank liquidity served as a major constraint for commercial bank financing
of private sector activity. A reflow of capital took place in 1984 with the
lifting of interest rate ceilings that made interest rates in Kiribati

competitive with international rates. There was a moderate outflow of capital
in 1988 with the transfer offshore of funds of the National Provident Fund
(NPF) 7/ formerly held in the form of time deposits with the Bank of Kiribati.8/

Savings and Investment

2.16   Kiribati has a low savings propensity, which is not unusual among
low-income economies. However, the steep fall in GDP in 1980 without a
commensurate decline in consumption, resulted in negative gross domestic
savings which were sustained through much of the decade by a substantial
inflow of remittances (see Table 2.2). It was not until 1985 that the sum of
domestic savings and net factor income from abroad was sufficient to cover
total consumption, leaving external aid to meet investment costs.

2.17   The central Government and public enterprises accounted for roughly
95 percent of total investment in 1988. The wide gap between domestic
investment and savings was met mainly from external aid which reached a high
of US$243 per capita or 75 percent of GDP in 1987. Information on private
sector investment is sketchy but was clearly small and concentrated in the
primary and service sectors. The Government has been exploring the
possibility of attracting private foreign investment for large-scale
commercial projects but has registered little progress on this front to date.

Foreign Trade

2.18   The vulnerability of the Kiribati economy is reflected in the
composition of its balance of payments (see Tables 2.2 and 2.4). Imports have
equalled GDP in recent years while export earnings (which accrue from the very
narrow product base of copra and fish) constitute around 20 percent of GDP.
Official transfers (equal to more than one-half of GDP) have more than offset
the deficit on merchandise trade yielding a positive current account balance
of US$6 million (20-25 percent of GDP) on average since 1985. The balance on
capital account tends to be slightly negative as RERF reinvestments and
financial investments of the National Provident Fund nominally exceed
concessional aid from multilateral agencies and some private transactions.
The overall balance of payments registered surpluses during most of the 1980s,
as the surpluses in the current account tended to outweigh capital account
deficits.

7/   The NPF operates a compulsory superannuation scheme to which all public
and private sector employees are obliged to contribute 5 percent of
wages and salaries with an equivalent amount paid by the employers.
The NPF operations have yielded surpluses since its inception and are
invested primarily in foreign government bonds and assets through a
London firm of stockbrokers, and in foreign mortgages through an
Australian financial institution.

8/   The Bank of Kiribati is a joint venture with Westpac of Australia which
owns 51 percent of the shares. It is the only licensed commercial bank
and foreign exchange dealer in Kiribati.

Table 2.4: KIRIBATI: MEDIUM-TERM BALANCE OF PAYMENTS, 1988-93
(In millions of US$)

	1988	1989	1990	1991	1992	1993
Exports, f.o.b.	4.5	4.7	4.6	4.7	5.0	5.1
Imports, f.o.b.	19.0	22.3	23.2	24.2	25.5	26.8
Trade balance	-14.5	-17.6	-18.6	-19.5	-20.5	-21.7
Services, net	3.2	4.0	2.8	3.1	3.5	3.7
Receipts	18.5	20.0	19.6	20.6	21.9	23.1
RERF interest receipts	9.1	9.0	8.8	9.1	9.5	9.9
Payments	15.3	16.0	16.8	17.6	18.5	19.3
Transfers, net	15.6	19.4	21.5	22.7	23.8	25.1
Private	2.4	2.9	3.3	3.6	4.0	4.4
Official /a	13.2	16.5	18.2	19.0	19.9	20.8
Current balance	4.3	5.8	5.8	6.3	6.8	7.3
Capital account	-5.5	0.5	-0.6	-0.8	-1.2	-1.4
Overall balance	-1.2	6.3	5.1	5.4	5.6	6.0
Monetary movements [increase in assets (-)]	0.5	-4.4	-5.4	-5.5	-5.8	-6.2
Commercial banks, net	3.8	-1.2	-0.9	-0.9	-1.0	-1.2
Monetary authorities	-3.4	-3.2	-4.4	-4.5	-4.6	-4.9
Changes in RERF /b	-3.6	-3.2	-4.4	-4.5	-4.6	-4.9
Government foreign accounts /c	0.4	..	..	..	..	..

/a Including aid-in-kind and technical assistance.
/b Interest received minus drawdown.
/c Excluding STABEX accounts held abroad.

Source: Data provided by the Kiribati authorities and staff estimates.

Exports

2.19   Kiribati's dependence on two primary exports--copra and fish, which
accounted for 71.8 and 27.4 percent of merchandise exports respectively in
1988--has had important implications for the country's economic development.
The sharp decline in copra prices in 1982-86 and a drought in 1984-85
significantly reduced export earnings leading to a severe deterioration in the
balance of payments. To offset the fall in export earnings, the governments
of UK, Canada and New Zealand assisted with projects to support copra and
related production as well as other agricultural and farm products.

2.20   The fishery sector provides an important source of wage employment
and fish is an important food source in the subsistence sector. In an effort
to spur development of this sector, in 1981 the government established Te
Mautari Ltd. (TML) in South Tarawa as a commercial fishing company to export
bulk frozen tuna. However, the initiative has encountered difficulties due to
inadequate financing, management practices, technical problems and a low catch
in 1987 due to bad weather.

2.21   Another government enterprise, the Marine Export Division, was set up
in 1987 in Christmas Island to export quality chilled fish (kingfish, milkfish
and lobster). Growth has been constrained by limited air service to Hawaii
and to other locations, including Japan. Additional problems include the lack
of quality control, inadequate managerial and marketing staff, and the absence
of banking facilities in Christmas Island for overseas transactions.

Developments in 1988-90 and Short-Term Outlook

2.22   Favorable weather and a sizable fish catch caused real GDP to jump by
17 percent in 1988, the best year of the decade for Kiribati in terms of
growth performance. However, in 1989 growth was lackluster. In that year
real GDP rose by merely 1 percent owing to a sharp, drought-related decline in
copra production that largely offset a rise of 50 percent in the fish catch
and expansion of construction and manufacturing. The Government's policy of
fiscal restraint continued in 1989 as current expenditures were held below the
level indicated in the budget. The overall budget showed a surplus of nearly
10 percent of GDP (Table 2.3), up from 8 percent in the previous year. In
view of the reduction in current expenditures, the drawdown of investment
income from RERF was limited to only A$5 million (about 3 percent of the
beginning year value of RERF). Consumer inflation rose moderately in 1989 to
4 percent from 3.1 percent in 1988, mainly reflecting the weakening of the
Australian dollar against other major currencies.

2.23   The balance of payments continued to reflect an overall surplus in
1989, primarily due to: (a) official transfers that financed virtually all of
the deficit in the trade account; (b) a net positive balance in services
transactions stemming from interest income of the RERF; and (c) a drawdown of
net foreign assets by commercial banks.

2.24   The only sources of monetary expansion in Kiribati are surpluses in
the balance of payments and expansion of credit to the private sector.
Following the onset of portfolio weakness in 1988, the Bank of Kiribati
pursued a more cautious approach to lending in 1989. On the side of deposits,
growth was sluggish and interest rates on savings and term deposits were
raised in order to attract more deposits and to prevent the transfer offshore
of deposits from the National Provident Fund.

2.25   The prospects for 1990 appear to be for little improvement over 1989.
Real GDP growth is likely to be only modest in view of the poor fish catch and
lower copra production. Although aid-financed construction activity will be
higher as will manufacturing output, the relatively small size of these
sectors limits their impact on overall growth. The fiscal and balance of
payments situations are expected to remain essentially unchanged in 1990 in
view of the continued restraint in demand management policies. No major
change in the inflationary picture is expected.

C. Medium-Term Outlook and Prospects

2.26   Given its exceptionally narrow resource base, the economic future for
Kiribati depends to a large extent on the degree to which policies can be set
on a path to exploit the country's few major development assets. These
include: fisheries resources, which are vast in terms of ocean area; the

lightly populated Line (and possible Phoenix) Islands; and, a small but highly capable workforce with overseas experience in mining operations (phosphates in Nauru), shipping and construction.

2.27   Fisheries development. The primary source of growth in Kiribati is expected to be in the maritime area. Further development of the fisheries resource depends primarily on the introduction of new techniques to extend the range, expand the volume and increase the market value of fish caught by domestic enterprises. For the time being, developments depend on what can be achieved by Te Mautari Ltd. (TML), the national fishing company based in Tarawa, and to a lesser extent, by the Marine Export Division (MED) of the Ministry of Natural Resources, operating from Christmas Island. TML generally operates pole and line vessels (and a mothership) with limited range because of the characteristics of bait available from the Kiribati lagoons. The addition of longline vessels (funded by the EEC) could greatly extend operations, improve efficiency and increase returns. Such developments have the potential to double the real value of fish exports within five years.

2.28   Kiribati should also seek greatly expanded revenues from licensing income derived from foreign fishing operations in its EEZ. In 1988, it received only A$1.8 million (US$1.5 million) for a reported catch of 15,000 tons, with Korea paying 45 percent (for 27 percent of the catch) and Japan 36 percent (for 56 percent of the catch); receipts under the regional US agreement were minimal. A more active policy to increase licensing revenues is warranted.

2.29   Increased fishing rents depends in substantial part on Kiribati's ability to police its EEZ more effectively. For this reason, the Australian offer to provide a patrol boat and contribute to its cost of operation should be considered. The offer was first made in 1987--at a time when several other Pacific Island countries accepted this type of aid. It is understood that the provision of the vessel, advisors and spare parts would be at no cost to Kiribati. In addition, support for operating costs during five years of expected usage would be provided under grant aid, as would maintenance and refitting costs for a further five years.9/ It may be noted that Australia is already providing grant assistance for the establishment of a national surveillance coordinating authority; the ability to carry out patrols would greatly improve the effectiveness of this operation.

2.30   Tourism is the second major development possibility in the Line Islands. To the east where people are few, land is relatively abundant and the Government wants to resettle a sizeable part of the total population. At the Kiribati Development Conference held on Kiritimati (Christmas Island) in October 1989, there were numerous indications of support from multilateral agencies and bilateral donors for the Government's policy of outer islands development, through resettlement of the Line and Phoenix Islands.

9/ With its own limited enforcement capacity, Kiribati managed in 1987 to earn A$1.35 million (US$1 million) from a fine paid on the release of an overseas purse seiner vessel caught fishing illegally. The fine represented the equivalent of 18 percent of tax revenue that year and possibly 10 years of the budgetary cost of operating the patrol boat.

2.31   Nevertheless, the possibilities are limited for further tourism development on Christmas Island, which already has a small but viable tourism trade based on sports fishing and bird-life. In addition, settlement is constrained by the prevalence of droughts that prohibit most agricultural development on that island. On the other hand, Tabueran (Fanning Island) appears to have significant potential for tourism development mainly for topographic reasons, if airport and related infrastructure can be developed.

2.32   The potential benefits from one or more major tourism ventures are substantial.10/ By 1994, as many as 2,000 resettled I-Kiribati could be employed in this type of development, a number equivalent to nearly 30 percent of the employed workforce in 1988 and well above the total currently employed in overseas mining and shipping. Appropriate tourism development would not limit resettlement programs, but would provide development opportunities needed to underpin the resettlement scheme. In addition, tourism would provide an outlet for the excellent local handicrafts industry, thereby widening the benefits of growth.

2.33   Several other possibilities exist for major development schemes including the resumption of phosphate mining on Banaba and satellite launching facilities on Kiritimati. The original proposal to re-mine Banaba for its residual phosphate deposits offered the promise of revenues in excess A$3 million a year for three years of operation, plus significant employment benefits.11/ A much expanded Kiritimati scheme to establish satellite launching facilities might be feasible, but the project has not advanced to the stage where is can be considered a firm possibility.

2.34   Employment Overseas. As noted, Kiribati has a sizeable overseas labor force, including (as of 1987) 1,070 seamen serving on South Pacific Marine Service (SPMS) vessels and about 500 working for the Nauru Phosphate Company. Cash remittances from these and other external sources appear to benefit up to one-third of Kiribati households; private transfers amounted in 1988 to A$4.5 million or about A$300 (US$250) per household. The 1,600 workers employed in overseas shipping and mining represent more than 20 percent of total employment in Kiribati. This external labor force is one of Kiribati's main assets. However, it is faced with the prospect of exhaustion of the phosphate deposits on Nauru, and by the probable easing of the demand for seamen through advances in marine technology. A national employment strategy should, it appears, include efforts to expand the amount of employment overseas as well as within the national boundaries.

_____

10/ One major scheme for tourism development on Fanning is being actively considered. Another possibility is for the Japanese Holiday Village Plan (sponsored by the Ministry of Transport and International Transport and Tourism Bureau) to develop international tourist facilities, financed by external aid and the private sector.

11/ Technical considerations are understood to have reduced somewhat the potential revenue and employment benefits.

2.35   In view of these prospects, the Government should consider discussing with its major partners in development, the possibilities for special provisions regarding employment and settlement of some I-Kiribati outside the country. These partners would include Australia, the United Kingdom, New Zealand and possibly Japan.

2.36   Other Development Potential. Despite substantial development financed by external aid over the last decade, there are still sizeable infrastructural gaps in Kiribati, especially as regards road and causeway construction in the outer islands, airport upgrading, and the improvement of telecommunications. The continued inflow of grant assistance for the above proposals will provide some growth in employment and income.

2.37   Prospects for growth in agriculture (excluding fisheries) are limited. No significant increase in copra production or exports can be expected and possibilities for export diversification are small. One notable exception is seaweed, which appears to be replacing copra production in some of the islands. However, with increased income from other sources, the demand for local fruits, vegetables and livestock should increase, stimulating private production and providing needed diversity in diets. Similarly, there will be increased demand for small manufacturers and for general trade and services. While these would not be leading sectors, they could provide considerable scope for private sector development on a scale appropriate to Kiribati.

2.38   As noted at the outset, GDP growth in Kiribati has been volatile during most of the 1980s, and the level of real GDP has yet to recover to its level of 1979, when phosphate mining ceased. The medium-term projections presented in Table 2.5 are based primarily on the proposed expansion of fisheries production, further infrastructure investment, and planned developments in tourism. This could be supported by small-scale private sector development in agriculture, manufacturing and service activities. On this basis, the GDP growth rate is expected to rise from an average of 1.9 percent in 1985-89 to 3.3 percent in 1990-94 and subsequently to 4.5 percent in 1995-99. Higher growth rates are expected to result in the first instance from a substantial increase in fisheries output (10-15 percent growth per annum), which is largely the result of greater capacity along with mechanization and other efficiency improvements. Expansion in the fisheries sector is expected to boost export growth to 5 percent per annum in 1990-94 and to 8 percent per annum in 1995-99.

2.39   The manufacturing sector, which is in a rudimentary state, contributes merely 2.5 percent of GDP. This minor contribution underscores the heavy dependence of the economy on imports of manufactures and the considerable scope that exists for import substitution in basic consumer items. To encourage private manufacturing investment, the government has streamlined licensing procedures, and undertaken the construction of an industrial estate in South Tarawa, to facilitate setting up of plants by private entrepreneurs and by foreign investors. Nevertheless, there seems to be no scope for large-scale industrial expansion as the small domestic market limits the scale of production, while high transport costs offset cost advantages provided by cheap labor. A strategy of small scale, labor intensive manufacturing for the home market is expected to yield industrial growth of 6 percent during 1990-94 and 7 percent in 1995-99.

Table 2.5: MEDIUM-TERM PROJECTIONS, 1990-99

	Estimates 1985-89	Projections 1990-94	1995-99
Growth Rates (% per annum)			
GDP	1.9	3.3	4.5
Agriculture and Fisheries	1.5	3.5	5.0
Industry	4.0	6.0	7.0
Services	1.8	3.0	4.0
Consumption	1.0	2.5	3.0
Gross Investment	7.0	7.5	8.0
Exports	2.4	5.0	8.0
Imports	7.8	4.1	4.5
Prices	5.1	5.0	5.0
Ratios to GDP (%)			
Gross investment	30.8	35.8	40.0
Gross savings	53.5	..	..
Other Indicators			
Debt service (%)	1.4	1.5	1.5
Terms of trade	-11.8	..	..

Source: Kiribati Statistical Yearbook 1988 and World Bank estimates.

2.40   The potential of the service sector to generate growth and employment remained underutilized in the 1980s. The projected growth rate of 3-4 percent for services during 1990-99 is predicated upon expansion of transport and retail services and rapid growth in tourism.

2.41   A fundamental problem of the economy concerns its high level of consumption, relative to income and savings. A key to achieving self-reliance in the long-term would be to restrain private consumption, primarily through taxation, keeping it well below GDP. Such a strategy would increase tax revenues, raise national savings and also limit import growth in the 1990s to 4-4.5 percent per annum.

2.42   High rates of investment (of the order of 30 to 40 percent of GDP) will be necessary to restore growth in the 1990s. External donor support and continued remittance inflows will be required to sustain investment at this level.

Financial Requirements

2.43   The balance of payments projections may be recast as shown in Table 2.6 to present external requirements and sources of financing. On this basis, total financial requirements rise from US$23.5 million in 1985-89 to US$28.6 million in 1990-94 and to US$32.1 million in 1995-99. This secular rise in financial requirements is explained by the large projected deficits in the balance of trade which are only slightly offset by a small surplus on services. The principal source of financing is expected to be external grants which need to be sustained on the order of US$15-16 million a year. Kiribati has taken steps to eliminate the need for external grants to finance current budgetary expenditures while dependence on foreign aid is contained through RERF interest payments and private remittances.

Table 2.6: EXTERNAL FINANCING REQUIREMENTS AND SOURCES, 1990-99
(US$ million per annum at current prices)

	Estimate	Projections	
Requirements	1985-89	1990-94	1995-99
	(23.5)	(28.6)	(32.1)
Merchandise imports	18.1	24.9	28.0
Merchandise exports	-3.5	-5.2	-7.0
Principal repayments /a	-	0.2	0.3
Interest payments /a	0.1	0.2	0.3
Other service payments /b	4.8	6.0	7.5
Change in NFA	4.0	2.5	3.0
Sources			
	(23.5)	(28.6)	(32.1)
RERF interest	7.6	8.7	10.0
Private transfers	2.1	2.7	3.5
External grants	15.5	15.6	16.1
Public loan disbursements	0.4	0.6	1.0
Other capital (net)	-2.1	1.0	1.5

Source: World Bank staff estimates.

/a Public MLT debt only.
/b Excludes RERF interest.

D. Development Issues: Constraints, Problems and Prospects

2.44   The fundamental challenge of development in Kiribati is to mobilize its limited human and natural resources, to lay the groundwork for a supportive economic and social infrastructure, and to generate the maximum possible growth of productivity in the medium and longer-term. Although the National Development Plan for 1987-91 makes self-sufficiency a key objective, it is doubtful whether dependence upon aid can be reduced significantly, even over the medium-term. Indeed, such a policy may not be advisable; the outlook for aid in the 1990s appears favorable (a possible increase of 75 percent would be realistic) and aid receipts could go a long way to building the physical infrastructure that Kiribati needs, but is unable to finance out of its own resources. The prudent policy in this respect would be to channel aid into the development of infrastructure and other projects that would contribute to the economy's future growth potential so that self-reliance could become a feasible goal for the subsequent decade.

2.45   To protect the investments of previous years, there is the growing need for increased recurrent expenditure to cover the costs of operation and maintenance (O&M) of these investments. Without adequate provision for these costs from local budgetary resources, aid-financed projects and equipment will either be under-utilized or will have an unnecessarily short life-span. There is also a need to make projections of recurrent costs in order to support projected medium- and long-term investment levels.

Fiscal Strategy

2.46   Although the budgetary policy for the 1980s avoided major fiscal imbalances, it must be recognized that for much of the decade, deficits on current operations were also covered by external grants. It is commendable that since 1986, external grants were only applied to development expenditures, leaving current expenditures to be financed entirely from domestic resources. To support long-term growth, it will be necessary to expand the domestic revenue base through reform of tax administration and the introduction of user fees and new forms of taxation, possibly including a value added tax. Greater demands on current expenditures are expected as infrastructure and production projects are completed, increasing local O&M financing requirements.

2.47   The experience of the 1980s underscores the extreme vulnerability of the Kiribati economy, owing mainly to its narrow resource base. In such circumstances, the development of a self-reliant economy presents enormous challenges, which requires a concerted effort and firm commitment on the part of government. This commitment has been set out in the National Development Plan: 1987-91 (see Table 2.7). Quite appropriately, the development strategy embodied in this Plan attaches high priority to resource development, particularly natural resource exploitation. Indeed, forty percent--a doubling of its share in 1980-85--of total public investment is allocated for this purpose, much of which will go to the development of the fisheries sector. Infrastructure investment requirements have been scaled down somewhat in view of the large earlier outlays in this sector (over 50 percent of development expenditures, 1980-85). Nevertheless, a substantial allocation (19 percent) is made to transportation, underscoring the continuing emphasis accorded this vital aspect of infrastructural development. The projections of 3-4.5 percent GDP growth in the 1990s appear achievable in view of the planned emphasis on the most productive sector (fisheries) and higher productivity expected to accrue from past infrastructural investments.

2.48   Other salient features of the Plan include (a) promoting private sector participation in investment, (b) a greater emphasis on rural and outer island development through settlement and development of the Line Islands, (c) strengthening family planning activities, and (d) ensuring fiscal discipline, balance of payments stability, and limiting future debt-service liabilities. Although Plan objectives and emphasis appear commendable, the challenge is to translate them into effective programs and policies. Serious deficiencies still exist in project preparation, monitoring and implementation of investment programs. The coordinating role of the National Planning Office (NPO) needs to be strengthened and further training of personnel in developing a comprehensive project monitoring system would be in order.

Public Sector Efficiency

2.49   The public sector dominates the Kiribati economy, accounting for 95 percent of gross investment and almost half of total GDP. Although the central government has been prudent in the conduct of fiscal policies, the same cannot be said of some public enterprises whose recurring losses have been a heavy drain on the government's budget. Until 1985, government subsidies to public enterprises ran upwards of 10 percent of GDP before falling to around 5 percent in 1988 due to the cost overhauls at Air Tungaru.

Table 2.7: NATIONAL DEVELOPMENT PLAN, 1987-91: PLANNED EXPENDITURE ON CAPITAL PROJECTS /a

	1987	1988	1989	1990	1991	Total 1987-91	% share 1987-91	% share 1980-85 /b
Production	8.6	10.4	10.5	10.3	5.8	45.6	41.1	19.2
Agriculture	1.4	1.2	1.8	2.0	1.6	7.9	7.2	4.5
Fisheries	6.5	6.6	6.4	7.3	2.7	29.6	26.7	13.8
Industry, Commerce and others	0.7	2.6	2.3	1.0	1.5	8.1	7.3	1.4
Social Services	2.6	2.8	4.8	4.5	2.8	17.5	15.8	17.5
Health and Family Planning	0.4	0.6	2.9	2.4	0.6	6.8	6.2	3.5
Education and Training	1.6	1.5	1.4	1.7	1.8	8.1	7.4	11.5
Culture and Community Development	0.6	0.6	0.5	0.4	0.4	2.6	2.3	1.2
Infrastructure	7.3	8.4	4.4	7.7	6.9	34.7	31.4	54.6
Economic	3.6	6.7	2.8	5.7	4.7	23.6	21.2	41.3
Transport	2.9	6.1	2.7	5.3	4.3	21.2	19.2	23.3
Communications	0.7	0.6	0.1	0.4	0.4	2.3	2.0	23.8
Social	3.8	1.7	1.5	2.0	2.2	11.2	10.2	13.4
Housing, construction and lands	0.4	0.6	0.6	0.9	0.8	3.3	3.0	0.2
Energy, Water and Sanitation	3.3	1.2	0.9	1.1	1.4	7.9	7.1	11.4
Administration /c	2.2	2.6	2.5	2.8	2.9	12.9	11.6	8.6
Total	20.7	24.1	22.2	25.4	18.4	110.7	100.0	100.0

/a This table includes only expenditure on capital projects.
/b Subsector average shares are for 1983-85.
/c Includes expenditure of a developmental nature on central and outer-island administration.

Source: Kiribati National Development Plan, 1987-91.

Between 1979 and 1985, subsidies grew at a rate of 7.3 percent per annum, a rate faster than the growth of either recurrent expenditures or revenue collections. Other public enterprises requiring heavy subsidies include the Public Utilities Board (in charge of water supply, sewerage, and electricity), Telecom Kiribati, and the Housing Corporation.

2.50   The appropriate strategy for reducing these costs is to shrink the size of the public sector while encouraging greater private sector participation in investment and enterprise. Evidence of the government's commitment in this respect may be seen in the privatization of a major public enterprise (the Ambarka Trading Company); five more companies are slated for privatization (Air Tungaru, Betio Shipyard, Government Printing, Telecom Kiribati and Kiribati Oil Company). A preliminary assessment of some 40 enterprises for transfer of ownership (or management contract) has been drawn up by a special Cabinet committee. Nevertheless, overall progress on privatization has been slow and there is a need for sharply increased pace of privatization; private sector initiatives are being crowded out, removing the stimulus of competition from an already limited range of business opportunities. To achieve greater progress, the government should concentrate its efforts on two goals: (a) divest full or majority ownership of state enterprises (excepting natural monopolies) to private sector interests, domestic and/or foreign; and, (b) refuse to initiate new enterprises in direct competition with the private sector except where the supply of essential goods and services is inadequate. The government's role in creating an efficient and productive economy lies in the provision of the basic physical and human infrastructure and improving the overall policy environment for the private sector.

Human Resource Development

2.51   High on the Government's list of priorities will be the need to increase investment in human resource development through manpower planning and training in those skills that are in short supply. At present, there is an oversupply of clerical and administrative staff but a shortage of skilled and professional staff. Current pay scales and promotional prospects do not encourage higher education, causing senior professional posts to be filled by expatriates. Training programs should be initiated or stepped-up in areas of great demand. For example, there is a shortage of secondary school teachers yet there are only three higher education institutions: Tarawa Teacher's Training College; Marine Technical Institute; and, Tarawa Technical Institute (TTI). The latter and its Rural Training Center are the principal centers for technical and vocational training; for higher education, scholarships are provided by foreign governments (Australia, New Zealand and UK) and students can be enrolled in the University of South Pacific Extension Centre in Tarawa. Others seeking higher education attend the University of Papua New Guinea. Higher education, vocational training and skill development are areas where foreign aid and technical assistance are required.

REFERENCES

Coppers & Lybrand Consultants (1989), "Country Paper - Kiribati" (draft paper for the Pacific Islands Regional Economic Report).

C. Browne (1989) with D. Scott, "Economic Development in Seven Pacific Island Countries". (IMF).

World Bank (1988), "Kiribati - Economic Developments, Issues and Prospects", Report No. 6889-KIR, May 1988.

Kiribati, Sixth National Development Plan, 1987-91, National Planning Office, Ministry of Financial Economic Planning, Tarawa 1986.

Kiribati Statistical Yearbook 1988, Statistics Office, Ministry of Finance and Economic Planning, Tarawa, June 1989.

Kiribati, 1989 Estimates of Revenue and Expenditure, Ministry of Finance and Economic Planning, December 1988.

Kiribati, "Recent Economic Developments", IMF, June 1989.

Kiribati Statistical Appendix

List of Tables

TABLE 1.1: POPULATION ESTIMATES (MID YEAR), 1979-88

	1979	1980	1981	1982	1983	1984	1985	1986	1987	1988
Banaba	900	100	80	70	60	50	48	48	49	50
Makin	1,442	1,455	1,516	1,578	1,644	1,713	1,784	1,822	1,861	1,900
Butaritari	3,227	3,294	3,358	3,424	3,491	3,560	3,630	3,707	3,786	3,886
Marakei	2,392	2,432	2,483	2,535	2,588	2,643	2,698	2,755	2,814	2,873
Abaiang	3,528	3,594	3,743	3,898	4,159	4,227	4,403	4,496	4,592	4,689
N. Tarawa	2,265	2,282	2,445	2,621	2,809	3,011	3,227	3,295	3,365	3,437
S. Tarawa	18,616	19,409	19,799	20,197	20,603	21,017	21,439	21,894	22,359	22,833
Maiana	1,752	1,833	1,892	1,953	2,015	2,080	2,147	2,193	2,239	2,287
Abemama	2,467	2,506	2,593	2,684	2,778	2,875	2,976	3,039	3,104	3,170
Kuria	818	824	868	910	957	1,006	1,057	1,079	1,102	1,128
Aranuka	874	900	916	933	950	987	986	1,007	1,028	1,050
Nonouti	2,333	2,365	2,470	2,581	2,698	2,818	2,942	3,004	3,068	3,133
N. Tabiteuea	3,043	3,092	3,107	3,123	3,139	3,155	3,172	3,239	3,308	3,378
S. Tabiteuea	1,214	1,247	1,262	1,277	1,292	1,307	1,323	1,351	1,380	1,409
Beru	2,242	2,239	2,326	2,417	2,511	2,609	2,711	2,769	2,827	2,887
Nikunau	1,884	1,888	1,922	1,957	1,992	2,028	2,065	2,109	2,154	2,199
Onotoa	2,075	2,097	2,081	2,025	1,990	1,958	1,923	1,984	2,005	2,048
Tamana	1,368	1,371	1,372	1,374	1,375	1,376	1,378	1,407	1,437	1,468
Arorae	1,545	1,545	1,529	1,514	1,498	1,483	1,468	1,499	1,531	1,563
Total Gilberts	53,963	54,473	55,740	57,071	58,547	59,879	61,375	62,677	64,009	65,388
Washington	419	424	429	435	440	446	452	461	471	481
Fanning	435	438	438	440	441	443	445	454	463	473
Christmas	1,299	1,366	1,434	1,507	1,583	1,663	1,748	1,785	1,823	1,861
Total Line	2,153	2,225	2,301	2,382	2,464	2,552	2,645	2,700	2,757	2,815
Phoenix Group Other nes							24	25	26	28
Total Kiribati	56,116	56,698	58,041	59,453	61,011	62,431	64,044	65,402	66,792	68,207

Source: Data provided by Kiribati authorities.

Notes: (1) Estimates shown in this table take into account the repatriation of
353 Tuvaluans, about 400 expatriates (including Chinese Laborers)
and over one thousand I-Kiribati from Banaba when the British Phosphate
Commission ceased its mining operation in 1979. Of the I-Kiribati
repatriated 948 were assumed to return to their respective home islands
in 1979 and the remaining 400 in 1980. The islands growth rates
calculated from the adjusted 1980 population and the 1985 figures are
then used to derive the intervening years' estimates. For 1986 onwards
a growth rate of 2.1% is used for all the islands.

(2) Note the 1985 figures are slightly higher than the 1985 census figures
because of the mid-year estimate adjustments.

TABLE 1.2: ACTIVITY STATUS OF THE INDIGENOUS POPULATION (15 YEARS & OVER)
BY SEX AND ISLAND, 1985

	MALE				FEMALE				TOTAL			
	Cash employ-ment	Village work	Home duties	Unem-ployed	Cash employ-ment	Village work	Home duties	Unem-ployed	Cash employ-ment	Village work	Home duties	Unem-ployed
Banaba	10	1	-	-	2	11	-	-	12	12	-	-
Makin	63	373	7	-	20	44	442	-	83	417	449	-
Butaritari	185	745	5	-	45	926	38	-	230	1,671	41	-
Marakei	89	581	2	5	27	633	78	1	116	1,214	80	6
Abaiang	194	850	6	2	47	167	911	1	241	1,017	917	3
N. Tarawa	90	718	14	-	28	736	117	2	118	1,454	131	2
Maiana	88	521	-	2	21	614	10	-	109	1,135	10	2
Abemama	133	600	11	-	52	597	187	-	185	1,197	198	-
Kuria	40	241	2	-	10	8	276	-	50	249	278	-
Aranuka	62	187	-	-	14	291	1	-	76	478	1	-
Nonouti	143	832	3	-	41	27	777	-	184	659	780	-
N. Tabiteuea	125	721	29	1	32	525	439	-	157	1,246	468	1
S. Tabiteuea	77	280	8	1	14	246	116	-	91	528	122	1
Beru	122	651	4	1	40	18	715	-	182	669	719	1
Nikunau	76	506	15	-	17	186	429	-	93	692	444	-
Onotoa	65	492	2	-	27	92	533	-	92	584	535	-
Tamana	57	346	2	3	22	170	303	8	79	516	305	11
Arorae	45	431	2	-	19	5	494	-	64	436	496	-
Outer Island	1,664	8,876	110	15	478	5,296	5,864	12	2,142	14,172	5,974	27
S. Tarawa	2,907	2,163	115	397	1,169	2,164	2,302	199	4,076	4,327	2,417	596
Washington	-	-	1	-	-	-	103	-	-	-	104	-
Fanning	104	18	4	-	3	1	311	-	107	19	315	-
Christmas	383	108	1	-	56	69	6	1	439	177	7	1
Canton	4	1	-	1	1	-	-	-	5	1	-	1
Outer Island	5,062	11,186	231	413	1,707	7,530	8,586	212	6,789	18,696	8,817	625

Source: 1985 Population Census.

Notes: (1) A significant proportion of those in 'cash employment' are wage and salary earners.

(2) Village work includes subsistence activities like fishing, cutting toddy, etc.

(3) The definition of un-employed here may be different from those adopted by other countries. Not included are the disabled, jail-inmates, students, old age persons, etc.

TABLE 1.3: CASH EMPLOYMENT BY INDUSTRY, SEX AND AGE GROUP, 1985

	Male					Female					Total
	15-24	25-34	35-49	50+	Total	15-24	25-34	35-49	50+	Total	
Agriculture & Fishing	159	160	115	33	487	3	6	3	2	14	481
Mining	5	3	5	1	14	-	-	-	-	-	14
Manufacturing	5	30	38	3	76	7	10	25	14	56	132
Electricity & Water	17	92	97	5	211	10	9	2	-	21	232
Construction	58	163	168	37	424	5	10	1	-	16	440
Distributive Trade	116	217	288	155	754	129	138	84	24	373	1,127
Transport & Communication	212	393	278	39	922	50	53	24	1	128	1,050
Finance Service	9	20	20	4	53	21	18	1	-	40	93
Public Administration	127	487	472	162	1,248	111	161	65	18	353	1,601
Education	43	135	187	11	378	94	162	52	3	311	687
Health	10	31	47	5	93	41	97	52	1	191	284
Other Services	77	157	248	115	595	88	80	49	38	255	850
TOTAL	836	1,888	1,939	570	5,233	559	742	358	99	1,758	8,991

Source: 1985 Population Census

TABLE 2.1: GROSS DOMESTIC PRODUCT BY ECONOMIC ACTIVITY, 1979-1989
(A$'000 at current prices)

	1979	1980	1981	1982	1983	1984	1985	1986	1987	1988	1989 Est.
Agriculture	6,694	4,860	6,823	7,393	9,053	12,083	8,939	7,561	6,600	11,550	10,939
Copra	3,385	1,167	2,242	1,982	2,304	5,223	2,764	-242	1,250	4,070	2,500
Fishing	897	1,115	1,467	1,798	2,925	2,920	2,040	3,500	950	3,000	3,870
Non-monetary	2,412	2,578	3,114	3,613	3,824	3,940	4,135	4,303	4,400	4,480	4,569
Phosphate mining	15,031	-	-	-	-	-	-	-	-	-	-
Manufacturing	494	494	535	572	649	670	705	723	761	760	836
Monetary	244	229	232	218	224	214	183	170	180	180	..
Non-monetary	250	265	303	354	425	456	522	553	581	580	..
Electricity & water	473	289	356	358	595	763	797	732	760	769	775
Construction	1,214	1,330	1,480	1,510	1,417	1,379	1,607	2,227	1,980	1,600	1,760
Monetary	1,018	1,100	1,226	1,237	1,108	1,044	1,205	1,745	1,400	..	..
Non-monetary	196	230	254	273	309	335	402	482	580	..	..
Trade and Hotels	2,533	3,687	3,884	4,886	3,902	4,251	4,439	4,634	5,000	5,500	6,050
Transport, Communication	2,234	3,908	3,862	6,278	5,600	4,683	5,341	5,727	5,750	6,100	6,344
Transport	1,823	3,480	3,487	5,837	5,054	4,237	4,653	4,775	4,794	5,086	..
Communications	411	428	375	441	546	446	688	952	956	1,014	..
Finance, Insurance	178	135	628	686	619	877	1,470	1,932	1,980	2,000	2,400
Real estate	121	112	152	108	234	-21	251	265	270	280	a/
Owner-occupied dwelling	358	390	427	473	542	580	645	687	700	710	1,010
Government	6,598	7,938	7,301	7,355	8,129	7,962	8,351	8,837	9,530	10,470	11,276
Community services	364	398	455	703	767	714	836	1,040	1,093	1,148	1,205
less											
imputed bank charges	-114	-111	-572	-643	-496	-832	-1211	-1602	-1850	-1900	-2280
GDP (at factor cost)	36,178	23,430	25,331	29,679	31,011	33,109	32,170	32,763	32,574	38,987	40,315
Indirect taxes	4,085	3,925	3,992	3,960	3,850	3,996	4,360	4,980	5,700	5,000	5,100
less subsidies	-2136	-2821	-3818	-4906	-4632	-3570	-3733	-1800	-1400	-1400	-700
GDP (at market prices)	38,127	24,534	25,505	28,733	30,229	33,535	32,797	35,943	36,874	42,587	44,715
of which:											
Monetary GDP	34,911	21,071	21,407	24,020	25,129	28,224	27,093	29,918	30,613	36,047	38,046
Non-monetary GDP	3,216	3,463	4,098	4,713	5,100	5,311	5,704	6,025	6,261	6,540	6,669

Source: Data provided by Kiribati authorities and staff estimates.

a/ Included in "Owner-occupied dwelling".

Note: The BPC phosphate mine in Banaba ceased operating in 1979.

TABLE 2.2: GROSS DOMESTIC PRODUCT BY INCOME AND EXPENDITURE, 1979-88
(A$'000 at current prices)

	1979	1980	1981	1982	1983	1984	1985	1986	1987	1988
Compensation of employees										
local salary & wages	15,040	13,008	13,548	14,194	15,258	15,263	16,152	16,704	17,500	18,000
expatriate supplements	836	1,478	1,114	1,284	1,350	1,056	1,141	1,735	1,800	1,500
Operating surplus										
monetary	15,616	3,981	4,560	6,852	6,414	8,001	5,252	4,135	2,813	9,858
non-monetary	3,218	3,463	4,098	4,713	5,100	5,711	5,704	6,025	6,281	6,372
Consumption of fixed capital	1,471	1,501	2,009	2,655	2,890	3,076	3,919	4,168	4,400	5,200
Indirect taxes	4,085	3,925	3,992	3,960	3,850	3,998	4,360	4,980	5,700	5,400
less subsidies	-2136	-2821	-3818	-4906	-4632	-3570	-3733	-1800	-1400	-1200
Gross Domestic Product	38,128	24,533	25,503	28,732	30,230	33,533	32,795	35,947	36,874	44,930
Final Consumption Expenditure of Households										
monetary	17,495	18,603	18,554	19,735	19,562	20,624	21,589	22,836	23,000	23,500
non-monetary	3,338	3,601	4,259	4,894	5,305	5,930	5,930	6,262	6,500	6,700
General Government	11,741	14,521	14,775	14,894	16,419	16,409	18,432	19,164	20,540	20,800
Private Non-Profit agencies	453	507	569	1,108	1,240	1,254	1,447	1,785	2,000	2,500
Gross Fixed Capital formation	4,782	6,815	12,583	12,401	8,714	6,636	10,260	11,979	11,000	12,000
Increase in Stocks	812	1,309	88	1,343	575	-100	82	263	300	500
Gross Resident Expenditure	38,601	45,356	50,826	54,375	51,815	50,753	57,720	62,289	63,340	66,000
Exports of goods & services	23,366	5,750	7,597	8,405	8,690	16,797	12,034	7,963	8,314	11,420
less										
Imports of goods & services	-22721	-27037	-31280	-32732	-30228	-33571	-35303	-36047	-36000	-34000
Errors & Omissions	-1118	484	-1660	-1316	-49	-446	-1658	1742	1220	1510
Expenditure on GDP	38,128	24,533	25,503	28,732	30,230	33,533	32,795	35,947	36,874	44,930

Source: Data provided by Kiribati authorities and staff estimates.

Note: Errors and omissions is the balancing item in the two approaches, i.e. GDP by income method versus the expenditure approach.

TABLE 2.3: INVESTMENT AND SAVINGS, 1979-88
(A$'000)

	1979	1980	1981	1982	1983	1984	1985	1986	1987	1988
Gross Fixed Capital Formation										
Private Sector	400	858	758	570	410	537	477	885	800	600
Public Enterprises	788	374	6,089	10,711	6,819	3,513	6,977	1,417		
General Government	3,574	5,785	5,738	1,121	1,683	2,586	2,806	9,697	10,200	11,400
Increase in Stocks	812	1,309	88	1,343	575	-100	62	263	300	500
Net lending to ROW a/	16,793	2,392	-915	-1854	6,742	13,555	18,443	20,148	21,378	22,355
Gross Accumulation	22,367	10,516	11,754	11,891	16,029	20,091	28,765	32,390	32,678	34,855
Savings	15,084	3,333	1,673	2,886	5,970	7,643	14,354	19,751	16,065	18,025
Consumption of fixed capital	1,471	1,501	2,009	2,855	2,890	3,078	3,919	4,188	4,400	5,200
Capital transfers from ROW, net	4,714	6,146	6,412	5,034	7,120	8,928	8,836	10,213	13,433	13,140
Errors and Omissions	1,118	-484	1,660	1,316	49	446	1658	-1742	-1220	-1510
TOTAL FINANCE	22,367	10,516	11,754	11,891	16,029	20,091	28,765	32,390	32,678	34,855

Source: Data provided by Kiribati authorities.

a/ Derived as a residual.

TABLE 3.1: CENTRAL GOVERNMENT BUDGET, 1979-88
(A$'000)

	1979	1980	1981	1982	1983	1984	1985	1986	1987	1988
Recurrent revenue	17,849	16,769	17,039	16,356	16,965	15,783	19,124	13,740	18,053	18,560
Development revenue	5,622	4,615	4,031	3,789	4,313	3,596	1,965	1,812	4,315	6,387
TOTAL REVENUE	23,271	21,384	21,070	20,145	21,278	19,379	21,089	15,552	22,368	24,947
Recurrent expenditure	15,632	14,363	17,978	18,016	16,439	15,738	16,815	16,635	17,833	18,029
Development expenditure 1/	3,365	4,804	5,188	5,057	5,382	3,796	1,111	1,731	2,336	3,405
TOTAL EXPENDITURE	18,997	19,167	23,164	21,073	21,821	19,534	17,926	18,366	20,169	21,434
Recurrent balance	2,017	2,406	-939	340	528	45	2,309	-2895	220	531
Development balance	2,257	-189	-1155	-1268	-1089	-200	854	81	1,979	2,982
OVERALL BALANCE	4,274	2,217	-2094	-928	-543	-155	3,163	-2814	2,199	3,513

Source: Central Government Accounts.

1/ Excludes aid in-kind and other aid flows going directly to the project implementing agency.

TABLE 3.2: CENTRAL GOVERNMENT REVENUE AND GRANTS, 1979-88
(A$'000)

	1979	1980	1981	1982	1983	1984	1985	1986	1987	1988
Direct tax										
Personal	1,284	909	793	747	1,067	954	1,038	1,180	1,215	1,232
Company	45	111	128	273	211	100	184	401	1,144	984
Indirect tax										
Import duty	3,315	3,380	3,483	3,428	3,299	3,472	3,739	4,023	5,124	4,837
Export duty	47	77	4	2	15	-	-	-	-	-
Licences	88	13	11	15	18	10	11	12	38	3
Hotel tax	-	-	-	-	-	-	28	43	72	20
TAX REVENUE	4,759	4,490	4,417	4,465	4,610	4,536	4,952	5,618	7,519	7,058
Entrepreneurial Income										
House rent	144	248	201	-	1	1	19	58	-	-
Philatelic sales	457	489	590	1,047	-	2	2	-	-	-
Shipyard sales	107	147	191	66	145	37	-	-	-	-
Telecom	112	136	151	183	171	243	-	-	-	-
Fish sales	36	121	33	73	57	22	26	47	219	44
PWD income	254	370	307	221	500	361	184	20	28	33
Property Income										
Phosphate tax	8,354	1,669	-	-	-	-	-	-	-	-
Fish licence	614	618	1,255	-	983	1,930	3,105	3,760	2,149	2,449
RERF drawdown	-	4,250	5,751	4,750	5,500	5,500	7,700	2,800	5,002	8,000
Interest received	286	801	455	428	265	133	375	393	161	35
Bank of Kiribati	-	-	-	-	-	-	22	83	148	96
Administrative Fees, Charges										
Aircraft landing fees	47	6	30	-	-	2	-	-	-	-
School fees	90	90	104	108	104	103	98	97	96	102
Nasda contribution	154	241	275	318	223	830	229	104	290	-
Other	2,152	1,097	1,148	1,087	906	509	901	721	2,371	725
Grants										
UK budgetary aid	-	2,000	2,017	3,500	3,500	1,774	1,485	-	-	-
Stabex drawdown	103	-	114	114	-	-	-	-	-	-
TOTAL REVENUE	17,649	18,769	17,039	16,358	16,965	15,783	19,098	13,697	17,981	18,540

Source: Data provided by Kiribati authorities.

Notes: (1) The significant decline in the 'Entrepreneurial' income since 1985 resulted when the
respective divisions became self-accounting organisations.

(2) Stabex drawdown is used for copra freight subsidy.

(3) Included in 'other' in 1987 is the fine of $1.35 million paid for the release of
a confiscated overseas purse seiner vessel.

TABLE 3.3: CENTRAL GOVERNMENT RECURRENT EXPENDITURE: 1979-88
(A$'000)

	1979	1980	1981	1982	1983	1984	1985	1986	1987	1988
Salaries	3,988	4,398	4,387	4,156	4,972	5,277	5,397	5,497	5,927	6,281
Wages	1,543	914	916	813	702	473	448	460	439	343
Allowances	308	377	361	238	288	319	337	288	334	466
Overtime	129	273	205	183	180	299	212	223	349	344
Provident fund	381	322	288	310	325	313	402	223	304	251
Pensions & gratuities	155	189	135	139	169	179	105	88	128	88
Land rents	37	78	345	238	218	212	229	221	248	252
Water supplies	335	331	330	330	330	330	280	230	180	130
S. Tarawa sewerage	-	6	-	96	139	139	140	140	200	310
Maintenance of government housing	898	505	508	473	380	280	380	315	148	98
Other subsidies	784	1,493	1,253	1,896	1,184	696	1,189	546	186	
Outer islands grant	58	112	151	230	258	253	257	297	343	366
Transfers to non-profit institutions	38	38	41	66	75	58	71	72	80	84
Transfers to household	109	26	14	39	385	3	25	94	19	40
Trasfers abroad	143	271	377	179	362	268	166	579	393	251
Office expense	134	134	148	164	163	179	199	323	319	333
Travelling	953	1,120	1,277	1,412	1,198	1,401	1,581	1,874	1,616	1,695
Hire of vehicles	4	748	1,174	865	1,006	1,057	1,288	825	1,023	628
Overseas travel	65	103	124	132	98	135	196	197	171	308
Utilities	161	325	405	529	556	528	507	569	468	522
Others n.e.c.	5,815	2,802	5,559	3,530	3,473	3,343	3,406	3,574	4,958	5,241
TOTAL	15,632	14,363	17,978	16,016	16,439	15,738	16,815	16,635	17,833	18,029

Source: Data provided by Kiribati authorities.

Notes: (1) Magistrate's sitting allowance, volunteer assistance and special constabulary payments all included in 'allowances'.

(2) Government contributes half of its employees total provident fund payments to the Kiribati Provident Fund (KPF).

(3) 'Furniture for houses' expenditure is included with 'maintenance of government housing'.

TABLE 4.1: BANK OF KIRIBATI'S INTEREST RATES AS OF DECEMBER, 1979-1989
(percent)

	1979	1980	1981	1982	1983	1984	1985	1986	1987	1988	1989
LENDING											
Secured	..	..	..	10.50	10.50	12.00	12.00	12.00	12.00	12.00	12.00
Unsecured	..	..	..	10.50	10.50	13.00	13.00	13.00	13.00	13.00	13.00
IBD'S < 50000											
3-6 months	..	..	..	7.00	7.00	6.00	6.00	6.00	..	..	..
6-12 months	..	..	..	7.25	7.25	7.00	7.00	7.00	7.50	7.50	8.00
12-24 months	..	..	..	7.50	7.50	8.00	8.00	8.00	8.50	8.50	8.50
IBD'S > 50000											
7 days	..	..	..	..	..	9.00	14.00	13.75	9.12	11.50	14.30
14 days	..	..	..	..	..	9.00	14.00	13.75	9.12	11.80	14.50
1 month	..	..	..	..	..	9.37	15.81	14.27	10.15	12.53	15.10
2 months	..	..	..	..	..	10.45	16.44	14.21	10.27	12.75	15.20
3 months	..	..	..	..	..	10.37	16.62	14.09	10.52	12.91	15.40
6 months	..	..	..	..	..	11.12	16.19	14.15	11.12	13.38	15.60
Savings a/c	..	..	..	4.00	4.25	5.00	5.00	5.00	5.00	5.50	5.50
Island a/c	-	-	-	-	-	-	-	-	6.50	6.50	7.00

Source: Data provided by Kiribati authorities.

Note: Sometimes funds are lodged with Westpac, Sydney on behalf of the customers.

TABLE 4.2: INDEX OF CONSUMER PRICES, 1979-89
(annual average percentage change)

	Food 500	Alcohol & Tobacco 140	Clothing 80	Transport 80	Housing & Household 75	Misc. 125	All Items 1,000
1979	6.1	17.1	3.7	1.3	5.1	4.9	6.5
1980	15.7	20.4	14.3	15.2	21.3	3.3	16.1
1981	6.8	0.6	8.7	24.7	14.0	6.5	7.7
1982	3.7	10.4	4.7	8.9	9.6	5.1	5.5
1983	3.5	14.5	3.9	7.5	11.4	4.4	6.3
1984	4.6	5.1	8.9	1.2	10.4	6.0	5.4
1985	4.2	3.5	14.0	11.3	2.5	2.6	4.5
1986	7.3	8.0	1.6	10.3	4.8	7.1	6.6
1987	6.0	4.0	6.0	3.1	14.9	1.5	6.5
1988	4.1	2.6	7.4	0.5	-7.5	-1.6	3.1
1989	3.9	0.4	4.9	5.3	8.9	15.7	3.9

Source: Data provided by Kiribati authorities.

TABLE 4.3: AVERAGE AUSTRALIAN DOLLAR EXCHANGE RATE (AVERAGE MID RATE) 1979-1988

	US $	UK $	DM	YEN	DUTCH GUILDER	NZ $	ECU	FRENCH FRANC	CANADIAN
1979	1.1179	0.5276	2.0490	244.6395	2.2421	1.0936	0.8123	4.7921	1.3095
1980	1.1395	0.4897	2.0695	257.6358	2.2620	1.1699	0.8110	4.8105	1.3320
1981	1.1494	0.5704	2.5924	252.9679	2.8620	1.3242	0.0178	6.2274	1.3774
1982	1.0173	0.5802	2.4627	252.3722	2.7091	1.3522	1.0356	6.6491	1.2537
1983	0.9025	0.5942	2.2991	213.9210	2.5678	1.3485	1.0139	6.8508	1.1111
1984	0.8782	0.6568	2.4890	207.9622	2.8050	1.5352	1.1152	7.6383	1.1341
1985	0.6988	0.5450	2.0567	166.6529	2.3189	1.4080	0.9404	6.2705	0.9515
1986	0.6681	0.4547	1.4538	112.8294	1.6376	1.2863	0.8908	4.6197	0.9287
1987	0.6977	0.4261	1.2529	100.7229	1.4093	1.1782	0.6074	4.1826	0.9234
1988	0.8475	0.4793	1.5491	113.7083	...	1.1994	...	...	1.1101

Source: IMF, IFS.

TABLE 5.1: BALANCE OF PAYMENTS, 1979-88
(A$ million)

	1979	1980	1981	1982	1983	1984	1985	1986	1987	1988
Exports, f.o.b.	22.0	2.6	3.6	2.4	4.0	12.5	6.1	2.5	2.9	6.6
Imports, f.o.b.	15.7	18.3	22.8	22.8	19.8	20.9	21.6	21.5	25.1	27.5
Trade Balance	6.3	-15.7	-19.2	-20.4	-15.8	-8.4	-15.5	-19.0	-22.2	-20.9
Services (net)	-0.8	-2.2	-2.4	-2.5	-3.4	0.1	1.3	9.2	4.4	4.0
Receipts	7.6	9.1	12.5	12.0	12.8	15.2	18.4	26.4	24.6	23.7
of which RERF Interest	4.7	4.3	5.8	4.8	5.5	6.7	5.5	10.9	11.1	11.7
Payments	8.2	11.3	14.9	14.6	16.0	15.1	17.1	17.2	20.2	19.6
Private transfers, net	-0.1	-0.1	1.2	1.8	1.3	1.5	1.3	2.4	3.1	3.4
Official transfers	9.6	15.1	18.7	13.8	18.4	16.2	17.8	22.0	23.4	21.1
Current Balance	15.2	-2.9	-3.7	-7.3	0.7	9.4	4.9	14.6	8.7	7.6
Capital balance	-2.5	-1.4	2.1	-0.4	-2.8	2.2	-1.0	-1.4	-5.0	-5.5
Borrowing, net	0.3	0.0	1.5	-0.1	-0.3	-1.3	0.0	0.1	0.7	-0.3
Stabex accounts abroad	-1.7	-0.7	0.9	0.4	-0.9	3.3	0.0	0.0	-3.1	1.9
Non-bank finance institutions	-1.4	-0.7	-0.3	-0.7	-1.6	-0.7	-0.9	-1.8	-2.5	-6.4
Others	0.3	0.0	0.0	0.0	0.0	-0.2	-0.1	0.3	0.0	-0.7
Errors and Omissions	..	4.7	-0.8	6.4	5.8	1.2	3.0	-5.6	4.6	-2.7
Overall Balance	..	0.4	-2.4	-1.3	3.7	12.8	6.9	7.4	8.3	-0.6
Monetary Movements (increase in foreign assets)	..	-0.5	2.5	1.4	-3.6	-12.7	-8.8	-7.4	-8.2	0.6
Commercial bank	..	-0.5	2.5	1.4	-3.5	-11.5	-8.6	-0.5	-0.6	4.8
Monetary authorities	..	0.0	0.0	0.0	-0.1	-1.2	1.8	-6.9	-7.6	-4.2
Reserve Fund	..	0.0	0.0	0.0	-0.2	-1.2	2.2	-7.1	-7.1	-4.7
Government foreign accounts	..	..	..	0.1	0.1	0.0	-0.4	0.2	-0.5	0.5
Reserve position in the IMF	..	0.0	0.0	0.0	0.0	0.0	0.0	-1.0	1.0	0.0

Source: Data provided by Kiribati authorities.

Note: Entries for the Reserve Fund are defined as interest receipts minus withdrawals for
budgetary purposes, and changes arising from transactions with the IMF in 1986-87.

TABLE 5.2: EXPORTS BY COMMODITY: 1979-89
(US$'000)

	1979	1980	1981	1982	1983	1984	1985	1986	1987	1988	1989
Phosphate	20,070	--	--	--	--	--	--	--	--	--	--
Copra	4,118	2,474	3,032	1,479	1,947	6,146	3,306	308	822	3,279	2,474
Handicrafts	7	3	3	2	1	4	6	2	2	..	..
Shark fins	28	22	17	31	16	43	25	15	11	13	38
Fish	169	215	806	524	1,356	1,511	713	1,191	577	1,196	1,551
Other domestic nes	22	23	23	17	8	9	8	23	72	67	90
Domestic Exports	24,414	2,737	3,881	2,053	3,329	7,712	4,058	1,539	1,485	4,542	4,153
Re-exports	224	228	230	341	284	3,243	186	136	526	605	692
TOTAL EXPORTS	24,637	2,965	4,111	2,394	3,613	10,955	4,244	1,675	2,011	5,147	4,845

Source: Data provided by Kiribati authorities and staff estimates.

TABLE 5.3: DOMESTIC EXPORTS BY DESTINATION, 1979–88
(A$'000)

	1979	1980	1981	1982	1983	1984	1985	1986	1987	1988
OCEANIA										
Australia	10,077	19	15	31	18	50	38	22	108	15
New Zealand	7,876	-	-	-	6	2	6	28	56	13
Fiji	254	116	74	211	247	2	202	1,140	451	1,356
Marshalls	179	-	407	321	51	1,668	710	32	1	5
A. Samoa	-	-	-	281	1,133	1,489	245	140	-	-
Tonga	-	-	-	-	-	-	-	-	131	144
Other	157	50	46	70	143	721	209	22	10	11
TOTAL OCEANIA	18,543	185	542	914	1,598	3,932	1,410	1,384	757	1,544
ASIA										
Japan	50	487	36	887	239	-	101	-	-	-
Other	25	347	524	-	-	2	1,171	-	1	3
TOTAL ASIA	75	834	560	887	239	2	1,272	-	1	3
AMERICAS										
USA	51	121	619	216	371	230	484	481	324	247
TOTAL AMERICAS	51	121	619	216	371	230	484	481	324	247
EEC										
Denmark	-	778	-	-	1,482	4,604	-	-	-	-
W. Germany	817	-	-	-	-	-	1,161	-	-	-
Netherlands	1,478	-	-	-	-	-	-	161	1,037	4,054
Other EEC	2	1	-	-	-	-	-	-	-	-
TOTAL EEC	2,297	779	-	-	1,482	4,604	1,161	161	1,037	4,054
OTHER nes	871	483	1,657	-	-	-	1,469	268	-	-
GRAND TOTAL	21,837	2,402	3,378	2,017	3,690	8,768	5,796	2,294	2,119	5,848

Source: Data provided by Kiribati authorities.

Note: Exports to Fiji consist mainly of fresh tuna from Te Mautari Ltd.
– the national fishing company.

TABLE 5.4: IMPORTS BY COUNTRY OF ORIGIN, 1979-88
(A$'000)

	1979	1980	1981	1982	1983	1984	1985	1986	1987	1988
Australia	9,097	10,774	10,961	9,639	9,120	8,490	8,366	8,683	10,983	12,352
New Zealand	983	882	1,108	1,682	2,316	2,141	1,376	1,065	1,819	1,382
Fiji	1,034	858	1,579	1,563	1,269	1,692	1,322	2,543	1,833	4,313
Other	616	255	584	351	383	1,498	2,101	1,891	2,256	1,570
TOTAL OCEANIA	11,730	12,769	14,210	13,235	13,088	13,819	13,165	14,182	16,891	19,617
Japan	924	2,480	2,682	3,995	3,572	3,478	4,566	4,155	2,980	3,088
Hong Kong	497	321	305	316	363	354	422	421	724	810
China	-	119	223	231	396	410	780	591	1,121	1,473
Other	245	278	183	173	205	274	575	461	1,051	848
TOTAL ASIA	1,666	3,198	3,393	4,715	4,525	4,514	6,343	5,628	5,876	6,217
USA	694	1,226	4,255	2,239	1,285	548	560	698	1,076	1,356
Other	231	85	10	5	4	6	3	95	142	22
TOTAL AMERICAS	925	1,311	4,265	2,244	1,289	554	563	793	1,218	1,378
UK	1,261	947	906	560	622	899	1,192	570	281	427
Other	100	27	35	48	79	1,067	150	188	137	503
TOTAL EEC	1,361	974	941	606	701	1,966	1,342	758	418	930
Other countries nes	69	11	22	1,974	22	24	169	91	740	43
GRAND TOTAL	15,751	18,263	22,831	22,774	19,605	20,877	21,582	21,452	25,143	28,185

Source: Data provided by Kiribati authorities.

TABLE 5.5: IMPORTS OF MAJOR COMMODITIES, 1983-89
(US$ million)

	1983	1984	1985	1986	1987	1988	1989
Food and Live Animals	4.64	4.95	4.18	3.81	5.46	6.11	6.97
Beverages and Tobacco	1.04	0.99	0.73	0.83	1.07	1.25	1.20
Crude Materials	0.47	0.24	0.13	0.22	0.18	0.62	0.35
Mineral Fuels	2.28	2.72	2.26	1.50	1.87	1.92	2.53
Animal and Vegetable Oil and Fats	0.02	0.03	0.02	0.01	0.03	0.03	0.10
Chemicals	0.74	0.96	0.76	0.76	0.88	1.32	1.88
Manufactured Goods	3.05	1.91	1.44	2.96	2.55	2.90	2.35
Machinery and Transport Equipment	4.01	5.33	4.46	2.85	3.66	5.75	5.38
Miscellaneous Manufactured Articles	1.37	1.16	1.00	1.31	1.72	1.55	1.86
Other Miscellaneous	0.10	0.08	0.14	0.11	0.21	0.09	0.21
Total	17.70	18.37	15.13	14.37	17.62	21.54	22.83

Source: Data provided by Kiribati authorities and staff estimates.

Table 6.1: EXTERNAL GRANTS AND LOANS, 1982-89
(In millions of US$)

	1982	1983	1984	1985	1986	1987	1988	1989 Est.
United Kingdom	8.5	9.0	5.2	4.9	3.5	3.7	2.4	2.4
Budgetary grant	3.5	3.2	1.5	1.0	--	--	--	--
Project aid	1.9	3.2	1.9	1.3	0.8	1.2	1.1	1.0
Technical assistance	3.2	2.6	1.7	2.4	2.7	2.7	1.5	1.3
Australia	2.3	2.0	2.5	1.6	1.9	1.8	2.0	4.9
Sewage project	1.1	0.4	0.1	--	--	--	--	--
Water project	--	0.5	1.0	1.0	1.3	1.2	0.3	1.2
Other aid	1.1	0.9	0.9	0.4	0.5	0.5	0.9	3.1
Bank of Kiribati equity loan	--	--	0.3	--	--	--	--	--
Defense cooperation program	--	--	--	--	--	--	0.5	0.1
Technical assistance	0.1	0.1	0.1	0.1	0.1	0.3	0.3	0.5
New Zealand	0.4	0.4	0.5	0.8	1.6	1.8	1.7	1.8
Of which: Technical assistance	--	--	--	--	0.1	0.1	0.3	0.3
Japan	1.1	2.1	1.4	2.5	4.2	3.6	1.6	2.6
Fishing vessels	--	1.2	1.3	2.1	--	--	--	--
Cold storage facilities	0.7	0.7	--	--	--	--	1.5	0.6
Causeway	--	--	--	--	3.9	3.1	--	--
Other	0.3	0.2	--	0.3	0.2	0.4	--	1.5
Technical assistance	0.1	0.1	0.1	0.1	0.1	0.1	0.1	0.4
European Community	0.3	1.5	2.2	0.7	0.8	2.1	3.6	0.3
Direct	0.3	0.6	0.9	0.6	0.7	0.1	2.7	0.3
Regional	--	--	1.2	--	0.1	0.1	0.0	--
STABEX	--	0.9	--	0.1	--	1.8	0.8	--
Training	--	--	--	--	--	--	--	--
Asian Development Bank	0.2	0.2	0.4	0.4	0.5	1.0	0.9	0.5
Loans	--	--	--	0.2	0.2	0.6	0.8	0.4
Technical assistance	0.2	0.2	0.4	0.2	0.2	0.4	0.1	0.1
Other	1.1	1.5	1.9	1.5	2.1	2.2	3.4	4.5
WHO	0.3	0.3	0.3	0.3	0.2	0.3	0.3	0.3
UNDP/UNFPA/UNICEF	0.1	0.1	0.2	0.1	0.4	0.5	0.9	1.4
Save the Children/FSP	0.2	0.3	0.3	0.3	0.4	0.4	--	0.1
Canada/Fed. Rep. of Germany	0.3	0.3	0.4	0.3	0.4	0.4	0.3	0.4
China	--	--	0.3	0.1	0.2	0.3	--	--
France/Korea	--	--	--	--	--	--	--	0.1
SPC/SPEC/ESCAP	0.1	0.2	0.2	0.2	0.2	0.3	0.1	0.1
USAID/Peace Corps	0.1	0.3	0.3	0.2	0.4	0.3	0.4	0.8
Others	--	--	--	--	--	--	1.2	1.3
Total	14.0	16.6	14.2	12.5	14.8	16.4	15.7	16.9
Memorandum items:								
Development expenditure 1/	6.5	8.9	9.6	7.7	11.0	10.2	11.4	13.1
Technical assistance	7.5	7.8	4.6	4.8	3.8	6.2	3.5	3.8

Source: Data provided by Kiribati authorities and staff estimates.

1/ Based on central government budget data.

Table 6.2: EXTERNAL ASSETS AND LIABILITIES , 1982-88
(In millions of SDRs)

	1982	1983	1984	1985	1986	1987	1988 Est.
Total external assets	84.43	92.41	103.97	108.17	117.19	128.41	139.88
RERF	74.49	77.63	82.00	85.92	95.96	105.63	111.95
Reserve position in the IMF	--	--	--	--	0.57	--	--
Government bank accounts abroad							
STABEX accounts abroad	2.13	2.87	--	--	--	1.60	0.79
Other 1/	0.17	0.11	0.09	0.31	0.18	0.40	0.19
National Provident Fund	3.73	5.00	5.49	4.59	5.00	5.96	11.51
Bank of Kiribati	3.91	6.81	16.38	17.36	15.49	14.82	15.45
External liabilities	1.80	1.60	1.70	1.34	1.05	1.30	1.17
Memorandum items:							
Reserve Fund							
Changes, net	9.57	3.14	4.37	3.92	10.04	9.67	6.32
Interest received	4.42	4.64	5.75	3.80	6.23	6.02	6.83
Valuation gains 2/	9.57	3.14	3.34	5.44	5.41	6.36	3.58
Transfer to the budget	-4.42	-4.64	-4.72	-5.31	-1.60	-2.71	-4.08
Outstanding amount							
Real value (1981=100) 3/	110.0	119.1	125.1	132.3	144.9	159.8	169.0
(in years of imports)	3.5	4.7	4.6	5.8	7.8	7.8	7.0
Currency composition							
U.S. dollars	24.18	22.83	26.43	20.15	19.67	13.75	26.38
Deutsche mark	10.93	10.17	9.71	19.46	27.61	18.95	13.79
Japanese yen	19.91	23.00	24.41	28.58	28.64	22.77	12.14
Pounds sterling	13.16	12.67	10.98	8.43	5.92	20.78	10.87
Australian dollars	6.31	9.05	9.37	9.42	13.64	17.62	25.30
Other	--	--	--	--	--	11.76	23.46
Portfolio							
Bonds	74.49	77.63	82.00	85.92	95.96	105.63	94.47
Equities	--	--	--	--	--	--	17.48
External debt service	--	0.34	0.12	0.25	0.26	0.22	0.23
(In percent of exports of goods and services)	--	2.50	0.50	1.50	1.60	1.50	1.30

Source: Data provided by Kiribati authorities and staff estimates.

1/ Consists of the Crown Agent Account, Coinage Account, and until 1987, Surplus Revenue Account.
2/ Including accrued interest not received, unrealized capital gains, and the effects
  of exchange rate changes.
3/ Deflated by prices of manufactured goods in industrial countries.

SOLOMON ISLANDS

DEVELOPMENT SURVEY

SOLOMON ISLANDS

CURRENCY EQUIVALENTS
Annual Averages

1981	$1 = SI$0.8702
1982	$1 = SI$0.9711
1983	$1 = SI$1.1486
1984	$1 = SI$1.2737
1985	$1 = SI$2.4808
1986	$1 = SI$1.7415
1987	$1 = SI$2.0033
1988	$1 = SI$2.0825
1989	$1 = SI$2.2932

FISCAL YEAR

January 1 to December 31

ABBREVIATIONS AND ACRONYMS

CDC	-	Commonwealth Development Corporation
CEMA	-	Commodities Export Marketing Authority
DBSI	-	Development Bank of Solomon Islands
EEC	-	European Economic Community
ICSI	-	Investment Corporation of Solomon Islands
LDA	-	Livestock Development Authority
MAL	-	Ministry of Agriculture and Lands
NFD	-	National Fisheries Development
SOE	-	State-owned enterprise
SIEA	-	Solomon Islands Electricity Authority
SIHA	-	Solomon Islands Housing Authority
SIPA	-	Solomon Islands Ports Authority
SIPL	-	Solomon Islands Plantations Ltd.
SOLAIR	-	Solomon Airlines
SOLRICE	-	Solomon Rice Company
SOLTEL	-	Solomon Telecom

Table of Contents

This report was prepared by a World Bank mission which visited Solomon Islands in December 1989. The mission members were Mark Baird, Paul Flanagan (AIDAB), Colin Pratt (consultant) and Bill Smith (consultant). A draft of the report was discussed with government officials in July 1990.

SOLOMON ISLANDS

DEVELOPMENT SURVEY

A. Background

3.1   Solomon Islands is an archipelago with a land area of 28,000 square kilometers spread across 1,500 kilometers of the South Pacific Ocean. The six main islands account for about 80 percent of the total land area and population. The population has grown rapidly by 3.5 percent per annum over the past decade and now exceeds 310,000. Internal migration has resulted in even higher rates of population growth in the capital city of Honiara and the surrounding areas of Guadalcanal. High population growth, in turn, has led to a rapid expansion of the labor force. As a result, basic wage rates are relatively low 1/ and unemployment is a problem around Honiara. Although there are encouraging signs that fertility is on the decline, this will not ease pressure on the labor market for the foreseeable future. Emigration opportunities are also limited. Hence, the priority for raising and sustaining economic growth.

3.2   About 10 percent of the population lives in Honiara. Most of the population lives in rural areas and is dependent upon agriculture for food and cash income. Including subsistence activities, agriculture accounts for about one-third of GDP. The major crops are coconut, cocoa and oil palm. In addition, Solomon Islands has a rich base of forestry and fishing resources. These two sectors account for about 10 percent of GDP and two-thirds of export earnings. There is also potential to develop mineral resources, including gold, bauxite and copper. Although the manufacturing sector has grown strongly in recent years, it is still small, accounting for only 4 percent of GDP and 6 percent of formal employment. Most manufacturing activity is based on the processing of primary products (including a new coconut mill and animal feed plant).2/ Transport and communications account for only 5 percent of GDP, but are an essential part of the economy. Given the large number of islands, and the high proportion of the rural population living in small isolated villages, most travel is by sea. Road transport is concentrated in Honiara and the surrounding areas of Guadalcanal. Better maintenance and further development of transport services is urgently needed.

3.3   Based on World Bank estimates, per capita GNP was about $430 in 1988, placing Solomon Islands in the low-income group of countries. The strong subsistence base and extended family system have helped to provide the basic needs of food and shelter for most of the population. However, health and education services are relatively undeveloped (see Table 3.1). There is a severe shortage of equipment, supplies and trained manpower (e.g., nurses and primary teachers). These problems are compounded by the increased demand for services from a rapidly growing population. Malaria remains the most important health problem in Solomon Islands and the leading cause of

---

1/ The Government pays SI$0.72 per hour for casual laborers.

2/ There are also a number of industries (e.g., flour milling, steel roofing) that process imported inputs for domestic consumption.

morbidity.3/ In the education sector, the primary attendance ratio is less
than 50 percent and only 27 percent of primary school leavers go on to
secondary school. Only 15 percent of the adult population is literate and
barely 1 percent of the population has been educated to degree or diploma
level. Human resource development will place heavy demands on budget
resources in the years ahead.

Table 3.1: SOCIAL INDICATORS, 1988 /a

Indicator	Units	Solomon Islands	Asia	Low-income
Crude birth rate	per 000	42.0	26.8	30.4
Crude death rate	per 000	10.0	8.8	10.0
Infant mortality rate	per 000 births		61.5	72.6
- Male		40.0		
- Female		36.0		
Life expectancy at birth	years		63.7	61.4
- Male		59.9		
- Female		61.4		
Population per:				
- Doctor	persons	9,542	1,422	1,462
- Hospital bed	persons	189	733	756
Gross enrollment ratios				
- Primary	%	48.0 /b	105.3	99.3
- Secondary	%	11.0 /b	37.5	33.4
Adult illiteracy rate	%	85.0	39.5	43.3

/a Or most recent estimate.
/b Attendance ratios from 1986 Census. These may be affected by Cyclone
    Namu. Enrollment ratios are usually higher.

Source: Statistics Office and World Bank, "Social Indicators of Development,
         1989".

3.4   Solomon Islands, which had been a British Protectorate, became
independent in 1978. The legislative assembly is elected by popular vote
every four years. The present Government of the People's Alliance Party came
to power in March 1989. Pending preparation of new aid guidelines, the
Government initially suspended all aid negotiations and froze technical

3/ In 1987, the incidence rate of malaria was 245 per 1,000 population.

assistance appointments. Priority has also been given to decentralization of government functions to the provinces. In line with this policy, responsibility for bilateral aid (mostly grants) has been given to the Ministry of Provincial Government and special grants for area councils have been included in the budget for 1990. At the local level, the traditional system of kinship groups (wantok) has an important influence on economic activity. About 87 percent of the land in Solomon Islands is under customary ownership. This system of land tenure has tended to reduce incentives for smallholder development and limit the supply of land for plantation, timber and tourism development.

B. Recent Economic Developments

3.5   Solomon Islands' natural resource base helped to sustain an average GDP growth rate of 4.5 percent per annum during 1981-84 (see Table 3.2). Joint ventures for copra, cocoa, palm oil, timber and fish made major contributions to primary production and export performance. An improvement in the terms of trade in 1983-84 also strengthened the overall balance of payments position, reducing the current account deficit to less than 10 percent of GDP. Expenditure restraint by the Government reduced the budget deficit to only 3 percent of GDP in 1984. As a result, the Government's use of domestic credit was limited. However, the money supply continued to grow strongly, due to private sector demand for credit (at negative real interest rates) and the accumulation of foreign assets. This fueled inflation, with consumer prices rising on average by 12 percent per annum during 1981-84.4/

3.6   The external environment for Solomon Islands deteriorated dramatically in 1985-86. Lower commodity prices for copra, palm oil and timber reduced the terms of trade by 25 percent over these two years. In May 1986, Cyclone Namu severely damaged crops and infrastructure. As a result, palm oil production fell sharply. At the same time, rice production by SOLRICE was abandoned and Levers Pacific stopped forestry operations (due to land access problems). The overall effect was to slow GDP growth to only 1.4 percent per annum in 1985-86 and reduce export earnings by 29 percent. The Government attempted to support the economy through higher levels of expenditure. The current budget was expanded to cover wage increases, transfers to the provinces, and subsidies to public enterprises. Development expenditure also rose due to cyclone reconstruction and large investments in fishing vessels and airport expansion. This additional spending was largely financed by higher levels of external grants, including STABEX funds from the EEC. These grants also helped to finance the widening current account deficit (25 percent of GDP in 1986). Foreign assets were also drawn down in 1985. This helped to contain money supply growth. Inflation remained around 12 percent per annum.

4/ Inflation is measured by the Honiara Retail Price Index. This does not reflect prices for the economy as a whole and is subject to large seasonal fluctuations.

Table 3.2: ECONOMIC INDICATORS, 1981-89

	1981-84	1985-86	1987	1988	Est. 1989
Production and Expenditure					
Growth rates (% per annum)					
GDP	4.5	1.4	1.7	4.3	5.2
- Subsistence	2.9	1.8	4.6	3.1	3.0
- Agriculture	7.5	-12.3	-4.9	13.3	10.0
- Forestry and fishing	6.0	7.4	-23.5	3.8	5.7
- Manufacturing	-4.1	9.5	20.8	0.0	5.0
- Other	4.0	6.0	10.3	2.0	4.0
Ratios to GDP (%)					
Gross investment		26.6	27.3	38.6	38.0
- Private		17.8	10.5	16.3	18.0
- Government		8.8	16.8	22.3	20.0
Domestic savings		4.8	-0.1	-0.8	0.7
National savings		2.3	-2.0	-0.1	-0.2
Central Government Budget (% of GDP)					
Revenue	22.3	22.5	23.7	24.8	25.6
- Tax revenue	19.3	20.4	21.7	22.2	22.8
- Nontax revenue	3.0	2.1	2.0	2.7	2.8
External grants	3.8	6.2	10.3	7.7	4.1
Expenditure	30.3	34.4	42.7	35.0	34.3
- Current	23.3	25.5	26.2	27.5	27.6
- Capital	7.0	8.9	16.5	7.5	6.7
Net lending	1.8	0.5	2.7	3.9	1.1
Overall balance	-6.9	-6.2	-11.4	-6.4	-5.7
Financed by:					
External borrowing (net)	3.3	5.1	11.9	4.8	2.1
Domestic credit /b	3.6	1.1	-0.5	1.6	3.6
Money and Prices (Growth Rates, % per annum)					
Domestic credit	19.0	27.2	13.3	30.3	31.7
Private credit	12.6	20.7	18.4	32.1	20.8
Broad money	13.4	6.1	34.3	31.3	-1.2
Money	16.8	3.6	22.4	32.0	2.0
Consumer prices /c	11.6	11.5	10.7	16.7	15.4
GDP deflator'		4.2	13.3	21.2	4.6
Terms of trade		-13.5	7.8	14.4	-11.1
Balance of Payments (US$ million)					
Exports (fob)	69.9	68.1	64.0	81.9	74.7
Imports (cif)	-79.2	-82.9	-84.8	-120.9	-111.5
Trade balance	-9.3	-14.8	-20.8	-39.0	-36.8
Services (net)	-12.5	-21.1	-22.2	-30.4	-31.9
Private transfers	-3.9	-1.2	-0.1	-1.4	1.2
Current account	-25.7	-37.1	-43.1	-68.0	-67.5
Official grants	14.7	21.7	41.6	42.4	36.6
Public loan disb. (net)	5.3	8.7	14.5	9.9	10.5
Other capital (net)	5.6	2.6	-1.5	18.8	5.0
Use of net foreign					
assets (- = increase)	-0.1	4.1	-11.5	-3.1	15.4
Ratios					
Current account/GDP (%)	-17.4	-24.3	-29.3	-38.6	-38.3
Debt service/exports (%) /d	0.4	1.6	2.0	3.5	6.1
DOD/GDP (%) /d	15.6	20.2	27.0	23.6	23.9
Net foreign assets					
(months of imports)	3.4	2.9	3.3	3.9	2.2

/a Includes forestry and fishing.
/b Includes discrepancy.
/c Based on Honiara Retail Price Index.
/d For public debt only.

Source: Statistical Appendix (with estimates added for 1989).

3.7   Over the past three years, Solomon Islands has been gradually recovering from the effects of Cyclone Namu. In the agriculture sector, palm oil production is now back to pre-1986 levels and copra production is responding well to improved price incentives. Fish production has benefitted from strong growth in the catch over the past two years (after being affected by colder ocean temperatures and rough seas in 1987) and construction of a new 18,000 ton fish cannery (which began operations in 1989). Although timber production has fallen well below the peak levels of the mid-1980s, more timber is now being processed. Manufacturing and construction activity have both done well over the past year. Overall, GDP growth remained low in 1987 but has recovered to 4.3 percent in 1988 and an estimated 5.2 percent in 1989. This has probably been sufficient to support real growth in per capita consumption over the past two years. At the same time, higher levels of foreign savings, channeled through the budget, have raised the investment rate to around 38 percent of GDP.

3.8   The Government has been less successful in restoring fiscal discipline. A number of tax measures were announced in 1988 and 1989, including higher duty rates (and a 3 percent levy) on a range of imported goods.5/ However, the effect on revenues was partially offset by weaknesses in tax administration and a growing list of exemptions from customs duties. Overall, revenues rose only moderately from 23 percent of GDP in 1986 to 26 percent in 1989. At the same time, current expenditure continued to rise, due to a series of wage increases for civil servants and teachers, and higher interest payments on external loans. Capital expenditure was boosted in 1987 by a large payment for the purchase of two purse seiner fishing boats,6/ but fell back to a more normal level in 1988. In 1989, the level of capital expenditure was constrained by the decision of the new Government to suspend aid. Allowing for the related fall in disbursements of external grants and loans, the Government has had to draw increasingly on domestic sources to finance the budget.

3.9   Domestic inflation rose from 11 percent in 1987 to 17 percent in 1988. This trend reflects the effect of wage increases in the civil service, higher import duty rates, shortages of locally-produced vegetables (toward the end of the year), the depreciation of the SI Dollar and the rapid expansion of domestic credit. To reduce the pressure on prices, the authorities temporarily slowed the depreciation of the SI Dollar during 1989. Bank liquidity was absorbed by imposing a 5 percent statutory reserve deposit, introducing a Central Bank bond and raising the liquid asset ratio to 30 percent. Although government use of domestic credit has continued to expand at a rapid rate, private credit growth slowed somewhat during 1989. Monetary expansion has also been contained by the drawdown of foreign assets. As a result, the annual rate of inflation fell to 15 percent during 1989 (and further to about 9 percent by mid-1990).

5/ At the same time, the basis for import duty assessment was changed from fob to cif and the 20 percent surcharge was abolished. These measures were expected to be revenue neutral.

6/ The purse seiners were delivered in mid-1988 at a total cost of SI$33.8 million, of which SI$27.3 million was financed on commercial terms.

3.10   Solomon Islands' export performance over the past three years has been supported by improved commodity prices (except for cocoa).7/   Currency depreciations in the mid-1980s also had a positive effect on producer incentives. Although the real effective exchange rate appreciated during 1989, it is still about 30 percent lower than in 1984. The revival of copra and palm oil production after Cyclone Namu and the steady rise in fish production have raised export volumes by about 8 percent per annum over the past two years. Solomon Islands has also benefitted from higher tourist receipts and private transfers. However, import growth has also been strong, boosted by the purchase of two purse seiners in 1988 and the recovery in consumer demand. The current account deficit remained around 38 percent of GDP. Net receipts from official grants and public loans fell from a peak of $56 million in 1987 to $47 million in 1989. This decline reflects the completion of disbursements for the purse seiners, lower receipts of STABEX funds and the recent suspension of aid. Net foreign assets were maintained at 3-4 months of imports through 1988, but fell during 1989 and early 1990 (to less than 2 months of imports).8/ Debt payments on the purse seiner loan pushed the public debt service ratio up from 1.8 percent in 1986 to 6.1 percent in 1989.

C. Development Prospects and Issues

Economic Prospects and Financing Requirements

3.11   The medium-term projections presented in Table 3.3 are intended to illustrate Solomon Islands' development prospects and to provide a framework for discussing related policy issues. In line with the Government's objectives, priority has been given to reducing macroeconomic imbalances and achieving sustainable economic growth (to absorb the rapidly growing labor force). GDP is projected to grow by 4-5 percent per annum. This is above the average for the past five years, when the economy was affected by Cyclone Namu. Some further recovery in palm oil and copra production is expected over the next couple of years. However, sustained agricultural growth will require crop diversification, based on the policies for smallholder development discussed in paras. 3.17-3.18 below. Although conservation policies are likely to constrain timber production, value added will gain from the development of milling activities. The current fish catch is well below sustainable levels and is expected to continue growing strongly. The new cannery will increase value added in the sector. The small manufacturing sector is expected to respond to improved incentives for private sector development, with several new investments already planned (e.g., the brewery).

The boats are now operated by Solomon Taiyo and NFD. Their performance to date has been disappointing.

7/   There has been a sharp drop in export prices for copra and cocoa during the first half of 1990. This recent development is not fully reflected in the price projections used in this report.

8/   About half of the net foreign assets are offset by unspent STABEX balances.

Table 3.3: MEDIUM-TERM PROJECTIONS, 1990-99

	Estimates 1985-89	--- Projections --- 1990-94	1995-99
Growth Rates (% per annum)			
GDP	2.8	4.6	4.7
- Subsistence	2.9	3.0	3.0
- Agriculture	-1.8	4.0	4.0
- Forestry	-5.8	4.0	4.0
- Fishing	3.9	6.0	6.0
- Manufacturing	8.8	8.0	8.0
- Other	5.6	5.0	5.0
Consumption		1.4	2.7
Gross investment		3.5	3.5
Merchandise exports	-3.8	8.1	6.0
Merchandise imports	2.9	2.6	3.4
Consumer prices	13.1	6.2	4.0
Terms of trade	-3.9	0.4	-0.4
Ratios to GDP (%)			
Gross investment	31.4	37.7	37.3
Domestic savings	3.1	9.9	13.0
National savings	0.4	9.4	13.0
Other indicators (%)			
Current account/GDP	-31.0	-29.5	-24.2
Debt service/exports /a	3.0	4.4	2.0
DOD/GDP /a	23.0	51.9	57.7
Net foreign assets (months of imports)	3.0	1.7	2.3

/a For public debt only.

Source: World Bank staff estimates.

Other sectors with good growth prospects are gold mining, construction and tourism.9/

3.12   The higher growth rate is generated by improvements in productivity and maintenance of the current high investment rate (about 38 percent). Most of the new investment is assumed to come from the private sector. However, there will also be significant demands on government resources to develop and maintain basic economic and social infrastructure. Consumption is projected to fall in 1990 but then recover, growing on average by about 3 percent per annum after 1991. With constraint on government consumption and some success in reducing the population growth rate, this would provide scope for modest improvements in per capita private consumption. More rapid consumption growth is precluded by the need to maintain a manageable balance of payments position. For the same reason, the high levels of investment need to be supported by an increase in domestic and national savings. Tight fiscal and monetary policies are assumed to reduce domestic inflation further over the next five years and then hold it in line with international rates (4 percent per annum).

3.13   The terms of trade for Solomon Islands are projected to decline in 1990, because of stable or falling prices for copra, palm oil, cocoa and logs. However, improving export prices are expected to bring the terms of trade back to the current level by the mid-1990s. Export incentives could be further improved by more active exchange rate management, supported by measures to improve marketing and transport services. Export volumes are expected to benefit from steady growth in the agriculture and fishing sectors, and increased processing of agricultural, timber and fish products. There are also prospects for mineral exports (e.g., gold), and sales of new agricultural and manufactured products in "niche" markets. Overall, the volume of exports is projected to grow by 6-8 percent per annum. Import volumes are expected to fall in 1990, but then grow by 3-4 percent per annum. These projections lead to a steady reduction in the trade deficit over the medium term. The current account deficit stabilizes around 30 percent of GDP in 1990-94 and then falls to 21 percent by 1999.

3.14   The balance of payments projections can be reorganized to show external financing requirements and sources (see Table 3.4). Total annual requirements rise from an average of $50 million over the past five years to around $70 million during the 1990s. This rising trend reflects the rising deficit on the services account, including the counterpart of technical assistance grants. The major financing item will continue to be external assistance. New commitments of project grants and loans are projected to return to more normal levels in 1990 (after the recent suspension of aid), then rise in real terms by 2 percent per annum in 1991-92 and remain constant in real terms in later years. In addition, $10-15 million of program aid (e.g., STABEX funds) will be needed in each of the next five years to maintain

---

9/   Visitor arrivals have remained around 12,000 per annum in recent years, of which about two-thirds are tourists. There is ample scope for tourism development based on Solomon Islands' natural attractions. However, this will require improved air links (to and within the country), more first-class hotel accommodation (especially outside Honiara), and better marketing overseas. The National Tourism Policy supports tourism development in a "controlled and sensitive" manner.

Table 3.4:   EXTERNAL FINANCING REQUIREMENTS AND SOURCES, 1990-99
($ million per annum at current prices)

	Estimates	Projections	
	1985-89	1990-94	1995-99
Requirements	50.3	68.4	69.3
Merchandise imports	96.6	136.5	205.5
Merchandise exports	-71.3	-114.1	-195.2
Principal repayments /a	2.1	5.0	3.8
Interest payments /a	0.9	1.6	1.3
Other service payments (net)	23.8	37.7	46.3
Change in net foreign assets	-1.8	1.7	7.6
Sources	50.3	68.4	69.3
Private remittances	-0.5	1.4	1.7
Official grants	32.8	52.6	49.7
Public loan disbursements	12.5	8.7	10.8
Other capital (net)	5.5	5.7	7.1

/a On public debt.

Source: World Bank staff estimates.

a manageable balance of payments position. Because all new loans are assumed
to be provided on concessional terms, the public debt service ratio falls
steadily to an average of 4.4 percent in 1990-94 and 2.0 percent in 1995-99.

3.15   Even with the program aid built into the projections, some drawdown
of external reserves is projected during 1990. As a minimum assumption, the
level of net foreign assets is projected to arise back to two months of
imports by 1994 and four months of imports by the end of the decade. However,
past experience suggests that these reserve levels may be insufficient to
cover the country's foreign exchange requirements in the event of an
unexpected deterioration in the terms of trade or another natural disaster
such as Cyclone Namu. A 30 percent decline in export earnings (as occurred in
1985-87) would add more than $30 million (50 percent of current aid
disbursements) to financing requirements in 1990. This magnitude underscores
the importance of maintaining fiscal and monetary restraint, mobilizing
domestic resources and strengthening export incentives. Under such
conditions, it would also be essential for the donor community to support the
Government's policy actions with temporary emergency and program aid.

Development Issues and Policies

3.16   The Government's approach to development is set out in the "Program
of Action 1989-93". The program commits the country to a free enterprise
economic system and encourages the private sector to play an important role in
development. To this end, the Government proposes to set up several new
financial institutions and privatize the commercial activities of the

Investment Corporation. Macroeconomic policies are to be geared toward reducing the fiscal deficit and achieving "economic growth with stability". Sectoral priorities are focused on the development of smallholder agriculture, human resources and economic infrastructure. Government policy also emphasizes the importance of improving land tenure arrangements and the management of natural resources, and the decentralization of government functions to the provinces. These broad objectives and priorities are appropriate. The challenge now is to translate them into effective programs and policies. Some areas for action are summarized below.

3.17   Smallholder development is essential for the sustained growth of the agriculture sector. Smallholders make up the bulk of the rural population and opportunities for further development of commercial plantations are limited by land constraints. The Government can support smallholder development in a number of ways.10/ First, research and extension services need to be strengthened. Under the Rural Services Project, four new research substations have been established and the research program reoriented toward farming systems (including intercropping of cash and food crops). Given the limited personnel and resources available, the emphasis on adaptive (rather than basic) research is appropriate. More use of farm trials would help develop relevant technologies. The extension service is based at the provincial level. However, training of extension workers remains the responsibility of the Ministry of Agriculture and Lands (MAL) and a new National Agricultural Training Institute (now under the College of Higher Education) has been established for this purpose. A stronger role for MAL in coordinating and supporting extension activities (including links to the research program) is needed. At the moment, extension workers spend too much time appraising DBSI loans and providing advice to individual farmers. More use of on-farm demonstrations and female extension workers would help improve the effectiveness of the service. The Government's proposal to develop Agricultural Opportunity Areas, 11/ if properly developed, could provide focus for the limited resources available for extension work.

3.18   Second, producer incentives need to be maintained through a competitive exchange rate and effective marketing arrangements. Commercial traders and cooperatives are active in the marketing of all crops in Solomon Islands. However, the Commodities Export Marketing Authority (CEMA) has a monopoly on copra exports. Efforts to stabilize producer prices when world copra prices collapsed in 1986 severely eroded CEMA's reserves. Although CEMA's financial position has subsequently improved, continued vigilance will be required to avoid such episodes in the future. There is also scope for reducing CEMA's fixed costs by improving accounting systems and stock controls, and reducing surplus staff in buying centers. Over the longer term, the Government should consider converting CEMA into a regulatory body without

---

10/ This discussion is based on the World Bank Review of Agricultural Programs in 1986. An internal desk review of the agricultural sector, undertaken for the World Bank in 1989, proposed the development of clan-based agriculture and of closer links between smallholders and plantations (through nucleus estates or contract growing).

11/ Agricultural Opportunity Areas cover 12 percent of the country's land area. Only about 30 percent of this area is currently used for agricultural production.

an export monopoly for copra. Marketing of other crops, including cocoa and palm oil, should be left in the hands of private traders. Finally, smallholder development will require a substantial improvement in transport facilities. An efficient inter-island shipping service at key collection points is essential in the outer islands. More efficient management of the government-owned shipping fleet is needed, and private operators should be encouraged to expand their services on key routes (if necessary, through budget subsidies). Better maintenance of wharves and access roads would also help reduce transport costs.

3.19   As already noted, land tenure arrangements have tended to reduce incentives for smallholders to develop their land, and limit the supply of land for plantation, timber and tourism development. In recent years, land problems have led to the closure of Lever Pacific's forestry operations and of the Anuha beach resort (following a fire). Land disputes can be expected to intensify as population pressures increase and the cash economy grows in importance. The only lasting solution is to demarcate, survey and record customary land. This process will allow the land to be used by the communal owners or leased out (with greater security to the tenant than in the past). To facilitate this process, the Government proposes to introduce the Customary Land Act during 1990 and strengthen the Lands Division of MAL. It will take some time to gain the trust of customary landowners, as past efforts at recording have been associated with the alienation of land by the Government, often for lease to foreign companies. Therefore, progress will be slow. First priority should be given to areas where smallholder resettlement or plantation development are planned, including the identified Agricultural Opportunity Areas. The Government is also leasing to farmers the land owned by SOLRICE. Possible uses for the land include oil palm, cash crops and livestock development.

3.20   Appropriate policies are required to manage and conserve the country's rich base of natural resources. Of prime importance is the forestry sector. Forests cover about 2.4 million hectares, or 85 percent of the total land area in Solomon Islands. However, only about 200,000 hectares are exploitable, the balance being on very steep slopes or in inaccessible areas. At present, logging operations clear about 10,000 hectares of natural forest each year. Replanting operations, almost entirely on government land, cover only about 1,000 hectares per year. At this rate, it is estimated that Solomon Islands' forest resources will be exhausted in 15 to 25 years.[12] In response, the Government has imposed a milling requirement on timber exports (currently 20 percent, to be raised to 80 percent by 1991).[13] There is also an export tax on logs. Reforestation programs are being prepared for customary land (with New Zealand assistance) and at Kolombangara (with CDC assistance). In addition, the Ministry of Natural Resources has prepared a comprehensive forest policy. This includes proposals to:

---

[12] Some estimates are more pessimistic. CSIRO, for example, has predicted that the rainforest will be eradicated by 1996 at 1986 logging rates.

[13] Regional studies by the World Bank suggest that milling requirements may neither conserve forest nor promote efficient milling. See World Bank, "Market Prospects for Forest Products from the Pacific Islands," 1990.

- prepare a forest inventory, to determine the extent of forest resources, identify areas of natural forest for protection and establish sustainable cutting rates;

- change licensing procedures and timber charges, to improve logging company operations (including incentives for replanting and milling); and

- strengthen the Government's institutional capacity to plan forestry development, implement replanting programs and enforce logging regulations.

These proposals warrant urgent consideration and implementation. Similar policies are being developed to protect the country's fishing and mineral resources.

3.21   Human resource development is essential for individual welfare and the country's economic prospects. The Government introduced, for the first time, a population policy in 1988. Although the average population density is low (10 per sq km), land pressures are starting to appear in some areas, such as Malaita, where fallow periods are shortening and women have to walk long distances to their gardens. Rapid population growth places extra demands on social services and the labor market. Closely spaced births are also detrimental to the health of mothers and children. The 1986 Census provides some evidence that fertility rates may be on the decline.14/ However, contraceptive use is still low and mostly limited to urban areas. Experience in other countries suggests that religious and cultural resistance to family planning can be gradually overcome through an effective information and education program. Such a program should be linked to efforts to improve basic health services (including the training of more nurses) and the control of malaria. The education system is already under strain and this situation will be aggravated by population growth. About half of primary teachers are untrained. The late and non-payment of salaries led to a series of teacher strikes in 1989. The Government has now introduced a revised salary structure for teachers, and efforts are underway to upgrade teacher conditions and skills. Proposals to provide free education through form five should be considered carefully in light of the funding constraints in the sector and the urgent need to increase spending on school maintenance and supplies.

3.22   The public sector plays a dominant role in Solomon Islands. The Government accounts for about 60 percent of gross investment and 40 percent of total expenditure. In addition, there is extensive involvement by state-owned enterprises (SOEs) in virtually all sectors of the economy. The four statutory corporations 15/ have generally been able to finance their operating expenses without subsidies, while their capital expenditure is largely financed by onlending of external assistance. The Government's equity in

---

14/ The fertility rate declined from 7.2 in the 1976 Census to 6.0 in the 1986 Census. Further study on the causes of this decline is warranted.

15/ The Solomon Islands Electricity Authority (SIEA), the Solomon Islands Port Authority (SIPA), the Livestock Development Authority (LDA) and the Solomon Islands Housing Authority (SIHA).

other SOEs is held by the Investment Corporation of Solomon Islands (ICSI).16/
Although the financial performance of these enterprises has improved since the
early-1980s, they still represent a significant claim on budget resources,
with transfers averaging 5 percent of GDP over the past five years.
Recognizing this burden, the Government is considering selling off or
liquidating some of the enterprises under the ICSI. The Mendana Hotel has
already been sold to a Japanese company, and bids have been sought for SOLRICE
(rice trading) and NFD (fishing). The remaining divestiture program should
proceed on a realistic timetable, with clear procedures to ensure an open
tendering process and a smooth transition of ownership. Divested firms should
operate in a competitive policy environment. In some cases, it may be
desirable to keep SOEs as joint ventures, but with clear commercial objectives
and independence from the budget.

3.23   The Government has also made major changes in the structure of the
civil service. The old Ministry of Economic Planning has been abolished and
an Economic Planning Unit established under the Ministry of Finance. This
unit also has responsibility for multilateral aid. However, as already noted,
responsibility for bilateral aid has been given to the Ministry of Provincial
Government. The revenue functions of the Ministry of Finance (Customs and
Excise, and Inland Revenue) have been separated off into the Ministry of
Housing and Government Services. This fragmented structure for planning and
budgeting increases the need for effective coordination. The Policy
Evaluation Unit in the Prime Minister's Office has played this role during the
transition period. More generally, it is doubtful whether the Government has
enough trained manpower to manage such a fragmented structure. Several key
officials have recently left the civil service and others are not fully
integrated into the decision making process. The recent decision to put all
senior officials on contracts linked to the election cycle will increase the
risk of political appointments and further reduce continuity in key positions.

3.24   The suspension of aid during 1989 provided a much needed opportunity
to establish clearer priorities for financial and technical assistance. The
new guidelines ask bilateral donors to finance 100 percent of project costs
(either through new commitments or reallocations within ongoing projects) and
to focus their assistance by province or sector. The Government recognizes
that a provincial focus may not be appropriate for smaller donors or national
programs (such as scholarships). It is also prepared to consider the
definition of project costs in a flexible manner. The real concern is whether
the new planning process will be able to define priorities clearly. While
there is a need to get aid administration closer to the local level, the split
between multilateral and bilateral aid will make project evaluation and
appraisal difficult. This problem is compounded by weak project preparation
and implementation capacity in the line ministries. The Government and donors
need to work together to find practical solutions to the current weaknesses in
aid administration.

3.25   The draft budget for 1990 was presented to Parliament in December
1989. The budget estimates are expansionary. The payroll bill is one-third

---

16/ ISCI investments include plantations (SIPL and Solomon Lever), fishing
     companies (Solomon Taiyo and NFD), the national airline (SOLAIR), the
     international telecommunications company (SOLTEL) and a marina (for
     boat construction and repair).

higher than budgeted for last year, due to the 17.5 percent pay rise for civil servants in mid-1989, the revised salary structure for teachers, the expansion in the number of key ministries, and the regrading of posts. In line with the new aid guidelines, no government contribution is budgeted for externally-financed projects. As a result, external loans and grants are projected to finance 93 percent of development expenditure. The budget is balanced with SI$20.5 million of domestic borrowing (equal to 16 percent of domestic revenues). The current budgetary situation requires action in three areas:

- It is essential to maintain tight control over the budget deficit and the Government's claims on domestic credit. Otherwise, the recent progress on containing inflation will be lost, the current account deficit will deteriorate further, and efforts to develop the private sector will be frustrated by credit constraints. The Government's decision to "reserve" all expenditures above 1989 levels, pending their justification, provides an opportunity to maintain fiscal discipline.

- Government expenditure should be focused on infrastructure and human resource development. These two sectors account for about half of the development budget for 1990, slightly down on their share for last year. The immediate priority is to provide adequate provisions for O&M. This might be best done by developing closer links between the recurrent and development budgets, and encouraging donors to finance multi-year sectoral programs (with declining contributions to recurrent funding).

- Revenues need to be increased without undermining private sector incentives. This can be done by improving tax administration and broadening the tax base. To this end, the Government introduced a sales tax on certain services (hotels, restaurants, telephones and overseas air tickets) in mid-1990. At the same time, a resident withholding tax was imposed on some forms of income. Income tax rates are already high (up to 42 percent), and could probably be reduced without any significant loss of revenue. However, tax exemptions should be limited. Import and export duties need to be adjusted to reduce distortions in protection rates.

3.26   The Government is committed to improving the environment for private sector development. Private sector demand for credit slowed in 1989 but is expected to grow strongly in the years ahead. To meet this demand, the Government proposes to strengthen the development role of the Central Bank and the Development Bank of Solomon Islands (DBSI), and establish two new institutions: a People's Bank (for rural credit) and an Industrial Development Corporation. It is questionable whether these new institutions are required. Rural credit could be channeled through the growing network of credit unions, while industrial lending could be handled by a strengthened Development Bank. DBSI has made losses every year since 1981, because of poor loan appraisal and supervision procedures, the difficulties of collecting arrears (due to the "wantok" system and the dispersed location of borrowers), and past weaknesses in management and staffing.[17/] However, recent improvements in the performance of DBSI suggest that it can play a more active

---

17/ Interest rates are guided by the Government, and range from 9-10 percent in agriculture to 14 percent in industry.

and profitable role in industrial lending, while leaving small-scale rural lending to the credit unions. The Central Bank also supports the private sector through interest rate subsidies for small and export credits. These subsidies would be more transparent if financed from the budget. Every effort should be made to target them on first-time borrowers and graduate as many borrowers as possible to market-related credit.

3.27   Investment incentives in Solomon Islands have been provided on an ad hoc basis, without adequate safeguards to the country or the investor. Foreign investor interest is still strong, despite land problems, but is often in areas where local capacity already exists (e.g., shells) or where strong resource management policies are needed (e.g., forestry). The Government is now considering a new package of investment incentives, that would provide tax holidays, import duty concessions and training assistance to projects approved by the Foreign Investment Board. In addition, there are plans to develop an industrial estate at Ranadi, including duty-free facilities for exporters. These are valuable initiatives. However, over the longer term, private investment decisions are likely to be more influenced by the Government's success in improving the overall policy environment (e.g., land tenure, taxation) and providing basic infrastructure (e.g., roads, water supply, power).

REFERENCES

Coopers & Lybrand Consultants (1989), "Country Paper - Solomon Islands" (draft paper for the Pacific Islands Regional Economic Report).

Browne, C. (1989), "Economic Development in Seven Pacific Island Countries" (IMF).

Central Bank of Solomon Islands (1989), "Mid-Year Review 1989".

Central Bank of Solomon Islands (1990), "Quarterly Review, March 1990".

Government of Solomon Islands (1989), "Programme of Action 1989-1993".

Hughes, A. (1988), "Climbing the Down Escalator" (NCDS Working Paper No. 88/2).

IMF (1988), "Solomon Islands - Recent Economic Developments" (confidential).

IMF (1989), "Solomon Islands - Staff Report for the 1989 Interim Article IV Consultation" (confidential).

McGowen International Ltd. (1989), Agriculture Sector Review of Solomon Islands" (a desk study for the World Bank).

Minister of Finance (1989), "1990 Budget Speech".

Ministry of Agriculture & Lands (1989), "Agricultural Plan of Action 1989-93".

Ministry of Health and Medical Services (1988), "Solomon Islands Population Policy".

Ministry of Natural Resources (1989), "Forest Policy Statement".

Ministry of Tourism and Aviation (1989), "The National Tourism Policy of Solomon Islands".

Office of the Prime Minister (1989), "Alternative Approach to Resolving Land/Development Disputes".

Statistics Office (1986), "1985/6 Statistical Yearbook".

World Bank (1986), "Solomon Islands - Review of Agricultural Programs".*

World Bank (1990), "Market Prospects for Forest Products from the Pacific Islands".*

* These documents are for internal use only.

STATISTICAL APPENDIX

LIST OF TABLES

No.   Title

           Population and Employment

1.1   Population of Solomon Islands, 1976 & 1986
1.2   Formal Employment, 1986

           National Accounts

2.1   GDP Prices, 1980-88
2.2   Expenditure on GDP at Current Prices, 1984-88

           Public Finance

3.1   Central Government Budget, 1980-89
3.2   Central Government Revenue, 1980-89
3.3   Central Government Expenditure, 1980-89

           Money and Prices

4.1   Monetary Survey, 1980-89
4.2   Interest Rates, 1984-88
4.3   Honiara Retail Price Index, 1980-89

           Balance of Payments and Trade

5.1   Balance of Payments, 1980-89
5.2   Merchandise Trade Indices, 1983-88
5.3   Merchandise Exports, 1980-89
5.4   Merchandise Imports, 1980-89
5.5   Direction of Trade, 1985-89

           External Assistance and Debt

6.1   External Public Debt, 1980-1988

Table 1.1: POPULATION OF SOLOMON ISLANDS, 1976 & 1986

Province	Land area (sq km)	Population 1976	Population 1986	Density (per sq km) 1976	Density (per sq km) 1986	Growth (% pa) 1976-86
Western	9,312	40,329	55,250	4.3	5.9	3.0
Isabel	4,136	10,420	14,616	2.5	3.5	3.2
Central	1,286	13,576	18,457	10.6	14.4	2.9
Guadalcanal	5,336	31,677	49,831	5.9	9.3	4.3
Honiara	22	14,942	30,413	679.2	1,382.4	6.8
Malaita	4,225	60,043	80,032	14.2	18.9	2.7
Makira	3,188	14,891	21,796	4.7	6.8	3.6
Temotu	865	10,945	14,781	12.7	17.1	2.8
Total	28,370	196,823	285,176	6.9	10.1	3.5

Source: Statistics Office (Population Census).

Table 1.2: FORMAL EMPLOYMENT, 1986

Industry	Employer	Self-employed	Wage earner	Other	Total	% share
Agriculture, forestry & fishing	14	9,118	8,865	360	18,357	46.3
Mining & quarrying		526	191	2	719	1.8
Manufacturing	13	1,037	1,224	16	2,290	5.8
Electricity, gas & water	1	7	418		426	1.1
Construction	14	195	1,978	25	2,212	5.6
Trade, hotels & restaurants	72	516	2,675	53	3,316	8.4
Transport & communications	7	214	1,800	5	2,026	5.1
Finance, industry & real estate	2	12	535	1	550	1.4
Community & personal services	13	106	9,210	73	9,402	23.7
Other	5	29	97	183	314	0.8
Total	141	11,760	26,993	718	39,612	100.0
-----	---	------	------	---	------	-----

Source: Statistics Office (Population Census).

Table 2.1: GDP BY INDUSTRIAL ORIGIN AT 1984 PRICES, 1980-88
(SI$ million)

	1980	1981	1982	1983	1984	1985	1986	1987	1988
Monetized sector	133.9	144.3	143.1	149.2	162.3	167.7	166.5	188.3	175.9
Agriculture	36.1	42.0	41.7	41.1	48.2	48.7	37.1	35.3	40.0
Forestry & sawmilling	12.0	12.3	13.7	14.0	13.9	13.5	15.6	11.6	10.3
Fishing	9.3	9.8	9.1	12.7	13.0	11.0	15.4	12.1	14.3
Gold mining /a	0.2	0.3	0.2	0.3	0.5	0.5	0.7	0.5	0.3
Manufacturing	7.1	6.4	6.6	6.6	6.0	6.8	7.2	8.7	8.7
Electricity & water	1.3	1.4	1.5	1.6	1.7	1.9	2.0	1.8	2.0
Construction	5.6	7.7	4.6	5.7	4.9	7.0	7.4	6.5	6.4
Retail & wholesale trade	17.2	18.5	19.1	17.6	22.1	22.1	21.5	22.4	20.2
Transport & communications	8.4	8.7	8.7	9.3	10.3	10.8	11.3	10.2	10.5
Finance & services	36.7	37.4	37.9	40.3	41.7	45.4	48.3	59.2	63.2
Non-monetized sector	31.9	33.4	34.1	35.4	35.7	36.5	37.0	38.7	39.9
Food	29.5	30.9	31.5	32.8	33.0	33.7	33.7	35.8	36.9
Construction	2.4	2.5	2.6	2.6	2.7	2.8	3.3	2.9	3.0
GDP	165.8	177.7	177.2	184.6	198.0	204.2	203.5	207.0	215.8
Growth rates (% pa)									
Monetized sector		7.8	-0.8	4.3	8.8	3.3	-0.7	1.1	4.5
Non-monetized sector		4.7	2.1	3.8	0.8	2.2	1.4	4.6	3.1
GDP		7.2	-0.3	4.2	7.3	3.1	-0.3	1.7	4.3

/a Excludes exploration.

Source: Statistics Office & IMF staff estimates.

Table 2.2: GDP BY EXPENDITURE AT CURRENT PRICES, 1984-88
(SI$ million)

	1984	1985	1986	1987	1988
GDP at factor cost	198.0	210.1	221.1	254.8	322.0
Net indirect taxes	23.7	26.8	31.4	39.8	44.5
GDP at market prices	221.7	236.9	252.5	294.6	366.5
Imports (GNFS)	129.3	163.8	202.6	247.2	350.9
Exports (GNFS)	127.5	114.6	144.9	173.6	225.2
Expenditure	223.5	286.1	310.2	368.2	492.2
Consumption	172.6	223.9	242.2	287.7	350.9
Government	52.1	66.6	84.1	90.8	123.8
Private sector	120.5	157.3	158.1	196.9	227.1
Gross investment	50.9	62.2	68.0	80.5	141.3
Government	12.2	14.3	29.6	49.5	81.6
Private sector /b	38.7	47.9	38.4	31.0	59.7
Domestic savings	49.1	13.0	10.3	6.9	15.6
Net factor income	-7.1	-3.5	-5.3	-12.4	-12.8
Current transfers	-3.2	-4.0	0.6	-0.3	-3.0
National savings	38.8	5.5	5.6	-5.8	-0.2
GNP	214.6	233.4	247.2	282.2	353.7
GNY	211.4	229.4	247.8	281.9	350.7

/a Includes change in stocks.

Source: Derived from Table 5.1 & IMF staff estimates.

Table 3.1: CENTRAL GOVERNMENT BUDGET, 1980-89
(SI$ million)

	1980	1981	1982	1983	1984	1985	1986	1987	1988	1989 Est.
Revenue	23.4	29.9	33.3	34.3	47.7	53.1	57.1	89.8	91.0	103.6
Tax	18.3	24.8	29.3	28.9	43.7	47.5	52.1	63.9	81.4	92.4
Non-tax	4.5	5.1	3.8	5.3	3.5	4.9	5.0	5.9	9.6	11.0
Capital	0.6	0.2	0.2	0.1	0.5	0.7	0.0	0.0	0.0	0.2
Grants	13.5	7.3	5.5	8.0	4.7	2.1	29.0	30.2	28.2	16.4
STABEX	..	..	..	--	0.0	0.0	16.7	25.1	20.4	9.5
Other	..	..	..	..	4.7	2.1	12.3	5.1	7.8	6.9
Expenditure	36.2	41.9	48.4	49.9	58.2	72.9	98.0	125.7	128.1	138.8
Current	24.4	30.9	34.5	39.2	46.1	59.2	65.7	77.1	100.7	111.6
Capital	11.8	11.0	11.9	10.7	10.1	13.7	30.3	48.6	27.4	27.2
Net lending	4.3	4.6	5.4	3.8	2.7	1.3	1.3	8.0	14.4	4.4
Overall balance	-3.6	-9.3	-13.0	-13.4	-8.5	-19.0	-11.2	-33.7	-23.3	-23.2
Financed by:										
Foreign borrowing (net)	3.1	3.3	5.4	7.7	4.6	8.8	18.3	35.1	17.5	8.4
Domestic financing	0.5	6.0	7.6	5.7	2.9	14.5	-0.6	1.9	5.0	15.9
STABEX account	..	..	..	..	--	--	-8.3	-14.9	-6.1	4.4
Other bank accounts	..	..	..	..	-1.8	9.4	5.2	13.5	7.5	8.0
Nonbank financing	..	..	..	..	4.7	5.1	2.5	3.3	3.8	3.5
Discrepancy /a	--	--	--	--	-1.0	-2.3	-6.5	-3.3	0.8	-1.1

/a Due to differences in timing, float and transactions outside the cash budget.

Source: Ministry of Finance and IMF staff estimates.

Table 3.2: CENTRAL GOVERNMENT REVENUE, 1980-89
(SI$ million)

	1980	1981	1982	1983	1984	1985	1986	1987	1988	1989 Est.
Taxes on income & profits	7.4	9.6	10.8	10.6	14.2	17.1	17.7	22.7	25.5	28.5
Companies	4.3	4.9	4.2	4.5	5.8	6.8	5.7	5.8	4.7	6.5
Individuals	3.1	4.7	6.6	6.1	8.4	10.3	12.0	16.9	20.8	22.0
Taxes on goods & services	0.9	1.2	1.2	1.2	1.1	2.1	1.7	1.8	3.7	3.8
Excise duties	0.2	0.3	0.2	0.3	0.2	0.4	0.4	0.4	0.5	0.8
Other /a	0.7	0.9	1.0	0.9	0.9	1.7	1.3	1.4	3.2	3.0
Taxes on international trade	10.0	13.8	17.3	17.1	28.4	28.3	32.7	39.4	52.2	60.1
Import duties	5.6	9.3	13.1	12.5	17.3	20.4	25.8	31.4	39.9	44.4
Export duties	4.4	4.5	4.2	4.6	11.1	7.9	6.9	8.0	12.3	15.7
Total tax revenue	18.3	24.6	29.3	28.9	43.7	47.5	52.1	63.9	81.4	92.4
Nontax revenue	4.5	5.1	3.8	5.3	3.5	4.9	5.0	5.9	9.6	11.0
Property income /b	2.8	3.1	1.9	3.4	1.7	1.8	2.7	3.7	5.6	8.3
Fees & charges	1.6	1.9	1.8	1.9	1.7	2.5	2.0	2.0	2.9	2.8
Other	0.1	0.1	0.1	0.0	0.1	0.6	0.3	0.2	1.1	-0.1
Total current revenue	22.8	29.7	33.1	34.2	47.2	52.4	57.1	69.8	91.0	103.4
Capital revenue	0.6	0.2	0.2	0.1	0.5	0.7	0.0	0.0	0.0	0.2
Total revenue	23.4	29.9	33.3	34.3	47.7	53.1	57.1	69.8	91.0	103.6

/b Includes business licenses & stamp duties.
/c Includes surpluses of public enterprises.

Source: Ministry of Finance and IMF staff estimates.

Table 3.3: CENTRAL GOVERNMENT EXPENDITURE, 1980-89
(SI$ million)

	1980	1981	1982	1983	1984	1985	1986	1987	1988	1989 Est.
Current expenditure	24.4	30.9	34.5	39.2	46.1	59.2	65.7	77.1	100.7	111.6
Wages & salaries	10.8	13.1	15.6	18.0	21.4	28.0	30.8	34.9	47.5	51.5
Purchases of goods & services	7.6	9.1	8.9	10.1	11.3	14.9	11.9	15.0	20.1	22.6
Interest payments	0.2	0.6	0.8	1.0	2.1	3.9	4.3	7.5	11.3	13.1
Subsidies & current transfers	5.8	8.1	9.2	10.1	11.3	14.4	18.7	19.7	21.8	24.4
- To public enterprises	1.7	2.3	2.5	2.8	3.0	3.7	5.9	5.8	6.1	7.2
- To local governments	2.8	4.2	5.3	5.5	6.9	9.0	8.4	8.0	8.5	8.3
- Other	1.3	1.6	1.4	1.8	1.4	1.7	4.4	5.9	7.2	8.9
Capital expenditure	11.8	11.0	11.9	10.7	10.1	13.7	30.3	48.6	27.4	27.2
Purchase of fixed capital assets	10.5	9.8	10.1	9.4	9.2	13.0	29.6	47.2	24.6	21.0
Capital transfers	1.3	1.2	1.8	1.3	0.9	0.7	0.7	1.4	2.8	6.2
- To nonfin. public enterprises	0.5	0.5	0.7	0.7	0.5	0.7	0.7	1.4	1.4	2.2
- Other	0.8	0.7	1.1	0.6	0.4	0.0	0.0	0.0	1.4	4.0
Total expenditure	36.2	41.9	46.4	49.9	56.2	72.9	96.0	125.7	128.1	138.8

Source: Ministry of Finance & IMF staff estimates.

Table 4.1: MONETARY SURVEY, 1980-89
(SI$ million)

End of period	1980	1981	1982	1983	1984	1985	1986	1987	1988	1989
Net foreign assets	23.3	12.6	19.3	28.8	41.5	24.7	40.8	61.6	79.7	49.8
	---	---	---	---	---	---	---	---	---	---
Domestic credit	19.2	27.2	29.2	25.4	38.5	61.7	62.3	70.8	92.0	121.2
	---	---	---	---	---	---	---	---	---	---
Government (net)	-3.3	-1.0	3.7	-0.9	2.3	12.7	9.6	8.2	9.6	21.7
Private sector /a	22.5	28.2	25.5	28.3	36.2	49.0	52.7	62.4	82.4	99.5
Other items (net)	-3.5	-7.8	-8.7	-4.3	-15.4	-20.1	-30.4	-34.8	-43.6	-44.5
	---	---	---	---	---	---	---	---	---	---
Broad money	39.0	32.2	39.8	47.9	64.6	66.3	72.7	97.6	128.1	128.5
	---	---	---	---	---	---	---	---	---	---
Money supply	15.2	14.2	15.8	18.4	28.3	28.3	30.4	37.2	49.1	50.1
Quasi-money	23.8	18.0	24.0	29.5	36.3	38.0	42.3	60.4	79.0	76.4

/a Including public enterprises.

Source: Central Bank of Solomon Islands & IMF staff estimates.

Table 4.2: INTEREST RATES, 1984-88
(% per annum)

End of period	1984	1985	1986	1987	1988
Central Bank					
Advances to banks /a	10	14	14	..	..
Commercial bank deposits	8	8	8	6	6
Statutory reserve deposits	..	..	..	..	10
Commercial banks					
Deposit rates (average)	6	6	7	7	7
Lending rates (average)	14	17	18	18	18
Treasury bond yield	9	10	12	11	11
Development bond rate	11	12	13	12	12

/a Minimum ordinary rate.

Source: Central Bank of Solomon Islands.

Table 4.3: HONIARA RETAIL PRICE INDEX, 1980-89
(fourth quarter 1984=100)

Period average	Weights	1980	1981	1982	1983	1984	1985	1986	1987	1988	1989
Food	51.0	60.2	72.0	81.3	86.6	99.8	106.0	118.0	127.4	153.8	166.0
Beverages & tobacco	10.0	64.1	77.7	90.2	92.1	100.7	109.6	151.1	196.8	228.2	265.5
Clothing & footwear	4.9	63.7	68.0	76.0	82.1	89.5	105.5	111.2	117.6	137.1	154.4
Transport	6.6	57.4	68.1	77.9	84.9	94.0	107.1	127.1	148.4	153.4	176.5
Housing	12.5	75.8	82.7	93.2	99.4	99.7	103.1	111.8	115.2	118.5	124.3
Miscellaneous	15.0	58.2	63.6	70.4	76.6	84.3	103.9	112.4	125.0	148.6	168.7
Overall index	100.0	62.2	72.4	81.8	86.9	96.5	105.9	120.0	132.8	155.0	178.8
Of which:											
Imported items	53.7	..	..	..	..	..	105.8	118.0	128.2	156.4	180.8
% change											
Food		15.0	19.6	12.9	8.5	15.0	6.4	11.3	8.0	20.7	7.9
Beverages & tobacco		11.5	21.2	16.1	2.1	9.3	8.8	37.9	30.2	14.9	17.4
Clothing & footwear		4.3	6.8	11.8	8.0	9.0	17.9	5.4	5.8	16.6	12.6
Transport		13.3	18.8	14.3	9.0	10.7	13.9	18.7	15.2	4.8	15.1
Housing		9.4	9.1	12.7	6.7	0.3	3.4	8.4	3.0	2.9	4.9
Miscellaneous		9.5	9.3	10.7	8.8	10.1	23.3	8.2	11.2	18.9	13.5
Overall index		12.6	16.4	13.0	6.2	11.0	9.7	13.3	10.7	16.7	15.4
Imported items		..	..	..	..	..	..	11.5	8.6	22.0	15.6

Source: Statistics Office & IMF staff estimates.

Table 5.1: BALANCE OF PAYMENTS, 1980-89
(US$ million)

	1980	1981	1982	1983	1984	1985	1986	1987	1988	1989
Merchandise exports (fob)	73.8	66.2	58.3	62.0	93.1	70.1	66.0	64.0	81.9	74.7
Merchandise imports (cif)	-88.9	-91.1	-71.0	-73.8	-80.7	-85.2	-80.8	-84.8	-120.9	-111.5
Trade balance	-15.1	-25.0	-12.7	-11.8	12.4	-15.1	-14.6	-20.7	-39.0	-36.8
Non-factor services (net)	..	..	..	..	-13.8	-18.1	-18.5	-16.0	-21.4	-31.1
- Travel receipts	..	..	..	..	2.2	2.6	2.7	5.0	5.6	6.5
- Other receipts	..	..	..	..	4.8	4.7	14.5	17.6	20.8	23.5
- Payments	..	..	..	..	-20.8	-25.4	-35.7	-38.6	-47.6	-61.1
Resource balance	-16.4	-13.4	-4.6	-12.7	-1.4	-33.2	-33.1	-36.7	-60.4	-68.0
Factor services (net)	..	..	..	..	-5.6	-2.4	-3.0	-6.2	-6.1	-0.7
- Receipts	..	..	..	..	4.6	4.1	3.1	3.2	3.6	3.9
- Public interest payments	..	..	..	..	-0.2	-0.3	-0.5	-0.6	-1.2	-1.9
- IMF charges	..	..	..	..	-0.2	-0.2	-0.2	-1.0	0.0	0.0
- Other payments	..	..	..	..	-9.8	-5.9	-5.4	-7.9	-8.5	-2.7
Private transfers (net)	0.8	-5.8	-4.5	-2.6	-2.5	-2.7	0.3	-0.1	-1.4	1.2
Current account balance	-30.7	-44.2	-21.9	-27.0	-9.5	-38.3	-35.8	-43.1	-68.0	-87.5
Official grants	19.1	17.5	11.8	14.9	14.6	11.8	31.5	41.6	42.4	36.8
- STABEX	..	..	..	..	0.0	0.0	9.6	12.5	9.8	4.0
- Other cash	..	..	..	..	6.0	4.1	4.5	4.1	3.7	4.0
- Goods & services	..	..	..	..	2.7	2.7	9.6	10.2	12.0	12.0
- Technical assistance	..	..	..	..	5.9	5.1	7.8	14.8	16.8	16.8
Public loan disbursements (net)	3.9	4.2	4.1	6.8	6.2	6.9	10.4	14.5	9.9	10.5
- Gross disbursements	4.0	4.2	4.1	6.9	6.8	7.8	11.4	15.7	12.6	15.2
- Principal repayments	0.0	0.0	0.0	-0.1	-0.7	-0.9	-1.0	-1.2	-2.7	-4.7
Other (net) /a	-0.6	9.1	10.2	8.5	-4.9	7.3	-2.0	-1.5	18.8	5.0
Use of net foreign assets	8.2	13.5	-4.2	-3.2	-6.3	12.3	-4.1	-11.5	-3.1	15.4
Net foreign assets (end of period)	29.6	16.1	20.3	23.5	29.8	17.5	21.6	33.1	36.2	20.8

/a Includes private capital flows, valuation changes, & errors & omissions.

Source: Central Bank of Solomon Islands, IMF staff estimates & World Bank, Debtor Reporting System.

Table 5.2: MERCHANDISE TRADE INDICES, 1983-88
(1983=100)

	1983	1984	1985	1986	1987	1988
Value /a						

Exports	100.0	150.1	113.1	106.4	103.3	132.1
Imports	100.0	107.0	112.7	108.8	109.5	158.8
Volume						

Exports	100.0	121.9	109.0	117.9	93.1	99.3
Imports	100.0	109.6	118.6	113.6	100.4	138.8
Unit value /a						

Exports	100.0	123.2	103.7	90.2	110.9	133.0
Imports	100.0	97.7	95.1	95.7	109.1	114.4
Terms of trade a/	100.0	126.1	109.1	94.3	101.6	116.3

/a In US Dollar terms.

Source: IMF staff estimates.

Table 5.3: MERCHANDISE EXPORTS, 1980-89

	1980	1981	1982	1983	1984	1985	1986	1987	1988	1989
Value (US$ million)	73.8	66.2	58.3	62.0	93.1	70.1	66.0	64.0	81.9	74.7
Copra	12.6	9.2	8.3	7.3	25.3	15.9	3.4	4.2	7.5	9.1
Palm oil	8.1	8.1	7.1	6.7	12.0	8.4	3.2	3.4	5.9	7.9
Fish (fresh & frozen)	23.8	21.9	10.2	21.2	19.7	18.7	26.9	22.4	31.9	22.5
Fish (canned)	3.1	2.9	3.0	3.1	2.4	2.4	2.8	3.6	4.3	3.9
Logs	18.0	17.0	22.0	16.4	22.6	16.0	19.5	17.5	18.1	16.9
Sawn timber	1.3	1.5	1.5	1.1	1.0	0.7	1.0	1.1	1.0	1.1
Cocoa	0.8	1.1	0.9	1.9	2.8	3.4	3.7	4.6	3.6	3.5
Other	8.1	4.4	5.4	4.4	7.4	4.7	5.4	7.3	9.5	9.6
Volume ('000 metric tons)										
Copra	31.7	31.8	33.9	25.5	42.0	43.6	32.4	27.9	27.1	32.9
Palm oil	15.6	16.9	18.8	20.0	21.5	18.6	14.5	11.6	13.6	14.2
Fish (fresh & frozen)	21.8	23.7	15.3	30.8	33.2	27.2	39.6	28.6	35.0	27.9
Fish (canned)	0.8	0.8	0.9	1.1	0.7	0.9	1.0	1.2	1.2	1.3
Logs ('000 cubic meters)	258.0	315.0	333.0	337.0	392.0	330.0	434.0	281.0	261.0	260.0
Sawn timber ('000 cubic meters)	7.0	7.0	7.0	6.0	6.0	4.0	6.0	6.0	5.0	5.0
Cocoa	0.3	0.6	0.8	1.2	1.4	1.8	2.0	2.7	2.6	3.3
Unit value (US$/metric ton)										
Copra	398.3	289.2	244.2	285.1	601.3	363.9	105.4	149.0	277.0	278.3
Palm oil	517.3	481.4	379.9	336.7	560.9	448.7	222.4	298.0	436.1	561.4
Fish (fresh & frozen)	1102.7	925.4	663.8	687.2	592.8	685.7	680.5	843.0	912.2	805.8
Fish (canned)	3904.8	3684.9	3312.0	2818.3	3269.0	2570.1	2653.0	2959.3	3576.9	3075.3
Logs (US$/cubic meter)	69.6	53.9	66.0	48.5	57.6	48.5	44.9	62.3	69.2	65.0
Sawn timber (US$/cubic meter)	185.9	219.0	220.8	178.2	172.2	174.7	169.8	175.2	209.6	221.4
Cocoa	2603.0	1768.7	1472.0	1603.5	1876.6	1929.6	1824.4	1703.1	1364.5	1071.4

Source: Central Bank of Solomon Islands.

Table 5.4: MERCHANDISE IMPORTS, 1980-89
(US$ '000)

	1980	1981	1982	1983	1984	1985	1986	1987	1988	1989
Food & live animals	7.9	8.0	8.7	7.1	10.3	10.6	9.9	10.1	16.7	..
Beverages & tobacco	2.2	2.7	2.2	2.4	2.9	2.7	2.4	2.1	3.2	..
Raw materials	0.5	0.7	0.6	0.7	1.0	0.8	0.5	0.4	0.8	..
Mineral fuels	11.8	17.5	14.8	15.5	15.0	14.1	11.3	10.0	11.1	..
Oils & fats	0.5	0.4	0.8	0.8	0.8	1.2	0.5	0.4	0.5	..
Chemicals	3.8	4.4	3.9	3.7	4.0	4.1	2.9	4.5	6.7	..
Manufactured goods	12.2	13.9	9.4	11.0	10.6	10.9	9.4	13.8	19.3	..
Machinery & transport equipment	29.0	22.2	13.8	16.1	15.7	18.2	18.1	19.6	29.8	..
Miscellaneous manufactures	5.7	5.8	5.2	4.2	5.3	6.6	4.7	6.2	9.3	..
Other /a	0.3	0.5	0.3	0.2	0.4	0.3	7.3	0.3	0.4	..
Total (fob)	74.1	75.9	59.2	61.5	65.8	69.3	66.9	67.4	97.6	..
Freight & insurance	14.8	15.2	11.8	12.3	14.9	15.9	13.7	17.4	23.3	..
Total (cif)	88.9	91.1	71.0	73.8	80.7	85.2	80.6	84.8	120.9	111.5

/a Includes adjustment for cyclone relief in 1986.

Source: Central Bank of Solomon Islands.

Table 5.5: DIRECTION OF TRADE, 1980-89
(% of total)

Table 5.5: DIRECTION OF TRADE, 1980-89
(% of total)

	1980	1981	1982	1983	1984	1985	1986	1987	1988	1989
Destination of exports	100.0	100.0	100.0	100.0	100.0	100.0	100.0	100.0	100.0	100.0
Japan	26.1	37.4	58.8	42.9	33.2	51.9	37.0	35.6	34.5	33.2
Australia	2.3	3.1	2.7	1.9	2.3	2.3	4.0	3.7	4.7	7.2
Other Asian countries	2.1	2.2	3.1	14.1	14.3	11.1	33.1	21.6	22.2	20.1
United Kingdom	12.8	11.9	14.4	11.3	12.4	14.1	8.5	13.8	14.5	16.9
Netherlands	12.5	11.9	3.6	2.5	11.2	10.4	2.5	2.0	1.7	6.7
United States	3.4	0.6	0.1	0.1	0.0	2.5	0.1	5.2	0.1	0.1
Other countries	41.0	32.9	17.4	27.2	26.5	7.8	14.8	18.0	22.4	15.7
Origin of imports	100.0	100.0	100.0	100.0	100.0	100.0	100.0	100.0	100.0	...
Australia	30.8	27.9	33.8	33.0	36.3	37.2	40.0	41.4	45.5	...
Japan	19.7	15.2	13.9	19.5	15.0	19.6	16.9	19.1	16.2	...
New Zealand	7.0	8.4	8.3	6.9	8.1	9.0	7.7	7.9	8.3	...
Singapore	14.7	22.1	17.5	18.7	14.5	10.2	8.2	9.2	5.4	...
Other Asian countries	6.7	6.3	8.3	7.5	9.5	11.0	10.0	8.9	9.8	...
United Kingdom	8.6	8.1	4.4	3.0	3.3	4.0	4.1	4.4	5.3	...
Other countries	12.5	12.1	13.7	11.4	13.3	8.9	13.2	9.1	9.6	...

Source: Central Bank of Solomon Islands.

Table 6.1: EXTERNAL PUBLIC DEBT AND DEBT SERVICE, 1980-88 /a
(US$ '000)

	1980	1981	1982	1983	1984	1985	1986	1987	1988
Debt outstanding & disbursed	17,464	19,562	22,364	27,877	31,966	42,874	56,109	79,687	86,485
Multilateral loans	7,123	11,306	15,392	19,883	23,609	28,891	34,954	43,701	49,047
Bilateral loans	10,341	8,256	6,971	7,994	8,357	13,983	17,686	31,729	33,846
Private creditors	0	0	0	0	0	0	3,469	4,257	3,592
Gross disbursements	3,960	4,183	4,117	6,884	6,829	7,806	11,381	15,689	12,638
Multilateral loans	3,960	4,183	4,117	5,063	4,234	3,720	4,188	5,341	7,702
Bilateral loans	0	0	0	1,820	2,595	4,086	4,080	10,348	4,936
Private creditors	0	0	0	0	0	0	3,113	0	0
Interest payments	29	89	86	92	196	270	543	604	1,210
Multilateral loans	29	89	86	89	147	212	324	376	393
Bilateral loans	0	0	0	3	49	58	219	228	652
Private creditors	0	0	0	0	0	0	0	0	165
Principal repayments	16	18	16	61	657	904	969	1,238	2,694
Multilateral loans	0	0	0	50	100	350	350	420	534
Bilateral loans	16	18	16	11	557	554	619	818	1,967
Private creditors	0	0	0	0	0	0	0	0	193
Total debt service	45	107	102	153	853	1,174	1,512	1,842	3,904
Multilateral loans	29	89	88	139	247	562	674	796	927
Bilateral loans	16	18	16	14	606	612	838	1,046	2,619
Private creditors	0	0	0	0	0	0	0	0	358

/a Excludes borrowings by the Central Bank.

Source: World Bank, Debtor Reporting System.

TONGA

DEVELOPMENT SURVEY

TONGA

CURRENCY EQUIVALENTS

Annual Averages

1981	$1.00 = T$0.8702
1982	$1.00 = T$0.9859
1983	$1.00 = T$1.1100
1984	$1.00 = T$1.1395
1985	$1.00 = T$1.4319
1986	$1.00 = T$1.4960
1987	$1.00 = T$1.4282
1988	$1.00 = T$1.2799
1989	$1.00 = T$1.2637

FISCAL YEAR

July 1 - June 30

ABBREVIATIONS AND ACRONYMS

ADB	=	Asian Development Bank
BOT	=	Bank of Tonga
EIB	=	European Investment Bank
IFAD	=	International Fund for Agricultural Development
SIC	=	Small Industries Center
TCB	=	Tonga Commodities Board
TDB	=	Tonga Development Bank
TVB	=	Tonga Visitors Bureau

Table of Contents

This report was prepared by a World Bank mission which visited Tonga in November 1989. The mission members were Kyle Peters, John Kerr-Stevens, Paul Flanagan (AIDAB) and Bob Smith (consultant). A draft of the report was discussed with government officials in June 1990.

TONGA: ECONOMICS DEVELOPMENTS AND PROSPECTS

A. Background

4.1   The Kingdom of Tonga consists of about 170 islands in three main
groups: Tongatapu and 'Eua; Vana'u; and Ha'apai. The population was
estimated at 94,535 in 1986 (see Table 4.1). Despite a natural rate of
population growth of about 1.5 percent per annum, the population has grown by
only 0.5 percent per annum since 1976, because of substantial emigration.
Since 1986, the population has stagnated, if not declined, due to a major out-
migration of 4,500-5,000 Tongans to New Zealand which occurred immediately
after the 1986 Census as a result of a temporary abolition of visa
requirements for Pacific Islanders entering New Zealand.

4.2   Tongan society is relatively homogenous with the Tongan language
spoken throughout the country. There was an elaborate social system in Tonga
well before European exploration began in 1616. Following a period of violent
political struggles for power in the early nineteenth century, a
Constitutional Monarchy was introduced in 1875. The Kingdom of Tonga was a
British protectorate for seven decades from 1900 becoming completely
independent of the United Kingdom in 1970. Tonga's current sociopolitical
order is a blending of traditional and Western elements. Its social structure
is characterized by: (a) a three-class system consisting of the Royal Family,
33 nobles and the people (commoners); (b) the dominant role of religion and
churches (the Free Wesleyan church is the principal religion); and (c) strong
extended family ties. The political order of the country is based on the
equal sharing of representation between the nobles, the Ministers of the
Crown, and the people in the Legislative Assembly. The combined influence of
church, monarchical state and relative isolation from the outside world have
given Tongan society an unusually conservative and stable nature, which has
also influenced economic management to a large extent.

4.3   The Kingdom of Tonga has an estimated GNP per capita of $800, placing
it in the lower middle-income group. However, social indicators in Tonga are
generally far superior to those of other lower middle-income countries: the
infant mortality rate is 26 compared to an average of 59 for lower middle-
income countries; access to safe water is available to 99 percent of the
population which is substantially higher than other lower middle-income
countries; the daily calorie supply is 2,940 compared to 2,767 for lower
middle-income countries; and life expectancy at birth is 65.7 compared to
63.8. Given these social indicators, and the traditional Tongan social system
based upon extended family ties, the incidence of poverty is felt to be very
low.

4.4   Economic events in Tonga are dominated by the emigration of Tongans
abroad seeking economic opportunities and the substantial flows of official
assistance that Tonga receives. Emigration, both permanent and transitory, is
by far the most important. It is estimated that 35,000 to 45,000 Tongans have
migrated and are living abroad, primarily in New Zealand, the United States
(mainly Hawaii, California and Utah), and Australia. These emigrants send
substantial remittances to their relatives in Tonga. During 1987/88 and

Table 4.1: SOCIAL INDICATORS, 1988 /a

Indicator	Units	Tonga	Asia	Lower-Middle Income
Population /b	persons	94,535	-	-
- Growth rate /b	%	0.5	1.8	2.2
Crude birth rate	per 000	32.0	26.8	31.5
Crude death rate	per 000	6.8	8.8	8.6
Infant mortality rate	per 000 births	26.0	61.5	59.1
Life expectancy at birth	years	65.7	63.7	63.8
Population per:				
- Doctor	persons	1649	1422	1547
- Nurse	persons	557	1674	
- Hospital	persons	275	733	
Child immunization				
- Measles	%		41.0	62.6
- DPT	%		48.6	64.7
Access to safe water	%	99.0		
- Urban	%	100.0	72.5	76.7
- Rural	%	71.0		46.3
Gross enrollment ratios				
- Primary	%		105.3	106.8
- Secondary	%		94.4	101.3
Adult illiteracy rate	%		39.5	26.2

/a Or most recent estimate.
/b Preliminary estimates from 1986 census.

Source: World Bank, "Social Indicators of Development, 1989".

1988/89,1/ private remittance inflows averaged about $28 million, which was more than three times merchandise exports and about 30 percent of GDP. In

---

1/ The Tongan fiscal year begins on July 1 and ends on June 30.

addition to inflows of cash, remittances are also received in-kind; the proportion of "in-kind" remittances is perceived to have increased dramatically in the last couple of years. Therefore, actual remittances in cash and kind may be even higher than estimated in the balance of payments. These remittance inflows have had an adverse effect upon labor supply, leading to higher reservation wages and a corresponding reduction in the production of traditional export crops. In the last two years, remittances have declined as a proportion of GDP. Given Tonga's dependence on private remittances, there is a growing concern that this may reflect a longer term trend due to a weakening of family ties between Tongans living abroad and their relatives remaining in Tonga. The long term trend of remittances is difficult to assess; however, much of the apparent stagnation may reflect exchange rate movements as remittances have continued to rise in US dollar terms.

4.5   The Kingdom of Tonga also receives substantial levels of official assistance, about $173 per capita.2/ These flows have supported a large public sector which dominates domestic economic activity and the formal labor markets. During the last five years, bilateral grants have constituted the largest share of external assistance (about three-quarters). The major donors are Australia, New Zealand, Japan and the EEC. Disbursements of concessional loans have varied during the 1980s, but averaged about $2.3 million per annum The main suppliers of these loans has been the Asian Development Bank, the European Investment Bank, International Fund for Agricultural Development and, more recently, the World Bank. Currently, Tonga is probably absorbing less assistance than donors are willing to contribute, due to a lack of viable projects, and planning and implementation constraints.

4.6   Agriculture and services are the most important sectors of the Tongan economy. According to the national account statistics, agriculture accounts for about 40 per cent of GDP, and virtually all production originates on small-scale landholdings. Recent analysis by the World Bank, however, indicates that agriculture value-added is significantly underestimated and therefore constitutes a larger share of economic activity.3/ The small manufacturing sector, which accounts for only about 10 percent of GDP, includes the processing of coconut products and businesses located in the industrial processing zone near the capital. A large part of GDP is generated in the services sector, reflecting the importance of Government expenditure and official assistance. There are no statistics of investment and savings but the main trends are apparent. In recent years, a high level of public investment in relation to GDP has been maintained. Considerable economic infrastructure has been created, notably in the areas of shipping and air transport, ports and harbors, telecommunications, and flood protection. Financing for these projects has been provided almost entirely by external concessional assistance. Private sector investment has been limited, as

---

2/ Official inflows recorded in the balance of payments in 1987/88 were only $79 per capita. Thus, a substantial portion of the official aid is in the form of technical assistance and other training which does not necessarily result in a financial transfer to Tonga.

3/ See, Kingdom of Tonga: Agriculture Sector Strategy Review, World Bank Report No. 8544-TON, April 10, 1990, Volume 1, pp. 6-7. (This document is for internal use only.)

indicated by the modest amount of credit extended by the commercial and development banks. Some of the financing of these investments have been derived from the Tonga Development Bank with lines of credit from multilateral and bilateral agencies. Thus, domestic savings has been negligible, if not negative, throughout the 1980s.

4.7 The structure of the balance of payments also reflects the dependence of the economy on private remittances and official grants, and the dominance of agriculture in economic activity. Exports are equivalent to about 10-15 percent of GDP, consisting of a small range of goods because of the narrow productive base. Primary products represent about three fourths of the total. The largest categories are coconut products; bananas, output of which have benefitted from development support provided by New Zealand; and vanilla, exports of which have grown rapidly during the 1980s, partly in response to favorable world prices. Other primary product exports are root crops, watermelons, and fish. Industrial goods, account for about one fourth of total exports; the largest item is knitwear. Imports are equivalent to more than 50 percent of GDP, reflecting the open nature of the economy and the limited potential for substitution by domestic production. The composition of imports by main categories has been relatively stable during this decade. Food and beverages and manufactured goods constitute about half of the total, reflecting the strong consumption demand generated by private remittances. Imports of machinery and transport equipment and industrial materials, which average about one third of the total, are closely tied to disbursements of external assistance. The services account normally shows a small surplus. The main sources of receipts are tourism, interest earnings on external assets, and shipping services as a result of the lease of a vessel to the Pacific Forum Line. The largest category of payments is freight, which constitutes about 30 percent of the value of imports (fob). The large negative trade balance has been more than offset by remittances and official aid, allowing increases in reserves in most years.

B. Recent Economic Developments

4.8 Since 1981/82, the Tongan economy has expanded by about 2.5 percent per annum (see Table 4.2).[4] The economy experienced negative growth only in 1987/88, when Tongan suffered a severe drought. Given that the population has grown at 0.5 percent per annum during this period, per capita GDP has increased by about 2.0 percent per annum throughout the decade. With the exception of Fiji, this is one of the best performances of the World Bank's Pacific Island members. It is especially impressive, given Tonga's limited natural resource base and the steady, substantial migration of Tongan citizens. Two factors have been responsible for the Kingdom's growth

---

[4] The lack of official national accounts is a major constraint to determining recent trends in the economy. The data analyzed in this section are unofficial estimates from the World Bank, IMF and the Treasury. An effort is currently underway to reestimate a consistent set of national accounts for the 1980s. Preliminary results from this exercise suggest that the rate of growth may be lower than outlined in this report, but the level of GNP is higher. Improving the quality and timeliness of economic data should be an important objective of the Government, as this is likely to have a positive effect upon economic management.

Table 4.2: ECONOMIC INDICATORS, 1981-89

	1981/82-85/86	1986/87	1987/88	1988/89
Production (growth rates % p.a.)				
GDP	3.1	3.3	-1.9	3.6
Agriculture	0.7	3.6	-10.0	2.1
Manufacturing	6.7	3.3	0.0	4.8
Others	5.0	3.1	4.7	4.5
Central Government Budget (% of GDP)				
Revenue	26.1	29.2	31.3	30.9
- Tax revenue	18.3	20.1	22.0	20.5
- Nontax revenue	7.8	9.1	9.4	10.5
Expenditure & Net Lending	46.2	52.6	50.5	49.5
Current	24.2	28.3	27.9	26.7
Development	21.2	17.5	21.7	20.7
Net landing	0.8	6.8	0.9	2.1
Overall Balance	-20.1	-23.2	-19.3	-18.5
Financed by:	20.1	23.2	19.3	18.5
External grants	19.3	20.2	20.5	20.4
External borrowing (net)	0.8	6.7	1.7	2.1
Domestic credit	0.0	-3.6	-3.0	-4.0
Money and Prices (growth rates % per annum)				
Domestic credit	18.4/b	-6.3	25.4	39.9
Private credit /a	13.0/b	12.4	20.0	42.5
Broad money	18.8/b	33.3	-2.2	6.8
Money	19.6/b	26.5	8.4	-4.5
Consumer prices	6.8	7.5	11.2	4.0
GDP	9.6	7.6	11.1	2.9
Balance of Payments ($ million)				
Exports (fob)	6.4	7.1	6.4	8.7
Imports (fob)	34.7	35.1	44.1	50.3
Trade balance	-28.3	-28.0	-37.7	-41.6
Services (net)	2.7	3.6	1.4	-6.6
Private transfers (net)	19.3	22.5	21.3	24.9
Current account	-4.8	0.8	-12.1	-20.6
External grants (net)	5.5	6.6	5.7	10.9
Public MLT (net)	1.3	0.6	3.6	..
Other capital (net)	3.8	-0.5	1.6	..
Use of net foreign assets (- = increase)	-2.1	-7.5	0.3	1.3
Ratios				
Current account/GDP (%)	7.4	1.1	-13.8	-19.8
Debt service/exports (%)	4.0	4.9	5.2	5.2
DOD/GDP (%)	39.2	47.7	44.7	38.9
Net foreign assets (months of imports)	6.3	8.6	7.0	6.5

/a Includes public enterprises.
/b 1982/83-1985/86 only.

Source: Statistical annex.

performance during the 1980s. First, the Government has pursued prudent fiscal policies, in order to preserve internal and external stability. The cornerstone of macroeconomic policy has been a budget law which requires a balanced recurrent budget.5/ Strict adherence to this policy is reflected in low levels of foreign borrowing and an increase in Government assets with the domestic banking system during the 1980s. Second, the Government has pursued a set of adjustment policies designed to restructure the economy towards more efficient export-oriented activities. Furthermore, the agriculture sector has also undergone a restructuring from relatively inefficient agriculture (such as coconuts) towards higher value agricultural activities.

4.9   During the 1980s, the sources of this economic growth were broad based. The manufacturing sector, outside of the desiccated coconut factory operated by the Tongan Commodities Board, has experienced significant growth. The performance of the manufacturing sector has been stimulated by: a stable macroeconomic environment; the Industrial Development Incentive Act, enacted in 1978, which provides attractive incentives to foreign investors within a simple and uncomplicated administrative environment; a number of fiscal measures which lowered personal income taxes and offered tax incentives to prospective foreign investors and exporters; the availability of credit finance through the Tongan Development Bank (TDB) for export-oriented industries; and, the establishment of a Small Industries Center (SIC), a 20-acre industrial estate in Nuku'alofa, which provides basic infrastructure (roads, water, power and telephone connections) plus simple standard factory shed buildings. Employment in manufacturing is estimated to have grown at an annual average of 8 percent during 1983-88.6/ The tourism sector also grew rapidly, with air visitors increasing by 25 percent since 1982. Growth was also bolstered by the service sector, particularly Government services, construction, telecommunication, power, and wholesale and retail trade. The latter was propelled by private remittances which averaged 20 percent of GDP during this period. Large investments in infrastructure funded by official assistance spurred growth in the other subsectors.

4.10   The agriculture sector has generally stagnated during the 1980s.7/ However, this stagnation has been wholly due to the declining trend in commercial exports, particularly coconut and banana exports, whereas the production, consumption and export of staple foods have been rising, largely offsetting the declining trend in commercial exports. Regarding commercial agriculture, coconut production has slowly declined throughout the 1980s reflecting the low returns from its cultivation and the aging tree stock. In the early 1980s, banana and vanilla production provided an impetus to the sector. However, in the past couple of years, a number of factors have

---

5/ The Government also set aside funds for development expenditures through the Development Fund. These funds are considered recurrent expenditures by the Tongan authorities. Therefore, in most years during the 1980s, "balanced" budget policy has led to positive government savings.

6/ This growth occurred despite the closing of the desiccated coconut factory, which resulted in a decline of about 200 workers in 1988.

7/ An analysis of the performance of the agriculture sector is contained in "Kingdom of Tonga: Agriculture Sector Strategy Review.", op. cit. (This document is for internal use only.)

hampered the performance of commercial agriculture: (i) a severe drought adversely affected agricultural performance in 1987; (ii) the local poultry industry collapsed as a result of a change in the duty structure which allowed duty free entry of chicken pieces; (iii) the banana crop has been continually affected by strong winds; (iv) overcropping resulting from the high production levels in 1987 left the vanilla crop overstressed; and (v) the desiccated coconut factory has discontinued operation.

4.11   The overall performance of the economy, however, slowly weakened towards the end of the 1980s. Several factors accounted for this trend. As discussed above, the underlying performance of export agriculture continued to weaken; in particular, production of bananas collapsed with the cessation of the New Zealand scheme. The slowdown in agriculture was exacerbated by the severe drought in 1987/88. Furthermore, the initial burst of activities in the manufacturing sector in the early 1980s also began to abate due to a lack of progress in implementing further structural policies to preserve competitiveness. Moreover, the recent upturn in economic activity in 1988/89 and 1989/90 largely reflected activities related to the King's birthday celebration and the South Pacific games, that were held in Nuku'alofa. The effects of these activities are expected to be transitory and the economic slowdown is likely to continue into the 1990s without a determined effort to revive the productive sectors.

4.12   Throughout the 1980s, the balance of payments has been financed without difficulty. Export performance, however, has been generally disappointing, reflecting the stagnant growth of traditional agricultural exports. Manufacturing export growth was relatively strong, but from a very small base. Rising private remittances and official grants financed a high level of imports. The trade deficit averaged almost 36 percent of GDP in the last several years. Large private remittance and official assistance inflows financed the large negative trade balance and allowed reserves to rise to about six months of imports. The underlying weakness in the economy which became apparent during 1987/88-1989/90 was also reflected in the balance of payments by the emergence of a negative overall balance and a drawdown of official reserves.

4.13   The conduct of fiscal policy during the 1980s has been dominated by the Government's balanced recurrent budget policy. Maintaining a balanced recurrent budget has been particularly difficult, because the Government has had difficulty in effectively taxing private remittances. In the early 1980s, the Government was able to contain spending, so that current expenditures were stable in relation to GDP. But, since trade and income tax revenues did not keep pace with GDP growth, the Government was forced to continue increasing import duties.8/ It was becoming apparent by the mid-1980s that the combination of the Government's balanced recurrent budget policy, the low and declining elasticity of trade and income taxes, and the Government's inability

---

8/   The elasticity of income taxes was eroded because of concessions to encourage productive activities and personal savings, such as lower corporate taxes for export-oriented industries, higher income tax exemptions and education allowances. By the mid-1980s, trade taxes were also reaching levels that affected the competitiveness of the economy and that further increases might be counter-productive.

to tax remittances, would necessitate continuing reductions in current expenditures. Therefore, the Government in 1986/87 introduced a major tax reform in which personal income taxes were reduced to promote savings and investment--the maximum rate for individuals is now 10 percent, while for resident corporations it is 30 percent and for nonresident companies 42.5 percent. A broad-based retail sales tax of 5 percent was also introduced to compensate for the revenue loss and to tax private remittances more effectively. As a result, revenues remained relatively stable for several years and the Government continued to maintain restraint on current expenditures. However, revenues in 1989/90 have again stagnated, forcing the Government to exert substantial pressure on Ministries to reduce further recurrent expenditures, leading to a further decline in expenditures on the already underbudgeted recurrent expenditure.

4.14   Throughout the 1980s, the Tongan economy has experienced erratic bouts of inflation despite its tight fiscal policy stance. For example, inflation as measured by the CPI was about 2 percent in 1984/85, but rose to 31 percent in 1985/86. These movements in the rate of inflation have been destabilizing to the economy and complicated interest rate policy and monetary management. There are two main reasons for the erratic behavior of prices. First, weather conditions, such as cyclones and droughts, have increased the variability of food prices, which constitute a large proportion of consumer expenditures. For example, in 1984 food prices plummeted by 15 percent after the recovery of food production from the effects of the 1982 cyclone, and in 1987 domestic food prices rose by 34 percent due to the effects of a severe drought. Second, inflation has moved substantially in relatively short periods due to exchange rate policy. The value of the Pa'anga (the Tongan currency) is tied at par to the Australian dollar. However, a large proportion of Tonga's imports (almost 40 percent) are from New Zealand. During 1984-87, the New Zealand economy experienced a rate of inflation in excess of 50 percent, while the New Zealand dollar was also appreciating substantially against the Australian dollar. The net effect on Tonga was to raise the price of imports substantially leading to high rates of inflation. Subsequently, as the Australian dollar has appreciated vis a vis the New Zealand dollar, inflation has abated in Tonga.

C. Development Prospects and Policies

4.15   Prospects and Financing Requirements. Despite achieving modest increases in per capita GDP--a better performance than the other small Pacific Island countries discussed in this report--during the 1980s, there is a need for adjustment policies to address the structural impediments to higher economic growth and export performance. Government policies to induce structural changes in the economy were initially successful in stimulating the performance of manufacturing and tourism, but recently the manufacturing sector appears to be slowing. The process of structural change in the economy needs to be intensified with much greater attention devoted to the agriculture sector than in the past. Overall, Tonga's economy has the potential to return to a growth rate of 3-4 percent per annum (see Table 4.3). Given the projected slow rate of population growth, this would permit reasonable increases in income per capita.

4.16   Achieving this rate of growth will be closely tied to the performance of the agriculture sector, because of its importance in the economy. This will be especially difficult given that the contribution of coconuts and bananas is likely to continue to decline, with the best prospects for higher growth arising from vanilla and non-traditional export crops (such as traditional food crops). Returns from the exports of <u>coconuts</u> are too low, given other wage opportunities and remittance receipts. As a result, copra production is not likely to grow. Production declines on Tongatapu will likely be offset by increases on some of the other islands where alternative sources of cash income are not available. The Tongan <u>banana</u> industry is also likely to stagnate. This is because the New Zealand aid program for bananas is ending and deregulation of the previous monopoly of banana importing agents in New Zealand will adversely affect Tonga. Previously, a monopoly had been

Table 4.3: MEDIUM-TERM MACROECONOMIC PROJECTIONS, 1990-99

	1984/85-88/89	1989/90-93/94	1994/95-98/99
Growth rates (% p.a.)			
GDP	2.6%	3.2%	3.5
percent			
Agriculture	1.4%	2.6%	2.7%
Manufacturing	5.7%	5.8%	5.9%
Others	3.9%	3.1%	3.4%
Consumer prices	10.3%	5.3%	4.8%
Other indicators			
Current account/GDP (%) /a	-22.4	-16.6	-16.9
Debt service/exports	5.2	8.4	8.3
DOD/GDP (%)	38.9	37.5	35.2
Net foreign assets (as months of imports)	6.5	5.4	4.1

/a For the last year of the period.

Source: World Bank staff estimates.

granted in return for a guarantee by the importers that they would purchase all the bananas that Tonga would supply. This monopoly was to be abolished in November 1990, and importers are likely to demand a lower price and higher quality from Tongan exporters. As a result, returns to growers in Tonga will fall. There will, however, remain a niche market for Tongan bananas in New Zealand because of the distinctive characteristics of the Tongan banana. Those Tongan farmers who are able to improve cultivation practices and yields through the New Zealand aid scheme will remain viable. In aggregate, however, the banana industry is likely over the next year to undergo a shakeout with production declining and then stabilizing at a lower level. Vanilla production should continue to grow, despite the recent fall in prices. Significant plantings in recent years will lead to continued growth in output and export earnings. Moreover, there have been promising developments in the export of traditional crops, such as taro to New Zealand and squash to Japan. Growth has been especially rapid with these crops and this is expected to continue. In aggregate, the agriculture sector will grow at a slightly lower level than the economy; however, this would be significantly higher than the rate achieved during the 1980s.

4.17   Higher growth in the 1990s will need to be supported by an improved performance of manufacturing and tourism. The sources of growth, therefore, would be similar to the early 1980s. This would require manufacturing growth of almost 6 percent per annum. As commercial agriculture, such as the processing of coconut products will contribute less than in the early 1980s, the role of export-oriented manufacturing will need to be enhanced. Government policies to improve the incentive structure in manufacturing are discussed below. Tourism growth could also be high, if Tonga improves its tourist infrastructure and gradually develops an image. If tourism reaches its potential, tourist arrivals will increase by about 6 percent per annum, reaching almost 30,000 by 1995. Furthermore, private remittances and official assistance are expected to remain constant in real terms providing an underpinning to growth in the service sector.

4.18   Given this growth performance and a maintenance in real terms of private remittance and official assistance flows, Tonga's external financing requirements are shown in Table 4.4. Despite significant growth in export receipts from an improved agriculture performance and an increase in manufacturing exports, the trade balance will remain large. This is due to the expected buoyancy of imports, resulting from the inflows of foreign assistance and private remittances. Under this scenario, official reserves remain at only 4 months of imports and there is little room to increase these reserves without recourse to higher amounts of external borrowing. Therefore, there is a significant downside risk in this scenario which can arise from three sources: (i) a decline of private remittances in real terms; (ii) the inability of the Government to contain the level of imports; and (iii) a stagnant export performance. Without immediate corrective policy, any of these events could easily exhaust Tonga's reserves and thereby, threaten economic stability.

4.19   Development Issues and Policies. Achieving the relatively favorable growth and balance of payments scenario outlined above would require a series of structural policies to foster growth in agriculture, manufacturing and tourism, as well as supporting macroeconomic policies. Given the economy's vulnerabilities to changes in the flow of remittances and the recent weakening of the economy's productive base, the Government needs to move quickly in strengthening its economic performance. Because of agriculture's large share of GDP and employment, policies in this sector will be particularly important.

Table 4.4: EXTERNAL FINANCING REQUIREMENTS AND SOURCES, 1984/85-1998/99
($ million per annum at current prices)

	1984/85-88/89	1989/90-93/94	1994/95-98/99
Requirements	34,021	48,067	65,549
Merchandise imports	38,694	55,354	78776
Merchandise exports	-7,153	-11,151	-18653
Principal repayments /a	59	1,636	2865
Interest payments /a	846	802	1324
Other service receipts	-539	1,281	687
Change in NFA	1,582	144	551
Sources	34,021	48,067	65,549
Private transfers	21,693	27,876	34,592
External grants	5,843	12,181	15,421
Public loan disbursements	3,577	3,142	6,264
Other capital (net)	2,909	4,867	9,271

/a Public MLT debt only.

Source: World Bank staff estimates.

4.20   The poor performance of commercial export crops in Tonga during the 1980s can be explained by several factors. First, there have been poor incentives for commercial crops, because of low world market prices, inefficiencies in the activities of the marketing board and the effects of official assistance and private remittances on the reservation wage and the exchange rate. This can be contrasted with the performance of traditional foodcrops, where the returns to labor are higher. Second, there have been administrative and management difficulties in the agriculture sector: inadequate disease and quality control as evidenced by the watermelon crop; and, too rapid expansion of new crops (e.g., bananas and watermelons). Third, there have been a number of inconsistencies in the policy environment. This is illustrated by the imposition and sudden withdrawal of import protection for pigs and poultry. The effect of which has been to virtually wipe out the poultry industry overnight. And finally, labor is clearly a constraint. Many family workers are not available due to schooling, other employment opportunities, or emigration. As a result, rural wages are relatively high and labor is scarce, particularly when large infrastructural projects are being undertaken. However, the land tenure system and availability of agricultural credit are no longer constraints on the development of the agriculture sector. Despite the rigid land tenure system in Tonga, the practice of leasing (formal and informal) is well established and appears to be working reasonably well. Likewise, credit is available to farmers, either through the Tonga Development Bank (TDB) or through self-finance as most families have access to money from remittances.

4.21   These considerations suggest a strategy for fostering sources of growth in agriculture, which is necessary to achieve Tonga's growth and development objectives during the 1990s. First, the export of coconut products are not likely to be viable at projected world prices and therefore, further attempts at commercially-oriented replanting, rehabilitation, or hybridization schemes need to be carefully reviewed for their economic viability. Second, while the Government should continue to foster the growth of vanilla production since its market prospects are relatively good, the best strategy is to develop high-value products that can bear high transport costs and give an attractive return to the farmer. This would mean the establishment of "niche" markets, such as squash to Japan and root crops to New Zealand, in which Tonga is able to exploit its potential for off-season production, small size and flexibility of response. Third, since Tonga's economy depends to a large extent on the traditional mixed subsistence/commercial smallholder farming system, the Government needs to recognize the importance of the system and guard against policies which threaten the sustainability of traditional farming. The growing use of tractors, provided by a subsidized Government service, have unknown future consequences on soil structure and fertility. Therefore, action is needed to eliminate these subsidies, which provide an undue incentive, and to undertake research on appropriate methods of land cultivation and mechanisation. Finally, the Government needs to improve its service capabilities to the agriculture sector. In this regard it should effect a financial restructuring of the commodity board to put it on a sound financial footing or allow the private sector to take over some of it functions; strengthen agricultural research and extension to support the emerging sources of growth in the agricultural sector; promote more actively Tongan agricultural products abroad; and, put into place an effective quality control system to ensure that exports are of a uniform quality and free of pests and disease. The latter is especially important, as demonstrated by the effect of the New Zealand ban on watermelon exports because of pests.

4.22   The manufacturing sector has the potential to contribute, albeit modestly, to economic growth and exports in the future. This would require an improvement in the overall incentive framework as the current situation is one of high protection for import-substituting industries, leading to a bias against exporting activities. The level of tariff protection is high and highly variable. The current set of incentives is administered on a company-by-company basis, leading to obvious distortions in the incentive framework. Encouraging export-oriented manufacturing needs to be an important objective of Government policy over the medium term. Government policy could also concentrate in the following key areas: an expansion of the existing SIC and possibly the establishment of another industrial center on Vava'u, as a number of firms have expressed an interest in locating on an industrial estate; an examination of the existing incentive structure to ensure that export-oriented activities are encouraged (there has been a recent tendency to encourage import substituting industries through tariff policy); and to ensure that exchange rate management provides adequate incentives to the manufacturing sector.

4.23   The tourism sector also has some potential for growth. Tourist arrivals (including holiday and business travelers) have increased by about 9 percent per annum since 1983. Moreover, tourism receipts as measured by the

Tonga Visitors Bureau (TVB), have also been increasing. Future growth in this sector is likely to be achieved as a result of three factors: (i) improvement and extension of the main runway on the island of Tongatapu, as well as an upgrading of the international terminal; (ii) further improvements to the existing hotel infrastructure; and (iii) a positive change in the attitude of the Tongan Government towards tourism. With these improvements, tourism will probably experience steady, but not spectacular, growth over the medium term. The sector's contribution to economic growth could be further enhanced by: (i) infrastructure development in Vava'u (the island with the highest tourist potential). The EEC funds that have been allocated for regional development on Vava'u could be used in this regard; (ii) fostering private sector development of ancillary industries to complement tourism infrastructure; and, (iii) allocate larger amount of resources to the TVB for the promotion of tourism in Tonga.

4.24   In support of these structural policies, the current policy of macroeconomic restraint would n   eed to be continued. In particular, two aspects of exchange rate management need to be carefully examined. First, the link between the Pa'anga and the Australian dollar has caused wide fluctuation in both the rate of inflation and the real exchange rate. The Government needs to consider moving towards an exchange rate system which better reflects Tonga's trading partners and developments in competitor countries. Second, the appropriateness of the level of the real exchange should be assessed in view of medium-term objectives to promote exports and tourism. Recent analysis undertaken by the Treasury suggests that the real effective exchange has appreciated and is at its highest since 1975 against all major trading partners. Support for this is provided by the apparent slowdown in export-oriented activities in the manufacturing sector.

4.25   There is also a need for further public resource mobilization, in order to relax existing restraints on recurrent expenditures to enable adequate resources for operations and maintenance expenditures and to finance an increasing portion of development expenditures. Without immediate corrective action, the Government will have to resort to a further drawdown of its deposits with the banking sector, or higher levels of external borrowing.9/ Adequate resources can be mobilized by the public sector through improved tax administration and a slight widening of the tax base. The goods and services tax (GST) is the first area for administrative improvements. Enforcing the provision for full auditing of GST returns is likely to have substantial benefits in terms of increased tax collections. Furthermore, widening the GST base to include small traders and the informal market also would increase revenues. Much of the increased activity in informal markets is a result of remittances received in kind rather than cash, and widening the GST in this manner could be an effective mechanism for taxing these inflows. Second, the loss of custom duties is a major drain on Government revenues. It is estimated that an increase in staffing, more stringent valuation of goods, and enforcing payment could result in almost T$2 million in additional revenues

---

9/ A significant drawdown of the Government's domestic balances is likely
    to have adverse implications for the economy due to the tight liquidity
    position of the Bank of Tonga (BOT), resulting from the slow growth of
    demand deposits in recent years.

per annum. Finally, adjustments in the duty structure on fuel, alcohol, and tobacco products also need to be considered. In particular, the decline in imported beer due to the establishment of the Royal Tongan Brewery and the lower level of the excise tax on domestically produced beer is estimated to cost the economy about T$3 million per annum. The increases in revenues resulting from these measures would allow the Government to fund its own development activities and to increase expenditures for maintenance. However, recurrent costs are likely to continue to be severely underbudgeted leading to a situation in which investment projects financed by official aid have a shortened economic life. After several years, donors are, therefore, asked to finance rehabilitation or reconstruction of these physical assets. A more balanced approach would be for donors to finance a portion of Tonga's operating and maintenance budget as a complement to improvements in domestic resource mobilization. This would enable Tonga to absorb more effectively available aid flows, while also improving Government finances over the medium term.

STATISTICAL APPENDIX

LIST OF TABLES

Table 1.1:   POPULATION OF THE KINGDOM OF TONGA, 1976 & 1986
(persons)

I. POPULATION DATA	------ 1976 -----		----- 1986 ------		growth rate p.a. 1976-86
	persons	percent	persons	percent	
Age:					
0 - 4	12,536	13.9	13,916	14.7	1.0
5 - 9	14,375	16.0	12,674	13.4	-1.3
10 - 14	13,127	14.6	11,852	12.5	-1.0
15 - 19	10,532	11.7	12,390	13.1	1.6
20 - 24	17,825	19.8	8,951	9.5	-6.7
25 - 34	7,529	8.4	11,156	11.8	4.0
35 - 49	11,997	13.3	11,531	12.2	-0.4
50 and above	9,693	10.8	12,106	12.8	2.2
Not specified			73	0.1	
Sex:					
Male	46,036	51.1	47,611	50.3	0.3
Female	44,049	48.9	47,038	49.7	0.7
Total population	90,085		94,649		0.5

Source: 1976: Statistical Abstract of Tonga, 1983, 1987.
        1986: Statistical Office, unpublished estimates from 1986 Census.

Table 1.2: EMPLOYMENT BY INDUSTRY, 1976 & 1986
(population aged 15 and above)

	1976		1986		growth rate p.a. 1976-86
	persons	percent	persons	percent	
Agriculture, forestry & fishing	9,529	51.2	10,607	49.1	1.1
Mining			28	0.1	n.a.
Manufacturing	402	2.2	587	2.7	3.9
Electricity and water	114	0.6	316	1.5	10.7
Building and construction	1,153	6.2	1,698	7.9	3.9
Wholesale and retail trade	825	4.4	1,523	7.0	6.3
Transport and communication	829	4.5	1,120	5.2	3.1
Financial services	61	0.3	448	2.1	22.1
Social & personal services	5,713	30.7	5,086	23.5	-1.2
Unenumerated		191	0.9	n.a.	
TOTAL EMPLOYMENT(WAGE+SALARY)	18,626		21,604		1.5

Source: 1976: Statistical Abstract of Tonga, 1983, 1987.
         1986: Statistical Office, unpublished estimates from 1986 Census.

Table 2.1: GROSS DOMESTIC PRODUCT BY INDUSTRIAL ORIGIN, 1981/82-1988/89
(Constant 1981/82 prices, Pa'anga millions)

	1981/82	1982/83	1983/84	1984/85	1985/86	1986/87	1987/88	1988/89
Agric., for. & fish.	24.28	21.80	22.21	24.24	25.00	25.90	23.30	24.20
Mining & Quarrying	0.41	0.39	0.40	0.36	0.40	0.40	0.50	0.60
Manufacturing	4.67	4.77	5.01	5.31	6.10	6.30	6.30	6.50
Electricity & water	0.35	0.37	0.44	0.47	0.60	0.60	0.70	0.80
Construction	2.26	3.54	4.11	4.39	3.30	3.40	3.70	4.00
Wholesale & retail trade	5.74	5.68	5.66	6.33	6.70	6.90	6.90	6.90
Transport, storage & Comm.	3.47	3.50	3.35	3.38	3.50	3.60	4.00	4.40
Finance & real estate	2.24	2.44	2.06	2.60	2.60	2.70	2.80	2.90
Comm., soc. & pers. services	8.87	9.87	10.72	10.79	11.60	12.00	12.40	12.50
GDP @ factor cost	52.29	52.36	53.96	57.87	59.80	61.80	60.60	62.80
Indirect taxes (- subs.)	8.40	9.00	8.90	8.49	8.70	9.00	8.70	9.00
GDP @ market prices	60.69	51.36	62.86	66.36	68.50	70.80	69.30	71.80
Memo items:								
GDP @ current prices (Pa'anga mil)	60.70	66.90	74.50	80.00	98.90	110.00	119.60	127.00
GDP deflator (1981/82=100)	100.00	109.00	118.50	120.60	144.40	155.40	172.60	177.60
(annual % change)		9.0	8.7	1.7	19.8	7.6	11.1	2.9

Source: Unpublished estimates by the Treasury and the World Bank.

Table 2.2: GDP GROWTH RATES BY SECTOR, 1981/82 - 1988/89
(growth rate per annum)

	1981/82 - 1982/83	1982/83 - 1983/84	1983/84 - 1984/85	1984/85 - 1985/86	1985/86 - 1986/87	1986/87 - 1987/88	1987/88 - 1988/89	1981/82 - 1988/89 p.a.
Agric., for. & fish.	-10.21	1.88	9.14	3.14	3.60	-10.04	3.86	-0.28
Mining & Quarrying	-4.88	2.56	-10.00	11.11	0.00	25.00	20.00	5.59
Manufacturing	2.14	5.03	5.99	14.88	3.28	0.00	3.17	5.07
Electricity & water	5.71	18.92	6.82	27.66	0.00	16.67	14.29	12.54
Construction	56.64	16.10	6.81	-24.83	3.03	8.82	8.11	8.88
Wholesale & retail trade	-1.05	-0.35	11.84	5.85	2.99	0.00	0.00	2.66
Transport, storage & Comm.	0.86	-4.29	0.90	3.55	2.86	11.11	10.00	3.45
Finance & real estate	8.93	-15.57	26.21	0.00	3.85	3.70	3.57	3.76
Comm., soc. & pers. services	11.27	8.61	0.65	7.51	3.45	3.33	0.81	5.26
GDP @ factor cost	0.13	3.06	7.25	3.34	3.34	-1.94	3.63	2.65
Indirect taxes (- subs.)	7.14	-1.11	-4.61	2.47	3.45	-3.33	3.45	0.50
GDP @ market prices	1.10	2.44	5.57	3.22	3.36	-2.12	3.61	2.37

Source: Unpublished estimates by the Treasury and the World Bank.

Table 3.1: CENTRAL GOVERNMENT BUDGET, 1983/84-1987/88
(Pa'anga millions)

	1982/83	1983/84	1984/85	1985/86	1986/87	1987/88	1988/89 Est.
Revenue	17.8	17.6	22.0	27.6	30.7	34.7	37.6
Tax revenue	12.0	12.4	15.8	18.5	21.1	24.4	24.9
Nontax revenue	5.8	5.2	6.2	9.1	9.6	10.4	12.7
Expenditure and net lending	30.4	33.0	41.4	43.7	55.2	56.1	60.1
Current expenditure	15.8	16.7	19.9	25.6	29.7	31.0	32.4
Development expenditure	14.2	15.4	20.4	17.8	18.4	24.1	25.1
Net lending	0.4	0.9	1.1	0.2	7.1	1.0	2.6
Overall balance	-12.6	-15.4	-19.4	-16.1	-24.4	-21.4	-22.5
Financing (net)	12.6	15.4	19.4	16.1	24.4	21.4	22.5
External grants	13.1	16.2	15.9	15.7	21.2	22.8	24.8
External borrowing (net)	0.2	0.7	1.4	0.1	7.0	1.9	2.5
Domestic credit (net)	-0.7	-1.5	2.1	0.3	-3.8	-3.3	-4.8
Ratios (% of GDP)							
Revenue	26.6%	23.6%	27.5%	27.9%	29.2%	31.3%	30.9%
Tax revenue	17.9%	16.6%	19.8%	18.7%	20.1%	22.0%	20.5%
Nontax revenue	8.7%	7.0%	7.8%	9.2%	9.1%	9.4%	10.5%
Expenditure and net lending	45.4%	44.3%	51.8%	44.2%	52.6%	50.5%	49.5%
Current expenditure	23.6%	22.4%	24.9%	25.9%	28.3%	27.9%	26.7%
Development expenditure	21.2%	20.7%	25.5%	18.0%	17.5%	21.7%	20.7%
Net lending	0.6%	1.2%	1.4%	0.2%	6.8%	0.9%	2.1%
Overall balance	-18.8%	-20.7%	-24.2%	-16.3%	-23.2%	-19.3%	-18.5%
Financing (net)	18.8%	20.7%	24.3%	16.3%	23.2%	19.3%	18.5%
External grants	19.6%	21.7%	19.9%	15.9%	20.2%	20.5%	20.4%
External borrowing (net)	0.3%	0.9%	1.8%	0.1%	6.7%	1.7%	2.1%
Domestic credit (net)	-1.0%	-2.0%	2.6%	0.3%	-3.6%	-3.0%	-4.0%

Source: Treasury Department, IMF Consultation Reports and World Bank staff estimates.

Table 3.2: TONGA: CENTRAL GOVERNMENT REVENUE, FISCAL YEARS 1982/83-1987/88
(In millions of pa'anga)

	1982/83	1983/84	1984/85	1985/86	1986/87	1987/88	1988/89
Tax revenue	12.0	12.4	15.8	18.5	21.1	24.4	24.9
Income and poll tax	2.4	2.4	2.4	2.8	2.7	3.6	3.9
Goods and services	0.3	0.3	0.4	0.4	2.6	2.9	3.0
Sales tax	0.1	0.1	0.1	0.2	2.3	2.8	..
License fees	0.2	0.2	0.2	0.2	0.3	0.2	..
International transactions	9.3	9.7	13.0	15.3	15.8	17.8	18.0
Import duties	4.9	5.1	6.4	6.9	7.6	9.0	..
Wharfage on goods	0.4	0.4	0.5	0.5	0.6	0.6	..
Ports and services tax	4.0	4.1	6.1	7.8	7.5	8.4	..
Airport tax	0.1	0.1	0.1	0.1	0.1	0.1	..
Nontax revenue	5.8	5.2	6.2	9.1	9.6	10.4	12.7
Government services /a	4.6	3.9	4.3	5.6	5.3	5.8	..
Rents and investment income	0.9	0.9	1.5	1.8	2.3	3.4	..
Other /b	0.3	0.4	0.4	1.7	2.0	1.2	..
Total	17.8	17.6	22.0	26.3	29.5	35.9	37.6

/a Excludes gross income from the post office.
/b Includes net income from the post office, transfers from duty-free shops, and revenue earmarked
    for the Tonga Trust Fund.

Sources: Data provided by the Tongan authorities; and Fund staff estimates.

Table 3.3: TONGA: CENTRAL GOVERNMENT CURRENT EXPENDITURE, FISCAL YEARS 1982/83-1987/88
(In millions of pa'anga)

	1982/83	1983/84	1984/85	1985/86	1986/87	1987/88	1988/89
Public administration	5.1	6.0	7.0	9.2	12.2	12.3	..
General administration	2.9	3.6	4.3	5.9	8.2	8.1	..
Fiscal administration	0.5	0.6	0.5	0.7	0.9	1.1	..
Law and order	1.7	1.8	2.2	2.6	3.0	3.1	..
Social and community services	5.0	5.3	6.1	7.6	8.5	9.8	..
Education	2.3	2.4	2.9	3.7	4.2	5.2	..
Health	2.2	2.3	2.6	3.2	3.3	3.6	..
Pensions and gratuities	0.4	0.4	0.4	0.5	0.6	0.7	..
Other	0.1	0.2	0.2	0.3	0.3	0.3	..
Economic services	5.5	5.0	6.0	7.1	7.4	7.7	..
Agriculture, forestry & fishing	1.5	1.5	1.7	2.0	2.1	2.3	..
Tourism	0.2	0.2	0.2	0.2	0.2	0.3	..
Transport and works	3.2	2.8	3.9	4.7	5.0	5.1	..
Communications /a	0.6	0.6	0.2	0.2	0.1	0.1	..
Other /b	0.2`	0.4	0.8	1.6	1.7	1.2	..
Total	15.8	16.7	19.9	25.6	29.7	31.0	32.4

/a Excludes post office expenditures.
/b Includes STABEX transfers to the Commodities Board; excludes amortization on public debt
and appropriations for the development budget and sinking funds.

Sources: Data provided by the Tongan authorities; ;and Fund staff estimates.

Table 4.1: TONGA: MONETARY SURVEY, 1983/84-1988/89 /a
(In millions of pa'anga: end of period)

	1983/84	1984/85	1985/86	1986/87	1987/88	1988/89
Net foreign assets	21.5	25.0	25.1	36.9	34.6	33.1
Domestic credit	6.1	8.5	12.6	11.8	14.8	20.7
Government (net) /b	-4.0	-5.2	-4.3	-7.2	-8.0	-11.7
Nonfin. public enterprises	...	...	...	...	...	...
Private sector /c	10.1	13.7	16.9	19.0	22.8	32.5
Other items (net) /d	8.3	9.5	10.0	12.6	14.2	16.2
Total liquidity	19.4	24.1	27.0	36.0	35.2	37.6
Currency	2.8	2.9	4.2	4.4	5.6	5.4
Demand deposits	6.2	7.3	7.1	9.9	9.9	9.4
Savings deposits	5.0	7.1	8.2	10.5	11.3	12.2
Time deposits	5.5	6.8	7.5	11.3	8.5	10.6
			Annual percentage change			
Memorandum items:						
Domestic credit	-1.3	38.7	48.1	-6.6	25.7	39.9
Private credit	3.9	35.4	23.0	12.4	20.1	42.5
Total liquidity (M2)	21.0	24.2	12.1	33.6	-2.2	6.7

/a Incorporates the relevant accounts of the Treasury, and the Boards of Currency and Coinage
/b Includes aircraft loan to the Government,.
/c Includes public enterprises.
/d Includes bills payable.

Source: Data provided by the Tongan authorities and staff estimates.

Table 4.2: BANK OF TONGA
Deposit Interest Rates

Term	Deposits <$100,000	Pre 2/10/89 interest rate	Post 2/10/89 interest rate
3 months		5.25%	6.750%
6 months		5.50%	7.000%
12 months		5.75%	7.250%
24 months		6.00%	7.500%
36 months		6.50%	8.000%
48 months		...	8.250%

Term	Deposits >$100,000	Pre-2/10/89 interest rate	Post 2/10/89 interest rate
3 months		6.00%	7.500%
6 months		6.25%	7.750%
12 months		6.50%	8.000%
24 months		6.50%	8.250%
36 months		6.75%	8.375%
48 months		...	8.500%

. Savings Accounts		5.00%	6.250%
. Target Savers		5.75%	6.750%
. School Agency		5.00%	6.250%

Source: Data provided by Tonga authorities.

Table 4.3: BANK OF TONGA
Lending Interest Rates

Classifications	Pre 1/7/89 interest rate	Post 1/7/89 interest rate
Agriculture, Fishing and Manufacturing	10.0%	12.50%
Tourism	10.0%	12.50%
Retail Trade, Wholesale Trade and Retail/Wholesale mixed	10.0%	12.75%
Building and Construction	10.0%	13.00%
Transport, Storage and Communication	10.0%	13.00%
Other Business Activities	10.0%	13.00%
Housing - Residence	8.0%	9.00%
- Rental	10.0%	13.00%
Personal Sector Finance	10.0%	13.00%
Churches, Schools, Sporting Groups	10.0%	11.00%
Government - Overdraft	10.0%	12.50%
- Term Loan	8.0%	10.25%
Semi-government - Loans and Overdrafts	10.0%	12.50%
All other lending	10.0%	13.00%

Source: Data provided by Tonga authorities.

Table 4.4: CONSUMER PRICE INDEX, 1976 - 1989
(Dec. 1984=100, quarterly data)

	MARCH	JUNE	SEPT	DEC	Annual Average		Percentage Change	
					Calendar Year	Fiscal Year /a	Calendar Year	Fiscal Year /a
1976	40	41	43	44	42.0			
1977	47	49	50	51	49.3	45.8	17.0	
1978	54	54	54	54	54.0	52.3	10.0	14.0
1979	55	55	57	61	57.0	54.5	6.0	4.0
1980	64	68	72	75	69.8	62.5	22.0	15.0
1981	77	80	80	83	80.0	76.0	15.0	22.0
1982	85	89	91	90	88.8	84.3	11.0	11.0
1983	92	93	104	103	98.0	91.5	10.0	9.0
1984	97	97	97	100	97.8	100.3	0.0	10.0
1985	103	108	123	134	117.0	102.0	20.0	2.0
1986	139	138	145	147	142.3	133.5	22.0	31.0
1987	142	141	151	162	149.0	143.8	5.0	8.0
1988	164	162	162	165	163.3	159.8	10.0	11.0
1989	168	168	--	--	--	165.8	--	4.0

/a Average CPI for the Tongan fiscal year, July 1 - June 30.

Source: Statistical Abstract, Statistics Office.

Table 5.1: BALANCE OF PAYMENTS, 1980/81-1988/89
(In thousands of pa'anga)

Item	1980-81	1981-82	1982-83	1983-84	1984-85	1985-86	1986-87	1987-88	1988-89/a
Balance of trade	-25,387	-27,638	-36,229	-28,905	-31,051	-37,835	-42,186	-51,596	-50,900
Exports, fob	6,572	7,140	3,754	7,942	9,849	8,397	10,655	8,844	10,700
Imports, fob	31,959	34,778	39,983	36,847	40,900	46,232	52,841	60,440	61,600
Balance of services, income and unrequited transfers	18,947	31,000	36,336	29,265	30,032	38,975	52,954	42,880	39,050
Total receipts	25,930	39,580	52,916	47,625	51,979	67,954	84,141	79,719	76,950
Private remittances	14,795	25,039	22,182	22,885	24,133	36,584	38,386	36,774	35,700
Official remittances	105	898	16,760	7,942	4,209	5,961	10,425	9,230	14,500
Travel	5,709	5,355	4,388	5,826	6,986	9,438	13,600	12,175	9,150
Transport	991	2,520	1,132	3,100	4,012	4,185	5,596	3,620	3,400
Investment income	3,858	3,901	3,334	3,558	3,893	4,287	5,986	8,000	3,700
Other	472	1,867	5,120	4,314	8,746	7,499	10,148	9,920	10,500
Total payments	6,983	8,580	16,580	18,360	21,947	28,979	31,187	36,839	37,900
Private remittances	938	1,610	5,857	5,605	2,798	3,378	4,573	7,542	5,150
Official remittances	1,083	1,309	594	581	53	1,623	843	1,410	1,150
Transport	2,773	2,857	4,448	5,553	10,599	15,651	15,887	18,103	22,250
Travel	1,047	1,092	2,300	3,423	3,715	4,770	4,768	4,161	3,100
Other	1,142	1,712	3,381	3,198	4,782	3,557	5,116	5,623	6,250
Current account balance	-6,440	3,362	107	360	-1,019	1,140	10,768	-8,716	-11,850
Financed by:									
Net Capital Inflows	7,048	-1,411	1,229	4,732	5,215	-804	345	6,613	10,206
Direct investment	0	0	0	0	25	167	300	82	--
Portfolio investment	0	0	0	0	33	5	0	-3	--
Long-term capital	1,730	6,282	-85	-322	1,019	-1,356	942	4,903	--
Short-term capital	5,318	-7,693	1,314	5,054	4,138	380	-897	1,631	--
Net errors and omissions	318	434	1,452	-1,075	452	-647	-230	460	--
Reduction in reserves	-290	-1,517	116	-6,167	-3,744	-983	-11,343	2,563	1,644

/a 1988/89 data include US$ 1.3 million in exports and capital outflows for unpaid fish exports.

Source: Reserve Bank of the Kingdom of Tonga.

Table 5.2: TONGA: EXPORTS BY MAJOR CATEGORY, 1983/84-1988/89 /a
(Value in thousands of US dollars, unit values in US dollars per metric ton, and volumes in metric tons unless otherwise indicated)

	1983/84	1984/85	1985/86	1986/87	1987/88	1988/89 Est.
Copra						
Value	--	--	--	101	--	--
Volume	--	--	--	1,000	--	--
Unit value	--	--	--	101	--	--
Copra meal						
Value	77	66	47	54	2	27
Volume	709	355	1,321	1,671	68	123
Unit value	109	186	36	32	32	219
Coconut oil						
Value	2,963	4,050	1,465	1,237	959	654
Volume	3,281	4,262	4,253	4,108	2,001	1,352
Unit value	903	950	344	301	479	484
Desicated coconut						
Value	529	521	413	461	310	278
Volume	532	463	575	875	414	309
Unit value	994	1,125	719	527	749	899
Bananas						
Value	442	578	729	1,230	563	363
Volume	1,558	2,381	3,149	4,974	1,795	970
Unit value	283	243	232	247	314	374
Vanilla beans						
Value	511	865	827	938	866	2,041
Volume	8	13	13	15	13	30
Unit value ($/kg)	64	67	64	63	67	68
Root crops /b						
Value	176	317	134	174	375	224
Volume	688	1,550	552	558	400	300
Unit value	255	205	243	311	937	747
Watermelons						
Value	552	350	136	1	12	5
Volume	238	131	77	1	17	9
Unit value	2	3	2	1	1	1
Fish						
Value	352	439	455	827	976	1,668
Volume	216	260	347	598	664	992
Unit value	1,631	1,688	1,310	1,383	1,470	1,682
Other exports /c	1,943	1,472	1,551	1,863	2,656	4,263
Total exports	7,544	8,657	5,757	6,886	6,718	9,523

/a Components may not add to totals because of rounding.
/b Root crops comprise taro, yams and cassava.
/c Includes squash in 1987/88 and 1988/89.

Sources: Data provided by the Tongan authorities; and staff estimates.

Table 5.3: MERCHANDISE IMPORTS, 1984/85 - 1988/89
(in thousands of Pa'anga)

	1984/85	1985/86	1986/87	1987/88	1988/89/a
FOOD AND LIVE ANIMALS	11,749	13,737	13,606	17,299	9,117
BEVERAGES AND TOBACCO	2,777	3,163	3,920	3,291	1,515
COPRA 221.2	550	0	0	274	0
TIMBER (DRESSED) 243.0	1,932	1,994	1,936	12,96	896
FERTILIZERS 271 & 56	132	123	33	67	47
OTHER SECTION 2	495	775	702	863	563
CRUDE MATERIALS INEDIBLE	3,109	2,892	2,671	2,500	1,506
MOTOR SPIRITS	2,150	2,394	2,353	1,559	946
AVIATION KERO & GASOLIN	815	1,830	998	1,424	337
KERO. (inc. power) 332.2	696	348	104	449	55
DISTILLATE FUE 332.3	3,260	2,801	2,446	2,287	1,493
BUTANE & OTHER GASES	204	201	287	188	170
OTHER SECTION 3	300	497	527	609	326
TOTAL FUELS AND LUBRICANTS	7,425	8,071	6,715	6,516	3,327
OILS AND FATS	116	129	126	153	103
CHEMICALS	3,357	4,075	5,234	4,924	2,123
CEMENT 661.2	831	1,068	1,201	1,167	404
OTHER MAN. GOODS	9,940	9,667	13,683	11,265	6,941
MANUFACTURED GOODS BY MATERIAL	10,771	10,735	14,884	12,432	7,345
VEHICLES 732.0 - 732.4	2,252	2,330	1,782	3,664	180,2
OTHER SECTION 7	4,869	9,547	11,109	11,280	6,892
MACHINERY & TRANSPORT EQUIPMENT	7,121	11,877	12,891	14,944	8,694
MISC. MAUFACTURED ARTICLES	4,906	5,392	5,292	6,331	3,278
COMMODITIES & TRANSACTIONS N.C.	221	254	230	302	302
TOTAL	51,552	60,325	65,569	68,692	37,310

/a For the first two quarters only.

Source: Statistical Abstract, Statistics Office.

Table 6.1: TONGA: EXTERNAL ASSISTANCE
(US$ '000)

	1982/83	1983/84	1984/85	1985/86	1986/87	1987/88	1988/89 Estimate
A. Bilateral Grants /a	10,204	11,433	9.389	7,873	9,870	10,916	15,490
Australia	3,914	4,653	5,319	2,534	3,595	3,710	4,224
New Zealand	2,583	2,564	2,346	2,400	2,664	3,200	3,704
Germany	187	750	743	518	298	598	670
United Kingdom	5	0	0	162	157	165	197
Canada	77	103	124	78	100	172	38
Japan	3,292	3,114	688	1,944	2,826	2,816	3,546
France	50	110	88	74	72	81	2,364
United States	96	139	88	162	157	172	244
Taiwan							
B. Multilateral Grants /a	5,170	3,580	3,383	2,335	3,497	3,336	4,198
EC regional	20	19	21	13	12	49	449
EC national	1	1	1,188	481	951	352	606
STABEX	2,868	1,019	0	0	816	1,000	1,102
FAO	120	245	106	16	53	137	158
UNCDF	173	284	138	-	-	-	-
UNDP/IFF	738	805	610	269	182	310	309
UNFDA	76	93	96	39	56	70	39
UNICEF	3	7	9	29	63	32	28
WHO	773	793	870	324	314	366	394
Other UN	-	-	-	713	597	704	867
CFTC	371	314	346	450	452	317	347
C. Multilateral Loans /a	555	1,038	1,475	373	791	1,760	3,145
ADB	419	923	1,116	49	182	704	1,332
EIB	137	115	223	0	295	352	552
World Bank	0	0	0	0	0	352	788
IFAD	0	0	135	324	314	352	473
D. Commercial Loans /a	-	-	-	-	4,409	380	441
E. Total Grants and Loans (A+B+C+D)	15,929	16,051	14,247	10,580	18,566	16,391	23,275
Cash	6,690	6,741	5,984	3,489	6,413	4,115	10,256
Aid in Kind	9,239	9,310	8.263	7.091	12,153	12,276	13,019
Memorandum Item: Exchange Rates (US$/T$)	0.9560	0.9260	0.801	0.648	0.628	0.704	0.788

/a Includes those cash and aid in kind which are passed through the Government account.

Source: Ministry of Finance.

Table 6.2: EXTERNAL PUBLIC DEBT, 1980-88
(US$ millions)

	1980	1981	1982	1983	1984	1985	1986	1987	1988
Debt outstanding and disbursed	18.9	20.4	21.4	20.0	19.2	23.5	32.3	44.3	43.8
Multilateral loans	3.4	4.2	5.8	6.5	7.6	8.9	9.9	12.6	14.4
Bilateral loans	15.5	16.2	15.6	13.5	11.6	14.6	17.8	22.1	20.3
Private creditors	0.0	0.0	0.0	0.0	0.0	0.0	4.6	9.6	9.1
Gross disbursements	13.2	4.1	2.5	0.9	1.8	1.3	5.5	6.5	3.3
Multilateral loans	1.3	0.8	1.7	0.9	1.3	1.1	0.7	1.9	2.5
Bilateral loans	11.9	3.3	0.8	0.0	0.5	0.2	0.4	0.6	0.8
Private creditors	0.0	0.0	0.0	0.0	0.0	0.0	4.4	4.0	0.0
Interest payments	0.0	0.1	0.1	0.2	0.2	0.2	0.3	0.4	0.4
Multilateral loans	0.0	0.0	0.0	0.1	0.1	0.1	0.1	0.1	0.1
Bilateral loans	0.0	0.1	0.1	0.1	0.1	0.1	0.2	0.2	0.3
Private creditors	0.0	0.0	0.0	0.0	0.0	0.0	0.0	0.1	0.0
Principal repayments	C.1	0.1	0.1	0.3	0.4	0.5	0.6	0.6	0.8
Multilateral loans	0.0	0.0	0.0	0.0	0.1	0.2	0.2	0.2	0.2
Bilateral loans	0.1	0.1	0.1	0.3	0.3	0.3	0.4	0.4	0.6
Private creditors	0.0	0.0	0.0	0.0	0.0	0.0	0.0	0.0	0.0
Total debt service	0.1	0.2	0.2	0.5	0.6	0.7	0.9	1.0	1.2
Multilateral loans	0.0	0.0	0.0	0.1	0.2	0.3	0.3	0.3	0.3
Bilateral loans	0.1	0.2	0.2	0.4	0.4	0.4	0.6	0.6	0.9
Private creditors	0.0	0.0	0.0	0.0	0.0	0.0	0.0	0.1	0.0

Source: World Bank, Debtor Reporting System

VANUATU

DEVELOPMENT SURVEY

VANUATU

CURRENCY EQUIVALENTS

Annual Averages

1981	$1.00 = Vt 87.83
1982	$1.00 = Vt 96.21
1983	$1.00 = Vt 99.37
1984	$1.00 = Vt 99.23
1985	$1.00 = Vt 106.03
1986	$1.00 = Vt 106.08
1987	$1.00 = Vt 109.85
1988	$1.00 = Vt 104.43
1989	$1.00 = Vt 116.04

FISCAL YEAR

January 1 - December 31

ABBREVIATIONS AND ACRONYMS

ADB	=	Asian Development Bank
CDC	=	Commonwealth Development Corporation
UNDP	=	United Nations Development Programme
VCMB	=	Vanuatu Commodities Marketing Board

Table of Contents

This report was prepared by a World Bank mission which visited Vanuatu in November 1989. The mission members were Kyle Peters and Colin Pratt, Te'o Fairbairn, and Bob Smith (consultants). A draft of the report was discussed with government officials in June 1990.

VANUATU: ECONOMIC DEVELOPMENTS AND PROSPECTS

A. Background

5.1   Vanuatu, formerly known as the New Hebrides, is an archipelago of some 80 islands, with a land area of 12,200 square kilometers. The population was 142,630 in 1989, according to preliminary results from the 1989 Census (see Table 5.1). This would imply a rate of population growth of 2.5 percent per anum since the last census in 1979. The underlying rate of population growth is higher, as the 1979-89 rate is biased downwards because of a significant decline in the expatriate population, particularly at the time of and immediately following Independence in 1980. If only ni-Vanuatu 1/ are considered, the rate of population growth is estimated at 2.9 percent per annum.2/ This is, however, a decline from previous periods, when the rate exceeded 3 percent per annum. Moreover, in contrast to Tonga and Western Samoa but similar to the Solomon Islands, emigration is virtually nonexistent because of cultural factors and limited opportunities.

5.2   Because of its geographical circumstances and recent colonial heritage, Vanuatu faces several severe constraints to economic development:

(a)   Prior to Independence, Vanuatu was governed by an Anglo-French condominium administration, which featured parallel British, French and joint services. Moreover, there was no integrated budget or expenditure program. The Government, therefore, inherited dual systems in many areas (for example, education) which were costly in monetary terms and in the human capital needed to administer them.

(b)   The country lies in an area of the Pacific which seems to be extremely vulnerable to cyclones. Periodically, the occurrence of cyclones inflict damage upon the country's economic, social and physical infrastructure, which causes major economic and social dislocation.

(c)   Human resource constraints are a major impediment to development. At Independence, adult literacy was estimated at 13 percent; while there have been improvements, adult literacy remains far below the regional average. Also at Independence, there were only 10 university graduates and there have been few additions since then. Moreover, about one-third of primary school teachers have had no training.

(d)   At the time of Independence, control of about one-fifth of the total land area and over half of the country's arable land was in the hands of expatriates. The Republic's Constitution prohibited foreign ownership of land and returned all land to ni-Vanuatu. Many of these

---

1/   The indigenous people of Vanuatu are known as ni-Vanuatu.

2/   This assumes that the expatriate population numbered 4,000 in 1989. In the 1979 census, there were 6,880 expatriates in Vanuatu.

Table 5.1: SOCIAL INDICATORS, 1988 /a

Indicator	Units	Vanuatu	Asia	Lower-Middle Income
Population	persons	142,630/b	-	-
- Growth rate	%	2.5/b	1.8	2.2
Crude birth rate	per 000	38.1	26.8	31.5
Crude death rate	per 000	7.7	8.8	8.6
Infant mortality rate	per 000 births	56.0	61.5	59.1
Life expectancy at birth	years	63.4	63.7	63.8
Population per:				
- Doctor	persons	5,248	1,422	1,547
- Nurse	persons	468	1,674	
- Hospital	persons		733	
Child immunization				
- Measles	%		41.0	62.6
- DPT	%	22.0	48.6	64.7
Access to safe water	%	61.0		
- Urban	%	95.0	72.5	76.7
- Rural	%	54.0		46.3
Gross enrollment ratios				
- Primary	%	87	105.3	106.8
- Secondary	%	12	94.4	101.3
Adult illiteracy rate	%	30	39.5	26.2

/a Or most recent estimate.
/b 1989 Population Census, preliminary estimate.

Source: World Bank, "Social Indicators of Development, 1989".

holdings were prime agricultural land, already under plantation cultivation. The once prosperous plantation agriculture (mostly copra) has been allowed to decay, as former foreign owners many of whom left the country at the time of Independence are unwilling to reinvest in their plantations. Furthermore because of land disputes among "customary owners", there is a backlog of unresolved cases, which hinders the full utilization of this land by ni-Vanuatu.

(e) Infrastructural constraints are also binding. A large proportion of the ni-Vanuatu population is scattered on numerous small "outer islands" where infrastructure is virtually nonexistent and communications are poor. On many of these "outer islands", the population is so small that infrastructure and communication services are prohibitively expensive.

5.3   The Republic of Vanuatu has an estimated GNP per capita of $820 (in 1988), which is slightly above the average for the region.3/ No figures are available for the incidence of poverty, but given the abundance of land it is felt to be relatively low. The available social indications, however, suggest that the quality of life in many rural areas is quite poor: child immunization rates are one-third the average for lower middle income countries, in a primary health survey conducted in 1985, about 47 percent of the population suffered from malaria, the control of which is a key health and budgetary issue; a nutritional survey in 1983 indicated that 40 percent of infants between the age of one and two were underweight; and the dietary pattern of rural ni-Vanuatu shows a relatively low consumption of protein foods. These statistics indicate that expenditures in the social sectors must remain a key priority in the 1990s.

5.4   The structure of the economy is highly dualistic. The traditional sector encompasses about 80 percent of the population; these activities comprise subsistence farming of root crops and tropical fruits, coastal fishing and livestock production. There is a small, but growing number of these traditional smallholders producing copra or vegetables for urban consumers on a commercial basis. In fact, smallholders accounted for 85% of all copra production in 1989. The modern sector is highly diversified for a Pacific Island nation and comprises chiefly plantation agriculture (copra, cocoa, coffee and livestock), tourism, government services and the offshore Finance Centre, which includes almost 100 banks and a number of nonbank financial institutions. Services account for about 70 percent of GDP, of which wholesale and retail trade, including tourism, is the most important subsector accounting for about one-third of GDP. Agriculture comprises 25 percent and industry accounts for the remainder. The economically active population is estimated to be about 60,000, of which 13,000 are employed in the modern sector. One-third of all modern sector employees are in the public sector. The diversification of the modern sector economy, the growing participation of subsistence farmers in cash cropping and the abundance of land (only 30 percent of arable land is currently cultivated) portend well for future economic development and growth.

5.5   Vanuatu's balance of payments exhibits the vulnerability and the structural weaknesses of the economy. Exports and imports are equivalent to about 16 percent and 44 percent of GDP, respectively. Copra comprises the bulk of commodity exports, and accounts for almost three quarters of total

---

3/   The Government has calculated that income per capita for the ni-Vanuatu population is only $365. This figure excludes data relating to expatriates, who receive much higher salaries than ni-Vanuatu and who repatriate a large portion of their earnings. This lower figure of $365 was accepted by the UN Committee on Development Planning which recommended Vanuatu for least developed country (LDC) status.

merchandise exports. Other principal exports include cocoa, beef, coffee, and timber. The reexport sector, which includes fish caught by foreign fishermen in both territorial and international waters, was thriving in earlier years, but has been depressed since 1986 primarily because of the closing of the South Pacific Fishing Company in 1986. The composition of imports is heavily weighted towards food, beverages, and other consumer goods, reflecting mainly the demands of a large expatriate population in Vanuatu and the tourist sector. A large portion of imports is also made up of capital and manufactured goods, which, to some extent, reflect Government imports financed by capital aid from donor countries. Since Independence, substantial deficits on merchandise trade have been more than offset by official transfers and earnings from services and other investments as well as by identified capital flows, permitting the accumulation of relatively large reserves.

5.6   As in the other Pacific Island countries, external aid is a dominant feature of the balance of payments and the economy. During 1984-87, Vanuatu received an annual average of about $27 million in external aid and official concessional loans; this is about $178 per capita. In 1987, as a result of the devastation of Cyclone Uma, external assistance rose to $51 million (this also included substantial STABEX flows), but has subsequently subsided to more normal levels. About 95 percent of development outlays are financed from external assistance and they comprise about half of Government revenues. Recurrent budget support from the French and the British was phased out in 1988, as agreed at the time of Independence. Vanuatu's official development assistance originates from more than 20 sources and represents an amount equivalent to slightly more than a quarter of GDP. The major bilateral donors are Australia, France, the United Kingdom, Japan and New Zealand. Multilateral assistance has been provided by the ADB, the World Bank, the UNDP, the European Community and other UN agencies. Given the low level of skills and shortage of trained personnel, aid coordination, in particular planning and implementation, is extremely difficult.

B. Recent Economic Developments

5.7   Economic and political disturbances associated with Independence resulted in a 10 percent contraction of GDP during 1980. As the political disturbances abated, economic activity gradually began to increase. During 1981-82, real GDP growth is estimated to have increased only slightly, by about 1-2 percent per annum.4/ Growth was constrained by low copra prices and unlike the other Pacific Island economies, declining external assistance due primarily to the reduction of recurrent budgetary support and technical assistance associated with Independence. By 1983, the economy had begun to recover with GDP growth of about 3 percent (see Table 5.2). The restoration of political stability supported a growth in tourism and offshore banking activities. Furthermore, the establishment of the Vanuatu Commodities Marketing Board (VCMB) in 1982 to stabilize copra prices helped to smooth fluctuation in farmers' incomes and arrest the decline in copra production. In 1984, extremely high copra prices, a steady growth of tourism, and an expansion of activities in the Finance Centre contributed to GDP growth of

---

4/ Reliable national accounts data are not available for 1980-82.

Table 5.2: ECONOMIC INDICATORS, 1983-89

	1983-84	1985-87	1988	Estimate 1989
Production & Expenditure				
(growth rates, % p.a.)				
GDP	6.8/a	0.0	0.5	2.5
Agriculture	6.9/a	-2.9	0.7	1.9
Industry	17.0/a	12.3	2.0	2.0
Services	5.7/a	-2.9	0.2	2.8
Expenditure				
Consumption	9.4/a	1.1	n.a.	n.a.
Government	7.3/a	-2.6	n.a.	n.a.
Private	10.7/a	3.3	n.a.	n.a.
Fixed investment	10.6/a	9.2	n.a.	n.a.
Indicators:				
Tourist visitors ('000s)	32.0	18.9	17.5	23.9
Copra production ('000 tons)	43.2	39.0	29.6	25.9
Cocoa production ('000 tons)	1.0	1.1	0.8	1.6
Beef ('000s heads)	12.8	13.4	14.6	13.9
Central Government Budget (% of GDP)				
Revenue	19.5	25.0	27.6	26.1
- Tax	15.5	19.6	22.3	21.3
- Non-tax	4.0	5.4	5.4	4.8
Expenditure & Net Lending	43.3	51.8	58.8	55.7
- Current	36.3	37.6	36.9	31.0
- Development	10.1	14.2	21.8	24.7
Overall Balance	-23.8	-26.8	-31.1	-29.5
Financed by:	23.8	26.8	31.1	29.5
External grants	25.5	25.7	29.0	22.7
External borrowing (net)	0.2	1.5	1.8	1.1
Domestic credit	-1.8	-0.5	0.3	5.7
Money and Prices				
(growth rates, % p.a.)				
Domestic credit	-2.2	-4.2	21.5	40.6
Private credit	3.7	5.3	9.0	9.9
Broad money	24.9	6.6	9.9	15.9
Money	20.5	9.1	-8.5	7.1
Consumer prices	4.0	7.9	8.7	7.7
GDP deflator	13.8	2.2	8.7	7.7

/a For 1984 only.

Table 5.2: ECONOMIC INDICATORS, 1983-89
(cont'd)

	1983-84	1985-87	Estimate 1988	Projection 1989
Balance of Payments ($ million)				
Exports (fob)	25.2	20.0	15.4	14.2
Imports (fob)	44.6	50.2	57.9	54.0
Trade balance	-19.4	-30.2	-42.5	-39.8
Services (net)	5.4	4.5	4.5	5.3
Private transfers	6.6	7.4	10.5	16.0
Current account	-11.5	-26.3	-27.5	-23.7
External grants	29.1	30.3	35.5	20.0
Public loan disbursement (net)	0.8	1.8	2.5	4.5
Other capital (net)	6.0	3.1	-19.9	0.5
Use of NFA (increase)	-24.4	-8.9	9.4	-16.7
Ratios				
- Current account/GDP (%)	-10.7	-22.4	-20.0	-19.6
- Debt service/exports (%)	0.7	1.2	1.9	2.3
- DOD/GDP (%)	3.9	8.3	11.2	13.4
- Official reserves (months of imports)	1.8	5.4	8.4	

Source: Reserve Bank of Vanuatu and World Bank estimates.

almost 7 percent. In aggregate, during 1981-84, real growth averaged about 4 percent per annum, allowing a modest increase in per capita incomes. Moreover, throughout this period, the balance of payments remained comfortable allowing a substantial accumulation of foreign reserves.

5.8   During 1985-87, a series of shocks reversed the relatively favorable growth and balance of payments performance of the early 1980s. In particular, devastating cyclones impaired agricultural production and damaged tourist facilities and other infrastructure. Low copra prices also contributed to a decline in agriculture output. The service sector was adversely affected by a series of external shocks. Tourism was depressed by a variety of factors:

    (a) contractual differences with a foreign airline lead to an interruption in airline services;

    (b) tourism from Australia (Vanuatu's largest market) fell sharply responding to weak domestic income and a depreciation of the Australian dollar; and

(c) confusion between Vanuatu and New Caledonia, a French Overseas
Territory near Vanuatu which had political difficulties in 1986-87.

A loss of investor confidence, as a result of a fishing agreement that Vanuatu
signed with the USSR and rumors of political ties between Vanuatu and Libya
also slowed the operations of the Finance Centre. Under these circumstances,
output stagnated during 1985-87. Inflation rose sharply to a peak of 16
percent in 1987, reflecting supply shortages following the cyclones and higher
import prices.

5.9   These trends were reflected in the balance of payments. Until 1985,
the economy had accumulated foreign reserves, because substantial deficits on
merchandise trade were offset by official transfers and earnings from
services. Beginning in 1985, the lower world price of copra, in combination
with depressed earning in tourism and the Finance Centre, led to deficits on
the overall balance. These deficits were financed through the use of net
foreign assets. The balance of payments position did strengthen in 1987, due
to a slight recovery in copra prices, and aid flows for cyclone
reconstruction.

5.10   By 1988, the recovery in world copra prices and postcyclone
rehabilitation reversed the decline in GDP; moreover, inflation slowed to an
annual rate of less than 9 percent in 1988. Tourism also began to rebound in
1988 but was cut short by adverse publicity relating to domestic political
developments. Events in 1989 appear to have been more favorable. Two factors
were crucial in this regard: (i) donor grant funding to help with the
purchase of an aircraft for Air Vanuatu and a promotional campaign to promote
Vanuatu as a tourist destination in Australia; and (ii) the subsiding of
political unrest by mid-year. These two factors led to a substantial recovery
in tourism from the very low occupancy rates that prevailed at the beginning
of 1989 to almost 100 per cent during the peak tourist season at the end of
1989.5/ Activities in the Finance Centre also experienced an upturn,
reflecting partly on easing of political tensions. Furthermore, steady copra
prices and a rebound in the beef industry contributed to the first significant
growth in the agriculture sector since the early 1980s.

5.11   Since Independence, the Government has experienced persistent fiscal
difficulties. These difficulties stem primarily from three factors. First,
the large public sector, that involved overlapping services in most areas,
inherited from the condominium powers. As a result, about 40 percent of
current expenditure is attributable to general public services. A second
factor is the structure of tax revenues. In order to develop Vanuatu's
offshore banking and related activities, there are no individual and corporate
income taxes, capital gains taxes or estate and gift duties. As a result,
foreign trade taxes account for more than 50 percent of revenues. Finally,
after Independence, there was a gradual withdrawal of budgetary support from
the United Kingdom and France. Technical assistance from abroad also
declined. As a result, foreign grants totalled less than 20 percent of GDP,
compared to about 50 percent at the time of Independence.

5/ Beginning in late 1989, the three main hotels in Port Vila have been
fully booked.

5.12   Deficits on the recurrent budget first occurred in 1982 and continued in 1983. In order to eliminate these deficits, the Government raised import duties on various items (e.g., coffee, beer, spirits, tobacco and gasoline) and broadened the tax base by introducing a departure tax, hotel and restaurant turnover tax, and work permit fees for non-residents. On the expenditure side, the Government streamlined many overlapping services and placed tight controls on government hiring. By 1984, a surplus was restored on the recurrent budget. However, the Government continued to face tremendous pressure to increase expenditures, particularly for development projects, because of the lack of public facilities and the need to integrate more fully the economy after achieving Independence.

5.13   Beginning in 1985, the recurrent budget was again in deficit. This resulted from a large decline in foreign grants for budgetary support, increased expenditures (on wages, transfers and as a result of Cyclone Eric & Nigel), and a slowdown in revenues due to the general slowdown in economic activity (lower copra prices and a decline in tourism). With a budget deficit, including grants, reaching 6 percent of GDP in 1986, the Government was forced to drawdown substantially its assets with the domestic banking sector, as well as float two domestic bonds issues for about Vatu 50 million. In order to preserve fiscal stability, the Government again undertook a series of austerity measures. This was made more difficult by the fact that many trade taxes had been raised during 1983, to such a level that further tax rate increases might be counterproductive. The following measures were undertaken:

(a)   a series of revenue-enhancing measures were introduced: increase in duty rates for a number of products, and the reduction of import-duty exemptions;

(b)   expenditure reduction measures were undertaken: a restriction on Government hiring without prior approval by a Government appointed panel; a freeze on civil service salaries since 1985, except for a small cost of living allowance in one year; and in 1989, across the board reduction in recurrent allocations to ministries by 10-15 percent; and

(c)   in 1989, the Council of Ministers adopted the following principles: that the Government must work towards a balanced recurrent budget and that no department may submit a social-community project that has recurrent costs implications unless it has identified cost-savings measures or the project generates revenues sufficient to cover its recurrent costs.

These measures have been effective in reducing the fiscal deficit, as the Government expects the 1989 recurrent budget to be in balance. Furthermore, in the 1990 Budget the Government presented a balanced recurrent budget, while increasing civil service wages and salaries and transferring monies from the recurrent budget into the Development Fund.6/

6/   The Development Fund is the account for development expenditures. Vanuatu has no "development" budget, just a recurrent budget.

5.14   As a result of these measures to restore fiscal stability and the recent favorable developments in the real sector, the economy of Vanuatu has a brighter outlook entering the 1990s, than at any time since Independence. Translating these favorable trends into a period of sustained economic growth and development will be a key challenge for policymakers in the 1990s.

C.   Development Prospects and Policies

5.15   For the medium term, Vanuatu needs to endeavor to achieve three interrelated development objectives. First, there is a need to achieve sustained economic growth and reverse the virtual stagnation of the 1980s. Per capita incomes, especially among the ni-Vanuatu population, are about the same entering the 1990s as they were at the time of Independence. Given that the ni-Vanuatu population is increasing very rapidly, the economy needs to expand at more than 4 percent per annum to ensure a meaningful increase in per capita incomes and to absorb the burgeoning labor force. Second, Vanuatu is currently almost totally dependent on foreign aid for it development. Increasing economic self-reliance, which would allow the Government a larger role in determining economic and developmental priorities, is therefore a second objective of Government policies in the 1990s. And finally, infrastructure and human resource development are extremely important, as a significant proportion of the population remains relatively isolated without access to the modern economy and with low levels of education. The first part of this section outlines a macroeconomic scenario which allows Vanuatu to achieve sustained economic growth with a modest increase in economic self-reliance. Moreover, the increase in domestic savings generated through this growth path, if coupled with continued restraint on current expenditures, would allow the Government to address the economy's needs in the areas of infrastructure and human resource development. In the last half of this section, the macroeconomic and sectoral policies necessary to achieve this economic growth are analyzed.

5.16   Prospects and Financing Requirements. Based on projections of the external environment affecting Vanuatu, our illustrative projections of key indicators of Vanuatu's medium-term prospects are contained in Table 5.3. Reflecting the momentum of growth begun in the late-1980s, and dependent upon appropriate macroeconomic policies, Vanuatu has the potential to grow by 4-5 percent per annum throughout the 1990s. Growth in the service sector, particularly tourism and the Finance Centre, can be expected to provide the primary impetus to economic growth. Projections for the tourism sector indicate that real growth could reach 10 percent per annum given the trend in visitor arrivals over the 1987-89 period. Growth in tourism would also spur growth in related services. The favorable image and publicity created by a strong growth performances in the tourism would also contribute to growth in the Finance Centre. Higher growth in these subsectors would offset slower growth in public services associated with the Government's ongoing adjustment program. In summary, services can be expected to grow by 5-6 percent per annum during the 1990s. Industry will also experience rapid growth, albeit from a low base, in support of developments in the tourist industry.

5.17   In the agriculture sector, copra output can be expected to grow only about at the rate of population growth, reflecting its importance in the subsistence economy and the relatively low returns from its cultivation.

However, both the beef industry and cocoa production are expected to grow significantly in the next decade. The increase in the tourism sector will provide a growing domestic market for Vanuatu's beef. Exports of beef are also likely to be robust, as new markets in the Pacific Islands develop and Japan would continue to purchase increasing quantities of Vanuatu's beef. Cocoa production is likely to reach about 3,000 tons by the end of the decade, as new plantings under an externally-financed cocoa project mature. Moreover, some stimulus to the agriculture sector will come from kava because of growing exports to satisfy demands of the pharmaceutical industry in European countries, and to Pacific Island countries, such as Fiji, Western Samoa and Tonga, which will have a deficit of this traditional crop. As a result of these trends, agricultural could be in the range of 3-3.5 percent per annum, reversing the stagnation of the 1980s.

Table 5.3: MEDIUM-TERM MACROECONOMIC PROJECTIONS, 1990-99

	1985-89	1990-94	1994-99
Growth rates (% p.a.)			
GDP	0.6	4.2	4.6
Agriculture	-1.3	3.0	3.5
Industry	8.1	4.1	4.5
Services	0.1	4.6	5.0
Consumption	0.1	3.7	3.9
Fixed investment	4.1	5.0	5.0
Exports of goods & services	-2.6	3.0	3.5
Imports of goods & services	-1.6	4.1	4.2
Consumer prices	7.5	5.0	4.6
Ratios to GDP (%) /a			
Gross investment	28.6	29.7	30.3
Domestic savings	10.1	12.2	14.9
Other indicators			
Current account/GDP (%) /a	-19.6	-17.8	-13.7
Debt service/exports (%)	2.3	2.8	2.4
DOD/GDP (%)	13.4	25.7	29.6
Net foreign assets (as months of imports)	27.9	32.2	30.1

/a For the last year of the period.

Source: World Bank staff estimates.

5.18   To support this pattern of economic growth an improvement in investment efficiency will need to be achieved. Higher levels of private sector investment, particularly in tourism and related-activities, will assist in attaining these efficiency improvements. But, the efficiency of public sector investments also needs to be enhanced. The composition of public investment will be extremely important in this regard; in particular, public investments needs to be concentrated in those areas which support private sector investment and assist the development of human resources. These projections imply that aggregate consumption increases at a slower rate than GDP, leading to a 5 percent of GDP increase in domestic savings, which reduces the dependence of Vanuatu on foreign savings. Private consumption, however, increases faster than population growth, permitting sustained increases in per capita consumption for the first time since Independence.

5.19   Faster growth in tourism, the Finance Centre and agriculture lead to a significant growth in export receipts. In combination with moderate import growth, the current account gradually improves over the medium term. As a percentage of GDP, the current account deficit (excluding external grants) gradually declines throughout the 1990s.

5.20   Projections of Vanuatu's external capital requirements and sources, based on the macroeconomic scenario outlined above, are shown on Table 5.4. The absolute external financing requirements are projected to grow to about $70 million per annum over the period 1994-99, compared to only $44

Table 5.4:   EXTERNAL FINANCING REQUIREMENTS AND SOURCES, 1990-99
($ million per annum at current prices)

	1985-89	1990-94	1994-99
Requirements	43.9	61.1	72.2
Merchandise imports	53.6	62.4	89.2
Merchandise exports	-14.2	-18.8	-30.6
Principal repayments /a	0.8	1.7	1.5
Interest payments /a	0.5	1.0	1.5
Other service payments	-3.7	-0.4	-5.5
Change in NFA	6.9	15.2	16.1
Sources	43.9	61.1	72.2
Private transfers	8.7	12.5	15.5
External grants	32.3	38.6	44.6
Public loan disbursements	3.2	7.8	8.6
Other capital (net)	-1.1	2.5	3.6

/a   Public MLT debt only.

Source: World Bank staff estimates.

million during 1985-89. External grants provide only an average of 60 percent of financing requirements during 1994-99, compared with about 75 percent during 1985-89. External grants also fall in real terms. Despite higher external borrowing, the debt service ratio and DOD/GDP ratio remain very low. Moreover, official reserves can be maintained at their present level, about 8 months of imports, and net foreign assets also remain very high but this reflects increased activities in the Finance Centre. The maintenance of high levels of official reserves is both prudent and appropriate because of Vanuatu's open capital account and its vulnerability to external shocks. This scenario implies that by following appropriate macroeconomic and sectoral policies as outlined in the next section Vanuatu can become increasingly financially self-reliant.

5.21   The scenario outlined in this section is sufficient to achieve Vanuatu's medium-term growth and developmental objectives. Reversing the economic stagnation of the 1980s and achieving more economic self-reliance, it will be necessary to initiate a program of structural reforms while continuing to undertake appropriate fiscal, monetary and exchange rate policies. These policies are discussed below.

5.22   Development Issues and Policies. Prudent macromanagement will continue to play a decisive role in Vanuatu's medium-term development prospects, especially given the economy's vulnerability to external shocks. As evidenced by economic management during the 1980s, the Government has acted decisively in response to economic events to preserve both external and internal stability. Fiscal austerity has reduced significantly fiscal imbalances, which could have easily destabilized the economy. The Government also managed the exchange rate flexibly, undertaking three devaluations during 1985-89 in order to protect the external position. Furthermore, in February of 1988, the Government moved to delink the Vatu from the SDR to which it was linked at Independence and to link it to a basket of currencies with weights that more closely resemble Vanuatu's overall trade and tourism receipts. The continuation of such appropriate exchange rate management in order to provide incentives to domestic investors and ensure the competitiveness of the tourist industry should remain an essential component of macroeconomic management.

5.23   With the complete elimination of French and UK budget support in 1988, and the high level of general administration, health and education expenditures resulting partly from the maintenance of a dual education system with an unavoidable duplication of facilities, the Government will need to maintain its austere fiscal policy stance for the medium term. As noted above, in a small, open economy like Vanuatu, a fiscal imbalance can quickly destabilize the economy. However, given that the economy has begun to revive and as a result, revenues are increasing, it is important that the Government carefully balance the need to maintain fiscal discipline with the longer term development needs of the economy. Recurrent budget savings generated from increased public resources mobilization and structural adjustments to recurrent expenditures need to be channelled into development expenditures. Government development expenditures then need to be focussed on infrastructure and human resource development. In this regard, the current Government policy of not funding any investment projects which cannot cover their recurrent expenditure after completion may not be compatible with Vanuatu's long-term development needs and should be reassessed. There is also a need for significantly higher levels of recurrent financing for maintenance outlays, particularly in transportation, and for health and education. Official assistance, which is largely restricted to investment projects, is undercommitted due to the lack of economically-viable projects and scarce local skilled manpower. The donor community should, therefore, consider providing recurrent cost financing and more technical assistance within the framework of sectoral expenditure strategies.

5.24   In addition to a stable macroeconomic environment and an appropriate incentive framework, sectoral policies also need to be developed to strengthen the performance of agriculture, tourism and industry. The macroeconomic scenario, outlined above, envisages a significantly stronger performance of the agriculture sector than was realized in the 1980s. The potential for agricultural development is high, as only about one-quarter of the total arable land is currently being used for agricultural purposes. Unlocking the potential of this unused land will require two types of policy actions. First, there is a need to improve the physical infrastructure in many of the outer islands in order to allow smallholders to market their crops. Rural roads are a major problem because of the inability of the Government to finance the recurrent costs. The Ministry of Public Works estimates that 15-20 percent of rural roads will become unusable if there is no increase in the level of maintenance funding over the next several years. Furthermore, a similar deterioration in wharfs and jetties is evident. Second, the agricultural extension services are constrained by a shortage of properly trained extension and other technical officers and the lack of recurrent funding to finance the cost of travelling. Promising agricultural developments, such as the export of kava and the potential of smallholder cattle, need to be disseminated more actively in the rural areas of Vanuatu. This will require a stronger agricultural research and extension service.

5.25   Resolution of existing land disputes will also be important to agricultural development, as much prime agricultural land is still awaiting a judicial decision. This slow resolution of land disputes is also a strong disincentive to further foreign investment in the sector. In this regard, the recent Government policy actions to allow for approved development to take place under a lease while the ownership of land is under dispute is a welcome step.

5.26   The activities of the Vanuatu Commodities Marketing Board (VCMB) have had a positive impact on agricultural development in Vanuatu. Unlike many other Pacific Island countries, the VCMB is professionally run and has stabilized prices in a manner that is consistent with national objectives and its own financial position. It currently plays a major role in collecting and marketing Vanuatu's principal export crops. The Board also has been actively involved in developing new export crops, such as kava, and inducing technological change in existing crops, such as hot air drying for copra and exploring the potential for alternative coconut products. The VCMB needs to continue to be managed in a sound manner, in order to ensure its financial viability.

5.27   As noted above, the _tourism_ sector will need to continue to provide a major impetus to economic growth both directly and as a stimulus for industrial and agricultural development. Vanuatu has significant tourist potential, with an apparent comparative advantage over all other countries in the region except possibly Fiji. The establishment of regular air service between Australia, Zew Zealand and Vanuatu, and an intensive public relations campaign in Australia have triggered a rapid growth of tourism in the last year. Ensuring that Air Vanuatu service remains reliable, while expanding further air links, is the most important need in this sector; interruption of air service, as occurred during 1985-88, will almost certainly trigger another economic slowdown. In securing other air links, the completion of the airport upgrading projects and the runway extension will be vital. Given existing occupancy rates and the projected growth of tourist arrivals, additional hotel accommodations will be required in a couple of years. While the Government should not be involved financially in this project, it does have, through the National Tourism Office, a role to play in attracting a suitable investor. A recent visitor's survey suggested the need for improvements in a couple of areas: (i) Australian and New Zealand tourists felt that Vanuatu was a relatively high cost destination, suggesting that the competitiveness of the tourist sector should be an important factor in exchange rate management; and (ii) both the road infrastructure and airport facilities were mentioned as needing upgrading. A key priority for promotional activities is to diversify gradually Vanuatu's tourist base, away from Australia. Currently, almost two-thirds of Vanuatu's holiday visitors are from Australia. This makes Vanuatu extremely dependent on domestic economic developments in that country. Finally, there is also need for attention to be given to the training of hotel staff.

5.28   The Government needs to finalize an Investment Act that was first formulated in the mid-1980s. The intention is to establish a set of incentives available to potential investors. This needs to be completed in a timely manner and should be extensively discussed with the business community prior to enactment. This could have a major impact upon activities in tourism and the Finance Centre. Moreover, while the potential for industrial growth in Vanuatu seems small, clearly formulated "rules of the game" will be important in attracting foreign investment.

STATISTICAL APPENDIX

List of Tables

Table 1.1: POPULATION OF VANUATU, 1979 & 1989
(persons)

	1979	1989
Ni-Vanuatu	104,371	142,630
Non Ni-Vanuatu	6,880	4,000 a/
Total population	111,251	146,630

a/ Preliminary estimate.

Source: Census of Vanuatu 1979 & 1989, National Planning and
Statistics Office (NPSO).

Table 2.1: GDP BY EXPENDITURE AT CONSTANT 1983 PRICES, 1983-87
(Vatu millions)

	1983	1984	1985	1986	1987
Government final consumption expenditure	3659	3927	4237	4123	3633
Recurrent expenditure	2306	2467	2698	2660	2333
Development expenditure (current)	1353	1460	1539	1463	1300
Household consumption expenditure	5450	6035	6598	6633	6654
Gross fixed capital formation	2142	2369	2619	2547	3081
Durable equipment	1196	1453	1545	1456	1613
Construction/land improvements	946	916	1074	1091	1468
Increase in stocks	463	435	634	559	267
Exports of goods and services	5934	6313	5695	4939	5325
Domestic merchandise exports, f.o.b.	1781	2032	1687	1879	2512
Re-exports, c.i.f.	928	947	937	456	177
Other goods and services	3225	3334	3071	2604	2636
Less: Imports of goods and services	7288	8245	8743	7745	7683
Imports for home consumption, c.i.f.	5156	5787	6252	5538	6210
Imports for re-exports, c.i.f.	310	347	282	212	182
Other goods and services	1822	2111	2209	1995	1291
Gross domestic expenditures	10360	10834	11040	11056	11277
Statistical discrepancy	-210	11	-73	-304	-455
Gross domestic product (producers' prices)	10150	10845	10967	10752	10822
Net factor income from abroad	-497	-385	373	460	-690
Gross national product (producers' prices)	9653	10460	11340	11212	10132

Source: NPSO.

Table 2.2: GDP BY EXPENDITURE AT CURRENT PRICES, 1983-87
(Vatu millions)

	1983	1984	1985	1986	1987
Government consumption	3659	4067	4501	4604	4546
Recurrent expenditure	2306	2555	2866	2979	2916
Development expenditure (current)	1353	1512	1635	1625	1630
Household consumption	5450	6306	7032	7406	8296
Gross fixed capital formation	2142	2491	2849	2903	4201
Durable equipment	1196	1478	1589	1583	2212
Construction/land improvements	946	1013	1260	1320	1989
Increase in stocks	463	458	695	620	320
Exports of goods and services	5934	7758	6391	4417	5142
Domestic merchandise exports, f.o.b.	1781	3222	1981	970	1503
Re-exports, c.i.f.	928	980	1036	479	186
Other goods and services	3225	3556	3374	2968	3453
Imports of goods and services	7288	8425	9074	8295	9014
Imports for home consumption, c.i.f.	5156	5796	6315	5821	7212
Imports for re-exports, c.i.f.	310	377	332	200	188
Other goods and services	1822	2252	2427	2274	1614
Gross domestic expenditures	10360	12655	12394	11655	13491
Statistical discrepancy	-210	-316	140	495	-348
Gross domestic product (producers' prices)	10150	12339	12534	12150	13143
Net factor income from abroad	-497	-399	402	511	-865
Gross national product (producers' prices)	9653	11940	12936	12661	12278

Source: NPSO.

Table 2.3: GROSS DOMESTIC PRODUCT BY INDUSTRIAL ORIGIN
AT CONSTANT 1983 PRICES, 1983-87
(Vatu millions)

	1983	1984	1985	1986	1987
Agric., For. & Fish.	2649	2831	2771	2606	2591
Plantations	246	259	239	252	251
Other comm. agr.	598	515	543	318	152
Smallholdings	786	922	827	902	865
Subsistence agr.	974	1006	1044	1065	1096
Forestry	45	129	118	69	227
Industry	772	903	940	1024	1282
Manufactuirng	311	419	466	466	588
Energy	158	191	192	190	180
Construction	303	293	282	368	514
Services	6729	7111	7256	7121	6948
Trade, Rst., Hotel	3627	3740	3753	3518	3599
Transport & comm.	757	808	770	741	762
Finance Center	819	772	967	1128	1087
Real est., bus. serv.	526	587	611	591	534
Gov't serv.	1393	1542	1629	1721	1614
Comm, soc., pers. serv.	72	72	74	76	79
less Imputed bank charges	-465	-410	-548	-654	-727
GDP at producers' prices	10150	10845	10967	10751	10821

Source: NPSO.

Table 2.4: GROSS DOMESTIC PRODUCT BY INDUSTRIAL ORIGIN
AT CURRENT PRICES, 1983-87
(Vatu millions)

	1983	1984	1985	1986	1987
Agric., For. & Fish.	2649	3543	3693	2983	3020
Plantations	246	358	365	303	280
Other comm. agr.	598	534	579	366	191
Smallholdings	786	1446	1517	1104	971
Subsistence agr.	974	1017	1070	1102	1162
Forestry	46	188	162	108	417
Industry	771	951	1018	1118	1498
Manufactuirng	312	431	481	471	612
Energy	157	196	202	200	189
Construction	302	325	335	446	697
Services	6729	7846	7822	8052	8627
Trade, Rst., Hotel	3627	4301	4046	3944	4499
Transport & comm.	757	867	872	895	967
Finance Center	819	800	1027	1254	1363
Real est., bus. serv.	527	626	659	694	678
Gov't serv.	1393	1597	1711	1893	1873
Comm, soc., pers. serv.	72	80	90	98	118
less Imputed bank charges	465	424	583	727	871
GDP at producers' prices	10150	12339	12534	12150	13143

Source: NPSO.

Table 2.5: OUTPUT OF MAJOR AGRICULTURAL COMMODITIES, 1978-1988

Commodity	1978	1979	1980	1981	1982	1983	1984	1985	1986	1987	1988
Copra (metric tons)	46,900	45,134	33,508	46,474	34,256	37,903	47,759	38,319	45,798	36,346	29,558
Cocoa (metric tons)	1,104	556	723	868	528	1,297	782	982	1,281	1,168	756
Coffee (metric tons)	0	100	54	61	21	38	25	49	57	53	15
Beef (slaughter numbers)				10,492	11,939	13,005	12,582	12,610	11,190	16,539	14,563
Forest products (cubic meters) a/						15.3	40.2	37.9	21.6	39.2	22.9

a/ Total logs and sawn timber.

Source: Central Bank Quarterly Economic Reports.

Table 3.1:   CENTRAL GOVERNMENT BUDGET, 1980-89
(Vatu millions)

	1980	1981	1982	1983	1984	1985	1986	1987	1988	1989
Revenue	1263	1367	1608	1892	2504	2970	2920	3647	3937	4168
Tax	943	1021	1265	1468	2038	2298	2241	2685	3387	3706
Nontax	320	346	343	424	466	672	679	962	550	462
Expenditure	4442	4786	5296	4551	5155	5822	6045	7480	..	..
Current	3563	3739	4225	3469	4222	4553	4794	4910	..	..
Development	879	1047	1071	1082	933	1269	1251	2570	..	..
Overall Balance	-3179	-3419	-3688	-2659	-2651	-2852	-3125	-3833	..	..
Financing	3179	3419	3688	2659	2651	2852	3125	3833	..	..
Foreign grants	3639	3934	3350	2601	3121	2740	2343	2857	..	..
Foreign Borrowing (net)	-21	-23	-28	-31	83	88	89	338	..	..
Domestic borrowing (net)	-439	-492	364	89	-553	24	693	638	..	..

Source: Data provided by Vanuatu authorities and staff estimates.

Table 3.2: CENTRAL GOVERNMENT REVENUES, 1980-89
(Vatu millions)

	1980	1981	1982	1983	1984	1985	1986	1987	1988	1989
Tax revenue	943	1021	1265	1466	2038	2298	2241	2685	3387	3706
Goods and services	124	151	247	317	460	489	576	521	547	579
Tourist services	61	95	63	93	105	94	70	68	83	135
Licenses	63	53	115	136	170	213	282	224	258	230
Registration fees		3	66	82	162	157	192	196	178	180
Work permit fees			3	6	23	25	32	33	28	34
International transactions	791	840	992	1100	1522	1724	1595	2042	2390	2512
Import duties	712	710	901	974	1245	1491	1523	1969	2305	2394
Export duties	79	130	91	126	277	233	72	73	85	118
Airport tax		13	15	23	25	43	34	32	37	42
Other	28	17	11	26	31	42	36	90	413	573
Nontax revenue	320	346	343	425	466	672	679	962	550	462
Public enterprises	77	80	84	136	129	278	308	334	342	195
Rents and interest	125	157	139	154	159	160	146	74	143	115
Fines and fees	30	26	28	37	50	83	92	117	a/	a/
Other	88	83	92	98	128	153	135	437	65	152
Total	1263	1367	1608	1891	2504	2970	2920	3647	3937	4168

a/ Included in rent and interest.

Source: Data provided by Vanuatu authorities and staff estimates.

Table 3.3: CENTRAL GOVERNMENT EXPENDITURES BY ECONOMIC CLASSIFICATION, 1981-89
(Vatu millions)

	1981	1982	1983	1984	1985	1986	1987	1988	1989
Wages and salaries	1171	1308	1362	1544	1735	1865	1970	2108	1866
Goods and services	857	923	952	960	990	1143	1094	1413	1504
Interest payments	28	25	19	23	33	28	41	92	114 b/
Other a/	48	474	105	425	433	398	495	347	799
Total	2104	2728	2438	2952	3191	3432	3600	3960	4283

a/ Includes STABEX funds
b/ Estimate.

Source: Data provided by Vanuatu authorities and staff estimates.

Table 4.1: MONETARY SURVEY, 1981-89
(Vatu billions)

End of Period	1981	1982	1983	1984	1985	1986	1987	1988	1989 e/
Net foreign assets	2.3	4.3	6.0	9.3	9.9	11.2	11.7	11.4	11.6
Domestic credit	1.8	2.4	2.9	2.2	1.9	2.7	2.0	2.3	2.3
Government (net) a/	-1.3	-0.9	-0.7	-1.3	-1.4	-0.9	-2.2	-2.1	-2.4
Private sector b/	3.1	3.3	3.6	3.5	3.3	3.6	4.1	4.4	4.7
Other	-0.3	-0.8	-1.8	-0.9	-0.7	-1.2	-0.9	-1.8	-2.0
Total liquidity	3.8	5.9	7.3	10.6	11.1	12.7	12.9	12.1	12.1
Money supply	1.3	1.5	1.8	2.1	2.2	2.2	2.8	2.6	2.8
Currency outside the banks	0.6	0.6	0.7	0.9	1.0	0.9	1.0	1.0	0.9
Demand deposits c/	0.7	0.9	1.1	1.2	1.2	1.3	1.8	1.6	1.9
Quasi-money	2.5	4.4	5.5	8.5	8.9	10.5	10.1	9.5	9.3
Time and savings deposits c/	0.7	1.5	1.9	2.2	1.8	2.7	2.0	2.3	2.1
Time and savings deposits d/	1.6	2.6	3.3	4.8	6.1	6.8	6.7	6.3	6.4
Demand deposits d/	0.2	0.3	0.3	1.5	1.0	1.0	1.4	0.9	0.8

a/ Includes Government foreign currency deposits with commercial banks.
b/ Includes public enterprises.
c/ In Vatu only.
d/ In foreign currencies.
e/ As of end-March.

Source: Data provided by Vanuatu authorities.

Table 4.2: STRUCTURE OF INTEREST RATES, 1981-89
(percent per annum, end of period)

	1981	1982	1983	1984	1985	1986	1987	1988	1989 a/
Vatu savings deposits	4.00-8.00	4.00-6.00	4.00-6.00	4.00-6.50	4.00-6.50	4.00-4.50	2.00-4.00	2.00-4.00	2.00-4.00
Vatu time deposits									
1 month	8.75-10.75	7.50-10.25	6.75-9.00	5.75-8.50	6.13-8.00	4.50-7.50	3.00-4.50	5.50-7.00	5.50-7.00
2-6 months	8.75-11.00	8.00-11.00	8.00-10.00	6.75-9.00	6.38-8.50	4.50-8.79	3.00-6.00	6.00-8.00	6.00-8.00
Above 6 months	8.50-11.00	8.50-11.25	8.50-11.50	7.00-9.50	6.00-9.00	4.85-8.50	3.00-6.75	7.50-8.00	7.50-8.00
Australian time deposits									
1 month	8.70-9.20	8.10-11.00	6.00-8.00	8.00-9.00	12.00-17.38	12.00-14.00	5.00-9.00	12.5-13.6	5.0-15.38
Vatu loans									
Commercial	12.00-18.00	12.00-18.00	12.00-18.00	12.00-16.00	12.00-16.00	12.00-16.00	8.00-16.00	8.00-17.00	8.00-17.00
Personal	15.00-18.00	15.00-18.00	14.00-18.00	14.00-21.00	14.00-19.50	14.00-16.50	8.00-17.00	8.00-17.00	8.00-17.00
Housing	11.50-18.00	11.50-18.00	11.50-18.00	11.50-16.00	11.50-16.00	11.50-16.00	7.00-16.00	8.00-17.00	8.00-17.00

a/ As of end-March 1989.

Source: Data provided by Vanuatu authorities.

Table 4.3: CONSUMER PRICE INDEX, 1983-89
(1st quarter 1976 = 100)

	1983	1984	1985	1986	1987	1988	1989 a/
High income							
Vila	191.3	204.1	210.1	222.8	259.5	282.8	297.8
Santo	176	187.3	189.9	202.1	231.9	249.7	262.4
Urban	188.8	201.4	207.4	219.4	254.9	277.4	292.1
Low income							
Vila	184.5	194.6	196.7	206.1	236.7	256.8	270.7
Santo	176.9	184.6	186.6	198	223.1	240.5	256.7
Urban	183.1	192.9	195	204.7	234.4	254	268.3
Composite	187.4	199.4	204.7	216.4	250.7	272.5	287.1
Annual rate of change (%)							
High income							
Vila		6.7	2.9	6.0	16.5	9.0	5.3
Santo		6.4	1.4	6.4	14.7	7.7	5.1
Urban		6.7	3.0	5.8	16.2	8.8	5.3
Low income		5.5	1.1	4.8	14.8	8.5	5.4
Vila		4.4	1.1	6.1	12.7	7.8	6.7
Santo		5.4	1.1	5.0	14.5	8.4	5.6
Urban							
Composite		6.4	2.7	5.7	15.9	8.7	5.4

a/ For the first quarter of 1989 only.

Source: Data provided by Vanuatu authorities.

Table 5.1: BALANCE OF PAYMENTS, 1982-1988
(Vatu millions)

	1982	1983	1984	1985	1986	1987	1988
1. Exports (f.o.b)	1027	1781	3221	1981	935	1502	1807
of which: copra	710	1308	2734	1392	443	719	955
2. Imports (f.o.b)	4163	4563	5103	5541	4965	6270	6045
of which: home consumption	3814	4305	4806	5291	4847	6113	5798
3. Trade balance (1-2)	-3136	-2782	-1882	-3560	-4030	-4788	-4438
4. Services & investment income (net)	415	550	524	884	597	-44	478
- Receipts	5002	5565	6621	6849	7897	7189	6603
- Payments	-4587	-5015	-6097	-5965	-7100	-7233	-6125
of which: Travel (net)	1854	1996	2155	1762	1270	1392	1659
- Receipts	2050	2200	2361	2000	1520	1544	1853
- Payments	-196	-204	-206	-238	-250	-152	-194
Direct investment income	-775	-1119	-1223	-720	-841	-1973	-1596
Value of expatriates services (debit)	-1497	-1050	-1270	-1362	-1362	-1377	-1370
5. Unrequited transfers	4160	3197	3883	3428	3120	5674	4805
of which: Official (grant aid & technical assistance)	3350	2802	3173	2665	2341	4817	3712
Private	810	595	710	763	779	857	1093
6. Current account balance (3+4+5)	1439	965	2525	752	-313	882	845
7. Capital account (net credit)	834	318	821	333	267	1541	1214
- Long term (including reinvested earnings)	644	794	805	333	202	1541	1214
- Identified short term	190	-476	16	--	65	--	--
8. Errors and omissions	-456	313	518	-623	1504	-1930	-2338
9. Overall balance	1817	1596	3884	1085	-46	2403	2059
10. Change in net foreign assets (- = increase)	-1817	-1596	-3864	462	1458	473	-279
of which: Monetary authorities (net)	523	85	-450	681	655	1672	208
Commercial banks (net)	-2340	-1681	-3414	-218	803	-1099	-487

Source: Central Bank of Vanuatu and Statistics Office, NPSO.

Table 5.2: EXPORTS BY MAJOR COMMODITIES, 1982-88

	1982	1983	1984	1985	1986	1987	1988
Copra							
Volume (metric tons)	34798	38538	46682	34930	40612	31846	31704
Unit Value (US$)	212.07	341.56	590.21	375.85	102.83	205.53	288.45
Value (US$ millions)	7.4	13.2	27.6	13.1	4.2	6.5	9.1
Cocoa							
Volume (metric tons)	548	1232	791	814	1197	1243	813
Unit Value (US$)	1081	1495	1720	1541	1543	1516	1378
Value (US$ millions)	0.6	1.8	1.4	1.3	1.8	1.9	1.1
Beef							
Volume (metric tons)	776	1054	681	1134	502	1044	964
Unit Value (US$)	2465	1843	2101	1647	2442	2189	2337
Value (US$ millions)	1.9	1.9	1.4	1.9	1.2	2.3	2.3
Timber							
Volume (metric tons)	652	3900	19161	17423	7839	19283	7001
Unit Value (US$)	361.87	82.57	77.31	73.62	75.76	98.19	144.98
Value (US$ millions)	0.2	0.3	1.5	1.3	0.6	1.9	1.0
Coffee							
Volume (metric tons)	..	..	..	84	22	44	19
Unit Value (US$)	..	..	..	2236	2923	1698	1839
Value (US$ millions)	..	..	..	0.2	0.1	0.1	0.0

Source: NPSO.

Table 5.3: IMPORTS BY COMMODITY GROUP, 1982-88
(Vatu billions, cif)

	1982	1983	1984	1985	1986	1987	1988
Imports for home consumption	4.81	5.25	5.87	6.02	5.57	6.78	6.77
Food and live animals	1.19	1.03	1.18	1.14	1.03	0.93	1.21
Beverages and tobacco	a/	0.27	0.31	0.28	0.24	0.19	0.35
Crude materials excl. fuel	0.88	0.05	0.05	0.06	0.06	0.21	0.08
Minerals, fuels etc.	0.65	0.57	0.61	0.61	0.54	0.58	0.56
Animal & vegetable oils/fats	b/	0.02	0.04	0.04	0.03	0.02	0.03
Chemicals	b/	0.32	0.41	0.37	0.34	0.41	0.40
Basic manufactures	1.20	0.85	0.91	1.02	1.00	1.48	1.37
Mach. and trans. equipment	0.76	1.08	1.36	1.31	1.42	1.75	1.72
Misc. manufactured goods	b/	0.81	0.87	0.92	0.77	0.89	0.81
Other	0.14	0.25	0.14	0.27	0.13	0.33	0.22
Imports for re-export	1.07	1.07	0.99	1.00	0.19	0.17	0.33
Total	5.89	6.32	6.87	7.03	5.76	6.95	7.10

a/ Included under food and live animals.
b/ Included under basic manufactures.

Source: NPSO.

Table 6.1: EXTERNAL GRANTS, 1981-87
(Vatu Millions)

	1981	1982	1983	1984	1985	1986	1987
Foreign receipts							
Grants:							
Recurrent grants	899	743	559	437	275	133	36
Technical assistance	1,635	1,479	1,050	1,270	1,362	1,362	1,310
Development grants	985	1,079	992	906	1,059	845	1,240
In cash	443	431	447	491	524	410	584
In kind	554	648	545	415	535	435	656
Stabex grants	415	31	..	366	..	..	1,487
Cyclone grants							
In cash	..	..	..	..	..	40	307
In kind	..	..	..	..	..	..	370
Other grants	..	..	..	142	4	..	..
Total grants	4,931	4,411	3,593	3,885	3,755	3,185	5,313

Source: NPSO

Table 6.2: EXTERNAL PUBLIC DEBT, 1980-88
(US$ millions)

	1980	1981	1982	1983	1984	1985	1986	1987	1988
Debt outstanding and disbursed	4.1	3.0	4.0	3.5	5.3	7.0	8.3	14.1	15.4
Multilateral loans	0.0	0.0	0.0	0.1	0.7	1.5	2.5	6.3	7.3
Bilateral loans	3.9	2.8	3.9	2.9	2.8	3.7	4.3	6.5	6.8
Private creditors	0.2	0.2	0.1	0.5	1.8	1.8	1.5	1.3	1.3
Gross disbursements	0.0	0.0	1.9	0.6	2.5	1.1	1.2	5.0	3.4
Multilateral loans	0.0	0.0	0.0	0.2	0.6	0.6	0.8	3.3	1.5
Bilateral loans	0.0	0.0	1.9	0.0	0.5	0.5	0.4	1.7	1.6
Private creditors	0.0	0.0	0.0	0.4	1.4	0.0	0.0	0.0	0.3
Interest payments	0.2	0.2	0.2	0.2	0.1	0.1	0.4	0.4	0.5
Multilateral loans	0.0	0.0	0.0	0.0	0.0	0.0	0.1	0.1	0.1
bilateral loans	0.2	0.2	0.2	0.2	0.1	0.1	0.2	0.2	0.3
Private creditiros	0.0	0.0	0.0	0.0	0.0	0.0	0.1	0.1	0.1
Principal repayments	0.3	0.3	0.3	0.3	0.4	0.4	0.6	0.9	1.0
Multilateral loans	0.0	0.0	0.0	0.0	0.0	0.0	0.0	0.2	0.2
Bilateral loans	0.3	0.3	0.3	0.3	0.3	0.3	0.4	0.5	0.5
Private creditors	0.0	0.0	0.0	0.0	0.1	0.1	0.2	0.2	0.3
Total debt service	0.5	0.5	0.5	0.5	0.5	0.5	1.0	1.3	1.5
Multilateral loans	0.0	0.0	0.0	0.0	0.0	0.0	0.1	0.3	0.3
Bilateral loans	0.5	0.5	0.5	0.5	0.4	0.4	0.6	0.7	0.8
Private creditors	0.0	0.0	0.0	0.0	0.1	0.1	0.3	0.3	0.4

Source: World Bank, Debtor Reporting System.

WESTERN SAMOA

DEVELOPMENT SURVEY

WESTERN SAMOA

CURRENCY EQUIVALENTS

	Annual averages
1981	WS$1 = $0.9649
1982	WS$1 = $0.8297
1983	WS$1 = $0.6496
1984	WS$1 = $0.5441
1985	WS$1 = $0.4557
1986	WS$1 = $0.4474
1987	WS$1 = $0.4716
1988	WS$1 = $0.4810
1989	WS$1 = $0.4408

FISCAL YEAR

January 1 to December 31

ABBREVIATIONS AND ACRONYMS

ADB	-	Asian Development Bank
EEC	-	European Economic Community
PMD	-	Produce Marketing Division
OECD	-	Organization for Economic Cooperation and Development
SCPL	-	Samoa Coconut Products Ltd
SFP	-	Samoa Forest Products Ltd
SOE	-	State-owned enterprise
WSTEC	-	Western Samoa Trust Estates Corporation

Table of Contents

This report was prepared by a World Bank mission which visited Western Samoa in November 1989. The mission members were Mark Baird, John Kerr-Stevens, Ranji Salgado (consultant) and Paul Flanagan (AIDAB). The report also draws on the findings of a World Bank agricultural mission and the IMF consultation mission, both of which visited Western Samoa at the same time. A draft of the report was discussed with government officials in June 1990.

WESTERN SAMOA

DEVELOPMENT SURVEY

A. Background

6.1   Western Samoa has a population of about 160,000, most of which is located on the two main islands of Upolu and Savai'i. At least 20 percent of the population lives in the urban area of Apia. Because of large net emigration flows (3-6,000 per annum since 1984),1/ population growth has been negligible in recent years. It is estimated that there are now at least 100,000 Samoans living overseas in New Zealand, Australia and the United States (including American Samoa). Many of the migrants are males aged 20 to 30, who have gone overseas to work. As a result, Western Samoa faces a high dependency rate (81 percent) and a growing shortage of labor.2/ Although most of the migrants become permanent residents overseas, they maintain strong cultural ties to Western Samoa and transfer funds back for family and social purposes. In 1989, recorded remittances totaled $38 million, significantly more than receipts from exports and aid combined. Actual remittances in cash and kind were probably substantially higher.

6.2   There are no official national account estimates in Western Samoa and it is difficult to measure the value of subsistence activities. Based on World Bank Atlas estimates, per capita GNP was about $580 in 1988. Through the extended family network and social services provided by the Government, basic needs are generally well satisfied and most social indicators are at reasonable levels (see Table 6.1). Although Western Samoa has few doctors, the coverage of basic health services (including the immunization program) is good. As a result, infant mortality is low and life expectancy high relative to the comparator countries. About two thirds of the population has access to safe water. Most children receive nine years of basic education and at least three years of high school education. Adult literacy is almost universal.

6.3   Western Samoa gained independence in 1962, following a period as a United Nations trust territory administered by New Zealand. Parliamentary elections are held every three years, with the right to vote restricted to about 20,000 village chiefs (matai) and 2,000 registered voters in Apia.3/

1/ These numbers are based on total arrivals and departures as recorded by the Immigration Office. Assuming net arrivals by foreigners are close to zero on average, they provide an indication of net migration by Samoans. There is probably also some unrecorded emigration to American Samoa.

2/ The recent agricultural sector review found that agricultural wage rates are as high as WS$10-16 per day, when both cash and payments in kind are taken into account. Labor shortages seem to be less acute around Apia, where unskilled workers are abundant at less than WS$1 per hour.

3/ A referendum on universal suffrage is expected to be held later this year.

Table 6.1: SOCIAL INDICATORS, 1988 /a

Indicator	Units	Western Samoa	Asia	Lower-Middle Income
Crude birth rate	per 000	33.2	26.8	31.5
Crude death rate	per 000	6.9	8.8	8.6
Infant mortality rate	per 000 births	36.7	61.5	59.1
Life expectancy at birth	years	65.4	63.7	63.8
Population per:				
- Doctor	persons	3,750	1,422	1,547
- Nurse	persons	411	1,674	
- Hospital bed	persons	229	733	
Child immunization				
- Measles	percent	78.1	41.0	62.6
- DPT	percent	84.3	48.6	64.7
Access to safe water	percent	69.0		
- Urban	percent	75.0	72.5	76.7
- Rural	percent	67.0		46.3
Gross enrollment ratios				
- Primary	percent	99.0 /b	105.3	106.8
- Secondary	percent	82.0 /c	37.5	52.0
Adult illiteracy rate	percent	2.0	39.5	26.2

/a Or most recent estimate.
/b For 10-14 years. The ratio is 88 percent for 5-9 years.
/c For 15-19 years.

Source: World Bank, "Social Indicators of Development, 1989" and National
         Planning Office.

The holder of a matai title is the elected head of an extended family (aiga).4/
The ditionally the matai has had nearly complete authority over the use of
customary land, which accounts for about 75 percent of land holdings in
Western Samoa and 80 percent of agricultural production. This system of land
tenure is often cited as a major constraint on agricultural development.

4/ For an interesting discussion of the economic effects of this social
    structure, see Yusuf & Peters (1985).

However, there is also evidence that the system is changing in response to income opportunities from cash cropping. Under the modified system, tenure is "by direct descent from the person who first cleared and planted the land, regardless of matai title".5/ The dramatic spread of matai titles in the last two decades has also allowed more individuals to gain access to land. As a result, there are now more opportunities for farmers to develop their land or to lease it out for commercial purposes.

6.4   Agriculture is the mainstay of the economy, accounting for about 50 percent of GDP and 80 percent of export earnings, according to official estimates.6/ However the statistical base is very weak. The recent agricultural sector review concludes that agriculture's contribution to GDP is significantly underestimated, particularly in the value of home consumption and domestic sales of taro and koko Samoa. It also appears that exports, especially of traditional foods to expatriate Samoans and exports to American Samoa, are also underrecorded.

6.5   The major cash crops are coconut, taro and cocoa (including koko Samoa). Copra production and exports have declined because of the poor return to labor, and banana exports have been greatly reduced by disease. On the other hand, taro and koko Samoa have probably expanded at a faster rate than indicated by official data, due to an expanding export market among Samoans overseas. Production of bananas, which was traditionally a major export item, has virtually ceased. The manufacturing sector is relatively small, accounting for less than 15 percent of GDP. Most production is for the small domestic market and based on imported inputs (e.g., beer, cigarettes). An important exception is coconut cream, which has become a major export item in recent years. The largest component of the service sector is government administration (about 15 percent of GDP). Tourist-related services have also become more important in recent years, following investments in airport and hotel facilities.

6.6   As with all small island economies, Western Samoa is highly vulnerable to external shocks. This vulnerability was all too evident in the destruction caused by Cyclone Ofa in February of this year. Estimates by the Samoan authorities place the cost at $140 million.7/ Fortunately, loss of life was minimal. But damage was widespread on both main islands; 25,000 were rendered homeless and several villages were completely destroyed. Schools, hospitals, water and power supplies were all severely affected. In the transport sector, one interisland ferry has been grounded, port facilities

---

5/ From O'Meara (1983). O'Meara also notes that "most of the agricultural lands which were created under the old tenure system have been divided among heirs and are now inherited strictly by the new principles of descent from the present occupants."

6/ Agriculture is defined to include all subsistence activities, forestry and fishing.

7/ This estimate is based on the cost of repairing damage to assets (excluding forests). No allowance is made for the cost of lost production.

have been damaged, and a quarter of the country's sealed roads have been destroyed or require major reconstruction. The agricultural sector was devastated. Tree crops and forestry plantations on the north coasts of both islands have been badly hit. The response of the people, with the support of the Government and the donor community, has been courageous. Emergency supplies have been sufficient to meet critical food and medical needs. Rebuilding is evident in all regions and sectors of the economy. The effects of the cyclone on Western Samoa's prospects are discussed below. But first, we review economic developments through 1989.

B. Recent Economic Developments

6.7   Western Samoa faced major macro imbalances in the early 1980s, due to a decline in the terms of trade and a rapid expansion of government expenditure (see Table 6.2). Lower prices for copra and cocoa, and a fixed exchange rate, affected production incentives, resulting in lower export volumes. As a result, despite the imposition of import controls, the current account deficit rose to 22 percent of GDP in 1981-82. By the end of 1982, the country faced a foreign exchange crisis, with payment arrears equal to one year's exports. The budget deficit after grants (16 percent of GDP) and the consolidated deficit of public enterprises (7 percent of GDP) had also risen to unsustainable levels. These deficits were financed in part by a rapid expansion of domestic credit, which fueled consumer price inflation of close to 20 percent per annum.

6.8   Action was finally taken in 1983-86 to improve the fiscal position. Revenues were raised dramatically through changes in import duties, a new goods and service tax, the collection of income tax arrears, and higher government charges. Public sector imports were made subject to duty and most excise duties were converted to an ad valorem basis. Curbs on the growth of public sector employment and wages, the postponement of lower priority projects, and the transfer of others to the private sector helped to contain expenditure levels. An improved system of expenditure control was also introduced. Higher inflows of external grants, including STABEX funds, have helped to generate a budget surplus since 1986. The deficit of public enterprises has also been substantially reduced.

6.9   The improvement in the fiscal position has enabled the Government to reduce its use of domestic credit and build up deposits with the Central Bank. Borrowing by public enterprises has also been substantially reduced. Although the money supply has been augmented by the accumulation of net foreign assets since 1985, consumer prices have risen on average by only 7 percent per annum over the past five years. The recovery of food production in 1989 helped to contain the inflationary impact of higher civil service salaries. There is also evidence that the general slowdown in economic activity has reduced the private sector's demand for credit.

6.10   The Government's program of fiscal restraint and higher interest rates helped to contain import demand. To improve export competitiveness, the Government devalued the Tala in 1983 and 1984, and has managed the exchange rate flexibly in subsequent years.[8] However, these measures have failed to

---

[8] The real effective exchange rate appreciated slightly in 1989 but is still about 30 percent below its 1982 level.

Table 6.2: ECONOMIC INDICATORS, 1981-89

	1981-82	1983-86	1987	1988	Est. 1989
Production & expenditure (growth rates, percent per annum)					
GDP		3.3	1.2	-0.1	-0.1
Subsistence		1.5	-1.5	-2.6	3.9
Agriculture /a		2.6	-6.1	-9.4	10.0
Manufacturing		7.8	1.6	1.6	-10.3
Other		3.5	7.2	5.5	-3.5
Expenditure		2.8	7.6	-1.4	-2.1
Consumption		2.6	5.2	-0.1	-2.5
- Private		0.2	5.8	-0.4	-5.5
- Government		22.3	2.1	1.2	12.8
Gross investment		3.6	17.2	-5.6	-0.7
- Private		4.1	22.4	-15.9	20.3
- Government		3.5	16.0	-3.3	-4.9
Central government budget (percent of GDP)					
Revenue	22.6	33.3	41.5	44.4	41.3
- Tax revenue	19.0	27.4	31.4	30.3	31.8
- Nontax revenue	3.6	5.9	10.1	14.1	9.5
External grants	12.6	15.5	17.1	15.4	14.7
Expenditure	47.8	45.4	49.0	44.4	50.4
- Current	24.3	19.9	21.1	20.3	23.0
- Development	23.5	25.5	27.9	24.1	27.4
Net Lending	3.3	4.7	6.2	7.7	2.5
Overall balance	-16.0	-1.3	3.4	7.6	3.1
Financed by:					
External borrowing (net)	6.9	1.4	2.8	1.0	5.1
Domestic credit	9.1	-0.1	-6.2	-8.6	-8.2
Money and prices (growth rates, percent per annum)					
Domestic credit	46.2	-6.7	-31.0	-60.8	-128.3
Private credit	11.7	17.3	23.1	22.4	6.0
Broad money	30.9	19.3	27.7	7.8	16.6
Money	33.9	7.0	32.7	5.4	9.6
Consumer prices	19.4	10.7	4.6	8.7	6.2
GDP deflator		10.3	4.1	9.7	3.4
Terms of trade		-4.8	6.4	18.9	-14.0
Balance of payments ($ million)					
Exports (fob)	12.1	15.8	11.8	15.1	12.9
Imports (cif)	-53.2	-49.5	-61.3	-74.6	-75.5
Trade balance	-41.0	-33.7	-49.6	-59.5	-62.6
Services (net)	-0.5	1.0	5.2	16.6	20.8
Private transfers	18.6	23.3	36.4	35.5	38.2
Current account	-23.0	-9.4	-5.5	-7.4	-3.6
External grants	15.1	14.9	17.7	17.7	16.0
Public loan disb. (net)	4.5	1.5	3.0	1.0	5.3
Other Capital (net)	4.5	-2.5	-1.1	1.6	-5.2
Use of net foreign assets (- = increase)	-1.1	-4.5	-14.1	-12.9	-11.7
Ratios					
Current account/GDP (percent)	-22.0	-10.0	-5.3	-6.4	-3.3
Debt service/exports (percent) /b	15.1	18.6	13.5	10.4	9.7
DOD/GDP (percent) /b	56.3	67.5	69.4	61.6	68.9
Net foreign assets (months of imports)	-1.1	0.8	4.5	6.5	6.7

/a Includes forestry and fishing.
/b For public debt only.

Source: Statistical Appendix.

achieve any lasting reduction in the trade deficit. In particular, agricultural export performance has continued to suffer from volatile commodity prices (e.g., copra and passion fruit), declining demand (coconut oil in New Zealand) and poor quality control (bananas). Despite the strong growth of coconut cream and taro exports, total export volume and earnings are still no higher than in the early 1980s. On the positive side, Western Samoa has benefited from strong growth in remittances (during the mid-1980s) and tourist receipts. These two items have ensured a steady improvement in the current account deficit which was reduced to 3 percent of GDP in 1989.

6.11   The Government has been able to finance its budget and the balance of payments through relatively high levels of aid on concessional terms. According to OECD data, net disbursements of Official Development Assistance totaled $216 per capita in 1987.9/ About 75 percent of gross disbursements are in the form of grants; the major donors are Australia, New Zealand, Japan and the EEC (STABEX funds). The balance are primarily soft loans from multilateral agencies (including ADB and the World Bank). The public debt service ratio peaked at over 20 percent in 1985-86, but has subsequently been reduced to around 10 percent. All payment arrears were settled by the end of 1985. Aid flows have remained basically flat in nominal terms in recent years. As a result, with the improvement in the current account, reserves have been accumulated. By the end of 1989, net foreign assets totaled $52.8 million, equivalent to 6.7 months of imports.

6.12   GDP growth has averaged less than 2 percent per annum since 1982, and has been negligible over the past three years. Although agricultural production recovered in 1989, the sector has grown by only 0-1 percent per annum during the 1980s. Performance has been constrained by depressed commodity prices, adverse weather conditions (e.g., drought in 1987-88), and poor management of the plantations managed by the Western Samoa Trust Estates Corporation (WSTEC). The manufacturing sector has been affected by the slowdown in domestic demand in recent years, with value added down sharply in 1989. Many firms suffer from poor management and several ventures (e.g., footwear, veneer) have recently stopped operations.

6.13   The growth of domestic expenditure slowed in the mid 1980s in response to the Government's program of fiscal restraint and economic adjustment. After a brief recovery in 1987, spurred by a temporary rise in the terms of trade, domestic expenditure has fallen over the past two years. The bulk of the adjustment has fallen on private consumption. Aid-financed projects have helped to maintain the investment rate at around 33 percent. Note that domestic savings are negative, because of the high propensity to consume out of remittance income. However, the improved fiscal position of the Government has boosted national savings to around 26 percent of GDP (20 percent of national income) over the past five years.

9/   Flows recorded in the balance of payments are substantially lower, because of the high levels of technical assistance and training provided in donor countries.

C. Development Prospects and Issues

Economic Prospects and Financing Requirements

6.14   The medium-term projections presented in Table 6.3 are intended to illustrate Western Samoa's development prospects and to provide a framework for discussing related policy issues. The short-term outlook is dominated by the effects of Cyclone Ofa. Agricultural production will decline because of crop damage, while manufacturing production will be affected by cyclone-related power cuts. Although there will be offsetting increases in construction and some service activities, overall GDP is expected to fall by at least 3 percent in 1990. However, barring any further shocks, the economy should recover strongly over the subsequent two to three years. For the medium term, priority has been given to achieving a satisfactory and sustainable rate of economic growth, without jeopardizing the recent gains in stabilization. Accordingly, annual GDP growth is projected to rise from an average of 1.9 percent over the past five years to 2.8 percent in 1990-94 and 3.5 percent in 1995-99. The key to this result is an improved performance from the agricultural sector, based on the policies discussed in para. 6.22 below. More rapid growth is precluded by the large size of the subsistence sector and, in the short term, by the long lead time for new investments in most commercial crops. Opportunities for growth outside agriculture are also limited. The best prospects would seem to be in tourist-related services, which are projected to benefit from a steady increase in arrivals and higher expenditures per tourist.[10] The small manufacturing sector is also expected to respond to improved incentives for private sector development, processing primary products for export (e.g., coconut cream, fruit juice) and supplying the domestic tourist industry (e.g., furniture, handicrafts).

6.15   The higher growth rate is largely generated by an increase in productivity. The investment rate rises to an average of 35 percent during the 1990s. Most of the increase in investment is assumed to come from the private sector. Government expenditure is assumed to be reallocated from investment to maintenance activities over the next few years. This leaves room for a modest rise in private consumption by about 3 percent per annum (after a post-cyclone adjustment in 1991). With little population growth expected over this period, per capita consumption would rise at a similar rate. Domestic savings are projected to remain negative because of the continuing influence of remittances from overseas. However, national savings are required to rise to around 30 percent of GDP (22 percent of national income). Because of the disruption caused by Cyclone Ofa, inflation is projected to rise sharply to 15 percent in 1990. Over the medium term, tight fiscal and monetary policies are assumed to hold inflation at 4-5 percent per annum, in line with international rates.

10/ Tourist development will require more flights (especially from the United States) and more competitive ticket prices compared to other destinations in the Pacific region. Hotel space is also a major constraint. The recent expansion of Aggie Grey's hotel has provided additional beds in Apia. But the Tusitala hotel is facing financial difficulties and two other hotel projects have not got off the ground. Accommodation outside Apia is very limited and there are no first-class beach resorts.

Table 6.3: MEDIUM-TERM PROJECTIONS, 1990-99

	Estimates 1985-89	-- Projections -- 1990-94	1995-99
Growth rates (percent per annum)			
GDP	1.9	2.8	3.5
Subsistence	0.8	1.0	1.0
Agriculture /a	0.5	1.9	3.0
Manufacturing	2.5	4.4	5.0
Other	3.2	3.9	4.5
Consumption	0.8	2.4	2.6
Gross investment	-0.4	3.5	2.4
Merchandise exports	0.5	4.6	6.1
Merchandise imports	4.2	3.1	2.6
Consumer prices	6.9	6.7	4.0
Terms of trade	-11.1	0.2	-0.4
Ratios to GDP (percent)			
Gross investment	31.7	35.5	34.9
Domestic savings	-6.4	-7.6	-6.7
National savings	19.2	29.8	29.3
Other indicators			
Current account/GDP (percent)	-6.3	-8.1	-5.6
Debt service/exports (percent)/a	15.4	8.2	5.6
DOD/GDP (percent)/a	68.7	98.4	100.9
Net foreign assets (months of imports)	4.2	10.8	11.8

/a For public debt only.

Source: World Bank staff estimates.

6.16   Cyclone Ofa is expected to cut the volumes of major export crops by 40-60 percent in 1990. It is clear that exports of treecrop products will be severely affected, and that surplus food production is likely to be diverted from export to domestic markets. At the same time, import volumes are project to rise sharply due to the related emergency and rehabilitation requirements. Although some of these imports will be financed by additional remittance flows, the current account deficit is projected to widen to 17 percent of GDP. Barring further shocks, it should be possible to reduce the current account deficit to the target range of 5-6 percent of GDP over a period of two to three years. Export volumes are expected to rebound strongly in 1991 and 1992. Over the medium term, export development will continue to be constrained by rising labor costs and the country's distance from markets.

However, these disadvantages can be reduced by maintaining a competitive exchange rate (with a more rapid pace of depreciation than over the past year), removal of domestic pricing distortions, and development of transport facilities. Overall, the volume of exports is projected to grow by 5-6 percent per annum, significantly higher than the recent trend. Import requirements are projected to fall back in 1991 and grow slower than exports in later years. Higher receipts from tourism and interest on reserves, together with a constant real (1989) level of remittance inflows, help keep the current account deficit at manageable levels.

6.17   The balance of payments projections can be reorganized to show external financing requirements and sources (see Table 6.4). Total requirements rise from an annual average of $53 million over the past five years to $70 million in 1990-94 and $78 million in 1995-99. This rising trend reflects the widening trade deficit, which is only partially offset by the improvement in the services account. The major financing item will continue to be private remittances. New commitments of project grants and loans are projected to remain flat in nominal terms through 1992, and then to grow in real terms by 2 percent per annum in later years. Provision has also been made for emergency and rehabilitation assistance in 1990 and 1991.11/ Because all loans are provided on concessional terms, the public debt service ratio falls steadily to an average of 8.2 percent in 1990-94 and 5.6 percent in 1995-99. However, disbursement of the ADB and World Bank loans raises the public DOD/GDP ratio to 100 percent.

6.18   The projections assume that external reserves are built up to a level equivalent to almost one year's imports. While this is a very high level, past experience suggests it could easily be eroded by unexpected changes in the terms of trade 12/ or the impact of weather on agricultural production. There is also a risk that remittance inflows will fall in real terms, because access to overseas employment is reduced 13/ or as second-generation Samoans lose their cultural ties. With remittances flat in nominal terms, and no corrective policy action, the current account deficit would widen sharply to 12 percent of GDP in 1990-94 and 17 percent of GDP in 1995-99. With no additional financing, reserves would be reduced to less than three months imports by the end of the decade. For these reasons, it is essential that the Government keeps reserves as a contingency, rather than drawing them down as a

---

11/ These include reallocation of the ADB program loan ($15 million), an emergency power loan from ADB ($0.5 million) and the road rehabilitation program from the World Bank ($14 million). A number of bilateral donors have also provided relief supplies and proposals to reallocate some project assistance are being finalized.

12/ There has been a sharp fall in world prices for copra and cocoa during the first half of 1990. This recent development is not fully reflected in the price projections used in this report.

13/ In 1988, more than 4,000 Samoans emigrated to New Zealand. An annual ceiling of 2,000 has now been set, although in practice this is unlikely to be met due to reduced demand for unskilled labor in New Zealand.

Table 6.4: EXTERNAL FINANCING REQUIREMENTS AND SOURCES, 1990-99
(\$ million per annum at current prices)

	Estimates 1985-89	-- Projections -- 1990-94	1995-99
Requirements	52.9	70.0	77.6
Merchandise imports	62.0	99.1	138.1
Merchandise exports	-13.3	-15.6	-28.1
Principal repayments /a	3.6	3.4	3.6
Interest payments /a	1.4	1.5	1.7
Other service payments (net)	-11.3	-30.7	-47.9
Change in net foreign assets	10.5	12.3	10.2
Sources	52.9	70.0	77.6
Private remittances	32.4	44.3	54.0
External grants	15.9	14.8	19.0
Public loan disbursements	4.8	17.8	13.0
Other capital (net)	-0.2	-6.9	-8.4

/a   On public debt.

Source: World Bank staff estimates.

development resource. The risks in the balance of payments also reinforce the
priority for fiscal and monetary restraint, strengthening export incentives
and improving domestic resource mobilization.

Development Issues and Policies

6.19   The Government's immediate preoccupation is understandably to restore
normalcy and rebuild basic services after the devastation of Cyclone Ofa. At
the same time, the above discussion suggests a number of areas were policy
action is needed to improve the medium-term development prospects for the
economy. These include: agricultural policies, public sector reform, aid
coordination, tax reform, fiscal and monetary policy, and private sector
incentives. In all of these areas, the Government has already prepared policy
proposals. The purpose of this discussion is to endorse the general thrust of
these proposals and to argue for their effective implementation.

6.20   Future growth in the economy will continue to be closely linked to
the performance of the agriculture sector. Coconuts will continue to be the
cornerstone of the traditional farming system, providing a wide range of
village consumption needs and raw materials. However, it is unlikely that
exports of basic coconut products will offer attractive returns at projected
world prices. There is also evidence that traditional cultivation is
encroaching into higher altitudes (often at the expense of lower land being
abandoned) and that herbicide use is expanding (in part to combat growing

labor shortages).14/ Further work is therefore required to establish the feasibility of rehabilitating village lands, curtailing further expansion on slopes, and developing alternatives to herbicides (such as more intensive use of ground covers).

6.21   As regards other export crops, the cocoa development program was severely affected by Cyclone Ofa. However, Western Samoa has the potential to develop further products like taro that can bear high transport costs and give an attractive return to the farmer. These products can often be sold in "niche" markets, where Western Samoa can exploit its potential advantages of off-season production and flexibility of response. There is also scope for further development of the country's forestry and fisheries resources, although this needs to be done in the context of a strong resource management policy.15/ The best prospects for import substitution would seem to lie in smallholder beef production, given the opportunities for grazing (on fallow land or under coconuts) in the smallholder farming system. Government and (current) WSTEC land is available to produce cattle on central ranches for fattening by smallholders.

6.22   In the budget statement for 1990, the Minister of Finance announced a number of important measures to support agricultural development. These measures include:

-    divestiture of governmental involvement in agro-based enterprises (SCPL, SFP and Samoa Feeds);

-    restructuring of WSTEC, by selling off non-plantation activities (e.g., beef) and leasing out of selected WSTEC estates;

-    linking domestic prices for commodity exports directly to the world fob price (without any levies for stabilization schemes);

-    rationalization of the marketing boards (PMD, Cocoa and Copra Boards), so that they eventually have only a passive role in providing information;

-    phasing out of Agricultural Store subsidies on fertilizers and agrochemicals;

-    elimination of import duties on agricultural machinery, fertilizers, agrochemicals and breeding animals (effective July 1990);

14/ Unlike Tonga, Western Samoa is too rocky in most areas for the use of tractors.

15/ In 1989, the Government established an environment division within the newly structured Department of Lands and Environment. This division has responsibility for conservation and environmental monitoring, and coordinates the environmental activities of other departments. New legislation on environmental planning is being prepared.

-   removal of all export taxes, including on copra, coconut oil, cocoa, taro, bananas, fruit and vegetables, livestock products and timber (effective February 1990);

-   establishment of credit schemes for purchasing agricultural inputs and for export finance; and

-   upgrading of the research and extension services of the Department of Agriculture.

This is an ambitious and comprehensive program and it is to be hoped that its implementation is not unduly delayed by the dislocation caused by Cyclone Ofa. A strong government commitment will be required to implement the proposed policy changes and to provide the needed institutional support. It will also be important to monitor the net impact of the various measures (e.g., lower subsidies and taxes) on farmer incentives to expand and diversify production.

6.23   Despite recent fiscal restraint, the public sector continues to play a dominant role in Western Samoa. The Government accounts for about 80 percent of gross investment and 35 percent of total expenditure. In addition, there is extensive involvement by state-owned enterprises (SOEs) in virtually all sectors of the economy. The Government recognizes that these enterprises have often not been run efficiently. This has led to a drain on budgetary resources and undermined incentives for private sector development. A SOE Monitoring Unit has recently been established to monitor performance, develop a system of controls and help identify candidates for divestiture. A number of enterprises have already been sold (e.g., the Food Processing Laboratory) 16/ or liquidated (e.g., Samoa Veneer Products).17/ As noted above, the Government also plans to divest its agro-based enterprises and the non-plantation activities of WSTEC. This divestiture program should proceed on a realistic timetable, with clear procedures to ensure an open tendering process and a smooth transition of ownership. Divested firms should operate in a competitive environment.

6.24   The need for reform also extends to the civil service. The highest priority in this area is human resource development. Western Samoa is fortunate to have a strong cadre of senior officials. But, as in other Pacific Island countries, there are too few staff at lower levels capable of implementing policies and projects. This is especially true in the line ministries. The recent salary increases will help to retain qualified staff and improve motivation. The Government is also introducing contracts for senior officials. This will be beneficial, provided it is not used for political appointments. Similar arrangements could be used to reward key staff at lower levels and offset the attraction of higher salaries overseas.

16/ The Food Processing Laboratory had virtually ceased exports of passionfruit juice prior to privatization in 1988. Now the new private owner has raised producer prices threefold and production has expanded significantly. Potential demand in New Zealand is still not fully satisfied.

17/ The sale of the Special Projects Development Corporation (SPDC) was stopped in July 1988. SPDC currently consists of a concrete plant and quarry, and is operating at a loss.

Technical assistance can help to fill critical gaps in the administration. However, to be effective, it needs to be structured so as to provide skills transfer and training for local counterpart staff.

6.25   Basic institutional changes are also required to improve planning and budget procedures. The recent decision to abolish the Department of Economic Development and establish a National Planning Office under the Prime Minister is a step in the right direction.18/ However, this change will only be effective if suitably qualified staff can be recruited and the functions of the National Planning Office are properly coordinated with the budget process, the availability of foreign aid and the operations of line agencies. The past emphasis on comprehensive five-year plans should be replaced with shorter strategic papers. Critical issues will be the policy framework for private sector development, the rehabilitation and maintenance of economic infrastructure, and the coordination of external assistance.

6.26   The case for the projected amounts of external assistance needs to be considered carefully. At the macro level, such large resource inflows could simply support a bloated public sector, while undermining incentives for export development and domestic resource mobilization. The Government has managed these pressures well in recent years, but continued progress on the policy agenda (as discussed in this section) is an essential element of the aid case. It is also essential that steps are taken by both the Government and donors to improve the effectiveness of aid utilization. At all levels, the capacity of the Government to absorb external assistance is stretched. Project design and selection is often left to the donors, without adequate coordination. Project implementation is hampered by human resource constraints and shortages of recurrent funding. More attention to cost recovery could improve recurrent funding in some sectors. The recent increase (13.7 percent) in power tariffs is an important step in this direction. However, given projected aid levels, it is unrealistic to expect all recurrent costs to be borne by the Government in the short term.19/ It is therefore desirable that donors finance a larger share of O&M expenditures.20/ Such assistance would be best provided within a multi-year program framework, with one donor playing a lead role in each sector. The program should provide for declining levels of recurrent funding by donors over time. Mechanisms for channeling aid funds to the private sector, such as two-step loans and financial sector operations, also need to be developed further.

6.27   Western Samoa has succeeded in raising tax revenues to 30 percent of GDP, one of the highest ratios among the Pacific Island economies. More than half of the revenues come from trade taxes (especially customs duties) and marginal income tax rates are very high.21/ In early 1988, a Commission of

---

18/ Other functions of the Department of Economic Development will be handled by a new Department of Commerce and Industry.

19/ External assistance has financed more than 80 percent of development expenditure in recent years.

20/ The alternatives are either lower levels of aid or the historical cycle of low maintenance, asset deterioration and then a new project for rehabilitation.

21/ The marginal tax rates on income rise to 45 percent for individuals, 48 percent for non-resident companies and 39 percent for resident companies.

Enquiry proposed a number of changes to broaden the tax base, reduce distortions and improve administration. Several of these proposals have been accepted by the Government and announced in the budget statement for 1990. These include:

- extension of the goods and services tax to all professional services;

- introduction of a capital gains tax and revised income tax brackets;22/

- rationalization of customs duties, to reduce the dispersion of rates; and (as noted above); and

- removal of all export taxes.

While these reforms may cause some short-term loss of revenues, the buoyancy of the tax system will be improved over the medium term (provided the whole package is implemented). This is an important element of the Government's program to improve domestic resource mobilization. At the same time, the reduction of income tax rates and rationalization of customs duties will improve the environment for private sector development.

6.28   For 1990, the Government's original budget projected a rapid increase in both current and development expenditure. Salaries were raised by 7 percent (with an additional payment of WS$260 for wage earners).23/ Higher levels of development expenditure are to be supported by disbursements from the ADB program loan. Following Cyclone Ofa, WS$18 million (including WS$12 million of reallocated funds) was earmarked for relief and rehabilitation. Additional spending of almost WS$12 million, to be financed in part from the sale of shares in the Bank of Western Samoa, was approved in June 1990. Although strict limits have been placed on operating expenses, the deficit (after grants) is expected to rise above 6 percent of GDP. At the same time, to provide funds for rehabilitation, the Central Bank has reduced the maximum lending rate from 17 percent to 12 percent. These measures are justified under the circumstances. However, it is essential that every effort is made to restore fiscal and monetary discipline as soon as possible. Otherwise, the short-term rise in prices could well lead to a persistent inflationary trend.

6.29   The private sector is expected to play a much larger role in the economy in the years ahead. Proposed reforms in agriculture, public enterprises and taxation will all help to improve the environment for private sector development. Credit is not a major constraint at this stage; private sector demand for credit was weak in 1989 (prior to the cyclone) and banks see few viable project proposals in the pipeline. In the short term, the private sector will benefit from the interest rate reductions noted above, as well as from a new scheme to provide exporters access to working capital at 9 percent interest. Over the long term, increased competition within the banking system would help to reduce margins. Lending rates could probably be reduced by

22/ The capital gains tax is 30 percent on all assets sold within three years (after allowing 5 percent per annum for inflation). The maximum tax on personal income (45 percent) now applies at WS$16,000 (previously WS$10,000).

23/ This amounts to an increase of about 25 percent at lower wage levels.

providing a higher return on statutory reserves and removing the credit ceiling for trading activities. As the demand for credit expands, additional resources could be mobilized by raising contributions to NPF and introducing foreign currency accounts.

6.30   Western Samoa provides investment incentives (in the form of tax holidays and customs duty exemptions) under the Enterprises Incentives Scheme. This scheme has assisted 200 enterprises to date, of which about half are still in operation. An Industrial Free Zone, approved in 1974, has never got off the ground. The Government has recently permitted greater flexibility for the siting of eligible enterprises (not necessarily within one area), and proposes to merge the administration of the Industrial Free Zone and the Enterprise Incentives Scheme. This is an important step toward a "one shop" approach to investment incentives. The new Department of Commerce and Industry can also play a useful role in promoting opportunities for foreign investment in Western Samoa. However, over the longer term, private investment decisions are likely to be more influenced by the Government's success in improving the overall policy environment and providing basic infrastructure. Special legislation (such as considered for the Royal Samoa Hotel) should be avoided. The case for custom duty exemptions should also be reviewed, in light of proposed changes in duty rates.

REFERENCES

ADB (1989), "Memorandum of Understanding on a Proposed Agricultural Development Program Loan".

Browne, C. (1989), "Economic Development in Seven Pacific Island Countries" (IMF).

Central Bank of Samoa, "Bulletin" (various issues).

Coopers & Lybrand Consultants (1989), "Country Paper - Western Samoa" (draft paper for the Pacific Islands Regional Economic Report).

Department of Statistics (1989), "Annual Statistical Abstract 1988".

Government of Western Samoa (1988), "Socio-Economic Situation Development Strategy and Assistance Needs" (for the Round Table Meeting, Geneva, October 1988).

Hassall & Associates (1989), "Tonga and Western Samoa Agricultural Sector Review" (prepared for the World Bank).

IMF (1989), "Western Samoa - 1988 Staff Report on the Interim Article IV Consultation Discussions" (confidential).

IMF (1990), "Western Samoa - Recent Economic Developments" (confidential).

IMF (1990), "Western Samoa - Staff Report for the 1989 Article IV Consultation" (confidential).

Minister of Finance (1989), "The 1990 Budget Statement".

O'Meara, J.T. (1983), "Why is Village Agriculture Stagnating?" (Department of Anthropology, University of California).

Yusuf, S. & Peters, R.K. (1985), "Western Samoa: The Experience of Slow Growth and Resource Imbalance" (World Bank SWP No. 754).

STATISTICAL APPENDIX

LIST OF TABLES

Table 1.1: POPULATION OF WESTERN SAMOA, 1981 & 1986

Age group	1981			1986		
	Male	Female	Total	Male	Female	Total
All ages	81,027	75,322	156,349	83,370	74,038	157,408
00-04 years	12,095	10,771	22,866	11,898	10,211	22,109
05-09	11,991	10,857	22,848	11,273	9,750	21,023
10-14	12,438	11,087	23,525	11,733	9,980	21,713
15-19	10,919	9,977	20,896	11,479	9,656	21,135
20-24	7,868	7,132	15,000	8,502	7,295	15,797
25-29	4,968	4,705	9,673	6,040	5,523	11,563
30-34	3,412	3,450	6,862	4,385	4,232	8,617
35-39	3,043	3,122	6,165	3,172	3,193	6,365
40-44	2,986	3,014	6,000	2,953	2,976	5,929
45-49	2,564	2,594	5,158	2,722	2,674	5,396
50-54	2,476	2,419	4,895	2,510	2,381	4,891
55-59	2,087	1,868	3,955	2,151	1,932	4,083
60-64	1,459	1,421	2,880	1,805	1,586	3,391
65-69	944	932	1,876	1,169	991	2,160
70-74	605	637	1,242	724	691	1,415
Over 75	678	940	1,618	839	943	1,782
Not stated	494	396	890	15	24	39

Source: Department of Statistics, Census.

Table 1.2: GOVERNMENT EMPLOYEES & SALARIES, 1986 & 1987

Department	Employees		Total salaries (Tala '000)		Average salary (Tala/person)	
	1986	1987	1986	1987	1986	1987
Agriculture, Forestry & Fisheries	255	255	1,447	1,153	5,673	4,522
Attorney General	11	14	103	151	9,343	10,802
Audit	13	13	107	117	8,268	9,008
Broadcasting	34	34	209	223	6,157	6,561
Customs	46	45	253	267	5,495	5,934
Economic Development	24	10	170	105	7,075	10,460
Education	1,700	1,818	8,134	8,265	4,785	4,546
Health	847	849	3,742	3,917	4,417	4,614
Inland Revenue	47	47	257	274	5,463	5,837
Justice	96	66	646	550	6,731	8,335
Labour	23	14	193	105	8,402	7,476
Lands & Survey	70	70	368	390	5,260	5,567
Post Office	219	219	998	1,013	4,559	4,624
Public Services Commission	28	28	226	265	8,084	9,458
Public Works	239	239	1,224	1,257	5,122	5,260
Prime Minister's	81	86	426	440	5,265	5,111
Statistics	31	31	132	146	4,273	4,706
Transport	37	36	182	184	4,914	5,123
Treasury	121	121	602	645	4,973	5,332
Youth, Sports & Culture		8		93		11,571
Land & Titles Court		36		185		5,149
Total	3,922	4,039	19,420	19,745	4,952	4,889

Source: Legislative Assembly (Approved Estimates).

Table 2.1: GDP BY INDUSTRIAL ORIGIN, 1982-89
(Tala million)

	1982	1983	1984	1985	1986	1987	1988	1989
At current prices	123.9	153.6	179.0	196.6	208.3	219.4	240.3	248.4
Subsistence	37.3	43.7	47.4	51.6	57.9	58.7	62.5	64.9
Agriculture, forestry & fishing	26.6	32.7	39.8	42.9	43.5	44.2	43.8	52.2
Manufacturing	13.9	21.3	29.0	32.0	28.9	31.1	36.5	31.6
Electricity	4.3	5.9	8.7	8.6	8.0	9.0	11.0	11.0
Construction	1.6	3.9	2.0	2.9	4.1	7.0	9.8	4.6
Distribution, rest. & hotels	9.4	11.4	13.2	15.7	18.8	20.2	22.4	25.6
Transportation	4.7	5.4	6.6	7.0	5.1	5.6	5.1	5.2
Other services	10.9	13.0	14.8	16.5	17.5	18.7	20.8	22.3
Government	15.2	16.3	17.5	19.4	24.5	24.9	28.4	31.0
At 1982 prices	123.9	131.7	129.5	134.1	140.9	142.6	142.4	142.3
Subsistence	37.3	37.9	37.9	37.6	39.6	39.0	38.0	39.5
Agriculture, forestry & fishing	26.6	27.5	26.9	25.8	29.5	27.7	25.1	27.6
Manufacturing	13.9	15.8	15.4	18.2	18.8	19.1	19.4	17.4
Electricity	4.3	4.4	4.6	4.9	5.2	5.5	5.9	6.0
Construction	1.6	4.1	2.0	2.9	3.8	5.9	7.4	3.4
Distribution, rest. & hotels	9.4	9.8	10.2	11.0	12.5	12.9	13.1	14.2
Transportation	4.7	4.8	5.4	5.4	4.9	5.4	5.6	5.7
Other services	10.9	11.1	11.2	11.5	11.7	12.0	12.1	12.5
Government	15.2	16.3	15.9	16.8	14.9	15.1	15.8	16.0
GDP deflator (1984=100)	100.0	116.6	138.2	146.6	147.8	153.9	168.8	174.6

Source: IMF staff estimates.

Table 2.2: GDP BY EXPENDITURE, 1982-89
(Tala million)

	1982	1983	1984	1985	1986	1987	1988	1989
At current prices								
GDP	123.9	153.6	179.0	196.6	208.3	219.4	240.3	248.4
Imports (GNFS)	63.4	87.6	107.5	129.5	126.7	151.4	175.5	194.6
Exports (GNFS)	21.4	41.6	50.0	59.4	53.3	59.8	84.5	94.3
Expenditure	165.9	199.7	236.5	266.7	281.7	311.0	331.2	348.7
Consumption	133.0	159.7	177.1	206.6	222.0	236.9	253.8	265.6
- Private	122.2	135.2	148.7	173.8	185.7	198.1	211.2	214.7
- Government	10.8	24.5	28.4	32.8	36.3	38.8	42.6	50.9
Gross investment	32.9	40.0	59.4	60.1	59.7	74.1	77.4	83.1
- Private	5.7	6.9	10.3	10.4	10.1	12.9	11.7	15.0
- Government	27.2	33.1	49.1	49.7	49.6	61.2	65.7	68.1
Domestic savings	-9.1	-6.1	1.9	-10.0	-13.7	-17.5	-13.5	-17.2
- Private	-10.2	-16.9	-24.0	-42.7	-54.3	-70.5	-76.6	-63.0
- Government	1.1	10.8	25.9	32.7	40.6	53.0	63.1	45.8
Net factor income	-1.7	-1.8	-3.0	-3.8	-2.3	2.6	1.6	5.4
Net current transfers	22.5	31.4	37.8	53.1	63.5	77.2	73.8	86.6
National savings	11.7	23.6	36.7	39.2	47.6	62.4	61.9	74.9
GNP	122.2	151.8	176.0	192.8	206.0	222.0	241.9	253.8
GNY	144.7	183.2	213.8	245.8	269.5	299.2	315.7	340.4
At 1982 prices								
GDP	123.9	131.7	129.5	134.1	140.9	142.6	142.4	142.3
Imports (GNFS)	63.4	73.8	77.1	83.2	80.7	91.1	95.0	96.5
Exports (GNFS)	21.4	27.7	19.6	27.5	36.6	34.5	40.9	46.4
Expenditure	165.9	177.8	187.0	189.8	185.1	199.2	196.5	192.3
Consumption	133.0	144.7	144.5	151.8	147.2	154.8	154.6	150.7
- Private	122.2	123.7	122.7	128.7	123.0	130.1	129.6	122.5
- Government	10.8	21.0	21.8	23.1	24.2	24.7	25.0	28.2
Gross investment	32.9	33.1	42.5	38.0	37.9	44.4	41.9	41.6
- Private	5.7	6.0	7.9	7.3	6.7	8.2	6.9	8.3
- Government	27.2	27.1	34.6	30.7	31.2	36.2	35.0	33.3
Net factor income	-1.7	-1.5	-2.2	-2.5	-1.5	1.6	0.9	2.8
Net current transfers	22.5	26.4	27.7	34.9	41.0	47.3	41.2	45.0
GNP	122.2	130.2	127.3	131.6	139.4	144.2	143.3	145.1
GNY /a	144.7	163.9	171.3	177.1	177.9	193.1	189.4	190.4

/a After terms of trade adjustment.

Source: Derived from Table 5.1 & IMF staff estimates.

Table 3.1: CENTRAL GOVERNMENT BUDGET, 1980-89
(Tala million)

	1980	1981	1982	1983	1984	1985	1986	1987	1988	1989
Revenue	24.9	24.3	28.3	41.0	58.6	73.7	75.4	91.1	106.7	102.6
Tax	20.4	20.3	23.9	34.1	49.9	59.5	60.8	69.0	72.7	79.0
Non-tax	4.5	4.0	4.4	6.9	8.7	14.2	14.6	22.1	34.0	23.6
External grants	12.9	14.9	14.3	26.3	25.3	26.5	36.0	37.8	36.9	36.4
STABEX	0.0	2.1	0.7	2.0	0.0	0.3	8.8	8.3	4.8	4.7
Other commodity	0.3	0.7	0.0	0.0	1.7	0.0	0.1	0.0	0.4	0.2
Project	12.6	12.1	13.6	24.3	23.6	26.2	27.1	29.3	31.7	31.5
Expenditure	47.6	52.0	59.4	68.0	82.9	91.0	93.3	107.6	106.7	125.2
Current	21.1	25.1	31.7	29.0	33.6	41.3	43.7	46.4	48.8	57.1
Development	26.5	26.9	27.7	39.0	49.3	49.7	49.6	61.2	57.9	68.1
Net lending /a	4.9	4.8	2.8	1.3	12.7	10.7	11.3	13.6	18.6	6.1
Treasury advances (net) \b	..	..	..	--	5.9	8.5	7.1	8.9	7.3	5.0
Capital accounts	..	..	..	..	6.8	2.2	4.2	4.7	11.3	1.1
Overall balance	-14.7	-17.6	-19.6	-2.0	-11.7	-1.5	6.8	7.5	18.3	7.7
Financed by:										
External borrowing (net)	7.3	7.9	8.2	3.2	3.0	1.7	2.1	6.1	2.3	12.7
Disbursements	..	..	..	..	5.5	5.6	6.8	11.6	8.3	19.7
Repayments	..	..	..	..	-2.5	-3.9	-4.7	-5.5	-8.0	-7.0
Domestic financing (net)	7.4	9.7	11.4	-1.2	8.7	-0.2	-8.9	-13.5	-20.6	-20.4
Banking system /c	..	..	..	..	8.4	-0.8	-15.4	-18.0	-21.5	-23.0
Nonbank /c	..	..	..	..	0.3	0.6	6.5	4.5	0.9	2.6

/a Includes net loans to public enterprises, capital subscriptions & land purchases.
/b Change in net foreign asset holdings of the Treasury.
/c Includes long-term treasury bonds & a residual item.

Source: Treasury Department & IMF staff estimates.

Table 3.2: CENTRAL GOVERNMENT REVENUE, 1980-89
(Tala million)

	1980	1981	1982	1983	1984	1985	1986	1987	1988	1989
Income tax	6.0	6.6	8.4	11.0	12.7	13.7	16.0	14.9	17.2	18.8
Taxes on goods & services	2.8	2.6	3.5	3.9	7.0	9.8	10.8	13.1	13.8	16.1
Excise tax	2.8	2.6	3.5	3.9	6.9	9.7	10.6	12.1	12.7	14.5
- Domestic	2.8	2.6	3.5	3.9	5.0	8.0	9.0	9.8	10.6	12.2
- Import	..	..	..	..	1.9	1.7	1.6	2.3	2.1	2.3
Goods & services tax	0.0	0.0	0.0	0.0	0.0	0.0	0.1	0.9	1.0	1.3
Business license	..	..	..	..	0.1	0.1	0.1	0.1	0.1	0.3
Taxes on international trade	11.3	10.9	11.8	18.5	29.3	35.1	32.4	40.8	41.2	44.1
Import duties	10.1	10.1	11.0	17.5	27.9	32.5	30.4	38.7	38.7	41.8
Export levy	0.6	0.2	0.2	0.3	0.3	1.3	0.7	0.6	0.7	0.6
Foreign exchange levy	0.6	0.6	0.6	0.7	1.1	1.3	1.3	1.5	1.8	1.7
Other taxes	0.3	0.2	0.2	0.7	0.9	0.9	1.6	0.2	0.5	0.0
Total tax revenue	20.4	20.3	23.9	34.1	49.9	59.5	60.8	69.0	72.7	79.0
Nontax revenue	4.5	4.0	4.4	6.9	8.7	14.1	14.7	22.1	34.0	23.6
Fees & service charges	1.5	1.5	1.8	2.0	2.6	2.7	2.6	3.4	3.5	4.0
Department enterprises	1.2	1.0	1.5	3.2	2.2	4.7	5.8	7.5	9.7	8.4
Rents, royalties & interest	1.0	1.2	0.5	1.3	2.8	3.2	4.8	8.9	19.0	8.7
Other /a	0.8	0.3	0.6	0.4	1.1	3.5	1.5	2.3	1.8	2.5
Total revenue	24.9	24.3	28.3	41.0	58.6	73.7	75.4	91.1	108.7	102.6

/a Includes sales of government supplies.

Source: Treasury Department & IMF staff estimates.

Table 3.3: CENTRAL GOVERNMENT EXPENDITURE, 1980-89
(Tala million)

	1980	1981	1982	1983	1984	1985	1986	1987	1988	1989
Current expenditure	21.1	25.1	31.7	29.0	33.6	41.3	43.7	46.4	48.8	57.1
Salaries & wages	10.9	12.9	13.3	14.8	16.7	17.7	23.1	23.5	26.9	31.9
Interest payments	2.3	2.9	3.0	4.5	6.5	6.3	6.3	6.5	5.7	5.7
– External					4.1	3.5	3.7	3.6	2.9	3.1
– Domestic					2.4	2.8	2.6	2.9	2.8	2.6
Other	7.9	9.3	15.4	9.7	10.4	17.3	14.3	16.4	18.2	19.5
Development expenditure	26.5	26.9	27.7	39.0	49.3	49.7	49.6	61.2	57.9	68.1
Domestically financed /a	7.6	8.3	8.9	7.1	12.8	17.9	15.7	20.3	17.9	26.9
Project-loan financed	6.3	6.5	5.2	7.6	12.9	5.6	6.8	11.8	8.3	9.7
Project-grant financed	12.6	12.1	13.6	24.3	23.6	26.2	27.1	29.3	31.7	31.5
Total expenditure	47.6	52.0	59.4	68.0	82.9	91.0	93.3	107.6	106.7	125.2

/a Data for 1984 onward include government payments of import duties.

Source: Treasury Department & IMF staff estimates.

Table 4.1: MONETARY SURVEY, 1980-89
(Tala million)

At end of period	1980	1981	1982	1983	1984	1985	1986	1987	1988	1989
Net foreign assets	-9.0	-19.1	-25.9	-1.3	1.2	6.4	31.1	56.8	88.4	121.0
Treasury	..	..	..	..	..	-15.7	-8.6	3.7	18.8	27.8
Central Bank of Samoa	..	..	..	..	..	18.1	32.0	44.1	59.4	82.7
Commercial banks	..	..	..	..	..	4.0	7.6	9.0	10.2	10.5
Domestic credit	27.1	41.9	57.9	48.4	50.3	54.9	43.9	30.3	11.9	-3.4
Government (net)	9.6	19.9	31.5	22.0	21.1	20.4	4.9	-13.1	-34.8	-50.0
Public enterprises	6.2	10.0	12.3	10.5	10.1	12.1	12.3	10.5	6.2	4.1
Private sector	11.3	12.0	14.1	15.9	19.1	22.4	26.7	32.8	40.2	42.6
Other items	0.1	0.2	-0.8	-5.6	-8.7	-9.3	-11.8	-8.3	-13.3	-16.2
Broad money	18.2	23.0	31.2	41.5	42.8	52.0	63.2	80.7	87.0	101.5
Money	9.2	14.0	16.5	16.5	18.6	19.5	21.6	28.7	30.3	33.2
Currency ouside banks	..	..	..	..	..	8.4	9.2	10.5	10.7	12.5
Demand deposits	..	..	..	..	..	11.1	12.5	18.2	19.5	20.7
Quasi-money	9.0	9.0	14.7	25.0	24.2	32.4	41.5	52.0	56.7	68.3
Savings deposits	..	..	..	..	..	7.9	9.9	11.9	12.8	14.9
Time deposits	..	..	..	..	..	24.5	31.6	40.1	44.0	53.4

Source: Central Bank of Samoa.

Table 4.2: FINANCIAL SYSTEM STRUCTURE, 1985-89
(% of total)

End of period	Balance sheets					Domestic credit				
	1985	1986	1987	1988	1989	1985	1986	1987	1988	1989
Treasury	12.6	9.9	6.4	3.0	1.3	14.6	8.6	-2.3	-15.6	-23.2
Central Bank of Samoa	14.3	16.5	20.4	22.2	25.9	5.3	0.9	0.9	1.5	1.4
Commercial banks	33.6	35.4	37.0	36.0	35.2	31.1	36.3	42.7	43.6	44.0
Bank of Western Samoa	26.5	27.6	28.9	27.7	28.2	23.5	27.8	32.3	33.1	33.5
Pacific Commercial Bank	7.1	7.8	8.1	8.3	7.0	7.6	8.5	10.4	10.5	10.5
Other financial institutions	39.5	38.2	36.2	38.8	37.6	49.0	54.2	58.7	70.5	77.8
National Provident Fund	18.6	18.2	16.8	19.0	17.6	21.2	22.6	21.2	29.6	30.4
Development Bank of Western Samoa	12.6	12.4	12.2	12.6	12.4	21.9	24.3	29.1	32.0	37.6
Nat. Pacific Insurance	3.4	3.0	2.6	2.6	3.0	0.4	1.3	1.6	1.4	1.4
Western Samoa Life Assurance Corp.	2.4	2.4	2.5	2.6	2.5	1.8	2.2	2.8	3.4	3.9
Public Trust Office	1.7	1.5	1.3	1.3	1.1	2.4	2.5	2.6	2.6	2.7
Post Office Savings Bank	0.8	0.7	0.8	0.7	1.0	1.3	1.3	1.4	1.5	1.8
Total	100.0	100.0	100.0	100.0	100.0	100.0	100.0	100.0	100.0	100.0
Amount in Tala million	206.6	235.5	277.9	305.6	363.5	113.4	112.1	109.2	114.1	114.7

Source: Central Bank of Samoa.

Table 4.3: INTEREST RATES, 1983-89
(% per annum)

As from	Feb 83	Feb 85	Mar 86	Sep 86	Jan 87	Nov 88
Deposit rates						
Savings deposits	8	7	7.5	7.5	7.5	7.5
Time deposits /a						
- 1 month		10	10.5	10	9.25	9.25
- 3 months	14	12	12.5	11	10.25	10.25
- 6 months	15	13	13.75	12	12	12
- 12 months	17	15	15	------- Negotiable ------		
- 24 months	17	15	13.75	------- Negotiable ------		
Lending rates						
Commercial banks /b	14-20	15-18/c	15-19	14-17.5	14-17.5	14-17
Development Bank of Western Samoa	8-17	10-16/d	10-16	8-16/e	8-16	8-16
National Provident Fund	8-17	10-17	10-17	10-17	10-17	10-17
Public Trust & WSLAC (housing)	10-12.5	12-15	12-15	12-15	12.5-16/f	12-16

/a Effective September 15 1986, the rates for term deposits in excess of WS$20,000 and all rates for terms over 6 months have been opened to negotiation.
/b Effective September 15 1986, a penalty rate of 19% to be charged on amounts in excess of agreed overdraft limits.
/c From September 1 1985 to March 16 1986, 21% for import financing.
/d From March 1 1985.
/e From October 1 1986.
/f From July 1 1987.

Source: Central Bank of Samoa.

Table 4.4: CONSUMER PRICE INDEX, 1980-89

Period average	Weights	1980	1981	1982	1983	1984	1985	1986	1987	1988	1989
Indices (1980=100)											
Food	58.8	100.0	120.2	145.6	167.6	182.3	200.2	213.1	219.1	239.4	246.5
Clothing & footwear	4.2	100.0	123.8	141.5	168.8	195.2	210.3	228.2	235.3	249.4	268.2
Housing & household ops	12.0	100.0	135.2	162.9	184.5	209.5	219.4	224.1	227.0	239.4	253.9
Transport & communications	9.0	100.0	112.2	128.0	149.8	152.0	160.5	159.1	168.8	167.3	209.0
Miscellaneous	16.0	100.0	114.7	124.6	157.4	196.8	220.4	238.5	268.4	300.3	333.8
Import component (all groups)	50.3	100.0			171.4	201.2	217.4	216.9	216.3	228.1	251.3
All groups	100.0	100.0	120.5	142.6	166.4	185.7	202.6	214.3	224.1	243.6	258.8
Annual changes (%)											
Food			20.2	21.1	15.1	8.8	9.8	6.4	2.8	9.3	3.0
Clothing & footwear			23.8	14.3	19.2	15.8	7.7	8.5	3.1	6.0	7.5
Housing & household ops			35.2	20.5	13.3	13.6	4.7	2.1	1.3	5.5	6.1
Transport & communications			12.2	14.1	17.0	1.5	5.6	-0.9	6.1	-0.9	24.9
Miscellaneous			14.7	8.6	26.3	24.9	12.1	8.2	12.5	11.9	11.1
Import component (all groups)						17.4	8.1	-0.2	-0.3	5.5	10.2
All groups			20.5	18.3	16.7	11.6	9.1	5.8	4.6	8.7	6.2

Source: Department of Statistics.

Table 5.1: BALANCE OF PAYMENTS, 1980-89
(US$ million)

	1980	1981	1982	1983	1984	1985	1986	1987	1988	1989
Merchandise exports (fob)	17.2	10.8	13.5	17.8	18.6	16.1	10.5	11.8	15.1	12.9
Merchandise imports (cif)	-62.2	-56.4	-49.9	-48.8	-50.7	-51.2	-47.1	-61.3	-74.6	-75.5
Trade balance	-45.0	-45.7	-36.4	-31.0	-32.1	-35.1	-36.6	-49.6	-59.5	-62.6
Non-factor services (net)	2.4	0.8	1.6	1.1	0.9	3.9	3.8	6.4	15.8	18.4
- Travel receipts	..	..	..	4.7	4.7	6.6	8.5	9.5	15.9	17.1
- Other receipts	..	..	..	4.4	4.0	3.8	4.8	7.0	9.7	11.6
- Payments	..	..	..	-8.1	-7.8	-6.5	-9.6	-10.0	-9.8	-10.3
Resource balance	-42.6	-44.9	-34.8	-29.9	-31.3	-31.3	-32.8	-43.2	-43.7	-44.2
Factor services (net)	-2.5	-2.0	-1.4	-1.2	-1.6	-1.7	-1.0	1.2	0.8	2.4
- Receipts	..	..		0.1	0.3	0.7	1.2	3.4	2.9	4.8
- Public interest payments	-2.3	-1.8	-1.1	-1.0	-1.4	-1.7	-1.4	-1.3	-1.3	-1.2
- IMF charges	-0.2	-0.3	-0.3	-0.3	-0.5	-0.6	-0.7	-0.6	-0.4	-0.3
- Other payments	..	..	..	..	-0.1	-0.1	-0.1	-0.3	-0.4	-0.9
Private transfers (net)	18.7	18.6	18.7	20.4	20.5	23.6	28.4	36.4	35.5	38.2
Current account balance	-26.4	-28.3	-17.6	-10.7	-12.4	-9.3	-5.4	-6.5	-7.4	-3.6
Official transfers (net)	17.4	15.9	14.3	17.0	13.4	11.4	15.3	16.9	17.1	15.2
- External grants	17.4	15.9	14.3	17.7	13.8	11.8	16.1	17.7	17.7	16.0
- Other				-0.7	-0.4	-0.4	-0.8	-0.8	-0.7	-0.8
Public loan disbursements (net)	8.6	3.7	5.2	1.9	7.0	-1.5	-1.5	3.0	1.0	5.3
- Gross disbursements	10.9	5.4	7.0	4.7	10.2	2.5	2.8	6.0	4.2	8.5
- Principal repayments	-2.3	-1.7	-1.7	-2.8	-3.2	-4.0	-4.3	-3.0	-3.2	-3.3
Other (net) /a	-3.5	9.7	-0.8	-5.2	-8.6	1.6	3.1	-0.3	2.4	-5.2
Use of net foreign assets	4.0	-1.1	-1.1	-3.0	-1.4	-2.2	-11.3	-14.1	-12.9	-11.7
Net foreign assets (end of period)	-8.1	-5.0	-3.9	-0.9	0.5	2.8	14.1	28.2	41.2	52.8

/a Includes private capital flows, valuation changes, and errors & omissions.

Source: Central Bank of Samoa, IMF staff estimates & World Bank Debtor Reporting System.

Table 5.2: MERCHANDISE TRADE INDICES, 1982-89
(1982=100)

	1982	1983	1984	1985	1986	1987	1988	1989
Value /a								
Exports /b	100.0	132.3	142.4	115.5	79.8	87.2	114.3	98.3
Imports	100.0	97.8	101.7	102.7	94.4	123.0	149.6	151.3
Volume								
Exports /b	100.0	124.2	94.8	110.7	113.3	104.4	103.7	97.3
Imports	100.0	102.6	109.2	118.3	110.1	128.8	141.1	133.9
Unit value /a								
Exports /b	100.0	106.5	150.2	104.3	70.5	83.6	110.2	101.0
Imports	100.0	95.3	93.1	86.8	85.7	95.5	106.0	113.0
Terms of trade a/	100.0	111.8	161.3	120.1	82.2	87.5	104.0	89.4

/a In terms of US Dollars.
/b Excludes re-exports.

Source: Central Bank of Samoa.

Table 5.3: MERCHANDISE EXPORTS, 1980–89

	1980	1981	1982	1983	1984	1985	1986	1987	1988	1989
Value (US$ '000)	17,215	10,759	13,481	17,806	18,584	18,132	10,508	11,775	15,102	12,874
Copra	9,112	3,786	2,290	908	0	425	469	31	948	1,427
Copra meal	..	..	317	437	322	250	294	357	447	288
Coconut oil	..	..	3,419	7,200	11,276	6,963	2,927	4,117	5,622	3,086
Coconut cream	632	613	615	778	899	1,263	1,263	1,466	1,863	2,245
Cocoa	3,297	1,386	818	2,999	1,229	1,050	1,425	1,237	606	945
Taro	1,140	2,061	1,808	1,540	1,498	2,279	1,939	2,394	2,502	2,578
Bananas	479	232	238	264	15	12	17	19	12	15
Timber	352	279	1,055	351	684	364	265	187	521	60
Veneer	..	..	261	306	177	75	215	17	..	..
Fruit juice	..	40	140	312	267	447	143	92	25	33
Beer	371	439	543	546	472	172	125	221	309	320
Cigarettes	166	289	303	329	314	249	308	291	329	306
Other exports	1,107	812	704	582	659	898	599	487	1,116	994
Re-exports	559	822	969	1,252	771	1,686	518	859	801	579
Volume (metric tons)										
Copra	25,657	18,323	10,536	4,864	..	2,798	3,350	570	3,282	5,944
Copra meal	..	..	3,963	5,200	4,290	5,928	6,152	5,170	5,281	3,058
Coconut oil	..	..	8,037	12,207	10,651	10,928	12,552	11,527	10,330	6,292
Coconut cream	..	..	..	..	589	924	923	1,002	1,166	..
Cocoa	1,527	902	782	2,157	862	590	898	852	474	605
Taro ('000 cases)	86	151	140	110	137	220	188	224	191	284
Timber ('000 bd.ft.)	1,288	941	2,627	1,409	1,724	1,277	612	309	955	112
Unit value (US$/metric ton)										
Copra	361	236	221	190	..	155	142	55	293	244
Copra meal	..	..	80	84	75	42	48	69	85	94
Coconut oil	..	..	425	590	1,059	637	233	357	544	490
Coconut cream	..	..	..	..	1,526	1,367	1,368	1,463	1,598	..
Cocoa	2,193	1,560	1,062	1,413	1,884	1,807	1,612	1,474	1,298	1,588
Taro (US$/case)	13	14	13	14	11	10	10	11	13	10
Timber (US$/'000 bd.ft.)	274	296	401	249	397	285	433	604	548	531

Source: Central Bank of Samoa.

Table 5.4: DESTINATION OF EXPORTS, 1980-89
(% of total)

	1980	1981	1982	1983	1984	1985	1986	1987	1988	1989
Pacific	38.0	59.2	54.2	47.4	46.5	57.1	66.5	71.7	63.4	62.8
New Zealand	25.7	34.0	27.1	25.4	21.6	29.7	30.3	37.0	27.5	34.5
Australia	2.0	2.5	9.8	12.7	14.1	17.5	21.3	19.5	16.5	8.7
American Samoa	10.3	22.7	17.3	5.3	6.8	6.0	8.0	9.3	7.1	9.5
Other				4.0	4.0	3.9	6.9	5.9	12.3	9.9
North America	8.0	9.7	28.6	31.3	38.1	31.5	9.3	13.3	4.7	9.0
United States	8.0	9.7	28.6	31.3	38.1	31.5	9.3	13.3	4.7	9.0
Canada	0.0	0.0	0.0	0.0	0.0	0.0	0.0	0.0	0.0	0.0
Europe	49.5	25.7	6.9	12.3	14.9	9.9	24.2	14.9	29.8	27.9
Germany, Fed. Rep.	10.6	8.7	5.8	10.2	3.3	8.3	21.3	14.9	29.5	23.2
United Kingdom	0.5	0.4	0.1	1.9	6.9	0.0	0.5	0.0	0.0	1.1
Netherlands	30.5	16.6	1.0	0.0	4.7	1.6	2.0	0.0	0.3	3.6
Other	7.9	0.0	0.0	0.2	0.0	0.0	0.4	0.0	0.0	0.0
Asia	6.5	5.4	10.3	9.0	0.5	1.5	0.0	0.1	2.1	0.5
Japan	4.4	5.3	7.9	3.6	0.5	1.5	0.0	0.1	0.4	0.4
Other	2.1	0.1	2.4	5.4	0.0	0.0	0.0	0.0	1.7	0.1
Total	100.0	100.0	100.0	100.0	100.0	100.0	100.0	100.0	100.0	100.0

Source: Central Bank of Samoa.

Table 5.5: ORIGIN OF IMPORTS, 1980-87
(% of total)

	1980	1981	1982	1983	1984	1985	1986	1987
Pacific	56.0	53.0	58.1	58.2	46.3	68.9	63.6	59.2
New Zealand	32.2	29.4	31.0	28.2	22.2	32.6	35.9	41.2
Australia	20.4	19.8	21.4	28.0	9.1	20.1	27.6	18.0
American Samoa		0.1	0.1	0.1	0.1	0.1	0.1	0.0
Fiji	3.4	3.7	5.5	3.8	14.8	16.0	0.0	0.0
Other		0.0	0.1	0.1	0.1	0.1	0.0	0.0
North America	8.6	8.3	9.8	14.1	5.9	3.8	6.2	5.6
United States	8.6	8.2	9.7	14.0	5.9	3.8	6.2	5.6
Canada	0.0	0.1	0.1	0.1	0.0	0.0	0.0	0.0
Europe	8.8	7.8	4.2	4.9	6.3	3.9	10.6	10.3
Germany, Fed. Rep.	2.0	2.6	2.1	2.4	1.8	1.2	7.4	3.5
United Kingdom	5.8	4.7	1.6	1.0	2.6	1.6	1.9	5.9
Netherlands	0.0	0.0	0.1	1.1	0.1	0.3	0.2	0.2
Other	1.0	0.5	0.4	0.4	2.0	0.8	1.1	0.7
Asia	20.3	28.8	27.6	22.7	41.3	23.1	19.6	24.9
Japan	9.3	10.7	11.9	10.5	9.0	13.9	12.3	12.8
Singapore	11.0	12.4	5.7	5.7	17.5	2.0	1.6	3.6
Other		5.7	10.0	6.5	14.8	7.2	5.7	8.5
Other	6.3	2.1	0.3	0.1	0.2	0.3	0.0	0.0
Total	100.0	100.0	100.0	100.0	100.0	100.0	100.0	100.0

Source: Central Bank of Samoa & IMF, Direction of Trade Statistics.

Table 6.1: EXTERNAL GRANTS, 1980-89
(US$ '000)

	1980	1981	1982	1983	1984	1985	1986	1987	1988	1989
Project grants	17.1	13.2	13.7	16.4	12.8	11.7	12.1	13.8	15.2	13.9
New Zealand	4.4	4.1	2.4	2.5	3.0	3.4	1.4	2.4	2.7	2.2
Australia	5.2	1.8	5.0	7.3	5.0	4.1	1.2	4.2	5.2	3.7
EDF	2.0	0.8	1.7	4.2	1.9	0.7	0.0	0.6	0.1	0.4
Germany, Fed. Rep.	2.0	1.0	0.5	0.1	0.9	0.4	1.2	1.5	1.3	1.2
Japan	2.0	3.5	2.7	1.3	0.2	1.8	8.1	4.2	4.2	4.5
Netherlands	0.2	0.6	0.1	0.1	0.2	0.2	0.0	0.0	0.0	0.0
UNDP	1.1	1.4	1.2	0.7	0.9	0.8	0.1	0.6	0.5	0.8
Other	0.3	0.1	0.1	0.3	0.8	0.4	0.1	0.4	1.3	1.2
Cash & commodity grants	0.3	2.7	0.6	1.3	0.9	0.1	4.0	3.9	2.5	2.2
EEC (STABEX)	0.0	2.0	0.6	1.3	0.0	0.1	3.9	3.9	2.3	2.1
Other	0.3	0.7	0.0	0.0	0.9	0.0	0.0	0.0	0.2	0.1
Total grants	17.4	15.9	14.3	17.7	13.8	11.8	16.1	17.7	17.7	16.0
Of which: Expenditures abroad	3.4	1.5	2.2	2.3	1.6	1.6	1.7	2.3	2.1	1.8

Source: Central Bank of Samoa.

Table 6.2: EXTERNAL PUBLIC DEBT AND DEBT SERVICE, 1980-88
(US$ '000)

	1980	1981	1982	1983	1984	1985	1986	1987	1988
Debt outstanding & disbursed	55,597	56,685	60,311	60,317	64,184	64,619	65,280	71,807	71,165
Multilateral loans	34,835	38,812	43,703	46,590	51,962	53,742	55,788	59,967	59,832
Bilateral loans	12,490	11,531	11,731	10,762	8,072	7,632	7,087	9,528	9,488
Private creditors	8,272	6,342	4,877	2,965	4,150	3,245	2,405	2,312	1,845
Gross disbursements	10,876	5,395	8,972	4,722	10,227	2,470	2,776	6,018	4,182
Multilateral loans	10,876	5,164	5,819	4,213	7,254	1,452	1,827	3,499	3,090
Bilateral loans	0	231	1,154	509	973	1,018	949	2,519	1,092
Private creditors	0	0	0	0	2,000	0	0	0	0
Interest payments	2,313	1,758	1,140	1,005	1,359	1,688	1,413	1,271	1,291
Multilateral loans	283	457	233	359	420	458	537	624	674
Bilateral loans	1,170	633	380	305	789	843	613	480	464
Private creditors	860	668	527	341	150	387	263	167	153
Principal repayments	2,293	1,672	1,745	2,845	3,247	3,951	4,316	3,001	3,220
Multilateral loans	321	341	417	587	968	1,308	1,496	1,812	1,978
Bilateral loans	149	221	335	729	2,262	1,644	1,896	789	845
Private creditors	1,823	1,110	993	1,529	17	999	924	400	399
Total debt service	4,606	3,428	2,885	3,850	4,606	5,639	5,729	4,272	4,511
Multilateral loans	604	798	650	948	1,388	1,766	2,033	2,436	2,650
Bilateral loans	1,319	854	715	1,034	3,051	2,487	2,509	1,269	1,309
Private creditors	2,683	1,778	1,520	1,870	167	1,388	1,187	567	552

Source: World Bank, Debtor Reporting System.

Distributors of World Bank Publications

ARGENTINA
Carlos Hirsch, SRL
Galería Guemes
Florida 165, 4th Floor-Ofc. 453/465
1333 Buenos Aires

AUSTRALIA, PAPUA NEW GUINEA,
FIJI, SOLOMON ISLANDS,
VANUATU, AND WESTERN SAMOA
D.A. Books & Journals
648 Whitehorse Road
Mitcham 3132
Victoria

AUSTRIA
Gerold and Co.
Graben 31
A-1011 Wien

BAHRAIN
Bahrain Research and Consultancy
   Associates Ltd.
P.O. Box 22103
Manama Town 317

BANGLADESH
Micro Industries Development
   Assistance Society (MIDAS)
House 5, Road 16
Dhanmondi R/Area
Dhaka 1209

   Branch offices:
   Main Road
   Maijdee Court
   Noakhali - 3800

   76, K.D.A. Avenue
   Kulna

BELGIUM
Jean De Lannoy
Av. du Roi 202
1060 Brussels

CANADA
Le Diffuseur
C.P. 85, 1501B rue Ampère
Boucherville, Québec
J4B 5E6

CHINA
China Financial & Economic
   Publishing House
8, Da Fo Si Dong Jie
Beijing

COLOMBIA
Infoenlace Ltda.
Apartado Aereo 34270
Bogota D.E.

COTE D'IVOIRE
Centre d'Edition et de Diffusion
   Africaines (CEDA)
04 B.P. 541
Abidjan 04 Plateau

CYPRUS
MEMRB Information Services
P.O. Box 2098
Nicosia

DENMARK
SamfundsLitteratur
Rosenoerns Allé 11
DK-1970 Frederiksberg C

DOMINICAN REPUBLIC
Editora Taller, C. por A.
Restauración e Isabel la Católica 309
Apartado Postal 2190
Santo Domingo

EL SALVADOR
Fusades
Avenida Manuel Enrique Araujo #3530
Edificio SISA, 1er. Piso
San Salvador

EGYPT, ARAB REPUBLIC OF
Al Ahram
Al Galaa Street
Cairo

The Middle East Observer
8 Chawarbi Street
Cairo

FINLAND
Akateeminen Kirjakauppa
P.O. Box 128
SF-00101
Helsinki 10

FRANCE
World Bank Publications
66, avenue d'Iéna
75116 Paris

GERMANY
UNO-Verlag
Poppelsdorfer Allee 55
D-5300 Bonn 1

GREECE
KEME
24, Ippodamou Street Platia Plastiras
Athens-11635

GUATEMALA
Librerias Piedra Santa
5a. Calle 7-55
Zona 1
Guatemala City

HONG KONG, MACAO
Asia 2000 Ltd.
6 Fl., 146 Prince Edward
   Road, W.
Kowloon
Hong Kong

INDIA
Allied Publishers Private Ltd.
751 Mount Road
Madras - 600 002

   Branch offices:
   15 J.N. Heredia Marg
   Ballard Estate
   Bombay - 400 038

   13/14 Asaf Ali Road
   New Delhi - 110 002

   17 Chittaranjan Avenue
   Calcutta - 700 072

   Jayadeva Hostel Building
   5th Main Road Gandhinagar
   Bangalore - 560 009

   3-5-1129 Kachiguda Cross Road
   Hyderabad - 500 027

   Prarthana Flats, 2nd Floor
   Near Thakore Baug, Navrangpura
   Ahmedabad - 380 009

   Patiala House
   16-A Ashok Marg
   Lucknow - 226 001

INDONESIA
Pt. Indira Limited
Jl. Sam Ratulangi 37
P.O. Box 181
Jakarta Pusat

ITALY
Licosa Commissionaria Sansoni SPA
Via Benedetto Fortini, 120/10
Casella Postale 552
50125 Florence

JAPAN
Eastern Book Service
37-3, Hongo 3-Chome, Bunkyo-ku 113
Tokyo

KENYA
Africa Book Service (E.A.) Ltd.
P.O. Box 45245
Nairobi

KOREA, REPUBLIC OF
Pan Korea Book Corporation
P.O. Box 101, Kwangwhamun
Seoul

KUWAIT
MEMRB Information Services
P.O. Box 5465

MALAYSIA
University of Malaya Cooperative
   Bookshop, Limited
P.O. Box 1127, Jalan Pantai Baru
Kuala Lumpur

MEXICO
INFOTEC
Apartado Postal 22-860
14060 Tlalpan, Mexico D.F.

MOROCCO
Société d'Etudes Marketing Marocaine
12 rue Mozart, Bd. d'Anfa
Casablanca

NETHERLANDS
InOr-Publikaties b.v.
P.O. Box 14
7240 BA Lochem

NEW ZEALAND
Hills Library and Information Service
Private Bag
New Market
Auckland

NIGERIA
University Press Limited
Three Crowns Building Jericho
Private Mail Bag 5095
Ibadan

NORWAY
Narvesen Information Center
Book Department
P.O. Box 6125 Etterstad
N-0602 Oslo 6

OMAN
MEMRB Information Services
P.O. Box 1613, Seeb Airport
Muscat

PAKISTAN
Mirza Book Agency
65, Shahrah-e-Quaid-e-Azam
P.O. Box No. 729
Lahore 3

PERU
Editorial Desarrollo SA
Apartado 3824
Lima

PHILIPPINES
International Book Center
Fifth Floor, Filipinas Life Building
Ayala Avenue, Makati
Metro Manila

POLAND
ORPAN
Palac Kultury i Nauki
00-901 Warszawa

PORTUGAL
Livraria Portugal
Rua Do Carmo 70-74
1200 Lisbon

SAUDI ARABIA, QATAR
Jarir Book Store
P.O. Box 3196
Riyadh 11471

MEMRB Information Services
   Branch offices:
   Al Alsa Street
   Al Dahna Center
   First Floor
   P.O. Box 7188
   Riyadh

   Haji Abdullah Alireza Building
   King Khaled Street
   P.O. Box 3969
   Damman

   33, Mohammed Hassan Awad Street
   P.O. Box 5978
   Jeddah

SINGAPORE, TAIWAN,
MYANMAR,BRUNEI
Information Publications
   Private, Ltd.
02-06 1st Fl., Pei-Fu Industrial
   Bldg.
24 New Industrial Road
Singapore 1953

SOUTH AFRICA, BOTSWANA
For single titles:
Oxford University Press
   Southern Africa
P.O. Box 1141
Cape Town 8000

For subscription orders:
International Subscription Service
P.O. Box 41095
Craighall
Johannesburg 2024

SPAIN
Mundi-Prensa Libros, S.A.
Castello 37
28001 Madrid

Libreria Internacional AEDOS
Consell de Cent, 391
08009 Barcelona

SRI LANKA AND THE MALDIVES
Lake House Bookshop
P.O. Box 244
100, Sir Chittampalam A.
   Gardiner Mawatha
Colombo 2

SWEDEN
For single titles:
Fritzes Fackboksforetaget
Regeringsgatan 12, Box 16356
S-103 27 Stockholm

For subscription orders:
Wennergren-Williams AB
Box 30004
S-104 25 Stockholm

SWITZERLAND
For single titles:
Librairie Payot
6, rue Grenus
Case postale 381
CH 1211 Geneva 11

For subscription orders:
Librairie Payot
Service des Abonnements
Case postale 3312
CH 1002 Lausanne

TANZANIA
Oxford University Press
P.O. Box 5299
Dar es Salaam

THAILAND
Central Department Store
306 Silom Road
Bangkok

TRINIDAD & TOBAGO, ANTIGUA
BARBUDA, BARBADOS,
DOMINICA, GRENADA, GUYANA,
JAMAICA, MONTSERRAT, ST.
KITTS & NEVIS, ST. LUCIA,
ST. VINCENT & GRENADINES
Systematics Studies Unit
#9 Watts Street
Curepe
Trinidad, West Indies

UNITED ARAB EMIRATES
MEMRB Gulf Co.
P.O. Box 6097
Sharjah

UNITED KINGDOM
Microinfo Ltd.
P.O. Box 3
Alton, Hampshire GU34 2PG
England

VENEZUELA
Libreria del Este
Aptdo. 60.337
Caracas 1060-A

YUGOSLAVIA
Jugoslovenska Knjiga
P.O. Box 36
Trg Republike
YU-11000 Belgrade